9/03

The Temptation
of Innocence in
the Dramas of
Arthur Miller

The Temptation
of Innocence
in the Dramas
of Arthur Miller

Terry Otten

University of Missouri Press
Columbia and London

Library of Congress Cataloging-in-Publication Data

Otten, Terry.
    The temptation of innocence in the dramas of Arthur Miller / Terry Otten.
        p.   cm.
    Includes bibliographical references (p.) and index.
    ISBN 0-8262-1406-1 (alk. paper)
        1. Miller, Arthur, 1915—Criticism and interpretation.   2. Innocence
    (Psychology) in literature.   3. Drama—Psychological aspects.   4. Temptation
    in literature.   I. Title.

    PS3525.I5156 Z84 2002
    813'.52—dc21

2002023840

♾™ This paper meets the requirements of the
American National Standard for Permanence of Paper
for Printed Library Materials, Z39.48, 1984.

Text Design: Stephanie Foley
Jacket Design: Susan Ferber
Typesetter: Bookcomp, Inc.
Printer and binder: Thomson-Shore, Inc.
Typeface: Goudy

For Jane, always,
for Keith and Maryellen,
for Julie and Ted—
and for both Alyces

Contents

Abbreviations viii

Preface ix

Acknowledgments xv

1. *All My Sons* and Before 1

2. *Death of a Salesman* 26

3. *The Crucible* to *A Memory of Two Mondays* 60

4. *The Misfits* and *After the Fall* 94

5. *Incident at Vichy* to *The Creation of the World and Other Business* 134

6. Other Plays of the 1970s and 1980s 165

7. Last Plays of the Century 210

Works Cited 251

Index 269

Abbreviations

The following abbreviations for Arthur Miller's works are used in parenthetical citations throughout *The Temptation of Innocence in the Dramas of Arthur Miller*. Complete bibliographical information for these texts appears in Works Cited.

AC	*The Archbishop's Ceiling*
ACl	*The American Clock*
AF	*After the Fall*
AMC	*Arthur Miller and Company*
AMS	*All My Sons*
BG	*Broken Glass*
C	*The Crucible*
Conv.	*Conversations with Arthur Miller*
CWOB	*Creation of the World and Other Business*
DM	*Danger: Memory!*
DS	*Death of a Salesman*
E	*Echoes down the Corridor*
GY	*The Golden Years*
IV	*Incident at Vichy*
LY	*The Last Yankee*
M	*The Misfits*
MPC	*Mr. Peters' Connections*
MTM	*A Memory of Two Mondays*
MWHAL	*The Man Who Had All the Luck*
P	*The Price*
PT	*Playing for Time*
RDMM	*The Ride down Mount Morgan*
SB	*Salesman in Beijing*
T	*Timebends: A Life*
TE	*The Theater Essays of Arthur Miller*
TWM	*Two-Way Mirror*
VB	*A View from the Bridge*

Preface

"Innocence kills."
Timebends

For more than fifty years, Arthur Miller has been more than a dramatist. He has been a chronicler of American culture, which he has both characterized and criticized. Though subject to the vagaries and vicissitudes of theater criticism—virtually disowned by many sixties reviewers for the seeming "bad taste" and self-pity of *After the Fall*, deemed hopelessly out of fashion by the new intellectuals devoted to the avant garde in the seventies, spurned by current postmodern academic theorists for his supposed sexism and naive belief in individual responsibility—he has somehow persevered, in his eighties still writing and producing works that reflect the transformation and yet consistency of his major themes. Until the recent revivals on Broadway, Miller suffered the near disregard of his work from the mid fifties to the last decade of the century by most of the New York theater world, even though he has remained among the most performed American playwrights in Europe, especially England, and other parts of the world. Surprisingly to some, no doubt, he was voted the most important English language playwright of the twentieth century, and *Death of a Salesman* and *The Crucible* were ranked the second and sixth best plays, according to a 1999 poll of playwrights, actors, journalists, and other theater professionals, conducted by the Royal National Theatre in London. Yet even when his recent play *Broken Glass* won the Olivier Award for the best new play in London in 1994, the *New York Times* barely made mention of the honor. A typical response to Miller's current work by many New York critics is represented by Michael Feingold's patronizing dismissal of *The Last Yankee* in 1996: "I don't mean to sneer at Miller's play, only to say that its view of life is that of an elder statesman, comfortably sheltered from the terrible griefs of our time. . . . [I]t's not Miller time anymore."[1]

Yet Miller's dogged determination and a growing body of insightful criticism, both laudatory and critical, have secured his place as one of the handful of truly major dramatists of the twentieth century. Critically successful new productions of his major plays in the nineties,[2] along with the Signature Theater's devoting its 1998 season to producing Miller plays, and the staging of new plays written in the nineties (*The Ride down Mount Morgan* in 1990, *The Last Yankee* in 1993, *Broken Glass* in 1994, and, most recently, *Mr. Peters' Connections* in 1998), give hope that Miller may once again claim his rightful place in the New York theater world more than a half century after his first major play was produced. Even his first failure on Broadway, *The Man Who Had All the Luck*, received a New York revival in 2001. Miller's stubborn insistence on individual choice and responsibility gives force to his plays even in a postmodern age of profound disillusionment, irony, and cynicism. Too few have appreciated the evolution of Miller's art over the past half century. As David Rabe has coyly commented, the critics "have maligned him for not growing when in fact what has happened is that they have refused to admit he has grown" (AMC, 145). Without abandoning his essential themes, he has attempted to accommodate but not surrender to the prevailing intellectual currents of the last few decades.

1. Michael Feingold, "Post-Miller Time." Feingold echoes the earlier claim of one of Miller's most vocal critics, Robert Brustein, that Miller's "concerns are curiously isolated from the world in which we now live" ("The Unseriousness of Arthur Miller," 39).

2. Including *The Crucible* produced by the National Actors Studio in 1991, *The Price* at the Roundabout Theater in 1992, *All My Sons* at the Roundabout in 1997, the Tony Award–winning *A View from the Bridge* at the Roundabout in 1998, and *Death of a Salesman* at the Paper Mill Playhouse in 1998 and the widely acclaimed production with Brian Dennehy and Elizabeth Franz at the Eugene O'Neill Theater in 1999.

My concern here is to explore the changing nature of Miller's quintessential theme of guilt and responsibility, to show how his adaptation of it reflects not stasis but extension, not mere repetition but continuity—variations on a theme that echoes the most ancient of myths, what James Dickey alludes to as "the oldest dream of all—the oldest and the most dreamlike—the one about starting to fall." For in virtually all Miller's major plays, characters struggle against debilitating self-knowledge; ultimately naked and East of Eden, they confront their own culpability and are threatened by what Miller considers the greatest temptation of all, "the temptation of innocence." To Miller the most destructive force is ignorance, ignorance masked as innocence. He understands, in Rollo May's words, that though "it is dangerous to know, it is far more dangerous not to know,"[3] that it is not guilt that causes moral havoc but denial and the spurious claim of innocence. The central threat underlying most of his plays is not the destruction *of* innocence but destruction *by* innocence and the subsequent evil it can generate. Virtually every Miller protagonist is in pursuit of an innocence that he or she knows, consciously or unconsciously, does not exist and cannot be earned.

Undoubtedly, any approach to Miller's work must broach the topic of tragedy, not only because it constituted the focus of the earliest critical commentary on the plays but also because Miller has so often written or spoken about it in essays and interviews, even into the nineties when his newer dramas seem far more aligned with the issues of postmodernism than with the tenets of tragedy. Indeed, although his plays have undergone enormous change and ventured into areas seemingly foreign to tragedy as a genre, they nonetheless echo the tragic themes and rhythms that provide the spine of his earliest work. Miller has not so much abandoned as transformed his tragic vision as he has incorporated the relativism and irony of the age, and inculcated tragic themes in a rich variety of eclectic yet experimental forms reflecting not only the conventions of traditional and Ibsenian tragedy but comedy and much of the substance of existential and postmodern drama. Nevertheless, despite the current vogue of dismissing the relevance of tragedy on the contemporary stage, it is no small irony that the recent critically successful revivals of early Miller texts have revitalized the old debates about the possibility of writing

3. James Dickey, *Deliverance*, 186; Rollo May, *Love and Will*, 165.

modern tragedy, a debate Miller has certainly exacerbated not only by his drama but also by his written and spoken pronouncements, and especially his reflections on how he first learned his craft by imitating and modifying Ibsen's conception of modern tragedy. In all their rich variety and experimentation, Miller's plays maintain the substance of tragic dramas, which, Larry Bouchard writes, "show theodicies to be manifestations and not explanations of the tragic dilemma of human experience and ultimate reality. The need to secure an explanation for catastrophe, suffering, injustice—is displaced when tragedy probes the irreducible sense of malevolence in humanity and divinity."[4]

As I discuss the theme of tragedy as it pertains to Miller's evolving sense of the tragic, I shall also address, at least indirectly, the question most commonly related to it, its significance in an age lacking a religious center. As Nietzsche once remarked, do away with God and it will go hard on the tragic poets. Yet Miller persistently reflects the close association between religion and tragedy, and his statements reveal his deep awareness of how the "death of god" has transfigured tragedy and shifted the motivation of dramatic action from the cosmos to a self measured against not some essentially transcendent code of morality but rather personal and socially constructed values.

Despite the seeming "secular humanism" that critics have often found in his works, Miller, as Neil Carson has written, "can best be described as a religious writer."[5] Although his dramas say little about God directly except in historical contexts like *The Crucible* or in fables like *The Creation of the World and Other Business*, they speak loudly about spiritual impoverishment and the consequences of moral choices. Discussing the viability of tragedy with Robert Martin, Miller once remarked that "what we are talking about really is maybe a function of man which goes back to the Bible and into earliest Western literature, like the Greek drama" (*Conv.*, 200). He envisions the tragic dilemma as a reflection of the Fall, a theme that surfaces directly and indirectly in many of his texts. Adam and Eve, after all, confronted the first tragic choice, in which they were fated to lose, either by eating the forbidden fruit of knowledge and

4. Larry D. Bouchard, *Tragic Method and Tragic Theology: Evil in Contemporary Drama and Religious Thought*, 2.
5. Neil Carson, *Arthur Miller*, 154.

violating the injunction against doing so or by obeying the injunction and denying the will to freedom. Living "after the fall," Miller's
characters exist in spurious gardens—often in the Eden of American
culture—and make choices, gain knowledge, and bear the consequences of choice.[6]

As the following discussions will show, Miller's major dramas sustain the rhythms of tragedy, influenced strongly by Ibsen no doubt
but undergirded by Miller's own sense of the crisis of identity in a
culture bereft of its spiritual roots. In an interview at the beginning
of the last decade of the century, when his work was enjoying a
lively revival and new plays were being produced, he reiterated a
still deeply abiding theme in all his works, that "The wages of sin
is still death. . . . [C]onsequences exist."[7] An elemental core of Puritan consciousness informs all of Miller's plays and defines their tragic
nature. His insistence on human depravity, the wages of sin, and the
necessity for personal responsibility make him part of that strain of
Puritanism that Robert Spiller traces, in his famous study *The Cycle
of American Literature*, from Jonathan Edwards to Poe, Hawthorne,
and Melville, to O'Neill, Steinbeck, and Faulkner. Even in plays of
widely differing contexts and textures—some short and some long,
some comic and some serious, some contemporary and some historical, Miller holds to his elemental conviction that one must confront
a past that is irrevocably bound to the present and endure the consequences of choice—that, inevitably, "the birds come home to roost"
(AMC, 49).

6. In reference to Miller's conception of American culture, Christopher Bigsby
perceptively concludes that, for Miller, "The myth of American society is that
the journey to America was a double journey, forward to the future but also back
through time towards innocence, a world free of history and ultimately, of course,
time, a movement which logically washed the individual free of responsibility and
hence a utopianism stained at source" ("Arthur Miller: Time Traveller," 3).

7. Steven R. Centola, " 'Just Looking for a Home': A Conversation with Arthur
Miller," 87.

Acknowledgments

I owe a debt of gratitude for financial assistance provided by the Faculty Research Fund and a stipend for research attached to the Kenneth E. Wray Chair in the Humanities at Wittenberg University. I wish to express my thanks to colleagues and friends in the Department of English who have assisted me, read portions of my manuscript, and made suggestions—though they are of course not responsible for my errors. I am also grateful for the encouragement of Steven Centola, Matthew Roudané, Brenda Murphy, Steven Marino, and other members of the Arthur Miller Society. My gratitude goes as well to the Harry Ransom Humanities Research Center at the University of Texas at Austin, to the Special Collections Library at the Harlan Hatcher Graduate Library, and, in particular, to Kathryn Beam, curator at the University of Michigan, for assistance in researching unpublished Miller materials housed at their libraries.

Earlier versions of Chapter 2 and parts of Chapters 3 and 4 first appeared in the journals listed below. I express my thanks to the editors of these journals for permission to use these materials:

"*Death of a Salesman* at Fifty—Still 'Coming Home to Roost,'" from *Texas Studies in Literature and Language* 41:3, pp. 280–310. Copyright 1999 by the University of Texas Press. All rights reserved.

"Historical Drama and the Dimensions of Tragedy: A *Man for All Seasons* and *The Crucible*," from *American Drama* 6:1, pp. 42–60. Copyright American Drama Institute 1996. All rights reserved.

"Coming Home to Roost Again: Tragic Rhythm in Arthur Miller's *Broken Glass*," from *South Carolina Review*

31:2, pp. 17–24. Copyright Clemson University, 1999. All rights reserved.

I especially express my appreciation to Arthur Miller for his patience with my requests, his allowing me to research his unpublished manuscripts, and his kind permission to quote freely from his published and unpublished works.

I am most indebted to my wife, Jane, for her careful reading, thoughtful suggestions, and constant encouragement.

The Temptation
of Innocence in
the Dramas of
Arthur Miller

1   *All My Sons* and Before

For more than a decade before *All My Sons* established his reputation on the American stage, Arthur Miller had already served an apprenticeship as a playwright and nearly abandoned his craft after the failure of his first Broadway production, *The Man Who Had All the Luck*, in 1944. *No Villain*, his initial play written as an undergraduate at the University of Michigan in 1936, won Miller his first Avery Hopwood Award, and he subsequently revised it as *They Too Arise* in 1938, Miller's senior year, when it won the Theater Guild National Award (he revised it again in the same year as *The Grass Still Grows*). Miller's second play, *Honors at Dawn*, won a second Hopwood Award in the next competition, and *The Great Disobedience* received a second place in the following year. Following graduation Miller coauthored *Listen My Children* with Norman Rosten in 1939, under the auspices of the New York Federal Theater Project. He then wrote his ambitious historical drama, *The Golden Years*, which, because of the termination of the Federal Theater Project, was not staged until 1990. He completed *The Half-Bridge*, begun in 1941, in 1943. In addition to these dramas, Miller wrote in the early forties what he now calls "some silly radio plays . . . just to make a living,"[1] including *The Pussycat and the Expert Plumber Who Was a Man; William Ireland's Confession; The Four Freedoms*; a patriotic one-act, *That They May Win*, which was published in 1943; and *Grandpa and the Statue*. In addition to writing dramatic scripts, Miller was formulating and exploring his themes in short stories, in his journalist reportage on soldiers in the war, *Situation Normal*, and most importantly,

---

1. Arthur Miller, "Responses to an Audience Question and Answer Session," 827.

in his novel *Focus*. In varying degrees these early texts contain the seeds brought to fruition in the plays to follow. Of these, the dramas and *Focus* especially explore the theme of spurious innocence and moral responsibility.

No Villain (and its revisions as *They Too Arise* and *The Grass Still Grows*) Miller has called "the most biographical play I ever wrote" (AMC, 28). The play treats a familiar family structure in Miller's plays: the Jewish, middle-class Simon family consisting of a father in the clothing business and his distant wife, Esther; two sons, Arnold, a student at the University of Michigan, and Ben, who discontentedly works for his father; and a thirteen-year-old daughter, Maxine (who disappears in the two later versions of the play). Agreeing temporarily to help his father, Arnie (Arnold) unwittingly crosses a picket line at his father's factory and is beaten up by the strikers. A Marxist sympathizer, Arnie claims sympathy for the men. Facing ruin because of the strike, Abe, the father, urges Arnie's brother Ben to marry the daughter of a rich manufacturer, and Ben reluctantly agrees. In the meantime, the Manufacturers Association, despite Abe and Ben's protests, vote to engage strikebreakers. Although Arnie begs Ben not to marry only to save his father's business, Ben overhears Esther's father volunteer to help Abe; out of shame, Ben asks Arnie to support his father along with him. Caught between family loyalty and his principles—a seminal conflict in Miller's dramas—Arnie refuses. At the point of greatest conflict, Esther's father melodramatically suffers a heart attack and dies. The grandfather now gone and the business destroyed, the family finally begins to come to terms with life, the anger fades, and for the first time Abe expresses tenderness for Esther as she grieves over the loss of her father. Ben gains independence from the flawed values of the capitalistic world represented by Abe and Esther, backs out of the marriage, and declares he will find his own way, much to the delight of his brother, Arnie.

As critics have noted, though simplistic, psychologically undeveloped, overtly didactic, and melodramatic, the play nonetheless foreshadows the essential conflicts and moral themes in *All My Sons*, *Death of a Salesman*, *The Crucible*, *After the Fall*, *The Price*, and other later works.[2] Though written at a time when Miller was drawn to

2. See especially Benjamin Nelson, *Arthur Miller: Portrait of a Playwright*, 29–45; and Christopher Bigsby, "The Early Plays."

Marxism, the play challenges the idea of human perfectibility and exposes the capacity for evil and necessity for moral action. Even the title *No Villain* conveys not the sense of innocence but its opposite. It points toward the idea fully developed in plays like *After the Fall*: If no one is a "villain," neither is anyone "good"; good intentions can be the source of evil as well as good. The title comes from an early scene when Abe ironically tells his cold and judgmental wife, "I ain't no . . . no . . . bad . . . no villain,"[3] even when his seemingly noble efforts to save the family and preserve the business for his sons have alienated his sons and created the moral crisis in the play. Of course, Miller minimally exploits the issue in this first text (as Bigsby observes, the revisions in *They Too Arise* make the play more substantial), but even here Miller introduces his trademark questions of guilt and responsibility and the naive assumption of innocence. To be sure, the first play, and even more so the other plays Miller wrote at Michigan, *Honors at Dawn* and *The Great Disobedience*, lean more toward melodrama than tragedy, not only in the dependence upon incidents of plot but in the emphasis on victimization. The "villains" appear less responsible for their moral impotence than the externally defined social system that incapacitates them as moral agents. In an essay, "About Theatre Language," appended to the 1994 republication of *The Last Yankee*, he refers to his first drama as "purely mimetic, a realistic play about my own family" (*LY*, 81).

Although neither *Honors at Dawn* (1937) nor *The Great Disobedience* (1938) marked major progress in Miller's skills as playwright, they were important apprentice works. A strike play like *No Villain*, reflecting Miller's own experiences working at an auto parts factory, *Honors at Dawn* reintroduces two brothers as contesting figures whose contrasting natures not only represent the conflict between capitalistic and individual values but also embody a much darker theme, what Bigsby calls "the process of betrayal" so central in Miller's works. Sons of a Polish immigrant, Max and Harry Zabriski foreshadow Biff and Happy Loman in particular. Max likes to work with his hands and is fully sympathetic with his fellow workers at the Castle Parts plant, who are demonstrating for higher wages. Offered

3. Quotes from *No Villain* and *The Great Disobedience* appear in unpublished manuscripts housed at the Harlan Hatcher Graduate Library at the University of Michigan. They are quoted with the permission of Arthur Miller.

a bribe to inform on other workers, he refuses, and he subsequently goes to join Harry at college to escape the conflict. He discovers that Harry totally embraces the ruthless capitalism he himself rejects and that Harry has been an informer for university officials beholden to the owner of the very factory where Max worked. When a professor is fired and radical students are suspended, Max returns to rejoin the factory workers in another strike. As the play ends, he is being brutally beaten but, as Nelson comments, he knows "that he has finally gained at a new 'dawn' the 'honors'—the personal integrity and social responsibility—he had falsely sought at the university." Superficially, as Bigsby concludes, Max's "noble sacrifice in the cause of humanity" aligns him with a "panoply of secular saints which was a product of 1930s literature." More significantly, perhaps, the play foreshadows *After the Fall*, according to Nelson, in which "the stress is not only on the loss of innocence, but more significantly on the events following the painful but providential fall."[4]

In *The Great Disobedience*, Miller attempted his first real experiment with "the problem of dramatic language"; he recalls in a 1994 essay: "I turned at once to a stylized treatment of life in a gigantic prison, modeled on Jackson State Penitentiary in Michigan. . . . The theme of that play was that prisons existed to make desperate workingmen insane" (*LY*, 81). The drama ostensibly describes the need for prison reform, but in effect it indicts the wider capitalistic society personified in Stephen Riker, the industrialist owner of the Riker Rubber Company who manipulates the prison system. When the company doctor, Victor Matthews, refuses to support Riker's denial of just compensation for his workers, Riker has Victor imprisoned for performing an illegal abortion on a girl who was threatening suicide. The prison becomes a metaphor for describing the corruptive and destructive power of the system.[5] The compensation racket Riker runs at his plants is imitated by the narcotics trade in the prison operated in part by the sadistic Deputy Warden McLean; here, too, people of conscience succumb to the power of the system. The prison psychiatrist, Dr. Karl Mannheim, a former college friend of Victor's

4. Bigsby, "Early Plays," 35; Nelson, *Arthur Miller*, 26; Bigsby, "Early Plays," 34; Nelson, *Arthur Miller*, 27.

5. In his autobiography, *Timebends: A Life*, Miller alludes to the prison as "a reflection of society, and what was wrong with it" (*T*, 27).

and former boyfriend of Victor's wife, Caroline, soon faces the moral dilemma of either helping Victor or following the dictates of Riker and his cronies at the prison.

Victor tells Karl of his persistent sense of guilt surfacing in night-mares where "twisted bodies came floating into the room. In the daytime, cripples followed me on the streets." Karl, too, confronts his own culpability with a growing sense of despair and hopeless-ness. Knowing he is morally corrupted, he vows to "train myself to see only what I choose to see." He compares himself to the artists of the paintings hanging on his office walls: "Rivera, Van Gogh . . . I'm sure they'd rather be blind than have to sit eight hours a day in an art gallery, with their hands cut off." "I've got too many inher-ited notions in my head about good and evil, right and wrong," he rationalizes. "A man who works in the society can't keep them."

Becoming more and more psychotic, Victor believes Caroline is carrying their child. In probably the most turgid lines in the play,[6] Karl eventually picks up the image of the symbolic child, evoking the Christ image to embody the vision:

> I feel . . . as though . . . something was actually born here. A new son, red with a new life in him. Victor's son . . . the one they couldn't kill with Victor because things like this are not the property of men. They belong to mankind. Long ago it was nailed to a cross, but it never died because its conception lies in the constant struggle of men with masters of men . . . there must be a new Jesus in tens of thousands walking the earth.

The rhetorical flourish matches the melodrama at the end of the play. It ends tenuously, at best. Although Karl has the sadistic Mc-Clean dismissed for running the narcotics racket in the prison, a new assistant arranged by Riker joins Karl, perpetuating Karl's own failed attempt to merge compromise with idealism. The play ends with "the sound of rivets closing in."

Miller never fully incorporates or adequately probes theme and character in this early work, although he again raises the moral issues that provide the core of his canon. The highly affected language,

6. According to Miller the judges denied him his third Hopwood Award because they thought the play too "turgid," a word which he claims described "my own feelings about Jackson" (*T*, 93).

stereotypical characterization, and awkward plotting identify *The Great Disobedience* as the work of an as-yet-immature writer wrestling with potentially powerful issues of personal development and moral consequences. Miller's next unproduced play, *The Half-Bridge*, proved no more successful as an artistic effort, but it again gave Miller the opportunity to work with his shaping concepts and ideas.

The Half-Bridge traces the growing self-awareness of Mark Donegal, the brooding and alienated son of a wealthy family, who serves as mate on a merchant ship, having found society dominated by "little people" and mediocrity. Tempted by a German agent, Dr. Luther, to commit piracy and insurance fraud, he nearly succumbs, driven by the need for self-aggrandizement in a world diminished by triviality and moral void. Finally he is rescued by the love of Anna Walden, a highly vulnerable woman who believes she killed someone in self-defense and is trying to escape; by the encouragement and goodwill of a German refugee Jew, August Kruger, and a fellow sailor named Carrol; and by the kindly—perhaps homosexual—attention of the captain of the ship. They all lead Donegal to understand that a meaningful existence depends upon the acceptance of responsibility for others, that his own self-identity impinges upon social consciousness. The play ends with Mark's bombastic assertion of self-determination to claim his name and his identity in the world. Although it is a precursor to later Miller plays in its concerns for self-authenticity, its embracing of social responsibility (the "half-bridge" alludes to the bridge projecting from the heart with which one must connect to others), and to some degree in its references to the Jewish question during the war, *The Half-Bridge* shows little promise of the works to follow. In many respects, however, Miller's next drama, *The Golden Age*, signaled a significant advance both in his art and in his ability to explore more complex characters and moral issues.

The Golden Years and The Man Who Had All the Luck

The Golden Years and *The Man Who Had All the Luck*, Miller's last major apprentice play and his first drama produced for the New York stage, were published together in a 1989 text with an introduction by Miller and afterword by Christopher Bigsby. Bigsby was instrumental in resurfacing the earlier play and was mainly responsible for its production on BBC Radio in November 1987. Miller has commented that "*The Golden Years* really came of Fascism" in the late thirties. It was "a kind of metaphor for the paralysis of the West. . . . Hitler was talked about as if he were simply another politician who was a bit crude now and then" (AMC, 30). Miller wrote the play thinking that the Federal Theatre would produce it; but when the government funding stopped, it became prohibitive to stage with its elaborate designs, costumes, and large cast, especially at a time when the popular stage was dominated by realistic social dramas. Miller has referred to *The Golden Years* as "a big, classical tragedy"[7] that pits the historical figures of Cortez and Montezuma as characters driven by contrasting illusions. Cortez convinces himself that he has come to Mexico to bring Christianity to the land as well as to acquire its wealth, and Montezuma believes himself ordained to be immortalized by the gods. When Cortez arrives, he appears to Montezuma as the incarnation of Quetzalcoatl, the great god who, like Christ, had advocated peace, healed the sick, walked on water, and promised to return. When Cortez comes under the sign of the cross, the very sign of Quetzalcoatl as well, Montezuma must believe him the god returning to assure Montezuma's own transfiguration. Captured by the illusion, Montezuma fails to act against the force coming to destroy him. He succumbs to the appearance of the seemingly transcendent conquistador; and like the Western nations paralyzed by Hitler in the late thirties, he ignores all the signs of Cortez's rapacity and ruthlessness.

In effect, Montezuma participates in and in large measure wills his destruction by a blind faith in his transformation, an immortality destined by the gods and seemingly conveyed in Cortez as a messenger of fate. Consequently, Montezuma reads the events of Cortez's coming, first signaled by the eclipse of the moon, as fulfillment of his own destiny. Satiated by the violence that has secured his reign and that Cortez's brutality ironically mirrors, he seeks for "a way to govern that does not end in ruins" (GY, 27). When he discovers that

7. In his introduction to the 1989 publication of *The Golden Years* and *The Man Who Had All the Luck*, Miller speaks of *The Golden Years* as a "tragedy" looking "toward a non-existent poetic theater inspired by the Elizabethan models" (5) and as a fable "based on an obsessive grip of a single idea bordering on the supernatural" (6).

Cortez's helmet matches that of Quetzalcoatl preserved in the temple, he knows "the gods have come." He seeks in the conquistador "The key to the riddle of the Universe" (64). He incorporates into his deluded vision his image of Cortez, growing so enamored of it he fails to act against him as enemy of his reign and people; he is rendered impotent to act. When the illusion finally shatters and Montezuma is captured as hostage by Cortez, he accepts his mortality and tells his people, "I am but an Aztec man who would preserve his countrymen from further butchery" (102–3). Dying from an arrow shot by his own people, Montezuma tells Cortez that "in my unmourned face see your face, and in my destiny, the destiny of all oppression that dares to dig its heels in the living heart of Mexico" (106), words that are to echo in similar images in later Miller plays, as when Procter tells Judge Danforth in *The Crucible*, "I hear the boots of Lucifer, I see his filthy face. And it is my face, and yours, Danforth" (C, 119–20).

Although a play with political significance, reflecting in Cortez's mesmerizing of Montezuma Hitler's capacity to freeze Western opposition against him, *The Golden Years* holds a larger meaning as well. As Miller explains in his introduction, the crucial idea in the drama is that of personal responsibility. That is, "the belief in the centrality of the individual and the importance of what he thought and did." Whatever tragic consequences emerge from the collision of these historical figures come not from the differences between opposing cultures or from some manifestation of historical inevitability, but from Montezuma's own belief "about himself and his role in the universe." In other words, "there is no force as powerful, politically as well as personally, as a man's self-conception" (GY, 8). Montezuma is therefore not so much the victim of Cortez or of history as of himself, of his own choices. He bears the primary responsibility for his tragic end even as it enlarges his stature by bringing him to full self-awareness and acceptance of his own culpability.

In *Timebends*, Miller writes about the genesis of his next drama, *The Man Who Had All the Luck*. Provoked by hearing from his mother-in-law's younger sister, Helen, the story of her apparently successful husband's suicide, Miller first wrote a failed novel before reworking the story through "endless drafts" into the play (T, 86–88), his first Broadway production. He conceived of it as a "fable" or a "myth" concerned with the workings of fate rather than as a realistic portrayal of characters. The draft as first performed in 1944 treats, as Miller notes, a Job-like figure in reverse. David Beeves is the beneficiary of extraordinary luck. When his intended's father violently opposes their marriage, he is suddenly killed in an accident. When David tries unsuccessfully to repair the expensive car of a man who could make his fortune, a total stranger—an Austrian immigrant named Gus Eberson—mysteriously appears and fixes the car for him, allowing David to take the credit. When David buys a modest garage, the state builds a highway in front of it. While others suffer, he prospers, even though he cannot understand the reasons for his good fortune and considers himself unworthy. Believing in some sense of cosmic justice, he is convinced he must somehow pay for his successes. "[I]s a thing really yours because your name is on it?" he asks. "Don't you have to feel you're smart enough, or strong enough, or something enough to have won it before it's really yours?" (MWHAL, 158). Like a Puritan hounded by guilt, he both fears retribution and seeks it, thinking it will at last free him from his fear that he must pay for his luck. Other characters in the story see life differently. Shory, the owner of the local Feed and Grain Store who first hired David and began his string of successes, expresses a more nihilistic view of an arbitrary universe: "You can't make anything happen any more than a jellyfish makes the tides," he tells David (121). "A jellyfish can't swim no matter how he tries; it's the tide that pushes him every time" (170). For Shory, whose legs were blown off in a freak explosion at the end of the war, the universe contains no prevailing justice. And when David confesses that he and Hester seem unable to have children, Gus, who now is David's employee and closest friend, remarks, "What has this got to do with right or wrong? There is no justice in the world" (155).

But David is driven by a puritanical need to find order in the universe. When his brother Amos fails to receive a professional baseball contract after years of obsessive training administered by his father, Pat, David again feels guilty. He knows he has not earned his luck, whereas Amos has worked ceaselessly but vainly to be a major league player. Again faced with an indifferent universe, David tries to assure Amos's dream by talking a pro scout into watching his brother play. The ploy fails, however, when the scout spots Amos's flaw, an inability to respond to game conditions, essentially, he surmises, because his father overtrained him by forcing him to pitch in the cellar in the winter months and dulled his sensitivity to adjust to real game pressures. Turning on his father, Amos blames him for his failure and for not teaching him how to do anything other than pitch, a foreshadowing of Chris and Biff's Oedipal rebellions against their fathers in *All My Sons* and *Death of a Salesman*. In the meantime, measuring his incredible luck against his unworthiness, David becomes even more obsessive about a pending judgment, even subconsciously willing the death of his and Hester's child, conceived after three barren years of marriage. Certain that the death of his child will come as evidence of a divine retribution he cannot evade, he is so shattered by its being "a perfect baby" that he cannot bear to touch it, feeling both shame for having willed its death and fear that some payment still awaits him.

The plot finally turns on the failure of David's mink farm, an enterprise he enters through the assistance of Dan Dibble, the wealthy farmer whose car David took credit for repairing on the day Gus Eberson arrived. Investing all his holdings and mortgaging all his property to invest in the breeding of his minks, he discovers that he has apparently fed them diseased fish that will wipe them all out just at whelping time. Although Hester learns about the contaminated feed before David gives it to the minks, she does not tell him, wanting them to die and so complete the catastrophe David lived in fear of occurring. Were he to choose to participate in their deaths, she reasoned, he would assume responsibility for his life rather than seeing himself as the victim of fate. She places the burden of choice on him: "It was you who made it all and destroyed it!" (*MWHAL*, 204).

In the 1989 version of the play, Miller has David cautiously discard any fish with the black specks that reveal their contamination and so unwittingly save the animals. Once again David is astounded by his luck. But Hester again insists that he alone must assume the responsibility for what happens: "This wasn't something from the sky. This was only you" (*MWHAL*, 207). Yet even at the end, David still lives with a fear of retribution that saps his will and reduces his personal responsibility for his life. Twice he responds with an ambiguous and ominous "For now": once when Gus insists he is lucky and should enjoy it, and once at the very end, when he calls up to Hester, "Yes, I'm here! . . . For now" (208). He still cannot fully claim free will and apparently still awaits the agency of some external force to determine his fate.[8]

Miller attributed the failure of the original play in part to the production itself, but mainly to his failed attempt to marry myth and realism. "I was trying to make this guy both mythic and ordinary at the same time," he has said of David, "and succeeded in making him more ordinary than mythic" (AMC, 40). Yet, as Paul Unwin, director of the Bristol Old Vic 1990 production, observes, Miller was stretching the bounds of realism to explore a wider issue: "At the same time when Europe seemed to be abandoning itself to tyranny and America abandoning Europe, Miller was testing the notion of individual responsibility. Do we affect events or are we simply their victims?" (41).[9]

Brenda Murphy sees in the play a "close affinity to Ibsen's *Master Builder*" in Miller's exploration of the question. Given the close similarities between David and Ibsen's figure Solness—both blessed by good fortune, both thinking their good luck undeserved, both fearing some catastrophe in payment—"it might seem an adaptation if it were it not for the fundamental thematic differences in Miller's play." The "fundamental" difference, according to Murphy, is that Solness is a "tragic" figure, "both guilty and victimized, the cause of a self-destruction that he cannot avoid," whereas David Beeves exists in a universe where luck is "a matter of random chance." Miller's focus falls on "the efficacy of praxis—willed action."[10] Yet Miller himself has written that the flaw in his play is that "it should have ended tragically . . . although I hadn't written it tragically, I hadn't set out to write a tragedy" (AMC, 40). Miller's artistic dilemma points toward the problematic question of the nature of tragedy that

8. In earlier versions of the play, David gains a fuller epiphany, and the play ends with a more complete and happier resolution.

9. Miller relates David Beeves to Montezuma in *The Golden Years* in that they both were "destroyed by an illusion of . . . powerlessness," which he again relates to "the paralysis of will in the democracies as Hitler moved week by week to the domination of all Europe" (T, 90). He also writes, "The fear of drift, more exactly a drift into some kind of fascism, lay hidden somewhere in the origins of *The Man Who Had All the Luck*" (86).

10. Brenda Murphy, "The Tradition of Social Drama: Miller and His Forebears," 16, 18. For a more extensive treatment of the topic, see Murphy's essay, "*The Man Who Had All the Luck*: Miller's Answer to *The Master Builder*."

was to inform so much of the criticism of his early successes—*All My Sons*, *Death of a Salesman*, *The Crucible*, *A View from the Bridge*—and has hounded him throughout his career: To what degree can free will and tragic choice coexist in a universe denied a moral agency or divine intervention?

In his autobiography, Miller describes a brief but telling meeting with John Anderson, a critic for the *Journal American*. Anderson told him that he sensed in *The Man Who Had All the Luck* "some strong shadow world behind the characters, a fascinating gathering of darkness that made me wonder if you have thought of writing tragedy. A doom hangs over this play, something that promotes tragedy." In fact, he said to Miller, "you've written a tragedy, you know, but in a folk comedy style." Miller concludes, "I held his words dear" (*T*, 104). With hindsight, Miller admits, "the truth was that the play's action did seem to demand David's tragic death, but that was unthinkable to my rationalist viewpoint" (*T*, 105). This fascinating observation describes the nexus of Miller's early artistic struggle with tragedy as genre. Clearly drawn to the Greeks and to Ibsen's conviction that there is an inexorable system of retribution, that the past always demands payment in the present, Miller at the same time located the hidden forces of retribution in the self, combining fate and free will without the machinery of the supernatural. *The Man Who Had All the Luck* sets in juxtaposition the "mythic" elements of tragedy and Miller's "rationalist viewpoint." Despite its failure, Miller reflects, "I learned . . . where I was positioned in the world" (*Conv.*, 347). *All My Sons* and the plays to follow reflect Miller's attempt to accommodate these seemingly opposing views and to forge a conception of tragedy that both builds on and severely strains the tradition of tragedy and Ibsen's redefinition of it.

All My Sons

Other than his experiments writing drama and radio plays before completing *All My Sons* in 1947, Miller wrote a number of prose works, most notably his novel *Focus*, which he penned partly in response to the stage failure of *The Man Who Had All the Luck*. Important among these was his book *Situation Normal*, essentially a series of "reports" that he first wrote to contribute to a war movie

(The Story of G.I. Joe) based on Ernie Pyle's *This Is Your War*. In his numerous interviews with soldiers, Miller was seeking confirmation of his assumption that the men were fighting out of principle rather than necessity or legal obligation, but he was disillusioned by his inability "to find men who betray a social responsibility as a reason for doing or not doing anything." This disturbing awareness was countered by his admiration of men transformed by an inordinate loyalty and commitment to comrades-in-arms and by his sympathy for those soldiers who found it difficult to return to the insularity of their previous lives. He "couldn't help believing . . . that somewhere in their subconscious they knew not only that America must win but that Fascism must be destroyed."[11] Miller's war reportage no doubt did much to mature his own moral sensibility. Good and evil could no longer assume the simplistic nature of moral certainty that informed his earlier work. *All My Sons* reflects Miller's evolving sense of moral complexity in tension with a form that constrains his ability fully to penetrate the moral ambiguity he exposes.

According to Miller, the idea for *All My Sons* came from his then-mother-in-law's incidental gossip "about a young girl somewhere in central Ohio who had turned her father in to the FBI for having manufactured faulty aircraft parts during the war" (*T*, 85). Vowing to make one more attempt to create a successful play, Miller intended to "do something which is first of all clear" (*Conv.*, 177). His efforts were rewarded by a New York run of 328 performances and receipt of the Drama Critics' Circle Award, which the play won in competition with Eugene O'Neill's *The Iceman Cometh*. Still stung by the pervasive criticism of *The Man Who Had All the Luck* as muddy and discursive, he set out with full deliberation to keep reworking the new play "until it seemed as tight as a drum" (*T*, 271).

All My Sons was first titled *The Sign of the Archer*, a reference to Keller's wife, Kate's desperate belief in astrology and perhaps as well to the linear structure of the play—the "*x* leads to *y* leads to *z*" trajectory of classical Greek tragedy. Committed from his study at Michigan to the Aristotelian form of Greek drama and the pattern of introspective illumination he found in the shaping influence of Ibsen, Miller considered the play's achievement to be "its revelation of process, and it was made a stitch at a time, so to speak, in

11. Arthur Miller, *Situation Normal*, 44, 40.

order to weave a tapestry before our eyes" (*TE*, 135). Often called his most Ibsenian play, *All My Sons* imitates Ibsen's conception of drama as "a lifting of the veil," in which "the past reaches into the present, usually destructively, but leaving some illumination behind" (486). Thematically, the play describes the devastating effects of innocence, both as a form of self-denial and as simple ignorance; but to some its excessive plotting and dependence on chance incidents, its strict obedience to the unities, and its adherence to a rigid architectonic structure, make it, in Hersh Zeifman's phrase, "straitjacketed by order."[12]

Miller has claimed that *All My Sons* was one of the plays he had to write "to master naturalism before I tried anything else" (*Conv.*, 7). But the play is infused with symbolism and mythical allusions that coexist with its naturalistic surface. The archetypal set, that remains the same throughout the play, evokes the image of Eden "after the Fall." Prominent in the right downstage corner is "a four-foot-high stump of a slender apple tree whose upper trunk and branches lie toppled beside it, fruit still clinging to its branches" (*AMS*, 5). A composite symbol, the split tree carries overt mythic significance. Yet when Joe Keller refers to the fallen tree in the opening scene, he speaks with the most quotidian language, responding to his neighbor Frank Lubey, "Ain't it awful? The wind must've got it last night" (7). Often accused of lacking poetry in his early plays, Miller in fact often employs the prosaic language of realism in dialogue, counterbalancing the poetic devices of symbolism and the subtle manipulation of stage imagery and form. Clearly, the wind is a metaphysical image, a coming of the forces of retribution, the plague signaling the gathering forces of the past in Ibsenian fashion. As Kate ironically senses, "there are meanings in such things" (22).

The fallen tree obviously alludes to the post-Lapsarian world of the Keller household. Planted in honor of Larry, the younger Keller son missing in action for three years, the tree furthers the plot and initiates much of the dialogue. The action often centers around the tree; characters touch it, and Larry pulls off the broken top of the tree as the second act begins, leaving the stump the insignia of their shattered Eden. The play, Enoch Brater rightly concludes, possesses

12. Hersh Zeifman, "All My Sons After the Fall: Arthur Miller and the Rage for Order," 107.

"mythological paraphernalia . . . entirely integrated with a natural-istic set." In this mundane setting—almost a quintessential depiction of American middle-class life in the post-war era—we sense, as Ben Brantley observes in his review of the Roundabout's 1997 produc-tion, that "the shame is as thick as fog."[13] The fallen Eden proves to be more than just the Kellers' lost paradise; it becomes an emblem of the failure of the American dream, which Miller captures with far deeper insight in *Death of a Salesman*.

Rooted in his dark vision of the war and, beyond that, the Depres-sion that the war ironically ended, Miller glimpses a society traveling "on some kind of obscene trip, looking to get rich at any cost," just as pre-Depression society moved blindly to the Crash. Indeed, he views the period as the "most materialistic moment in history since I've been around," driven by "a lot of sharks who were leading, not only the economy, but the spiritual side of the country" (AMC, 49). Part of the crass materialism that propelled the country, the Kellers confront the consequences of their choices. Their backyard becomes an arena of the dead and dying. Miller recalls how he complained to the set designer of the first Broadway production, Mordecai Gorelik, about a low bump placed on the stage that interfered with the actors' movements. "You have written a graveyard play," Gorelik retorted. "The play is taking place in a cemetery where their son is buried, and he is also their buried conscience reaching up to them out of the earth." The bump stayed, assuming "a certain power" that unified the performance and, in Miller's words, reminded the actors "that the play was indeed about a bad conscience" (T, 275)—one that is shared by virtually every character in the play.

As central figure, Joe Keller bears the heaviest weight of respon-sibility for the tragedy he has unwittingly brought upon his family. Despite his casual demeanor and feeble attempts to lighten the per-vading darkness that falls on the household, he expresses his sense of guilt from the opening minutes of the play. His concern about Kate's discovering the fallen tree and the compassion he feels for her when his son Chris informs him that she was up when the tree cracked at four in the morning partly disguise a deeper concern. He tells Chris that they cannot tell Kate that they believe the elder

13. Enoch Brater, "Ethics and Ethnicity in the Plays of Arthur Miller," 126; Ben Brantley, "Arthur Miller Visits the Sins of the Fathers upon the Children," C11.

son, Larry, is dead or insist that she face the truth because the finality of Larry's death would seal his own guilt. He is *"frightened at the thought"* of telling her because he knows she would associate Larry's death with those of the twenty-one pilots killed by faulty cylinder heads he ordered shipped. Clearly, he knows that Kate is aware of his culpability in the crime even though she never openly speaks of it.[14] When Chris tries to elicit his approval to marry Ann Deever, Larry's fiancée, Joe tries to evade commitment, apprehensive of how Kate would react and how such a union would resurrect a past he fears to confront. "Isn't it your business, too?" Chris asks. "You have a talent for ignoring things"—to which Joe admits with unintended irony, "I ignore what I gotta ignore" (AMS, 16).

Despite his seeming obliviousness to the past, he cannot stop playing "jail" and "police" with the neighbor's children; and when Kate insists "There's no jail here," expressing her own denial of guilt, Joe responds defensively that he has "nothing to hide" (AMS, 23).[15] Yet even his language betrays him, as he tells Chris he must take over the business because "The whole shootin' match is for you!" (13)—both an oblique reference to the war and an ominous foreshadowing of his suicide. Kate pointedly tells Joe, pricking his conscience, that he must continue to believe in Larry's survival—"You, above all, have got to believe; you . . ." "Why me above all?" he asks. "What does that mean, me above all?" (23).

As the first act closes, Joe continues to show his vulnerability. Boasting that he returned from the penitentiary "with a smile" and proudly walked down the street even though everyone thought he was guilty, Joe adds, "Except I wasn't and there was a court paper

14. Although this seems apparent on rereading the text, critics have only recently begun to recognize Kate's awareness of Joe's guilt, a fact made powerfully apparent in Julie Walters's performance in the highly acclaimed London restaging in 2000. Her performance, along with such performances as Elizabeth Franz's Tony-winning portrayal of Linda Loman and Joan Allen's depiction of Elizabeth Proctor in the 1999 film version of *The Crucible*, has helped establish a new appreciation of Miller's ability to create strong female characters despite occasional attacks in feminist criticism.

15. As critics have noted, references to *jail*, *crime*, *the law*, and similar terms appear throughout. Ann's brother George is a lawyer, and the father of the woman whom George is supposed to marry is a retired police inspector. As any reader of Miller knows, his works are filled with such references, and in some respect almost every play contains a literal or figurative courtroom and trial.

in my pocket to prove I wasn't" (AMS, 30). But he knows that the legality of a paper innocence holds no truth. He subconsciously uses his former employee Steve Deever to displace his own guilt, urging Deever's daughter, Ann, to show compassion for the surrogate who took the blame for Joe's own crime. He tells her that her father's shipping the faulty parts was "a mistake, but it ain't murder. You mustn't feel that way about him" (33). Just as his vigorous defense of Ann's father proves a form of self-exoneration, so does his insistence to Chris that Larry never flew a P-40 like the planes wrecked by the damaged cylinder heads. More evidence of his guilt surfaces in his fear of George, Ann's brother, who announces he is coming to see her after visiting their father in jail. Fearing a conspiracy, Joe tells Chris that George's going to see his father for the first time may be part of a plot to get him and that Ann "was sent here to find out something" (38). At the conclusion of the laborious first act, Joe once again reveals his sense of guilt when he tells Chris he wants to leave his wealth to Chris: "I mean with joy, Chris, without shame . . . with joy. . . . Because I sometimes think you're . . . ashamed of the money" (38).

Miller introduces a potentially tragic conflict in Joe Keller that he develops far more convincingly in the character of Willy Loman. Keller ultimately does embody conflicting forces, not, as Benjamin Nelson has written, of "good versus evil," but "family and society, each of which is inherently good." And Nelson goes on to say that tragic irony emerges in that Keller's "crime against the outside world eventually becomes a crime against his own family as well."[16] But Miller reaches for a moral complexity and tragic resolution in *All My Sons* that he never fully achieves, largely because of the limitation of the recognition scene and the underdeveloped motivation for Joe's suicide.

Keller's denial of responsibility extends to the end of the play when Chris dramatically reads Larry's last letter to Ann blaming his father and announcing his suicide. Just before this, Keller tells Chris he cannot send him to jail "Because you know I don't belong there." Asserting personal innocence by virtue of a corporate guilt, he demands, "Who worked for nothin' in that war? When they work for nothin', I'll work for nothin'. . . . Half the Goddamn country is gotta

16. Nelson, *Arthur Miller*, 86.

go if I go!" (AMS, 82). But when Chris reads Larry's letter and Keller rereads it in disbelief, he suddenly seems completely accepting of his guilt. After two very short exchanges with Chris, in which Joe insists that "a man can't be a Jesus in this world!" he decides he will accept judgment. Declaring he "thinks" he understands, he speaks his famous "all my sons" speech: "Sure, he was my son. But I think they were all my sons. I guess they were, I guess they were" (83). The language expresses an instantaneous but hardly convincing conversion. Miller, Alan Stambusky contends, "gives" Keller "the tragic insight of the classical hero."[17] It is an epiphany neither fully earned nor understood, although Miller's tragic sense dictates its occurrence. The extent of Keller's understanding is limited to a three-sentence response. Raymond Williams analyzes the artistic problem as a manifestation of Miller's attempt "to express so deep and substantial a personal discovery" in "the naturalistic form" that the form collapses "because the consciousness which the form was designed to express is in any serious term obsolete, and was already, by Miller himself, being reached beyond."[18] Keller's speech has the ring of tragedy but not the substance.

The suicide poses another dilemma that makes the play appear more melodramatic than tragic. Although we witness Keller's guilt throughout and Miller points clearly to the death it inevitably leads to, the suicide's motivation and ultimate meaning remain obscure. One asks if Keller seeks death as self-judgment or escape, whether, as Santosh Bhatia concludes, the death is "an act of self-purification" that "sets a seal on his heroism and provides a rich tragic import to the play," or whether it serves the function of a well-made plot without possessing the psychological or mythic authority of a modern tragedy. Tom Scanlon points to the perhaps unintentional irony that Keller wills death not because of his allegiance to "all my sons" but because he sees in Larry's rejection of his fatherhood a denial of his myopic vision about the primacy of the father-son relationship—"and if there's anything bigger than that I'll put a

17. Alan A. Stambusky, "Arthur Miller: Aristotelian Canons in the Twentieth-Century Drama," 97. Robert Bechtold Heilman calls Keller "an Uncle Ben . . . who is finally pushed, somewhat abruptly, into a quasi-tragic role—self-recognition and suicide" (The Iceman, the Arsonist, and the Troubled Agent: Tragedy and Melodrama on the Modern Stage, 142–43).

18. Raymond Williams, "Arthur Miller: An Overview," 10.

bullet in my head!"(AMS, 77).[19] The result is a measure of moral uncertainty in the play, which seems, on the one hand, to condemn Keller's narrow commitment to the family as the center of his value system and, on the other hand, to explain much of the action in terms of the exclusively family values the text seems to reject. Unlike *Death of a Salesman*, in which Willy's death projects an intended artistic ambiguity, in *All My Sons* the suicide ends in near equivocation as escape *or* suicide, rather than being either both or neither.

Like Keller, Kate has provoked lively debate among Miller critics. To some, like Harold Clurman, she bears heavy responsibility for the tragic consequences that emerge. To Clurman, "If there is a 'villain' in the piece, it is the mother—the kindly, caring mother who wants her brood safe and her home undisturbed." A victim of her blinding innocence, she "cannot consciously accept the consequences of the morality she lives by" even though "it is a morality that kills her children and even her husband."[20] Miller's own comments give some credence to Clurman's accusation and go even further. In response to Rosemary Harris's portrayal of Kate in a London production directed by Michael Blakemore, Miller commented that she is "a woman using truth as a weapon against the man who had harmed her son . . . rather ambiguously destroying him with her knowledge of his crime. . . . There's a sinister side to her in short" (*Conv.*, 369).[21] In *Timebends* he goes so far as to argue that "Her guilty knowledge, so obdurately and menacingly repressed, can be interpreted as a wish to deny her son's death, but also, and perhaps even primarily, to take revenge on her culpable husband by driving him psychically to his knees and ultimately to suicide" (*T*, 135–36).

19. Santosh K. Bhatia, *Arthur Miller: Social Drama as Tragedy*, 42; Tom Scanlon, *Family, Drama, and American Dreams*, 74. Steven R. Centola describes Keller's suicide as a failure "to transform guilt into responsibility; he dies as he has lived—in bad faith" ("Bad Faith and *All My Sons*," 128). Examples of the foreshadowing of the death include Chris's prediction that one day the kids Joe teases about jail will "all come in here and beat your brains out" (AMS, 14) and the "I'll put a bullet in my head!" statement.

20. Harold Clurman, *Lies Like Truth: Theatre Reviews and Essays*, 67.

21. In the same context Miller also comments on Hanna Marron's 1977 depiction of Kate in Jerusalem. The production "centered on Kate, the mother, which was an emphasis our original production had bypassed in favor of the father-son conflict" (*T*, 135).

Not surprisingly, feminist and other critics have been quick to attack Miller's portrayal of Kate, as well as his depiction of women like Linda Loman, Elizabeth Proctor, Beatrice Carbone, and Maggie in *After the Fall*. "Miller's male point of view defines women as Other, either a paper doll devoid of depth and warmth or a source of confusion and the locus of evil," one critic protests. Charging Miller with sexual bias, he concludes that Miller distributes "situations, options, and agony along gender lines, creating women who endure and survive and men who fail and fall. If Miller writes tragedy . . . he makes it a male preserve."[22] It would be difficult to argue that Miller does create many fully rounded female characters suitable to tragedy, especially in the early plays, but the same can be said of most playwrights in the long tradition of tragedy. In *All My Sons*, it can be argued, Kate is not simply marginalized as one who can only "endure and survive" but not "fail and fall" as a tragic figure. Although not a tragic protagonist who comes to larger awareness, she actually contributes to the tragic elements of the play, fully capable of making "tragic" choices and of suffering their consequences.

Kate's stiff, insistent nature bears witness to her guilt. Precisely because she subconsciously knows not only of Keller's guilt but of her own, she acts with near ruthless determination to keep the past at bay while at the same time desperately trying to freeze the moment of Larry's disappearance. Fully cognizant of Keller's crime, which she tacitly excuses by her silence, she projects her insistence on his innocence onto Ann's father, who is jailed in Joe's place, telling her, "What your father did had nothing to do with Larry. Nothing. . . . That's all, that's enough" (AMS, 31–32). Accepting Larry's death would not only mean the collapse of the family upon which she places all value, but would also acknowledge the presentness of a past testifying to the shared guilt of the family. As Miller emphasizes, she *knows* Keller's culpability and shares it by protecting the secret. Consequently, she futilely struggles to arrest time, to reject Larry's death in fear that it is a form of judgment.

Psychologically, she is bound to believe that Ann Deever has been "waiting" for Larry. Threatened by Chris's obvious intent to marry Ann, she proves capable of petty cattiness, telling Ann "I'm afraid

22. Jeffrey D. Mason, "Paper Dolls: Melodrama and Sexual Politics in Arthur Miller's Early Plays," 112–13.

you gained a little weight, didn't you, dear?" when Chris shows obvious admiration for Ann's new dress (*AMS*, 26). As Ann becomes more insistent, Kate ironically claims that Larry "has" to be alive because it is evidence of a cosmic order. "That's why there's God. Otherwise anything could happen" (28). She attempts to invert what she already knows but cannot admit. The evidence of moral order in the universe is in fact Larry's sacrificial death in expiation of his father's sin. So when Ann asks, "And do you know Larry wasn't one of them" killed by the faulty aircraft parts, Kate knowingly responds, "Put that out of your head!" (31–32), revealing her secret fear of retribution.

Of course, she does not gain tragic awareness; to the end she hopelessly tries to avoid judgment. Facing Chris's alienation, she places the full weight of guilt onto her husband: "I mean you might make it clear to him that you *knew* you did a terrible thing" (*AMS*, 76). But her effort to absolve herself by blaming Keller, like her need to believe that "the stars" determine fate rather than personal choice, finally confronts the truth of Larry's harsh judgment. Kate's foreknowledge is implicit in her reaction. Fiercely struggling to keep Chris from reading the letter, she obviously fears the implication of what it says. Showing no shock of recognition, she begs Joe not to go with Chris to jail and ironically pleads with Chris, "It's up to you, if you tell him to stay, he'll stay. Go and tell him!" (84). Even when Joe shoots himself, she tries to bury guilt. "Don't, dear," she tells Chris; "Don't take it on yourself. Forget now. Live" (83). She thus ends the play by muting judgment with a plea of innocence.

Chris, too, falls short of being a fully tragic figure. Miller speaks of the importance of his first discovering the centrality of the father-son relationship in writing *The Man Who Had All the Luck*, and *All My Sons* was no doubt fueled by this interest. Just as *The Man Who Had All the Luck* anticipates *All My Sons* in treating the theme, Miller's first successful play points to *Death of a Salesman*. But whereas in *Death of a Salesman* Biff, Happy, and Willy form a composite tragic hero, in *All My Sons* the characters never attain full integration. However ambiguously, Willy's death frees Biff as a representative of Willy's own best self, but Joe Keller's suicide leaves Chris's fate unresolved.

Like his father, Chris falls victim to innocence, although Miller makes him the moral spokesman in the play. In Christopher Bigsby's analysis, the "submerged theme" in *All My Sons* is "a concern with guilt as a principal mechanism of human behavior" poised against "self-interest as a spectre behind the mask of idealism." Although he takes on the role of moral conscience in the play, Chris betrays a capacity for self-delusion and denial even to the end. Miller's intent, however, was apparently to imbue Chris with the vision necessary to give the play its moral vision. Ostensibly, Chris grows in the play, gaining a knowledge about "the sins of the father" and the conspiracy of silence and finally pronouncing judgment on them. Edward Murray even declares that Chris is "primarily free from the sense of guilt and able to enjoy life again. . . . [H]is movement as a whole seems relatively steady and credible."[23] The counterview, however, portrays Chris as pompous, weak, even hypocritical, and driven as much by guilt as moral outrage.

The truth is that Miller himself intended to show in Chris "the guilt of an idealist who presents an impossible ideal"; but, he concludes, "I didn't know how to do it. I could only carry the impulse to a certain end" (AMC, 48). A David Beeves rendered more complex, Chris bears responsibility for being the interpreter of the moral ideal he himself fails to uphold. Unlike an Oedipus come to self-awareness and passing judgment on himself, Chris remains suspect even to the end of the play. Miller gives Chris virtue without a necessary heroism, allowing him to voice moral truths but limiting his acknowledgment of his own culpability. He appears to lack full integrity precisely because he remains to some degree innocently self-ignorant. It is such innocence that Miller was later to display as a debilitating virtue.[24]

Miller did not consciously make Chris an innocent character, however. He recognized the destructive potential of innocence in

23. Christopher Bigsby, A Critical Introduction to Twentieth-Century American Drama 2: Tennessee Williams, Arthur Miller, Edward Albee, 168; Edward Murry, Arthur Miller, Dramatist, 16.

24. A good indication of the artistic tension this produces surfaces in two reviews of the Roundabout's 1997 revival. Responding to Michael Hayden's portrayal of Chris, Howard Kissel complained that Hayden's Chris "has an openness that is just right for a man others dislike for his virtuousness, but he must also suggest a heroic stature, which Hayden does not" ("Sons Lacks Pop: Overacting Spoils Dated Miller Drama," 33). On the other hand, Ben Brantley contended that Hayden "turns his character's saintliness into a willful assumed ignorance that will shatter into devastating effect" and give "genuinely tragic life" to the play ("Arthur Miller Visits the Sins," C-13).

characterizing Chris, but his intent was often obscured by his use of Chris as moral spokesman.[25] Reflecting Miller's depiction of the capacity for heroism in ordinary men during war in *Situation Normal*, Chris says of the men he commanded that "they didn't die; they killed themselves for each other. . . . Everything was being destroyed, see, but it seemed to me that one thing was made. A kind of responsibility. Man for man." Returning to work for his father, he acknowledges, "I felt . . . ashamed somehow. . . . I felt wrong to be alive, to open the bankbook, to drive a new car, to see the new refrigerator" (AMS, 36). And Ann tells him, "Even in your letters, there was something ashamed" (35). Even at the end when he acts in righteous indignation at his father's crime, Kate undermines his moral virtue, commenting, "I always had the feeling in the back of my head, Chris . . . almost knew" (74). And if he already knew and neglected to act, he would share responsibility for the crime. Like the destructive Gregers in *The Wild Duck*, which surely must have influenced Miller, Chris is diminished as moral agent because his embracing of moral certitude is tinged with willful self-denial.

Chris's relationship with his father, as Biff's with Willy in *Death of a Salesman*, forms the nexus of the play, but whereas the later work depicts a genuine moral ambiguity, the earlier drama suffers from a lack of critical focus. Although Larry's condemnation provides the moral perspective in its judgment of Keller, Chris plays the hero of consciousness, pontificating to Kate that "This is the land of the great big dogs, you don't love a man here, you eat him! That's the principle; the only one we live by—it just happened to kill a few hundred this time, that's all. The world's that way . . ." (AMS, 81). But as Christopher Bigsby states, "Righteousness and self-righteousness become confused" in Chris, as Keller's "guilt becomes entwined with [Chris's] desire to declare his innocence." According to June Schlueter and James Flanagan, Keller and Kate's self-deluding belief in their innocence is mitigated in part by "their belief in the sanctity of the Keller family," but Chris's "is the more treacherous kind of self-delusion, for Chris believes religiously in the lie" of "the

---

25. Miller's commentary in *Timebends* in reference to Arthur Kennedy's performance as Chris in the original Broadway production reflects his awareness of Chris's duplicity. Miller notes that Chris's "sweet idealism in the first act must turn to murderous anger at the climax of the second" (T, 272).

purity of his father's behavior."[26] To guard his own innocence, Chris ultimately must make his father scapegoat for the accumulated guilt of the family.

Ironically, Jim Bayliss tells Kate that Chris could "never live" knowing the truth, because surviving "takes a certain talent . . . for lying. You have it, and I do. But not him." But in fact Chris is one of the conspirators in denial, along with Keller, Kate, and the neighbors (as Jim tells Kate, "I've always known") (AMS, 74). Suffering from guilt because he lived while those under his command died, because he betrays them by "doing business" with his father, because he wants to marry Larry's intended, he finds his father a scapegoat for his own passivity.[27] Having not acted himself, he accuses his father of his own sin of silence and fraudulently plays a "metaphoric Christ, a secular saint espousing universal love for all God's children."[28] At best he shares complicity in his father's death, which seems vaguely to be both an act of Oedipal destruction of the father and a moral judgment.

As the purveyor of much of the moral vision of the play, especially in his overtly moralistic speeches at the end, Chris courts a priggishness that subverts the moral force of his words. But while it is not altogether clear to what degree Miller intends us to see this duplicity, it becomes increasingly obvious that the idealistic characters in Miller's work, from Chris Keller on, are prone to lapsing into self-absorbing innocence, suspect even when they adhere to moral certainty. For Miller, the only evil greater than an act of evil itself is the claim of innocence that allows for self-deception to camouflage

26. Christopher Bigsby, Modern American Drama, 1945–1990, 78; June Schlueter and James K. Flanagan, Arthur Miller, 49.

27. Among critics who have noted this, see especially Nada Zeineddine's conclusion that "In seeking his father's punishment, Chris is actually atoning for his sins" (Because It Is My Name: Problems of Identity Experienced by Women, Artists, and Breadwinners in the Plays of Henrik Ibsen, Tennessee Williams, and Arthur Miller, 161); and Steven R. Centola's similar argument that "by destroying his father," Chris hopes "he can somehow expiate his own sin" ("All My Sons" 37).

28. Zeifman, "All My Sons After the Fall," 109. See also Raymond H. Reno's sarcastic depiction of Chris as "Christ the killer. The one he kills is his father [God], and it is this fact that organizes the allegory" ("Arthur Miller and the Death of God," 1070). To the contrary, Santosh Bhatia favorably compares Chris to Hamlet in his idealism and virtue: "He too, like Hamlet, confronts a world which is full of evil and betrayal" (Arthur Miller, 40).

the potential for evil in one's self—yet, paradoxically, the attempt to find the moral center, however fated to end in ambiguity, is the ennobling principle in Miller's heroes. His commitment to realism seldom allows his protagonists the comfort of surety, but the struggle to affirm a moral order can lead to a measure of victory more existential than transcendental. Chris contains far more subtlety of character than Miller's earlier idealists (like Arnie Simon or David Beeves), but the dependence on plot and the heavy-handed moralism he is designated to speak tend to restrict his psychological development as a character and to obfuscate the duplicity Miller hints at in his character. It was forceful enough, though, Miller points out, to motivate the Catholic War Veterans to demand the banning of all productions of Miller plays by the army (*E*, 279).

Despite the artistic flaws of *All My Sons*, it possesses an often compelling theatricality. Like its rival in 1947, *The Ice Man Cometh*, it still enjoys a powerful stage life, as recent revivals remind us. Given its close adherence to the practices of the well-made play as it was refined by Ibsen, it tends at times to substitute plot for character. Additionally, it blurs the line between "legal guilt" and "moral awakening," as Christopher Bigsby contends. Even Keller's recognition speech ("Sure, he was my son. But I think to him they were all my sons" [*AMS*, 82]) "follows proof of physical causality rather than moral conversion."[29] Be that as it may, the drama marks a crucial stage in Miller's development as playwright. It begins to probe deeper psychological levels, to explore a world of moral complexities, to test the limits of realism, and to dramatize more subtly the pervasive presentness of the past than the earlier texts. Miller recalls that "*All My Sons* had exhausted my lifelong interest in the Greco-Ibsen form, in the particular manner in which I had come to think of it" (*T*, 144); but his next great play, *Death of a Salesman*, is inextricably bound to the tradition of tragedy as he understood it and is in large measure a culmination of his own emerging tragic vision.

29. Christopher Bigsby, *Confrontation and Commitment: A Study of Contemporary American Drama, 1959–66*, 27–30.

2   Death of a Salesman

"Tragedy," Eric Bentley has warned, can "easily lure us into talking nonsense." If so, *Death of a Salesman* surely doubles the risk. For likely no modern drama has generated more such talk than Miller's classic American play. After two decades of strenuous debate had seemed to have exhausted the subject, critics began to complain about "the pointless academic quibbles" concerning whether or not *Death of a Salesman* is a "true" tragedy. Such topics, wrote Lois Gordon in 1969, "have been explored ad nauseam."[1] Yet, thirty years later and a half-century after the play's premiere, the question of its fitness as a tragedy continues to be a central critical concern.

Of course, Miller himself provided much of the impetus for the critical battles by writing his controversial 1949 essay "Tragedy and the Common Man," in defense of Willy Loman as a suitable subject for tragedy; an essay later the same year, "The Nature of Tragedy"; and a number of important essays in subsequent years, including the preface "On Social Plays," published in the 1955 one-act edition of *A View from the Bridge* and *A Memory of Two Mondays*. Furthermore, the issue was and still is raised one way or the other in many, if not most, interviews, often by Miller himself. He admitted in the 1957 introduction to the *Collected Plays* that he had "set out not 'to write a tragedy' " and called *Death of a Salesman* "a slippery play" to categorize; nevertheless, he defended it against "some of the attacks upon it as a pseudo-tragedy": "I need not claim

1. Eric Bentley, *The Playwright as Thinker*, 128; Gerald C. Weales, *American Drama since World War II*, 3; Lois Gordon, *"Death of a Salesman:* An Appreciation," 98.

that this is a genuine solid-gold tragedy for my opinions on tragedy to be held valid" (*TE*, 144, 146).[2]

By the time he wrote the foreword to his *Theater Essays* (which was first edited by Robert A. Martin in 1977), Miller admitted, "I have often wished I had never written a word on the subject of tragedy"— and then, "[t]he damage having been done," he went on to argue for the validity of modern tragedy, concluding, "I have not yet seen a convincing explanation of why the tragic mode seems anachronistic now, nor am I about to attempt one" (*TE*, lv).

The critical controversy, however, has never fully abated, and the topic inevitably continues to surface in interviews. By the time Matthew Roudané interviewed him in November 1983, Miller seemed less defensive and insistent. Responding to the question of whether or not *Death of a Salesman* was a Sophoclean tragedy, he commented, "I think it does engender tragic feelings, at least in a lot of people. Let's say it's one kind of tragedy. I'm not particularly eager to call it tragedy or anything else; the label doesn't matter to me" (*Conv.*, 361). And in 1997 he claimed that when people ask him what the play is about, he simply responds, "Well, it's about a salesman and he dies. What can I tell you?"[3]

But undeniably the "damage" *has* been done; one way or the other, *Death of a Salesman*, probably more than any other dramatic play, still provokes critical wars about the viability of tragedy in the modern age and particularly in American culture. Even as Miller seems to have moved more into the contemporary literary world in his recent dramas, and as more critics have begun to see his canon in postmodern terms alien to the concept of tragedy and traditional approaches to the genre, the question still remains dominant in evaluations of a work that Eugene O'Neill may well have prophesied in response to those who argued that tragedy is foreign to the American experience:

> Supposing someday we should suddenly see with the clear eyes
> of a soul the true valuation of all our triumphant, brass band

2. Miller earlier told Robert Corrigan that he was not "concerned about tragic form" in writing the play: "That is after the fact. Just to lay that to rest. The theatre gets too involved in analytical theory" (*Conv.*, 257).

3. Jonathan Mandell, "Renaissance Man: At 82 Arthur Miller Is Pleasing a New Generation of Theatergoers." Miller also has described the play as "absurdly simple! It is about a salesman and it's his last day on the earth" (*TE*, 423).

materialism, see the cost—and the result in terms of eternal verities? What a colossal, ironic, 100 percent American tragedy that would be, what? Tragedy not native to our soil? Why, we *are* tragedy the most appalling yet written or unwritten![4]

Miller has always admitted his predilection for tragedy, at times at the cost of obfuscating his plays by defending them as tragedies. The plays "that have lasted," he has insisted, "have shared a kind of tragic vision of man" (*Conv.*, 294). Although "tragedy is still basically the same" and can be traced back to the Bible and "the earliest Western literature, like Greek drama," he told Robert Martin in the late 1960s, "it is unlikely, to say the least, that since so many other kinds of human consciousness have changed that [tragedy] would remain unchanged" (200). He acknowledged to Steven Centola in a 1990s interview that his own later plays "may seem more tragic" than his earlier efforts in which "the characters' inability to face themselves gives rise to tragic consequences."[5] This awareness of an evolving form may partly explain why even those critics who share Miller's belief in the "tragic nature" of *Death of a Salesman* often stop short of declaring it (or other of his plays) an unequivocal or conventional tragedy. They instead allude to its "tragic situations," its evocation of "tragic feelings," its "tragic implications," or its "tragic rhythms"—or to other subthemes of the genre. But an extensive survey of criticism, coupled with an interpretation of the play's salient features as a modern "tragedy," reveals identifiable, seminal issues that have informed Miller scholarship throughout the decades and locates the shaping themes in the canon of his work.

Miller has long confessed that classical tragedy and Ibsen's adaptation of it in the post-Enlightenment period have provided the structural and thematic spine of his work. Looking back over his career in the middle 1980s, he remarked: "I think probably the greatest single discovery I made was the structure of the Greek plays. That really blinded me. It seemed to fit everything that I felt. And then there was Ibsen, who was dealing with the same kind of structural pattern— that is the past meeting the present dilemma" (*Conv.*, 386).[6] He

4. Eugene O'Neill, *Selected Letters*, 159.
5. Centola, "'Just Looking,'" 86–87.
6. Miller also told James J. Martine his often repeated admission that the Greeks and Ibsen were the "two sources for my form—certainly for my ideas of a theatre's

recalled that as an undergraduate he read "by chance . . . a Greek tragedy and Ibsen at the same time" and discovered that "something happened *x* years ago, unbeknownst to the hero, and he's got to grapple with it" (AMC, 49). His devotion to the tragic mode as he perceives it and his varied experiments with tragic form and matter have made him more vulnerable to critics bent on showing the deficiencies of his works as tragedies or his mere mimicking of an obsolete literary tradition.

Christopher Bigsby may be right in claiming that "the argument over the tragic status of *Death of a Salesman*, finally, is beside the point,"[7] but of all Miller plays *Death of a Salesman* has been the lightening rod that has most attracted the unending debates on Miller and tragedy, and any serious assessment of its endurance and significance after fifty years must engage the question. Most often paralleled with *Oedipus*, *Death of a Salesman* has also been compared with Shakespearean tragedies (especially *Lear* and *Othello*), Lillo's *The London Merchant*, and various plays by Ibsen, O'Neill, Williams, and others.[8]

---

purposes." He told Olga Carlisle and Rose Styron in a *Paris Review* interview published in 1966 that tragedy "seemed to me the only form there was" when he began writing drama and that he especially admired the Greeks "for their magnificent form, the symmetry. . . . That form has never left me; I suppose it got burned into me." He also called himself a "descendent of Ibsen" in an interview with Ronald Hyman: "What he gave me in the beginning was a sense of the past and a sense of the rootedness of everything that happens" (*Conv.*, 292, 88, 189).

7. Christopher Bigsby, introduction to Arthur Miller, *Death of a Salesman*, xviii.

8. For a general summary of major opening-night reviews of the play as "tragedy," see especially Brenda Murphy's *Miller:* Death of a Salesman (61–65), and her provocative commentary on the 1999 staging of the play directed by Robert Fall, "The 1999 Revival of *Death of a Salesman*: A Critical Commentary." Articles and books that directly address the question tend to include summaries of critical opinions on the topic. For an especially useful commentary placing the play against historical definitions of tragedy, see Stephen Barker's "The Crisis of Authenticity: *Death of a Salesman* and the Tragic Muse," particularly his pithy but useful appendix tracing the evolution of theoretical views of tragedy. For more sustained discussions of *Death of a Salesman* and *Oedipus*, see especially Paul N. Siegel, "Willy Loman and King Lear"; Charlotte F. Otten, " 'Who Am I . . .': Re-investigation of Arthur Miller's *Death of a Salesman*"; Bhatia, *Arthur Miller*; Judah Bierman, James Hart, and Stanley Johnson, "Arthur Miller: *Death of a Salesman*"; and Esther Merle Jackson, "*Death of a Salesman*: Tragic Myth in the Modern Theatre." In a recent interview, Joyce Carol Oates refers to Willy as "our domestic Lear, spiraling toward suicide as toward an act of selfless grace, his mad scene on the heath a frantic seed-planting episode by flashlight in the midst of which the once proud, now disintegrating

Attacks on the play as tragedy have spanned from casual dismissal to vitriolic antagonism. Representative views include Eleanor Clark's early severe condemnation of the play's "pseudo-universality" and "party-line" polemics in her 1949 *Partisan Review* essay "Old Glamour, New Gloom." Calling Miller's concept of tragedy "not feasible," Alvin Whitley, among other somewhat later critics, admonished Miller to realize "that he is extending the traditional interpretation [of tragedy] to embrace demonstrably different emotional effects" and that, "in the basic matter of personal dignity, Willy Loman may have ended where Hamlet unquestionably began." Richard J. Foster labeled Willy a "pathetic bourgeois barbarian" and concluded that the drama was "not a 'tragedy' or great piece of literature." Reflecting a common theme among Miller critics, Eric Mottram assaulted Miller's "muddled notions of Greek tragedy and modern psychology" that "lead him to plumb for that old stand-by for the American liberal, 'the individual.'" For a more recent indication of dismissive critical commentary regarding Miller's sense of tragedy, one might cite Harold Bloom's rather patronizing remark in his 1991 critical anthology *Willy Loman:* "All that Loman actually shares with Lear and Oedipus is aging; there is no other likeness whatsoever. Miller has little understanding of Classical or Shakespearean tragedy; he stems entirely from Ibsen."[9]

Because no concept of modern tragedy has ever attained the status of being the single standard measure of the genre the way Aristotle's *Poetics* was to classical tragedy, *Death of a Salesman* is subject to as many interpretations and evaluations as there are definitions. Most modern theories of tragedy severely modify Aristotle whether applied to *Death of a Salesman* or to any other modern drama;[10] but

---

man confesses, 'I've got nobody to talk to'" (quoted in Philip C. Kolin, *"Death of a Salesman:* A Playwrights' Forum," 613).

9. Alvin Whitley, "Arthur Miller: An Attempt at Modern Tragedy," 262; Richard J. Foster, "Confusion and Tragedy: The Failure of Arthur Miller's *Salesman*," 87–88; Eric Mottram, "Arthur Miller: The Development of a Political Dramatist in America," 32; Harold Bloom, introduction to *Willy Loman*, 1.

10. Among those measuring Miller against Aristotle, Rita Di Giuseppe argues most extensively and convincingly that *Death of a Salesman* is a modern Aristotelian tragedy. Her essay, "The Shadow of the Gods: Tragedy and Commitment in *Death of a Salesman*," might be compared with Stephen Barker's provocative reading of the play in "Crisis of Authenticity," which treats it as an essentially Nietzschean tragedy.

certain elemental subthemes have constituted the targets of critics, among them the loss of community and divine order, the victimization and diminution of the hero, the banality of language, the lack of choice, the protagonist's lack of awareness or epiphany, the irresolution of the ending, and the failure to effect a catharsis.

Perhaps the most sustained historical study of the development of tragedy is Robert Heilman's two-volume exploration of the genre, *Tragedy and Melodrama: Versions of Experience* and *The Iceman, The Arsonist, and The Troubled Agent: Tragedy and Melodrama on the Modern Stage*. Distinguishing between tragedies and what he calls "disaster" plays or serious melodrama, Heilman incorporates the thinking of many theorists, proposing that tragedy includes a hero divided by counter "imperatives" or "impulses," who chooses between unreconcilable opposites, gains awareness, accepts consequences, and evokes emotions of both defeat and victory (what Heilman calls a "polypathic" rather than "monopathic" response). He differentiates between such plays and "disaster" dramas, in which characters are mere victims whose deaths shed little or no light on the nature of human experience. Like all such formulaic criticism, Heilman's at times creates a Procrustean bed of criticism in which some plays of dubious merit are raised in stature as "tragic" and superior dramas receive the more pejorative label of "melodrama." Nonetheless, because his study, in addition to offering a useful survey of dramatic theory and major plays, provides a functional definition that allows for critical discriminations to be made, I shall occasionally use his critical terminology, while keeping in mind George Bernard Shaw's admonishment that critics can "become so accustomed to formula that at last they cannot relish or understand a play that has grown naturally, just as they cannot admire the Venus of Milo because she has neither corset nor high-heeled shoes."[11] To be sure, different critics using the very same elements cited by Heilman and others, have vociferously declared *Death of a Salesman* both "the great American tragedy" and an exemplum of cheap pathos.[12] In response to the play's fiftieth anniversary in 1999 and continued prominence as what many

11. George Bernard Shaw, "How to Write a Popular Play," 54.

12. Robert Heilman himself concludes that Willy is "so limited that this is a limitation of the play itself" (*Tragedy and Melodrama: Versions of Experience*, 237), a common view of many critics who identify the play with Aristotelian "low tragedy."

still consider "the great American tragedy," it seems appropriate to look once more at the issues raised in the critical debate as they have been amplified and qualified by different theoretical approaches.

Underlying any consideration of the play's tragic potential is the larger question of whether or not tragedy can exist in an age when "God is dead." Nietzsche warned that it would go hard with tragic poets if God is dead, and writers like Joseph Wood Krutch and George Steiner, in works like *The Modern Temper* (1929) and *The Death of Tragedy* (1961), have long since pronounced the demise of tragedy, largely on the grounds that the absence of some identifiable, universal moral law that locates the operation of a transcendent order against which to judge the tragic hero denies the possibility of tragic drama. Miller himself has certainly recognized the problem this poses. When asked if his plays were "modern tragedies," he admitted, "I changed my mind about it several times. . . . To make direct and arithmetical comparison between any contemporary work and the classic tragedies is impossible because of the function of religion and power, which was taken for granted in an *a priori* consideration of any classic tragedy" (*Conv.*, 88). In a seminal discussion on the nature of tragedy with Robert Corrigan, Miller identified society as "the only thing we've got in modern times that has any parallel to the ancient deities. . . . [A]nd what it lacks is sublimity because at bottom, I think, most people . . . have no sense of divinity . . . and this is what cuts down the tragic vision. It levels." And he went on to explain, "By society, I don't mean, of course, merely the government. It is the whole way we live, what we want from life and what we do to get it" (254). In the same interview he noted that the classic hero "is working inside a religious cosmology where there is no mistaking a man for God; he is conscious to begin with that he is in the hands of God. . . . We are in the middle of a scrambled egg and mucking about in it, and the difference between the points of contact with the man and his god, so to speak, are fused" (255). In effect, in a secular universe the moral center shifts to the individual in relationship to his social environment. As Miller told Robert Martin, "What we've got left is the human half of the old Greek and the old Elizabethan process" in which human beings were measured against the presence of the gods (202). As a consequence, Miller concluded, "if we're going to talk about tragedy at all . . . we've got to find some equivalent to the superhuman schema that had its names in the past, whatever they were. Whether they went under the name of Zeus's laws, or, as in Shakespearean times, reflected a different ideology toward man, they also had lying in the background somewhere an order which was being violated and which the character was seeking to come to some arrangement with" (201).

In *Death of a Salesman*, society assumes the role of the gods to whom Willy gives allegiance. It constitutes what Heilman calls an "imperative," an obligation to a given, externally located code, that compels the tragic hero to act in direct opposition to an opposing "impulse," which Heilman characterizes as a personal or egocentric need or desire. The dilemma is underscored with irony, though, because unlike the traditional gods of tragedy, Willy's gods prove to be morally indifferent. As Rita Di Giuseppe has written, they have "metamorphosed . . . into the fat gods of consumerism."[13] Miller's depiction of such a secular universe has inevitably led to the protesting cry of some critics who apparently want Miller to provide a transcendent moral force that would belie the realism of his conception.[14] He often frustrates them by contextualizing the play in a realistic, if expressionistic, form that seems too reductive to allow for the grandeur of tragedy; but he encloses within this realism a tragic rhythm that depends upon the integrity of his uncompromised realism. The "discovery of the moral law," he wrote in "Tragedy and the Common Man," is no longer "the discovery of some abstract or metaphysical quantity" but is grounded in the nature of human experience itself (*TE*, 5).

Eric Bentley offered the much-repeated view in his *In Search of Theater* that *Death of a Salesman* futilely attempts to align tragedy with social drama, the one conceiving of the hero as responsible

13. Rita Di Giuseppe, "Shadow of the Gods," 115.

14. The theologian-literary critic Tom F. Driver, for example, complains that "There being no objective good and evil, and no imperative other than conscience, man himself must be made to bear the full burden of creating his values and living up to them. The immensity of this task is beyond human capacity" ("Strength and Weakness in Arthur Miller," 111–12). In fact, Miller's depiction of the moral viability of characters surfaces in their pervasive sense of guilt and the compulsion shared by Willy and Biff to somehow redeem the past. Driver, like Foster and Mottram, among others, seemingly expects Miller to manufacture a god, a metaphysical reality that would somehow resolve the spiritual crisis. But Miller's refusal to identify "an ultimate truth" is more a matter of artistic integrity than a failure of moral vision.

for his own fate and the other as the pathetic victim of a severely flawed society.[15] But, as Christopher Bigsby has observed, surely *Oedipus* and *Hamlet* integrate social drama and tragedy (*DS*, xviii). For Miller, "there are certain duties and social fears that can create a tragic event," specifically when the dialectic develops "between the individual and his social obligations, his social self" (*Conv.*, 346). Miller has described Greek tragedies as "social documents, not little piddling private conversations" written by "a man confronting his society" (101). The differences that emerge in modern tragedy when realistically described social forces usurp the role of the gods transfigure tragedy profoundly—but not unrecognizably. Miller has called what emerges "the tragedy of displacement," in which "the tragic dimension" surfaces in the protagonist's struggle for a lost "personal identity" displaced by "the social mask" (347). In "Tragedy and the Common Man," he attributed "the terror and fear that is classically associated with tragedy" to the "inner dynamic" driven by the "total onslaught of the individual against the seemingly stable cosmos surrounding us" (*TE*, 4). As in *Hamlet*—though obviously different from it—the tragic conflict pits one imperative against another: The social imperative of success is in direct competition with the personal imperative or "impulse" of finding the authentic self. This transformation of the tragic conflict generates concomitant tensions in the form and focus of the text, between the outer and inner worlds, between Willy as hero and Willy as a psychological case study, between social commentary and personal experience, between the socially accepted view of morality and personal guilt, between suicide and self-sacrifice—in short, between melodramatic documentary and modern tragedy. Such tension plays out as well in other Miller texts.

Miller himself has sensed the precarious nature of his plays as tragedy, admitting in his essay "On Social Plays" that "The debilitation of the tragic drama . . . is commensurate with the fracturing and the aborting of the need of man to maintain a fruitful kind

---

15. Eric Bentley, *In Search of Theater*, 32. John Mander identifies a related unresolved conflict between Marxian and Freudian elements: "If we take the 'psychological' motivation as primary, the 'social' documentation seems gratuitous; if we take the 'social' documentation as primary, the 'psychological' motivation seems gratuitous" (*The Writer and Commitment*, 115).

of union with his society" (*TE*, 62). Furthermore, he has implied that his artistic end in *Death of a Salesman* was closer to Ibsen than to Sophocles. In *Timebends* he confesses that he "wanted to set off before the captains and the so seemingly confident kings the corpse of a believer," to plant "a time bomb under American capitalism" (*T*, 184); but he knew this differed from the Greek plays, which, at the end, "return to confirm the rightness of the laws" (*TE*, 6). His purpose was political and satirical, for he knew, as Christopher Bigsby has written, that "Willy Loman's American dream is drained of transcendence. It is faith in the supremacy of the material over the spiritual" (*DS*, xxiii). It is little wonder that Miller threatened a lawsuit when he was asked by Paramount Pictures to permit a twenty-five minute short subject to be shown before the film version of the play to assure the audience that "nowadays selling was a fine profession with limitless spiritual compensations as well as financial ones"—indeed, it *would* have made the play "*morally* meaningless, a tale told by an idiot signifying nothing" (*T*, 315). In his 1999 Massey Lecture at Harvard, he added, "Never in show business history has a studio spent so much good money to prove that its feature film was pointless" (*E*, 276).

Because Miller creates a naturalistic, almost Marxian view of American culture in the near-Depression era, some have reduced the drama, along with other Miller works, to social determinism. And the truth is, Miller *does* describe Willy as a childlike victim of the cultural values he adopts virtually without question. In Miller's words, he "carried in his pocket the coinage of our day" as a true believer in the American dream of success (*Conv.*, 176). The very embodiment of the myth, he carried an unidentified "product" in his case, "the cipher," in Stephen Barker's reading, "of an empty signifier."[16] And yet Miller grants Willy stature and significance because of—as much as despite—his dogged commitment to a pernicious ideal. One cannot take away Willy's dream without diminishing him, Miller has suggested: "[T]he less capable a man is of walking away from the central conflict of the play, the closer he approaches a tragic existence" (*TE*, 118). Ironically, like Oedipus, who at every point insists on fulfilling his obligation as king by unwittingly searching for his own father's murderer even though it finally destroys him

16. Stephen Barker, "Crisis of Authenticity," 88.

to do so, Willy unreservedly follows his imperative to its fatal end, similarly encouraged by all the others around him to abort his quest: Linda, Biff, Happy, Charley, and Bernard all urge him to give up, just as Teiresias, the Chorus, Jocasta, and the Shepherd plead with Oedipus to do the same. That Willy does not finally understand the corruptness of the dream exposes his intellectual failure, but he dies in defense of the imperative that consumes him. When in a symposium on the play John Beaufort and David W. Thompson argued that Willy "has no moral values at all," Miller contended that "The trouble with Willy Loman is that he has tremendously powerful ideals. . . . The fact is that he has values" (*Conv.*, 30). As he told the Chinese actors for the 1983 production in Beijing, Willy "hasn't a cynical bone in his body, he is a walking believer, the bearer of a flame. . . . He is forever signaling to a future that he cannot describe and will not live to see, but he is in love with it all the same." Even though the imperative devastates him as it does Oedipus, and even though it ironically proves false, Willy, "in his fumbling and often ridiculous way, . . . is trying to lift up a belief in immense redeeming human possibilities" (*SB*, 49).[17] What matters finally is not so much the validity of the ideal but that Willy offers himself up to affirm it. It motivates him just as the oracle compels Oedipus to fulfill his kingship. However ironically, Willy fulfills his role as salesman with the same determination that compels Oedipus to affirm his kingship.

But it would be absurd to argue Willy's tragic stature on the grounds of his innocent, misguided commitment to the American dream of success, even though his devotion to the code is no less consuming than Oedipus's or Hamlet's commitments to their imperatives. At a deeper level we must ask *why* he invests so totally and self-destructively in support of the dream. For Oedipus or Hamlet, of course, the moral imperative was a given—there was divine order, after all, a divinity that shapes human destiny. For Willy, however, the imperative was not so readily apparent or universally acclaimed. His fierce devotion to it was not for its own sake; rather, it was for Willy a means to an end. In a critically important comment, Miller

17. Or, in Helene Wickham Koon's words, "His principles may be unconscious and built upon fallacies, but he believes in them, practices them, and finally dies for them" (introduction to *Twentieth Century Interpretations of* Death of a Salesman, 7).

contended that "Willy is demanding of the market and of his job some real return *psychically*" (*Conv.*, 297–98, italics mine). He seeks self-dignity and with it something more, what most defines the counterpoint to the social imperative in the play, to recover the lost love of Biff and preserve the family. Willy does not want simply to fulfill the imperative for the dream's sake, but to express his love through "success." Because his will to succeed consistently frustrates his impulse to love, he suffers the division Heilman ascribes to the tragic hero.[18]

In a reversal of Aristotelian priorities, Miller dramatizes, in Browning's phrase, "Action in Character, rather than Character in Action." Or, to put it another way, plot enters character to create "the soul of the action" rather than the narrative or external plot. *Death of a Salesman* "removes the ground of the tragic conflict from outer events to inner consciousness," as Esther Merle Jackson has proposed, depicting "a *tragedy of consciousness*, the imitation of a moral crisis in the life of a common man."[19] This shift violates the linear, architectonic movement of classical tragedy by placing the impetus for the action not in the hands of the gods but in Willy's own consciousness. When he announces "I am tired to death" (*DS*, 2), he sets in motion an inexorable internal struggle between past and present. On the verge of neurosis and paranoia because he vacillates hopelessly between two poles, Willy shares an obsessive nature with other tragic figures who skirt madness. But Miller has always insisted that Willy is not insane. His well-known aversion to Frederic March's portrayal in the film version of the play emphasizes the point. "If he was nuts," Miller wrote of Willy in *Timebends*, "he would hardly stand as a comment on anything" (*T*, 325). March, who had been a "first choice for the role on stage," made Willy "simply a mental case," a neurotic, pathological case study, "an idiot" headed for the "looney bin," Miller complained to Christopher Bigsby—but Willy is not "crazy," and the audience recognizes that "This man is obviously going down the chute and he's telling them exactly what they believe" (*AMC*, 58).

---

18. Bernard F. Dukore asks tellingly, "does not the desire for love inhere in Willy's occupation, and does not the hope of success link to the family?" (Death of a Salesman *and* The Crucible: *Text and Performance*, 21).

19. Jackson, "*Death of a Salesman*: Tragic Myth," 68.

The internalization of the conflict is expressed in the staging of the play. We are on "The Inside of His Head," as Miller first proposed calling the work, on a stage expressive of the dialectical tensions between what Miller refers to as "social time" and "psychic time," city and country, home and workplace, as Willy's "daydreams" project the counterforces operating in his consciousness. On one hand, Miller maintained the dictum of tragedy he learned from the Greeks and Ibsen and coined "the birds coming home to roost" (AMC, 49), initiating the play in the rhythm of ancient tragedy with the appearance of "the x-factor," when Willy announces he cannot go on. But from there the play assumes more postmodern traits. As Matthew Roudané has suggested, the text is "Postmodern in texture but gains its theatrical power from ancient echoes, its Hellenic mixture of pity and fear stirring primal emotions." Although Elia Kazan recognized from the beginning that Willy creates his own history in the play, only recently have critics begun to appreciate Miller's postmodern view of history, an element increasingly apparent in one-act plays like *Some Kind of Love Story* and *Elegy for a Lady* and in works of the last decade like *The Last Yankee*, *The Ride down Mount Morgan*, and *Mr. Peters' Connections*. Miller collapses time in *Death of a Salesman*, rather than simply showing the past reasserting itself in the present, making past and present coexist so completely that neither we nor Willy can always distinguish between them. June Schlueter has observed how the extraordinary design "invites a recontextualizing reading of the play and a distinctly postmodern query: To what extent has Willy assumed authorial control of his own history, consciously or unconsciously rewriting and restaging it to suit his emotional needs?" In Miller's use of "re-memory," she surmises, the text challenges "the historicity of knowledge, the nature of identity, the epistemological status of fictional discourse."[20] Yet for all its postmodern elements, as Roudané has rightly asserted, it "gets its power from ancient echoes." Miller began the play with the conviction that "if I could make [Willy] remember enough he would kill himself" (TE, 138). The eruption of the past is vital in this sense because it reflects Miller's tragic view of causality, because it is "an

---

20. Matthew Roudané, *"Death of a Salesman* and the Poetics of Arthur Miller,"
63; June Schlueter, "Re-membering Willy's Past: Introducing Postmodern Concerns through *Death of a Salesman*," 143, 151.

acknowledgment," Christopher Bigsby has declared, "that we are responsible for, and a product of, our actions" (*DS*, xi).[21]

Inspired by seeing *A Streetcar Named Desire*, Miller developed what Brenda Murphy has termed "subjective realism," which she describes as "expressionistic with the illusion of objectivity afforded by realism."[22] It allowed him to project a concept of time in which "nothing in life comes 'next' but . . . everything exists together at the same time. . . . [Willy] is his past at every moment." As a result, the "form seems to be the form of a confession" (*TE*, 136). The form thereby conveys the moment of moral consequence when Willy must finally pay the price for his choices: "[Y]ou've got to retrieve what you've spent and you've got to account for it somehow" (AMC, 201). Miller has employed biblical language to define the moral significance of the drama, which shows us, "so to speak, the wages of sin" (*Conv.*, 31). Willy, in a way, confesses despite himself as his memory becomes an unwilled confession. A divided hero, he sins against both imperatives that motivate him. He violates the law of success, Miller has explained, "the law which says that a failure in society and in business has no right to live." But he also sins against "an opposing system which, so to speak, is in a race for Willy's faith, and that is the system of love which is the opposite of the law of success" (*TE*, 149). To be true to one set of values necessitates betrayal of the other. That is the tragic dilemma that Miller traced back to Eden when, either way they choose—either by disobeying the injunction not to eat the fruit or denying their impulse toward freedom—Adam and Eve are fated to suffer tragic consequences. Unable to accommodate diametrically opposite demands, Willy must and does make choices in response to the contending codes. He commits adultery in Boston to gain access to buyers, but consequently carries undeniable guilt for breaking "the law of love." In his annotations to the playscript, Miller recorded that Willy is in fact "craving to be liberated from his guilt."[23]

It is an essential question whether or not Willy *does* choose and, perhaps more importantly, whether he truly pays a price for his

21. In *Modern American Drama*, Bigsby has written, "the present cannot be severed from the past nor the individual from his social context: that, after all, is the basis of [Miller's] dramatic method and of his moral faith" (124).

22. Murphy, *Miller: Death of a Salesman*, 5.

23. Quoted in Kenneth Thorpe Rowe, *A Theater in Your Head*, 56.

choices. It is difficult not to see his moral viability in light of his pervasive sense of guilt. Even if he fails to make the right moral choices (though no choice can be "right" in relation to the contending poles in the dialectic), he is surely not amoral. The play demands an accounting for his actions. One may contend that Willy lacks intellectual awareness, of course, and is thereby diminished as a tragic hero, but not that he is morally moribund. Few characters in modern drama expose so vividly the presence of a guilty conscience.

When Willy returns "tired to death," Gerald Weales has concluded that he is "past the point of choice."[24] In a way he is right. The play begins when Willy must finally suffer "the wages of sin" for choices already made, in the same way that Oedipus must confront the consequences of a crime already enacted. But in fact he also makes choices within the time frame of the present. As Miller has insisted, he is unwilling to "remain passive in the face of what he conceives to be a challenge to his dignity" (TE, 4). To this end he chooses not to take Charley's repeated offer of a job, although he already depends on Charley's help and could resolve his immediate financial crisis by accepting the position. Almost without regard to Willy's rejection of the job, Charley ironically explains why when he remarks in the requiem, "No man only needs a little salary" (DS, 110). Willy chooses not to suffer the loss of dignity—to accept would demean him and, perhaps more, would deny the validity of the imperative by which he measures his worth. Most importantly, he chooses the car at the end of the play over the rubber hose, the latter representing both acceptance of defeat and escape from the consequences of failure, the former embodying an act of sacrifice, an ironic affirmation of the failed dream but, nonetheless, a conscious assertion of will. As we will see later, in the first case he would die *from* something, and in the second he would die *for* something. As noted, it is a distinction not clearly drawn in *All My Sons*, in which the motivation and ultimate meaning of Joe Keller's death remains nebulous rather than intentionally ambiguous. Without free will, tragedy cannot exist in Miller's view, for tragedy contests the idea that characters are only victims of external powers rather than participants in their own destiny. Just as we can conclude that Willy is morally alive, we must acknowledge that he possesses freedom of choice. He chose to follow

24. Gerald C. Weales, "Arthur Miller: Man and His Image," 172.

the imperative that finally defeats him, and he chooses to die in part to perpetuate the dream. "He brings tragedy down on himself," Raymond Williams has explained in his defense of the play as tragedy, "not by opposing the lie, but by living it."[25]

Willy might be considered a composite tragic hero in that his divided nature and tragic fate are inexplicably bound to his two sons, who represent the poles in the dialectic. Willy's choice to follow the dictates of the cultural ethos most directly affects his family, which provides the locus of the tragic action. The larger community and its unifying myth of universal order are projected in the altar, the palace, and the throne room in traditional tragedy; but the fragile Loman house, part externally real and part psychically real, houses a fragmented, dysfunctional family, where Willy's adherence to the law of success makes him, as Dan Vogel notes in *The Three Masks of Tragedy*, a petty "tyrannos" in his own house. But whereas "the family was subsumed by community, by public and even metaphysical-religious repercussions" in Greek drama, William Demastes has reminded us that, in the Loman household, family matters are disconnected from the larger human society or from a spiritually charged cosmos. Although Shakespeare's heroes all engage in psychological warfare at some personal level, they all see themselves primarily as agents of the larger community. Oedipus's or Hamlet's "Oedipus complex" is hardly the "soul of the action" in either text, however much both may be perceived in Freudian terms. But Miller has—in overtly Freudian terms—spoken of family as, "after all, the nursery of all our neuroses" (*Conv.*, 271), moving tragedy much more into the realm of the psyche and subjective reality, as O'Neill tried to do. Some critics, and most notably the psychiatrist Daniel E. Schneider, have read the play as centrally about the Oedipus complex, "an unreal Oedipal bloodbath," in which we witness the search for the father, violent sibling rivalry, castration fear, and crippling guilt over the death of a parent.[26] But while such themes doubtless appear, the rivalry between brothers and their struggles against the father are

25. Raymond Williams, *Modern Tragedy*, 104.

26. William W. Demastes, "Miller's Use and Modification of the Realistic Tradition," 77. Freudian readings appear incidentally in various interpretations of the play as well as being the primary approach of many studies, like Schneider's. See especially B. S. Field Jr., "Hamartia in *Death of a Salesman*"; John V. Hagopian, "Arthur Miller: The Salesman's Two Cases"; Karl Harshbarger, *The Burning Jungle:*

more important as manifestations of larger mythic forces operating in Willy himself. Biff's association with nature and desire to return to a pastoral world characterized by fecundity and openness parallel Willy's lyrical references to New England, the open windshield, and the warm air early in the play and, later in the play, his promise to Linda to someday buy a farm and his desperate attempt to "plant something." Hap's counter commitment to the idea of success, seen throughout in his unconscionable business dealings and sexual prowess, reaches full expression in the requiem in his vow to reclaim Willy's dream. But because Willy still naively convinces himself that he will eventually succeed and never doubts the dream Hap embodies, Willy does not need the assurances of his younger son or his forgiveness for not having been a success. It is Biff with whom he must be reconciled for the breach caused by his denial of "the system of love," a denial of his own other self.

Brenda Murphy has noted Miller's evolving conception of Biff. At first seeing the elder son as caught "between hatred for Willy and his own desire for success," the playwright had difficulty "developing a motivation for Biff's hatred." But especially under Kazan's direction, Miller came to see the work, in Kazan's words, as "a love story—the end of a tragic love between Willy and his son Biff. . . . The whole play is about *love*—Love and Competition."[27] When the Chinese actor playing Biff in Beijing wondered why Biff says "I don't know what I want," Miller, in a telling comment, replied, "You don't say 'I don't know what I want,' but 'I don't know what I'm supposed to want,' and this is a key idea. Biff knows very well what he wants, but Willy and his idea of success disapprove of what he wants, and this is the basic reason you have returned here—to somehow resolve this conflict with your father, to get his blessing" (SB, 71).

Willy and Biff form a symbiotic relationship. Biff cannot gain freedom from his father's imperative until his father somehow frees him from it—which, tragically speaking, he can do only through death. Similarly, Willy cannot succeed until he can align his love for Biff with the dream he follows. This explains why Biff returns, because, as

An Analysis of Arthur Miller's Death of a Salesman; and Schlueter and Flanagan, Arthur Miller.

27. Murphy, Miller: Death of a Salesman, 9; Kazan quoted in Rowe, Theater in Your Head, 44. Miller described the play in similar language: "Death of a Salesman, really, is a love story between a man and his son" (SB, 49).

Miller explained to the Beijing actors, he "sometimes feels a painful unrequited love for his father, a sense of something unfinished between them brings feelings of guilt" (*SB*, 79). Willy equally feels "unrequited love," which we see in his eagerness for Biff's return, and yet he also suffers "feelings of guilt." Biff has failed to meet Willy's imperative and feels estranged because of it; Willy has violated love for the sake of the dream by which he hoped to express it and feels alienated as well. Inextricably linked—both in Willy's subjective world, where he romanticizes Biff in the past to conform to his dream, and in the external realm of reality, where Biff has markedly failed to succeed—the two return to the crossroads, the place where *x* marks the spot, the hotel room in Boston where the law of success and the law of love collide, inflicting upon father and son a shared guilt that can only be redeemed by the death of the tragic hero.

Like the Greek chorus, whose plea for relief unwittingly leads to Oedipus's tragic end, Linda's supplications propel Willy and Biff toward their tragic destiny. She tells her son, "Biff, his life is in your hands!" (*DS*, 43). The character of Linda has always provoked intense critical reactions. Many see her as an enabler who "contributes to the truth-illusion matrix" by supporting Willy's "vital lie."[28] Some consider her an even more sinister figure. Guerin Bliquez has called her "the source of the cash-payment fixation" whose acquiescence "in all Willy's weaknesses" makes her a "failure as a wife and mother." Seeing Ben as a rival, Bliquez adds, she emasculates him and makes Willy a victim of her "ambition as well as his own." Calling her "stupid and immoral" for encouraging Willy's self-deceit, Brian Parker accuses Linda of possessing no higher ideal than Willy's dream and finds her "moral sloppiness" manifested in Hap "one degree farther"—"Hap is his mother's son." And Karl Harshbarger makes her an even more malevolent character, who coerces Willy "to relate to her as a small boy . . . by not allowing him to communicate his deeper needs to her," who sides with Biff against him, and who blames him "for his own feelings. She offers him his reward, love and support, only when he becomes dependent

28. Roudané, "*Death of a Salesman* and the Poetics," 70. David Morse also has noted Linda's reinforcement of Willy's "life-lie" ("The 'Life Lie' in Three Plays by O'Neill, Williams, and Miller"). William B. Dillingham, among others, has identified her as a "contributing cause" of the tragedy ("Arthur Miller and the Loss of Conscience," 344).

on her."[29] He goes so far as to claim that in her "extreme defensive-ness" against her own guilt she "must disguise the joy that she, not a man, has been victorious."[30] Linda is also commonly referred to as merely a sentimental sop, a cardboard figure, or "a mouthpiece for Miller's earnestness."[31] One critic has named her Jocasta as "mousy twentieth-century Brooklyn housewife," who, like Oedipus's wife-mother, prevents her husband "from asking the fateful question, 'Who am I?'"[32]

More recent feminist critics have found Linda a likely target for assaults on Miller, though as early as his 1970 book on Miller, Ben-jamin Nelson sounded a feminist chord that shows Linda helping "build a doll's house around [Willy] and, consequently, [doing] to Willy what he has been doing to Biff and Happy," making him as well as them "victims of her gingerbread house."[33] A number of studies published in the late 1980s deny Linda a significant role in a tragic pattern, depicting her as reflecting a male perspective, which "bor-rows the methods and espouses the sexual politics of melodrama. . . . If Miller writes tragedy . . . he makes it a male preserve."[34] Linda, according to Linda Ben-Zvi, "is the embodiment of society's per-ception of women" and of Miller's own conception, a view shared by Gayle Austin. Employing the feminist theory of Gayle Rubin, Austin laments Miller's reduction of women as "objects to be ex-changed" and denial of them "as active subjects in the play."[35] And

29. Guerin Bliquez, "Linda's Role in *Death of a Salesman*," 384, 386; Brian Parker, "Point of View in Arthur Miller's *Death of a Salesman*," 54; Harshbarger, *Burning Jungle*, 14.

30. In his extreme psychological reading, Harshbarger argues that Linda domi-nates Willy and attempts to reduce Biff "to the level of a dependent child" moti-vated by "a longing for Biff she has always had—a relationship which is symbolized by Biff taking 'her in his arms'" at the end of the play (*Burning Jungle*, 28–29).

31. Dennis Welland, *Miller the Playwright*, 50.

32. Otten, "'Who Am I . . . ,'" 87.

33. Nelson, *Arthur Miller*, 112–13. Related to feminist criticism, David Savran attacks the play from a different gender perspective, claiming that "the play eulo-gizes the contents of the Loman *imaginaire* by its romantization of a self-reliant and staunchly homosocial masculinity and by its corroborative and profound dispar-agement of women" (*Communists, Cowboys, and Queers: The Politics of Masculinity in the Work of Arthur Miller and Tennessee Williams*, 36).

34. Mason, "Paper Dolls," 113.

35. Linda Ben-Zvi, "'Home Sweet Home': Deconstructing the Masculine Myth of the Frontier in Modern American Drama," 224; Gayle Austin, "The Exchange

Kay Stanton concludes that Miller conflates all female characters in the play "in the idea of Woman: all share . . . in their knowing"; and, possessing "the potential to reveal masculine inadequacy," they "must be opposed by man."[36] More recently, Linda Kintz has explored Miller's "grammar of space," which projects "a nostalgic view of the universalized masculine protagonist of the *Poetics*," in whose conception women like Linda "wait at home, to console and civilize both husband and children, roles that provide a structural, narrative guarantee of masculine agency even in very different historical periods."[37] Tracing antifemale bias to the core of traditional tragedy itself, she raises a serious criticism not only of Linda's role but of the gender-biased nature of tragedy as genre.

These and subsequent feminist attacks on the characterization of Linda and the other women in the play,[38] and those in other Miller dramas, have not gone unchallenged; relative to seeing the play as tragedy, the issue is important, because Miller conceives of Linda as an essential contributor to the tragic meaning of the work. Janet

---

of Women and Male Homosocial Desire in Arthur Miller's *Death of a Salesman* and Lillian Hellman's *Another Part of the Forest*," 61, 63.

36. Kay Stanton, "Women and the American Dream of *Death of a Salesman*," 82. In a recent article, Rhoda Koenig concurs that Miller diminishes female figures, making Linda "a dumb and useful doormat" and reducing all women in the play to either the "wicked slut" or "a combination of good waitress and slipper-bearing retriever" ("Seduced by *Salesman*'s Patter," 10). To the contrary, in "Masculine and Feminine in *Death of a Salesman*," Heather Cook Callow, using Deborah Tannen's study of gender-associated linguistic patterns in *You Just Don't Understand: Men and Women in Conversation*, offers the interesting thesis that it is Willy's "concerns, values and expressions" that reflect "typically feminine" traits in the play.

37. Linda Kintz, "The Sociosymbolic Work of Family in *Death of a Salesman*," 106.

38. For other feminist interpretations, see especially Carol Billman, "Women and the Family in American Drama"; Charlotte Canning, "Is This Play about Women: A Feminist Reading of *Death of a Salesman*"; Charlotte Goodman, "The Fox's Cubs: Lillian Hellman, Arthur Miller, and Tennessee Williams"; Beverly Hume, "Linda Loman as 'The Woman' in Miller's *Death of a Salesman*"; Zeineddine, *Because It Is My Name*; and Austin, "Exchange of Women and Male Homosocial Desire." Along with feminist criticism, several recent studies have explored the issue of male gender as social construct; see especially Carla J. McDonough's *Staging Masculinity: Male Identity in Contemporary American Drama*; Savran's *Communists, Cowboys, and Queers*; and Eugene R. August's "*Death of a Salesman*: A Men's Study Approach," which discusses *Death of a Salesman* as "a profoundly male tragedy" depicting a man "destroyed by a debilitating concept of masculinity."

Balakian, for example, has argued that, rather than supporting a sexist view of women, *Death of a Salesman* is "accurately depicting a postwar American culture that subordinates women. . . . [It] cries out for a renewed image of American women." Although the drama realistically portrays America "through the male gaze," it "does not condone the locker-room treatment of women any more than it approves of a dehumanizing capitalism, any more than *A Streetcar Named Desire* approves Stanley Kowalski's brash chauvinism or David Mamet's *Glengarry Glen Ross* approves of sleazy real-estate salesmen."[39] Even if Linda's fierce will and love for Willy cannot save him, Christopher Bigsby has added, "this does not make her a 'useful doormat'" as some feminists have complained (*DS*, xx).

As Elia Kazan wrote in his directing notes on the play, Linda often appears as if she is ideally "fashioned out of Willy's guilt" and male ego as "Hard-working, sweet, always true, admiring. . . . Dumb, slaving, tender, innocent." In fact, "in life she is much tougher. . . . [S]he has *chosen* Willy! To hell with everyone else. She is terrifyingly tough."[40] Elizabeth Franz's portrayal in the widely acclaimed fiftieth-anniversary revival disclosed a strength in Linda that likely no other actress has fully exploited. Winner of one of the four Tony awards given the production (the others being for best actor, Brian Dennehy, best direction, Robert Fall, and best revival of a play), she attacked her sons with fierce indignation when they abandoned their father; and when she slammed the table in the "attention must be paid" speech, she seemed to transfer her assertive power to Biff, who later imitates her gesture. Certainly Miller did not think of her as a sentimental sop. Kay Stanton has suggested that Miller "seems not to have fully understood" her strength as a "common woman who possesses more tragic nobility than Willy,"[41] but at various times Miller has expressed his concern that Linda *not* be sentimentalized, beginning with Mildred Dunnock's original portrayal of the role.[42]

39. Janet N. Balakian, "Beyond the Male Locker Room: *Death of a Salesman* from a Feminist Approach," 115, 124.

40. Quoted in Rowe, *Theater in Your Head*, 47.

41. Stanton, "Women and the American Dream," 96.

42. Even in writing the play, Miller was intent on showing Linda's toughness. He even cut the famous "Attention must be paid speech" at one point for fear it made her too sentimental, and he took out of the original dialogue references she made to Biff and Hap as "darling" and "dear" (Murphy, *Miller: Death of a Salesman*, 45).

He recalls how Kazan forced Dunnock to deliver her long accusatory speech to Biff and Happy in act 2 in double time and then doubled the pace of the delivery again in order to straighten "out her spine, and has Linda filled up with outrage and protest rather than self-pity and mere perplexity" (*T*, 189).[43] He also observes how the Linda in the Beijing production, Zhu Lin, at first weakened Linda's character by "exploiting . . . the sentiments" that "will sink them all in a morass of brainless 'feeling' that finally is not feeling at all but an unspecific bath of self-love." Zhu Lin's interpretation reminded him of a Yiddish production in New York in which "the Mother was a lachrymose fount" like mothers "performed by actors of Irish backgrounds" in early film, "always on the verge of tears, too" (*SB*, 43).

For Miller, Linda's role was never merely ancillary, and although he acknowledged that she contributes to Willy's death—noting that "When somebody is destroyed, everybody finally contributes to it" (*Conv.*, 265), he conceived of Linda as "sucked into the same mechanism" as Willy.[44] Though not a "tragic hero," Linda contributes hugely to the tragic vision of the work. She functions in part as a chorus. In the crucial moments when she demands that "attention must be paid" and when she castigates her sons for abandoning Willy, she both provokes the action and provides a moral commentary on it. Perhaps more, as Gordon Couchman has contributed, she is "conscience itself" to her two sons—"she fixes responsibility for actions, something which, according to the playwright himself, must be done if our theater is to recover the spirit of tragedy." And, Bernard Dukore has added, "Far from demonstrating her stupidity, her comprehension of why [Willy] committed suicide derives from what she, not the audience, was aware of. When she last saw Willy, he was happy because Biff loved him."[45] Her essential recognition,

43. James Poling notes that Kazan jabbed at Dunnock with a fencing foil during rehearsals and shouted, "You've got more and damn it, you'll give it to me! You're a tigress defending her cub! Now, attack that scene—again, again!" ("Handy 'Gadget,'" 58).

44. Elsewhere, Miller has commented that "There is a more sinister side to the women characters in my plays. . . . [T]hey both receive the benefits of the male's mistakes and protect his mistakes in crazy ways. They are forced to do that. So the females are victims as well" (*Conv.*, 370).

45. Gordan W. Couchman, "Arthur Miller's Tragedy of Babbitt," 74; Dukore, Death of a Salesman *and* The Crucible, 28. Responding to an audience at the

though emotionally rather than intellectually expressed, illuminates the tragic implications of the text.

No mere passive victim, even though she is powerless to prevent Willy's end, Linda is primarily responsible for generating the tragic reunion of Willy and Biff. She can only respond to, not prevent, the fatal encounter she unwittingly prophesies when she tells Biff, with ironic accuracy, that Willy's fate is in his hands; and it is she who tells Biff about the rubber hose, thereby empowering him with the knowledge he needs to confront Willy at the end of the play. The climactic scene occurs at the restaurant, when Willy can no longer evade the memory that must return him, like Oedipus, to the crossroads that mark his betrayal. The scene in Howard's office that precedes it would surely be the pivotal moment in the action were this essentially a social or political drama, but rather than *being* the turning point, it leads directly to it, stripping Willy of his final hope and leaving him without reserves to combat the evidence of his failure as father and husband as well as salesman.[46] Christopher Bigsby has proposed that "There is no crime and hence no culpability (beyond guilt for sexual betrayal), only a baffled man and his sons trying to find their way through a world of images" (*DS*, xxvi); but the guilt Willy endures goes beyond mere infidelity, and Biff's culpability in abandoning his father both in Boston and at the restaurant adds a moral dimension that exceeds Willy's sexual indiscretions. The restaurant scene, which Miller once stayed up all night to rework during rehearsals (*T*, 189), brilliantly weaves together past and present by simultaneously showing Biff and Hap reenacting Willy's

---

University of Michigan, Miller reflected on Linda's extraordinary strength: "Linda is aware of the real story from the moment the curtain goes up. She knows Willy's suicidal. . . . If you make a single misstep, you would send him overboard. . . . When you're dealing with delicate mental imbalance, you have to be very careful. On the other hand, when Linda's alone with her sons, we can see the power of her feelings. . . . I regard Linda as a very admirable person. Outwardly, she's suffering more than anybody else in the play, and she's also doing more in her own way, to prevent the coming catastrophe" ("Responses to an Audience," 821).

46. Dukore rightly comments that even if Howard had given Willy a job in the city, it would not eliminate "the elemental source of Willy's discontent, which lies in his relationship with his older son and the world in which they live" (Death of a Salesman *and* The Crucible, 34). One might add that Willy cannot accept Charley's offer of a job for much the same reason. It would not resolve his existential crisis, and Willy's acceptance of it would in fact reduce him to a totally pathetic figure.

violation of love while Willy concurrently relives it. Again, were this only a social or polemical social play, the scene in Howard's office would constitute the nadir of Willy's hopeless existence, and the restaurant scene would begin the denouement. But the restaurant scene carries what Miller calls a "metaphysical" dimension, moving the play into the realm of tragedy by dramatizing the usurpation of the present by the past, the place where Willy must reenact rather than excuse or sanitize the past. In true tragic rhythm, every step forward leads back to that defining moment.

Biff's humiliating experience at Oliver's office mirrors Willy's at Howard's, Thomas Porter has noted,[47] and links their destinies as they meet at the restaurant. The scene opens with Hap seducing "Miss Forsyth" with the deception and exaggeration typical of the Lomans, directly establishing a parallel to Willy's sexual infidelity. When Biff arrives, he already has realized his inauthenticity after stealing Oliver's pen and is determined to force Willy and Hap to face the truth about all their self-deceit. Miller interestingly changed the early versions of the play, including the initial preproduction script distributed to the production team in 1948. Originally Biff intentionally lies both to Willy *and* Hap about having a lunch meeting with Oliver.[48] In the far more meaningful final version, Biff openly rebels against what he has become. Daniel Schneider, in his Freudian interpretation of the scene, calls it "the ultimate act of father-murder . . . [a] very adroitly designed Oedipal murder," in which Biff is "hero of the Oedipal theme" in rebelling against his father.[49] But while Biff comes in anger against what his father has made of him and does indeed rebel against him, he brings with him a deeper self-hatred and, with it, an understanding of Willy's desperation. Even as Hap competes for the girls, unmindful of his father's distress, Biff finds a compassion born of his self-awareness

47. Thomas E. Porter, *Myth and Modern American Drama*, 142.
48. Murphy, *Miller: Death of a Salesman*, 6.
49. Daniel E. Schneider, *The Psychoanalyst and the Artist*, 250–51. Field, Eisinger, and Harshbarger offer other Freudian analyses. Some critics especially note the Freudian importance of Biff's stealing Oliver's pen, a phallic symbol, thus expressing his assertion of manhood or fear of castration. More simply, the stealing of the pen is another reenactment of the past, when Biff stole the basketballs, like he stole lumber and the football. His existential self-questioning of his motives for stealing the pen makes him determined to coerce Willy to confront the truth about who he really is.

and Willy's agonizing cry that "the woods are burning . . . there's a big blaze going on all around" (*DS*, 83). Biff's consciousness of his own culpability—expressed in his plea to Hap to "help him. . . . Help me, help me, I can't bear to look at his face!"—bespeaks of something more than Oedipal revenge on the father. Calling Willy "A fine, troubled prince," he lies about the appointment with Oliver not to conceal his failure, as in the original script, but to alleviate Willy's suffering, even though he finally runs away from Willy in frustration *"Ready to weep"* (90). Biff wants to be free of the past and free of the imperative of success his father imposes on him, but he cannot achieve these ends without feeling guilt for failing his father, nor can he erase from the past the estrangement that occurred in Boston for which he feels partly responsible. In this modern tragedy, moral as well as psychological forces propel the scene.

As tragic protagonist, Willy, above all, must gain some measure of awareness, something now possible when he no longer possesses the capacity to reinvent, glamorize, or excuse the past. The "re-memory" of the experience in the hotel room is driven by guilt left unchecked without recourse to the defensive mechanisms of deceit and denial he has always employed. Consciously trying to fend off responsibility, he tells Bernard at Charley's office that the math teacher, "that son-of-a-bitch," destroyed Biff, but he knows subconsciously that Biff "laid down and died like a hammer hit him" because he lost all will when he caught Willy with the secretary (*DS*, 71). Willy's anger at Linda's mending stockings makes apparent his inability to wash his hands of guilt as well. His infidelity, echoed by Biff's prowess as a teenager and Hap's exploitation of his competitors' women, is ironically fused with its opposite. The same sexual exploits that violate "the system of love" Miller alludes to are a means to fulfill the imperative of success, whose ultimate end for Willy is, paradoxically, to secure the family and assert his fatherhood. The merging of Linda's laughter with that of the woman in the hotel represents the fatal union of imperative and impulse in Willy's mind, who is now unable to separate the contending forces that propel him. The sexual encounter with the woman is not the cause of Willy's violation of his love for Linda or for his sons but the symptom of a tragic conflict that he has created nonetheless. However much Willy struggles to live in denial consciously, he knows subconsciously that he bears responsibility, as his suffering bears witness. The play shifts after the restaurant scene into the future and out of Willy's unconscious, as Willy, having returned to the point of offense, seeks for some means to reconcile the conflicting "laws" that define him. The denouement inevitably follows the subjective reenactment of the encounter his memory will not let him evade—once again, "the birds come home to roost."

To what degree Willy really understands and accepts responsibility is a matter of unending debate among critics. In his prefatory essay to his *Collected Works*, Miller argued that "Had Willy been unaware of his separation from values that endure he would have died contentedly polishing his car. . . . But he was agonized by being in a false position, so constantly haunted by the hollowness of all he had put his faith in. . . . That he had not intellectual fluency to verbalize his situation is not the same as saying that he lacked awareness" (*TE*, 148). Nevertheless, in an earlier interview he acknowledged the "danger in pathos, which can destroy any tragedy if it goes too far," and confessed, "I feel that Willy Loman lacks sufficient insight into his situation, which would have made him a greater, more significant figure" (*Conv.*, 26). Miller's detractors, and in some cases defenders, have focused on the question. Heilman, for example, has written that *Death of a Salesman* is near to but not quite tragedy because "Willy is always in the first stage of the tragic rhythm—the flight from the truth; but he never comes to the last stage of the tragic rhythm, in which truth breaks through to him."[50] And Schlueter and Flanagan have argued that although Willy "casts an immense shadow over all of modern drama, he remains a pathetic 'low man.' "[51]

But even granting Willy's limited insight, it would be a mistake to claim that he is ignorant of himself or of his moral offenses. Certainly emotionally, as Lois Gordon contends, "he confronts himself and his world." Roudané persuasively argues that Willy "tragically knows at least part of himself," as is evidenced when he admits to Linda that he looks foolish, that he babbles too much, and that he feels estranged. He "mixes self-disclosure with external fact," as when he sarcastically responds to Hap, "You'll retire me for life on seventy goddam

50. Heilman, *Tragedy and Melodrama*, 234.
51. Schlueter and Flanagan, *Arthur Miller*, 63. Miller has denied that he intended the name as a pun, claiming he took it from a character in Fritz Lang's early film *The Testament of Mr. Mabuse* (*T*, 177).

dollars a week?" And his lyric cry, "The woods are burning!" further reflects Willy's "self-knowledge within the marketplace" as "he honestly assesses his overall predicament" when he meets his sons at the restaurant. "Such insights make Willy more than a misfit or a oversimplified Everyman" and "enhance his tragic structure precisely because they reveal to the audience Willy's capacity to distinguish reality from chimera." Granting that Willy himself does not comprehend the full meaning of his spiritual crisis or his guilt, Bernard Dukore asks, What if he did fully understand? "The play would then become too explicit and Willy the know-it-all protagonist of a drama with Uplift,"[52] devoid of tragic significance and at odds with the play's realistic portrayal.

Miller's commitment to the truthfulness of Willy's character in effect mitigates against his playing the role of the classical tragic hero—he "knows" in the Old Testament sense of experiencing reality, but there is no doubt that his intellectual vision is restricted. When he leaves the restaurant shattered by his painful return to the Boston hotel room, Willy is to a degree freed to act, to choose. Before his mental reenactment he was incapacitated by Howard's final humiliation of him, by his agonizing awareness that Bernard's success reflected on his own failure as father, by Charley's offer of a job that would come at the cost of any self-respect. Now he is galvanized into desperate action. Mobilized by the stinging awareness that he has utterly failed materially and morally, he impulsively tries to plant something, to nurture life amid walls of urban apartment houses that symbolize the domination of the nature he loves by the material world created by the selling mythos of American culture to which he is hopelessly tied.

His actions expose his sense of rather than understanding of his existential dilemma. In Miller's view of a world without transcendent mythic heroes, Willy alone cannot embody the tragic vision of the play. As part of a composite tragic figure, Biff assumes a dimension of the tragic protagonist Willy is too diminished to satisfy. As a projection of competing forces operating in Willy's psyche, Biff seeks freedom from the "phony dream" that he nonetheless carries as symbolically part of Willy. Joseph Hynes has expressed dismay that "The

52. Gordon, "Death of a Salesman: An Appreciation," 103; Roudané, "Death of a Salesman and the Poetics," 79; Dukore, Death of a Salesman and The Crucible, 37.

only one who gains self-awareness is Biff; but the play is Willy's. . . . [T]he showdown lights up the play's failure as tragedy."[53] But in fact "the play" does not turn on Willy as a single protagonist. Because Willy is so wedded to the dream, nothing less than his death can free him from it. Biff, however, can acquire freedom from the imperative Willy cannot abandon without self-destruction, but, paradoxically, he can only be freed *by* Willy. Possessing awareness of the corrosive nature of Willy's dream and its devastating effect on his father and himself, Biff pleads with Willy to "take that phony dream and burn it" (*DS*, 106). The "*anagnorisis* is there," declares David Sievers, but "is given . . . to Biff, who is purged of his father's hostility when he comes to see his father for what he is."[54] When he expresses his love for his father in a climactic embrace, he frees Willy to claim his tragic fate, as, paradoxically, Willy's death frees him.

Biff, then, provides the awareness Willy lacks, but he cannot himself resolve the tragic crisis. It may be true that Miller does not adequately develop Biff's character in relation to Willy or fully trace his moral development, although it is clear from the beginning that Biff returns home because he feels a sense of guilt and moral responsibility to heal the breach with his father. Miller himself has stated, "I am sorry the self-realization of the older son, Biff, is not a weightier counterbalance of Willy's character" (*TE*, 9–10), but his intent is not obscure. Biff is not a counterweight *to* but a counterweight *of* Willy's character. However unwittingly, Willy pays the price to free Biff from the imperative he ironically thinks he dies to defend: "[T]ragedy brings *us* knowledge and enlightenment" as audience, Dukore has wisely remarked, "which it need not do for the tragic hero."[55]

It is hardly surprising that the motivation for Willy's suicide is variously interpreted, for Miller himself substantially altered his earlier depiction of the death. The earlier version of the penultimate scene,

53. Joseph A. Hynes, "Attention Must Be Paid . . . ," 577. In another essay, Hynes calls Willy "insane," "a raving lunatic," "a victim of compulsion, and . . . mad to boot." Miller's construction of "the common man," he concludes, is "one who is economically of the lower or middle class, uneducated, unimaginative, inarticulate, and either mentally ill or uncommonly stupid" ("Arthur Miller and the Impasse of Naturalism," 331, 327, 333).

54. W. David Sievers, *Freud on Broadway: A History of Psychoanalysis and the American Drama*, 396.

55. Dukore, Death of a Salesman *and* The Crucible, 37.

Brenda Murphy has noted, occurs not when Biff confronts Willy with the rubber hose but when he confesses for the first time that he lied about the appointment with Oliver. The difference is important because the rubber hose, like the car accidents earlier, reveals Willy's flirtation with surrender to defeat. The car wrecks "were cowardly and escapist," Dan Vogel has rightly claimed, whereas his death at the end of the play is "purposeful, self-sacrificial, and epiphanic." Although it does nothing to achieve Willy's dream, it is not, as Schlueter and Flanagan conclude, simply "a deluded death gesture that only compounds the waste of his life."[56] Miller has identified the cause as Willy's "epiphany" in the penultimate scene when he realizes "He loves me!" and discovers "the resurrected knowledge of his vision with Biff, his seed and hope" (SB, 170). Having gained "a very powerful piece of knowledge, which is that he is loved by his son and has been embraced by him and forgiven," he can now choose death as fulfillment, not mere escape:

> That he is unable to take the victory thoroughly to his heart, that it closes the circle for him and propels him to his death, is the wage of sin, which was to have committed himself so completely to the counterfeits of dignity and the false coinage embodied in his idea of success that he can prove his existence only by bestowing "power" on his posterity, a power deriving from the sale of his last asset, himself, for the price of his insurance policy. (TE, 147)

The point is that Willy, however wrongly, chooses to die in such a way that he believes can restore the equilibrium between the imperative of success and the contesting will to love. "Unwittingly," Miller has written, "he has primed his own son Biff for his revolt against what he himself has done with his life and against what he has come

---

56. Murphy, *Miller: Death of a Salesman*, 6; Dan Vogel, *The Three Masks of American Tragedy*, 101; Schlueter and Flanagan, *Arthur Miller*, 65. Noting that *Death of a Salesman* is "about resistance, even unto death," contemporary playwright Tony Kushner explains, "A tragedy in which suffering and death are truly inexorable lacks drama; there needs to be a *what if*, a possible escape, or else the whole thing becomes grimly mechanical, pathetic, not exhilarating, grotesque rather than cathartic" (quoted in Kolin, "*Death of a Salesman*: A Playwrights' Forum," 608). It is precisely the choice between car and pipe, death by escape or death as affirmation, that provides the *"what if"* in the play and leads to catharsis at its conclusion.

to worship: material success" (*SB*, 135).[57] Anything less than death would make Willy's end purely melodramatic. As Kazan recorded, "it is a *deed*, not a feeling";[58] that Willy *chooses* rather than succumbs makes all the difference. In "The Nature of Tragedy" (1949), Miller wrote that "When Mr. B., while walking down the street, is struck on the head by a falling piano," we witness "only the pathetic end of Mr. B. . . . [T]he death of Mr. B does not arouse . . . tragic feeling" and produces no catharsis (*TE*, 9). Willy's death is neither accidental nor senseless. That he dies *for* something, however misconstrued, rather than *from* debilitating defeat, makes his end meaningful—and necessary. His death eliminates Biff's obligation to conform to his father's ideal. Although Christopher Bigsby is right in claiming that it is not "truth" but Willy's "commitment to illusion" that kills him,[59] the consummate irony is that he frees Biff from the very idea he himself holds in absolute allegiance. In the final analysis, the dream of success is not Willy's "ultimate concern" but a corruptive means to a higher end. That Willy remains ignorant of the truth that the dream subverts his end to reestablish the love between him and his son does not erase the fact that he dies as the agent of that love.

The effectiveness of the play's requiem has been another point of contention among critics: To some it is contrived and extraneous to the rest of the play; to others it is a necessary commentary on the consequences of the action. Miller has described a distinct breaking point at the end of the drama. When Willy "dies his consciousness vanishes and there is a space between the requiem and the play. . . . We've left Willy's head now; we're on the earth" (*AMC*, 59). In his view, crossing the distance between Willy's distorted internal point of view to external reality is essential to the resolution of the play. Without the requiem there would be only the death of a self-deluded salesman, whose end achieves nothing but blind self-annihilation. Willy's "tragedy" would provoke, as George Jean Nathan described it in his famous review of the play, an "experience [like] we suffer in contemplating on the highways a run-over and killed dog,

---

57. In the same work, Miller has claimed, "Willy is indeed going toward something through his dying, a meaningful sacrifice, the ultimate irony, and he is filled, not emptied of feeling" (*SB*, 196).

58. Quoted in Rowe, *Theater in Your Head*, 49.

59. Bigsby, *Critical Introduction*, 179.

undeniably affecting but without any profound significance."[60] Miller, though, does not portray Willy's death as meaningless, though it is certainly ironic. He has written, "We have abstracted from the Greek drama its air of doom, its physical destruction of the hero, but its victory escapes us. Thus it has become difficult to separate in our minds the ideas of the pathetic and of the tragic" (TE, 59).

In *Death of a Salesman,* Miller attempts to conjoin the pathetic and the tragic in a unique manner by uniting the destinies of Biff and Willy in a way he was never able to accomplish with the characters of Chris and Joe Keller. Chester Eisinger has argued that Biff's recognition "provides the contrapuntal release to life that we must see over against Willy's defeat in suicide."[61] But, in a larger sense, Biff's epiphany—that "I know who I am kid" (DS, 111)—is not one thing and Willy's death another; they are not a point/counterpoint but an integrated whole. Miller has acknowledged the seeming "rift" in the play between the focus of the dramatic action, which falls on Willy, and the recognition and moral resolution, which fall on Biff. He knew he could not give to Willy Biff's insight and be true to Willy's character, which is why he considered the funeral essential to rescue the play from pessimism. Willy's last conversation with Ben keeps his illusion intact,[62] but the requiem enlarges the vision. You go to a funeral because "You want to think over the life of the departed and it's then, really, that it's nailed down: [Biff] won't accept his life" (AMC, 56). Willy gains emotional awareness of Biff's love and consequently finds self-worth in dying for that love; Biff discovers freeing self-knowledge. His decision to go west may represent,

60. George Jean Nathan, "Review of *Death of a Salesman,*" 284.

61. Chester E. Eisinger, "Focus on Arthur Miller's *Death of a Salesman:* The Wrong Dreams," 171.

62. Ben represents what Porter has called "the older version of the Salesman, the ruthless capitalist," whose adventuresome brutality contrasts with Willy's "Dale Carnegie approach to success," most fully idealized in Willy's vision of Dave Singleman (*Myth and Modern American Drama,* 135). But Ben is also Willy's alter ego, as Sister M. Bettina, SSND, has discussed, "a projection of his brother's personality" whose presence provides "a considerable amount of tragic insight" ("Willy Loman's Brother Ben: Tragic Insight in *Death of a Salesman,*" 83). Willy's dependency on Ben's approval stems from his brother being a substitute father and the sole link to their peddler-father. Di Giuseppe concluded that Ben functions "much in the same manner as the 'gods' in classical tragedy who hover in the twilight zone uttering prophesies," both the embodiment of the success myth and its arbiter ("The Shadow of the Gods," 117).

as Nada Zeineddine has suggested, a "metaphorically killing of the father," a last expression of Oedipal rebellion against the father.[63] Biff confidently asserts that Willy "had the wrong dreams. All, all wrong" (*DS*, 111). His rejection of his father's ideal, however, emerges paradoxically from his embrace of his father and his father's ultimate act of love for him.

There is more uncertainty, more lack of resolve, at the end of the play than we ordinarily find in most conventional tragedies. Biff's heading west, Christopher Bigsby has written, "smacks a little of Huck Finn lighting out for the Territory, ahead of the rest. He is moving against history" (*DS*, xix). And both Bigsby and Gerald Weales have noted the irony that Biff's return to the West foreshadows the cowboy Gay's fate in *The Misfits*, who is displaced in the dying agrarian society.[64] Weales also has concluded that "there is no reason to assume that some of the irony" directed to Willy and the other Lomans "does not rub off on Biff."[65] Nevertheless, Biff most certainly moves "from something and to something." As he developed Biff's character, Miller clearly intended to show that Biff gains independence from rather than perpetuates his father's life of illusion. Bernard Dukore has implied that it is good that Miller does not more fully counterbalance Biff's perception against Willy's blindness because the play "might then become an italicized message." Those who say Biff's vision is "vague, trite and romantic, miss the point."[66] The tragic vision does not depend on being able to predict what will happen to Biff so much as on our awareness that Willy's death dissolves Biff's obligation to meet a spurious ideal, whatever the sequel might say.

Other parts of the requiem have also been debated vigorously. Charley's "A salesman is got to dream" speech has been variously called out-of-character and realistic, and Linda's often discussed last

63. Zeineddine, *Because It Is My Name*, 178. Matthew Roudané has agreed that Biff "still carries on an Oedipal resistance to his father" in the requiem ("*Death of a Salesman* and the Poetics," 81).

64. Weales, "Arthur Miller: Man and His Image," 178. In his *Critical Introduction*, Bigsby has alluded to Gay as "an ageing cowboy, as bewildered by the collapse of his world as Willy Loman has been" (185). Other critics, like Eisinger, have similarly contended that Miller sentimentally "romanticizes the rural-agrarian dream" ("Focus on Arthur Miller's *Death of a Salesman*," 174).

65. Weales, "Arthur Miller: Man and His Image," 169.

66. Dukore, *Death of a Salesman and The Crucible*, 25.

words "we're free . . . We're free . . ." (*DS*, 12) have been dismissed as a trite appeal for sympathy and too-obvious irony.[67] One might ask what the essential irony is: Is it that Linda thinks they are free when they are not? Or is it that they *are* free more than Linda knows—freed from the fear of Willy's death and freed from his illusory ideal? While some, like Ruby Cohn, have accused the requiem of being "jarringly outside" Willy's mind and devoid of any new insights, it introduces a metaphysical dimension at the end. Rita Di Giuseppe has proposed that Linda's remark about the insurance, "It's the grace period now," gives "the jargon of commerce . . . a metaphysical connotation."[68] And one might add that Miller considered calling the play *A Period of Grace*, as if to emphasize something transcendent that emerges in it.

The extraordinary richness of the text is seen in the protean nature of Willy as tragic hero. His role has generated dramatically compelling interpretations, from Lee J. Cobb's touchstone depiction of a towering but monumentally self-deluded character lost in a world of dreams and harsh reality; to Dustin Hoffman's feisty "shrimp" of a figure, a near-adolescent drained of mythical dimension, a "little boat looking for a harbor" but still a fierce fighter against an ever-widening doom; to Brian Dennehy's depiction of both a towering, monumental being who casts a huge shadow across the stage and a vulnerable child helplessly cowering with hands vainly folded over his head. What we are left with is perhaps a tragedy despite itself—Willy is a victim, but chooses nonetheless; he lacks self-knowledge, but is responsible for his son's self-awareness; his ideal is all wrong, but his commitment to it is aligned with a love he willingly dies for; his death lifts no plague and does not affect the larger community,

67. For example, Hynes has dismissed Charley's speech as "sheer sentimentality" and "untrue" ("Attention Must Be Paid . . . ," 283), whereas Welland has claimed that Charley alone understands Willy as salesman "in a wholly unsentimental way" (*Miller the Playwright*, 42). Miller himself considered the speech "objective information. . . . [I]t is absolutely real" and presents the obverse of Charley's earlier remark, " 'Why must everybody like you. Who liked J. P. Morgan?' . . . These are two halves of the same thing" (*Conv.*, 351–52). As several critics have noted, Miller's sympathetic portrayal of Charley as successful businessman, father, and neighbor mitigates against a simplistic reading of the play as an attack on American capitalism. Regarding Linda's last words, Hynes, for example, has described Linda and Charley's words as a "Hallmark Card flourish at the curtain" ("Attention Must Be Paid," 284).

68. Di Giuseppe, "Shadow of the Gods," 126.

but it rescues his family from the continuing anxiety of his death and releases Biff from a destructive imperative. Willy is petty, delusional, pathetic, but "Attention, attention must be finally paid to such a person" (*DS*, 43). However circuitously, the play completes the tragic pattern of the past becoming the present, and it affirms the tragic dictum that there are inevitable consequences to choices, that "the wages of sin" must be paid. Lacking a singular tragic protagonist, it offers a composite figure of father and sons who embody the tragic conflict between the imperative of success and the "system of love." Leaving society unredeemed, it ends in a sacrifice to reclaim the family and restore love. Although not "high tragedy" in Aristotelian terms, *Death of a Salesman* is something more than melodrama or "low tragedy" in its revelation of tragic vision, choice, awareness and consequence. At fifty years of age, Miller's play is still a play of enduring richness and mythic power.

3   *The Crucible* to *A Memory of Two Mondays*

Miller's next stage work was not his own play but an adaptation of Ibsen's *An Enemy of the People*. His admiration for Ibsen long established, he responded positively when Robert Lewis, Frederic March, and March's wife, Florence Eldridge, encouraged him to undertake the project. In addition to his respect for Ibsen's playwriting, Miller was attracted because he shared with the others involved in the effort a fear of growing pro-fascist sentiment that he thought Ibsen's play could question. The producer of the play, a wealthy Swedish businessman, Lars Nordenson, worked directly with Miller in producing the script, translating Ibsen into pidgin English, which Miller then reworked. Miller attributed the play's failure (it was restaged for a short run at Lincoln Center in 1971) not only to "Broadway's historic allergy to uplift masked as entertainment" but to Lewis's direction, which "encouraged a certain self-indulgent picturesqueness and choreographical quality," especially when "March stood over the townspeople with arms outspread like Christ on the cross" (*T*, 324).

The truth is more likely that Miller essentially misread the play as primarily "a teaching play" and "a message work" (*T*, 324). Miller wrote an essay entitled "Ibsen's Warning" in which he argues that *Enemy of the People* "is far more applicable to our nature-despoiling societies than to even turn-of-the-century capitalism, untrammelled and raw as Ibsen knew it to be." Emphasizing the play's polemical importance, he went on to say that "perhaps nature takes on even more of a pure moral value where religion itself has vanished into scepticism."[1] He seems

1. Arthur Miller, "Ibsen's Warning," 74.

largely to have ignored Ibsen's subtle irony and the near-comic incongruities with which Ibsen at times undercuts his idealistic hero, Dr. Thomas Stockmann. Miller claims that he was attacked for making Ibsen "a front for the Reds" by critics who "sprang to the defense of Ibsen's purity without bothering to read him" (*T*, 325). In truth, as David Bronson argues, Miller did make Ibsen's ambiguous protagonist into something of "a mouthpiece" and "a package of virtue,"[2] in some respects inviting the criticism the play evoked. Inspired by a political agenda, fearful like others of a rising McCarthyism, he tended to sacrifice Ibsen's more ambivalent view of Stockmann and to revert to his own earlier, more simplistic depiction of the moral idealist. When he found the inspiration for his next play buried in the historical records of the Salem witch trials, his image of the idealistic hero took on far greater complexity and richness. In the midst of a growing perspective of the fascist challenge to democratic principles, he discovered a character far more suited to his own tragic vision.

In *The Crucible* Miller again explores American culture in the perspective of tragedy, this time in the historical context of the McCarthy era. Like *All My Sons*, the play is constructed on a conspiracy of silence in which characters do not divulge the truth about others—or, more importantly, about themselves—and gradually fall prey to a deceit so pervasive as to be believed. "I was motivated in some great part by the paralysis that had set in among many liberals who . . . were fearful of being identified as covert Communists if they should protest too strongly," Miller has recently recalled. "Gradually, all the old political and moral reality had melted like a Dali watch. Nobody but a fanatic . . . could really say all that he believed."[3] Employing the historical context of the Salem witch trial like a Greek dramatist exploiting the mythic past, Miller reconstructs the historical moment in the present, transforming documentary records into modern tragedy.

2. David Bronson, "*An Enemy of the People*: A Key to Arthur Miller's Art and Ethics," 238.

3. Arthur Miller, "Why I Wrote *The Crucible*: An Artist's Answer to Politics," 159. In the 1999 Massey Lecture at Harvard entitled "*The Crucible* in History," Miller adds that the anticommunist rage was "paralyzing a whole generation and in a short time was drying up the habits of trust and toleration in public discourse" (*E*, 274).

In his well-known study *Historical Drama: The Relation of Literature and Reality*, Herbert Lindenberger acknowledges that in a strict sense historical dramas do not constitute a genre at all. But, he goes on to say, they "prove a special opportunity to examine the transitions between imaginative literature and the external world" by making "a greater pretense at engaging in reality than do writings whose fictiveness we accept from the start."[4] That grounding in reality no doubt explains the attraction Arthur Miller felt in writing about the Salem witch trials in *The Crucible*, excepting perhaps his early work *The Golden Years*, his most historically based drama. Inspired by a chance reading of Marion Starkey's *The Devil in Massachusetts*, Miller renewed an interest in the Salem trials that he had first experienced as an undergraduate at the University of Michigan (*T*, 330). As a consequence of his reading, Miller discovered in the trials a sort of "objective correlative," connecting him not only to the political inquisitions of the McCarthy era, in which he was increasingly embroiled, but also to something deeper—that same strain of American Puritanism that runs across American literature from Jonathan Edwards to Hawthorne to Faulkner and O'Neill. In his autobiography he recalls researching at the Historical Society in Salem in the spring of 1952 and seeing woodcuts and etchings of the 1692 trials; these exposed in him "a familiar inner connection with witchcraft and the Puritan cult, its illusions, its stupidities, and its sublimity too. . . . I felt strangely at home with these New Englanders." He remembers seeing in them "the same fierce idealism, devotion to God, tendency to legislate reductiveness," and "longings for the pure and intellectually elegant argument" he found in his Jewish heritage (*T*, 42). His personal affinity with characters and themes in the historical records and the corresponding political realities of the late forties and early fifties merged to form the matrix of what has become his most performed play and one of most frequently staged works in modern drama. Recently adapted as an opera by William Bolcom and successfully made into a film in 1996, the drama has also sold in excess of six million paperback books. Despite the cool reception to the premiere on Broadway, "I don't think there has been a week in

---

4. Herbert Lindenberger, *Historical Drama: The Relation of Literature and Reality*, x.

the past forty-odd years when it hasn't been on a stage somewhere in the world," Miller has recently written.[5]

By employing historical texts, Miller attempts to project his own experience and personal beliefs without violating the truth of the historical matter he surveyed. How a playwright manipulates and transforms the historical record of course determines the legitimacy of a play as historical drama. On one hand, as Niloufer Harben states, a playwright should "be free to approach his subject imaginatively," making "minor alterations such as transpositions of time and place, the telescoping of events and imposing of artistic form and movement." On the other hand, artistic license must be "controlled by an overriding respect for what is actually there in the evidence." Within its contexts, Lindenberger observes, historical drama assumes a protean character and may accommodate conventional and recognized genres such as tragedy or romance. In Miller's hands the historical play becomes a vehicle for modern tragedy in *The Crucible*, carefully sustaining the aura of the historical period but also projecting onto it the political realities of a dark era of modern American history and transfiguring an abbreviated reference to one John Proctor into an existential drama of self-discovery.[6]

To underscore the meaning of Miller's achievement, we might consider his play in juxtaposition with another drama written in the same period, Robert Bolt's *A Man for All Seasons*. Such a comparison is by no means arbitrary or tangential to the issues raised in this study, for despite the differing cultural and historical contexts out of which they wrote their plays, both Miller and Bolt attempted to employ historical drama to characterize a modern tragic figure. After Bolt's stage drama *A Man for All Seasons*, based on the controversy between Sir Thomas More and Henry VIII, won wide acclaim in London in 1960–1961 and enjoyed a run of 637 performances in New York, it

5. Miller, "Why I Wrote *The Crucible*," 165.
6. Niloufer Harben, *Twentieth-Century English History Plays*, 45; Lindenberger, *Historical Drama*, x. For varying assessments of Miller's use of historical texts, see especially David Levin, "Salem Witchcraft and Recent Fiction and Drama"; Henry Popkin, "Historical Analogy and *The Crucible*"; Robert Warshow, "The Liberal Conscience in *The Crucible*"; William J. McGill Jr., "*The Crucible* of History: Arthur Miller's John Proctor"; Robert Martin Jr., "Arthur Miller's *The Crucible*: Background and Sources"; Cushing Strout, "Analogical History: *The Crucible*"; and E. Miller Budick, "History and Other Spectres in Arthur Miller's *The Crucible*."

was turned into a highly successful screenplay in 1966—the movie won six Academy Awards. Although it gained its extensive popularity in the sixties, the work was first performed as a radio play in 1954, interestingly only a year following the opening of *The Crucible*. The close chronology does not constitute the major similarity between Bolt's and Miller's texts, however. Both writers attempt to describe a modern protagonist, specifically a hero of self; both depict him as a reluctant character who tries to evade martyrdom of any sort; despite a concern with recreating an accurate historical context, both playwrights conceive of personal character rather than political or economic factors as the chief determinant in the action; and, unlike Bertolt Brecht, whose historical play *Galileo* was staged just two weeks before the original stage production of *A Man for All Seasons*, both Bolt and Miller are less concerned with historical process than with the plight of the individual in a historical moment.[7]

Furthermore, the two playwrights both briefly flirted with communist ideology before writing their plays; perhaps more importantly, both saw their works as responses to the growing anticommunist sentiment in the West in the postwar period, especially in the United States. Miller's first unpublished dramas (*No Villain* or *They Too Arise*, *Honors at Dawn*, and *The Great Disobedience*) were strongly Marxian in character, and of course Miller was already feeling the heat of the McCarthy hearings at the time he seriously began to work on *The Crucible*, though he had considered writing about the witch trials much earlier in his career. Bolt, as William Free points out, had experienced and abandoned an early commitment to Marxism as well, emphasizing instead the capacity of the individual to color "the events which the forces of history determine." In the inevitable comparison with Brecht, some critics with Marxist leanings especially criticized Bolt's failure to, in Kenneth Tynan's words, "reveal [More's] convictions. . . . Mr. Bolt tells us nothing about More's convictions or how he came to embrace them." Such criticism echoes the objections of critics of Miller's play, like Eric Bentley and Tom Driver, that the American dramatist's "quasi-Marxist stamp" made

7. Kenneth Tynan complains that Bolt "looks at history solely through the eyes of his saintly hero," whereas Brecht "looks at Galileo through the eyes of history" (*Tynan Right and Left: Plays, Films, Places, and Events*, 163). See also his discussion of Bolt and Brecht in *A View of the English Stage, 1944–63*.

his plays "mere partisan critique," lacking the profundity of more authentic Marxian dramas by Brecht or Pirandello. But the criticism is ill-directed in reference to both writers, for neither Bolt nor Miller embraced Marxism to any significant degree. Although both accepted the reality of historical determinism in the shaping of events, they saw the individual caught in the historical moment as capable of independent, if ill-fated, choice. As Christopher Bigsby has written, for Miller, drama exists in "the nexus between determinism and free will."[8]

To be sure, despite the obvious similarities, *The Crucible* and *A Man for All Seasons* do differ in essential ways. Miller's use of a seemingly minor historical character certainly contrasts with Bolt's focus on one of the major shaping figures of the Renaissance. Miller is somewhat less bound by historical records than Bolt in developing his hero, though Bolt certainly uses considerable freedom in constructing his text. Miller found his play's center, he writes in *Timebends*, in a relatively abbreviated account of the breakdown of the Proctor marriage and in Abigail Williams's effort to discredit Elizabeth Proctor, as recorded in Charles W. Upham's *Salem Witchcraft* (*T*, 337). Assuming the artistic license accorded an author of historical drama, Miller created a fictional character riveted to a distinct historical frame but imbued with the traits of a modern existential hero. Borrowing especially from R. W. Chambers's biography of More, Bolt, too, took the liberty to remodel his historical hero, making him into a "man for all seasons."[9] But the dramatic distinction between the two creations is the discrimination between heroism given and heroism earned, and the difference indicates the potential of historical drama in the twentieth century to produce both eloquent melodrama and modern tragedy.

8. William J. Free, "Robert Bolt and the Marxist View of History," 53 (see also 51); Tynan, *View of the English Stage*, 289; Eric Bentley, "Miller's Innocence"; Driver, "Strength and Weakness"; Bigsby, *Critical Introduction*, 248. On Marxist criticism, see especially Driver's "Strength and Weakness," and Bentley's "Miller's Innocence." Far from being a "quasi-Marxist" play, Miller's work counters the basic socioeconomic determinism of Marxism with the force of self-will. Just how un-Marxian Miller's play is can best be seen by comparing it with Sartre's simplistic 1957 film adaptation, *Les Sorcières de Salem*, which makes it a heavy-handed polemical document.

9. For a discussion of Bolt's use of Chambers's biography, see Harben, *Twentieth-Century English History Plays*, 161–62.

As noted earlier, any attempt to define tragedy brings with it certain risks, as Miller's own commentaries on the subject surely suggest. On one hand, definitions tend to be reductive and exclusionary of works that can be wrongfully tainted as inferior because they do not measure up to some formulaic pattern; on the other hand, generic paradigms may well exaggerate the value of a work solely on the grounds that it fits a given model. Nonetheless, without some attempt at definition, no critical distinctions can be drawn—so the risk must be taken. For my purposes I again wish to employ the description of tragedy offered by the eminent Shakespearean scholar Robert Heilman, as discussed in the previous chapter. In an early but often-cited essay entitled "Tragedy and Melodrama: Speculations on Generic Form," Heilman summarizes the differences between tragedy and melodrama:

> In melodrama, man is seen in his strength or in his weakness; in tragedy, in both his strength and his weakness at once. In melodrama, he is victorious or he is defeated; in tragedy, he experiences defeat in victory, or victory in defeat. In melodrama, man is simply guilty or simply innocent; in tragedy his guilt and his innocence coexist. In melodrama, man's will is broken, or it conquers; in tragedy, it is tempered in the suffering that comes with, or brings about, new knowledge.[10]

These distinctions identify the major contrasts between Bolt's and Miller's plays and account for much of the durability and, arguably, superiority of Miller's forceful drama. To refine the distinction noted we can collapse the major differences between a melodramatic and tragic character to this: A melodramatic character is "whole," in Heilman's terms, whereas a tragic hero is "divided." A "whole"

10. Robert B. Heilman, "Tragedy and Melodrama: Speculations on Generic Form," 237. In *Iceman, Arsonist, and Troubled Agent*, Heilman labels *The Crucible* "superior melodrama," though "Miller hovers at the edge of tragedy." Although Miller "raises *The Crucible* in the melodramatic scale" over *Death of a Salesman*, he argues that "the basic pattern is that of a good man destroyed by forces of evil" (143–47). Other critics have complained that Proctor is "wholly good"; but although he, like most tragic heroes, possesses an elemental goodness, he also expresses a capacity for evil, pettiness, and cowardice that Miller goes out of his way to illuminate. And just as important, he bears the consequences of his *own* choices as well as the wrath of his oppressors.

character is weak *or* strong, innocent *or* guilty; a tragic character is both weak *and* strong, innocent *and* guilty.

At no point does Bolt's Sir Thomas More display weakness of character, though he is of course physically vulnerable. Bolt so elevates his character that when he first introduces him, he says, "the life of his mind . . . illuminated his body." And every character who encounters More, from King Henry to his beloved Daughter Meg, acknowledges his goodness and moral firmness. Moreover, if More is wholly good, his antagonist, Cromwell, is entirely evil. In Heilman's definition, the ultimate antagonist in a true tragedy is the self, but in *A Man for All Seasons*, Cromwell plays the conventional "bad guy," a "dockside bully" whose threats More easily dismisses as "terrors for children . . . an empty cupboard: to frighten children in the dark."[11] Cromwell is More's opposite, *not* his own other self; and lacking any of Cromwell in himself, More remains "whole." He instinctively recognizes Cromwell's crass Machiavellian devotion to political cunning, and at every turn he battles his enemy with the untarnished weapon of his moral purity. In short, More's innocence is never seriously jeopardized, not by Wolsey's argument of accommodation, not by the Spanish ambassador Chapuy's appeal of loyalty to the "Church," not by his loyal friend Norfolk's pragmatism or Cromwell's bullying threats or Henry's pleading, not even by the loving concerns of his son-in-law, Roper, or, above all, his beloved wife, Alice, or daughter, Meg—against every threat or temptation, he stands foursquare.

John Proctor, on the other hand, is clearly a divided character, driven by the counterdemands of "impulse" and "imperative," to again use Heilman's terms. Having succumbed to lust for Abigail Williams, he has sinned against his own values. Miller makes use of the brief reference to Proctor in recorded documents to place him in a historical context ripe for tragedy. According to Miller, the witch trials occurred at a time when "the idea of exclusion and prohibition" essential to theocratic ideology was being undermined by a sense that "the repressions of order were heavier than seemed warranted by the dangers against which the order was organized" (C, 6). Desperate to maintain tight control, the theocratic system asserted its absolutism, generating a historical conflict between what

11. Robert Bolt, *A Man for All Seasons*, xxii, 118.

Heilman calls the "imperative" for order and an "impulsive" will to power, a reflection of the Nietzschean dialectic of Apollonian and Dionysian principles described in *The Birth of Tragedy*. The conflict that results resides not alone in the society but more essentially in the self, as Miller conceives it, in John Proctor. Unlike Bolt's hero, Miller's endures a profound internal conflict that generates the tragic crisis in the play. Proctor is "a damaged man," Miller has said, at odds with himself as much as with the external forces that endanger him: "The most important thing is that Proctor is not to be heroic."[12] In the Massey Lecture of 1999, Miller relates Proctor's reluctance to speak out to the silence of the Left during the McCarthy era, which "bespoke a guilt that the Right found a way to exploit" (*E*, 285).

Although Miller, like Bolt, modified the historical accounts (reducing the number of girls in the "crying out," making Abigail Williams older and Proctor younger, limiting the judges to the primary characters Hathorne and Danforth), he claims in a brief headnote that "the fate of each character is exactly that of his historical model" and that the characters "play a similar—and in some cases exactly the same—role as in history." He adds that "little is known about most of the characters. . . . They may therefore be taken as creations of my own, drawn to the best of my ability in conformity with their known behavior" (*C*, 2). *The Crucible* thereby fulfills the definition of a historical play, as discussed earlier, and moves it toward the dimensions of tragedy.

Predictably some postmodern theorists have assaulted Miller's conception of "heroism" that simply does not mesh with the cynicism attached to much current theory. In his deconstructionist

---

12. Mel Gussow, "A Rock of the Modern Age, Arthur Miller Is Everywhere." Of course, critics debate whether or not Proctor is *really* guilty; some find his guilt unconvincing. See, for example, Bentley, "Miller's Innocence"; Herbert Blau, *The Impossible Theater: A Manifesto*; Popkin, "Historical Analogy"; and Stambusky, "Arthur Miller: Aristotelian Canons." However, in Arthur Ganz's reading, Proctor's "heroism is a comparatively easy matter" ("The Silence of Arthur Miller," 234). But Miller's defenders point out that the play depicts not only Proctor's past offenses but present ones as well. Marcel Aymé, who adapted the play for the 1954 French production *Les Sorcières de Salem*, notes that he not only violates an adolescent girl in the past of the play but attempts to redeem himself in the present by sacrificing her reputation to save his wife ("I Want to be Hanged Like a Witch"). As will be discussed, Proctor also continues to betray his own moral beliefs until the end of the drama.

reading of *The Crucible*, for example, Joseph Valente calls the play "a contradictory form of dramatic praxis," an "unwitting" portrayal that "purchases the legitimacy of its protest against . . . one witch hunt with its assistance in perpetuating [an]other." In fact, Miller knowingly creates the drama of a flawed hero. At one point Miller characterizes Proctor by describing him in terms of "the concept of unity" accepted by the physical sciences, "in which positive and negative are attributes of the same force, in which good and evil are relative, ever-changing, and always point to the same phenomenon" (C, 31). It is More's innocence that attests to his heroism; it is Proctor's lack of innocence that affirms his. That is, Proctor is capable of both good *and* evil. In an interview with Robert Lee Feldman on Nazi war criminals, Miller mirrors the distinction between melodrama and tragedy expressed by Heilman, observing that melodrama occurs in a play that "is primarily between a perfectly good and a perfectly evil personality" and embodies "a conflict between people rather than within people."[13] In this regard *The Crucible* portrays a tragic figure.

Unlike Bolt's hero, Proctor "is a sinner," Miller writes, and "not only against the moral fashion of the time, but against his own vision of decent conduct"—he "has come to regard himself as a kind of fraud" (C, 19). Whereas More, like Proctor, attempts to evade martyrdom, he does so only because he wills to save his life, not because he deems himself unworthy. Bolt describes him as "a man with an adamantine sense of his own self. He knew where he began and left off."[14] Proctor, however, exposes *"deep hatred of himself"*; he tells Mary Warren in a fit of rage, "Now Hell and Heaven grapple on our backs, and our old pretense is ripped away. . . . [W]e are only what we always were, but naked now" (C, 76). He shouts at Danforth, "A fire, a fire is burning! I hear the boots of Lucifer, I see his filthy face. It is my face, and yours, Danforth!" (111). He finds in Danforth a mirror image of his own criminality. In contrast, there is no such mirror for More, no other self to reflect his own capacity for evil. Yet, ironically, it is Proctor's consciousness of his complicity that generates his

13. Joseph Valente, "Rehearsing the Witch Trials: Gender Injustice in *The Crucible*," 134; Robert Lee Feldman, "Arthur Miller and the Theme of Evil: An Interview," 92.
14. Bolt, *Man for All Seasons*, xii.

authenticity as a tragic figure, for it provides the necessary "Other" that defines the measure of his heroism, a heroism gained by contesting the spurious innocence he first tries to claim and insure.

Even in the trial scene in act 3, though hounded by guilt, Proctor casts the blame on Abby, labeling her "whore" and "a lump of vanity." He acts neither heroically nor tragically. Only after fully acknowledging his own culpability can he assume the mantle of tragic hero. So it is that when Elizabeth attempts to blame her own frigidity for his adultery and its consequences, claiming "You take my sins upon you, John," Proctor, *"in agony,"* can respond, "No, I take my own, my own!" (C, 127).

Furthermore, even though Rebecca Nurse and other admirable characters recognize Proctor's essential goodness just as More's compatriots recognize More's nobility, Miller does not diminish his guilt. Like the other girls, Mercy Lewis both fears and is "strangely titillated by John Proctor," implying Proctor's sexuality as much as her moral looseness (C, 20). And his guilt is already known or assumed when the play opens. Abby's inability to secure a new position after being discharged by Elizabeth suggests that Proctor's adultery is already suspected by the community. Proctor's brutish treatment of Mary Warren also hints at his guilt. Her insistence that she will "not stand for whipping any more!" (56) suggests that she has been victimized by him before. And Proctor's spurning of the saintly Rebecca Nurse's plea that he clasp Reverend Parris's hand and heal the breach between them gives further evidence of his quick temper and vengefulness.

Above all, despite his avowed attempt to free himself from Abby, Proctor is apparently attracted to her even after she leaves his house. Abby tells him at the beginning of the play that she is drawn at night by "a sense of heat, John, and yours has drawn me to the window, and I have seen you looking up, burning in your loneliness"—and he must confess, "I may have looked up" (C, 21–22). In her intense feminist reading, Wendy Schissel charges Miller with "blaming the victim" and accuses Miller and his critics of experiencing "vicarious enjoyment . . . in a cathartic male character who has enacted their sexual and physical fantasies."[15] But Miller in fact uses Abby to

---

15. Wendy Schissel, "Re(dis)covering the Witches in Arthur Miller's *The Crucible*: A Feminist Reading," 463. Schissel goes on to attack Miller's "existential

expose, not conceal or excuse, Proctor's guilt, and he uses Elizabeth to reinforce rather than exonerate Proctor's culpability. Elizabeth tells her defensive husband with cutting truth, "She has an arrow in you yet, John Proctor, you know it well!" (59). Even when Abby admits to him that she and the others were dancing in the woods when Betty Parris took fright, he smiles widely at her and says half-flirtatiously, "Ay, you're wicked, yet, aren't y'!" (20). She reminds him that "John Proctor took me from my sleep and put knowledge in my heart! . . . You loved me, John Proctor, and whatever sin it is, you love me yet!" Significantly, he does not deny her claim but rather "*turns abruptly to go out*" (22).

Seven months after Abby's departure, in the very present of the play, Elizabeth catches Proctor dissembling, committing the same offense he condemns the theocratic leaders of employing. She reminds him that he said he saw Abby in a crowd but then later inadvertently admitted he talked with her alone. His anger at being found out in his deceit only verifies his guilt. According to Schissel, "we are meant to read" this as "understandably defensive anger," but in fact we are truly "meant to read it" exactly as Miller writes it, to show that Elizabeth is *right* in her condemnation of Proctor. Miller carefully does not let Proctor off the hook in the scene, as Schissel contends. Furthermore, by dropping Abby from act 4 (and excluding her from act 2), Miller emphasizes the internal crisis in Proctor and avoids diminishing his guilt by shifting blame onto Abby in the final scenes. Rather he places the full weight of responsibility onto Proctor himself. It is worth noting that until Proctor finally owns up to his own duplicity, it is Elizabeth who provides the moral focus in the play, a point given forceful emphasis in Joan Allen's portrayal of Elizabeth in the 1996 film adaptation. In Allen's interpretation, as *Boston Globe* film critic Jay Carr writes, Proctor's resolute wife "never courts his approval—or, more importantly, ours. She's cold . . . but she's honorable and she's right."[16] When Proctor tells Elizabeth, "I

---

mysticism" that projects "the paternalistic monotheism of the Puritans" (406). See also Valente's attack on gender injustice in the play in "Rehearsing the Witch Trials"; he predictably shares Schissel's view, claiming that "*The Crucible* treats the figure of the Salem witch . . . as metonymic of the figure of woman, whose victimization/vilification marks the very genesis of Judeo-Christian culture" (124).

16. Schissel, "Re(dis)covering the Witches," 466; Jay Carr, "*Crucible* Bewitches." Several months after the New York opening of the play, Miller added a

come into a court when I come into this house!" she rightly responds, "The magistrate sits in your heart that judges you" (C, 52). Elizabeth insists that he tell the court of the fraud, whereas he fears standing alone as accuser and, perhaps more than he realizes, wants to protect Abby. And there is clearly irony when Proctor accuses Hale of cowardice for letting Elizabeth be jailed when he himself has played the coward all along by denying his affair with Abby. When Proctor does go to court to expose the lies, he acts less out of principle than the need to protect Elizabeth, more out of fear than a sense of justice. However, in Bolt's play, Sir Thomas More acts courageously from the beginning; his heroism is a given. Proctor becomes a tragic hero despite himself.

Ostensibly, More, too, attempts to avoid martyrdom. And like Proctor he tries every legal means of escape. When the bill is issued requiring a loyalty oath to Henry (certainly an intended reference to the McCarthy hearings, which also cast their shadow in Miller's play), More insists it is "God's part" to bring us to martyrdom, but "Our natural business is escaping—so let's get home and study this Bill."[17] But More is undoubtedly "the stuff" of martyrdom from his very first appearance on stage. He cannot *not* be a martyr, because nothing in him serves as a polar opposite to his absolute but existentially untested faith. Consequently, in the trial scene in *A Man for All Seasons*, More has nothing to confess, and so he can only be unjustly condemned. He suffers death because of Rich's perjury, not because he committed offenses against the legal code and certainly not against himself.

Proctor, though, knows that he "lusted, and there *is* promise in such sweat" (C, 102), confirming what Elizabeth had told him: "There is a promise made in any bed—" (58). Although he still tries to protect his innocence by taking cheap shots at Abby in court, noting that "she were twice this year put out of this meetin' house for laughter during prayer" (96), he must accept the consequences of his own actions as well as the injustice of the corrupt system.

---

controversial scene between Abby and Proctor to the end of act 2 in an attempt to clarify their relationship. Most critics find it superfluous or damaging to the action, although it can be argued that the scene provides further evidence of Proctor's guilt in the affair. Miller dropped the scene from the collected works.

17. Bolt, *Man for All Seasons*, 126.

When he tries to escape martyrdom, therefore, he is motivated by his consciousness of his own unworthiness. Even to the very end, his self-judgment keeps him from playing the hero: "I cannot mount the gibbet like a saint. It is a fraud. I am not the man" (126). Not only does he not act heroically, he acts out of fear as well. Driven by self-preservation and self-judgment, he seemingly lacks More's capacity for heroism. "Let them that never lied die now to seek their souls," Proctor says of his condemned friends. "It is pretense for me . . ." (126). In his spirited attack on Tom Driver's position that Miller offers only "strident moralism" in defense of Proctor, E. Miller Budick notes that Proctor tries throughout not to acknowledge evil, including his own, and by his silence perpetuates it until the end of the drama when he discovers a morality "dependent upon recognizing and accepting" his own "humanness." Evil, Proctor finally comes to understand, "is more primary than the Devil who incorporates it," and it exists in the self. "Thus Miller puts the emphasis of his play on the importance of self-awareness, the recognition of evil within one's self, and the acknowledgment that this evil may be projected onto others through no fault of theirs."[18]

More attests to his heroic nature throughout the drama, so the action in the play turns not on self-discovery but on plot, which is in some respects the limitation of Miller's *All My Sons* and the earlier unpublished plays. When he therefore speaks eloquently to his family in the jail cell, More has already fully accepted his pending death without painful self-judgment. He represents a transcendent authority he has always claimed. Even when Meg offers up the greatest temptation, "doing the right deed for the wrong reason," in T. S. Eliot's famous phrase from *Murder in the Cathedral*,[19] More easily brushes it aside. Eliot's renowned play on the martyrdom of Thomas Becket is also an example of the history play as significant melodrama. Eliot forgoes the inner conflict to establish Becket's mythic heroism in language and deed, just as Bolt resorts to rhetoric and gesture to illuminate More. We never doubt for a moment that Becket will do the right deed for the right reason. In *The Crucible* the Fourth Tempter moves from static stage to dynamic reality. Miller gives us a historical figure in self-conflict, not an archetypal saint. We get

18. Budick, "History and Other Spectres," 547–48.
19. T. S. Eliot, *Murder in the Cathedral*, 44.

tragedy in Miller, spectacle in Bolt and Eliot. More remains unchallenged; when Meg warns, "if you elect to suffer for it, you elect yourself a hero," More answers confidently, "we *must* stand fast a little—
even at the risk of being heroes."[20] He endures no internal debate
and suffers from no self-doubt.

But whereas Bolt depicts no conflict in More, Miller brings Proctor
to a point of existential confrontation. He allows for the possibility
of self-deception as Bolt never does. When Proctor seeks Elizabeth's
forgiveness, she places the burden properly on him: "There be no
higher judge under Heaven than Proctor is!" (C, 127)—a truth she
ironically acquires because she has accepted responsibility for her
own failure as a wife. Coming to the awareness that he must judge
himself because he himself is responsible, Proctor must ask the existential question, "God in Heaven, what is John Proctor, what is John
Proctor?" (127). Christopher Bigsby rightly concludes that the process that most concerns Miller "is clearly . . . self-betrayal."[21] And
even to the end, as Proctor tries every avenue of escape, he betrays
his own moral principles. It is guilt that both debilitates him and
generates his heroism. More tries to evade his death by hiding in
the tangle of the law; but once the law itself is violated, he willingly,
almost eagerly, embraces his death. He would have been incapable of
perjuring himself like Proctor does when he offers his false confession
to save himself.

Proctor's heroism does not come so easily. It comes only when he
discovers he will be "used" to compromise the fame of those truly
martyred. Whereas the plot turns when Elizabeth lies to save Proctor, the essential "action in character" reaches the climax only when
Proctor destroys the signed confession. In the first case Proctor is subject to another's action, in the second to his own. Michael J. O'Neal
calls the tearing up of the confession "a bit of grandstanding."[22] But
Miller makes a critical distinction between confessing orally and
signing one's name—"How may I live without my name?" Proctor
asks; "I have given you my soul" (C, 133). More secures his soul
by not taking the oath; in confessing, Proctor willingly offers up his
"soul," negating any claim of transcendence. But the signed "name"

20. Bolt, *Man for All Seasons*, 141.
21. Bigsby, *Critical Introduction*, 197.
22. Michael J. O'Neal, "History, Myth, and Name Magic in Arthur Miller's *The Crucible*," 116.

attests to the here and now. It is an existential emblem, a personal affirmation, not a symbol of transcendental glory. Finally, when More dies he remarks to the Headsman, "Friend, be not afraid of your office. You send me to God."[23] Proctor dies with no such trust in the hereafter or God—"I say—I say—God is dead!" (111). He sees not God's assurance, but at least some degree of self-worth: "for I do think I see some shred of goodness in John Proctor. Not enough to weave a banner with, but white enough to keep it from such dogs" (133). His modest existential victory illustrates once again Miller's often-repeated dictum that in tragedy the "birds come home to roost. . . . You've got to retrieve what you've spent and you've got to account for it somehow. I don't mean to God, I mean to yourself, or else you are totally incomplete always. . . . You get existential justice, where you do your best, but that's about it" (AMC, 201).

According to Heilman's definition, melodramas (or what he labels "disasters") such as *A Man for All Seasons* end "monopathically," because we the audience experience a single strong emotion—we feel pathos for a good man victimized by injustice or fate. Tragedy ends "polypathically," because although we feel sorrow at the protagonist's death, we also feel that justice has somehow been satisfied, that the tragic figure pays a price for his own choices even though he also may be the unjust victim of powers beyond his control. Furthermore, his suffering ultimately ennobles him—we rejoice that suffering leads to a self-awareness, and so we experience a paradoxical "victory in defeat." An innocent victim but an absolute hero, More is totally victorious over a degenerate system; a divided character, Proctor gains self-recognition only through self-confrontation and self-judgment. Unlike More he moves from something and to something, from paralyzing innocence to a morally energizing guilt. If the focus in *The Crucible* were only on the horrors of the system that produced

23. Bolt, *Man for All Seasons*, 152. In an interview Miller concurred with Steven Centola's description of his central vision as "a kind of existential humanism—a vision that emphasizes self-determination and social responsibility and that is optimistic and affirms life by acknowledging man's possibility in the face of his limitations and even sometimes the dramatization of his failures" (*Conv.*, 343). Miller forgoes the realistic or Marxist drama with which he is too easily aligned to embrace tragic possibility, even though he moves the play more in the direction of existentialism than traditional tragedy. Proctor achieves a tragic dimension within the context of a world little able to affirm the presence of divine justice or retribution. Miller's work is tragic as much because of as despite his existential vision.

the witch trials and congressional hearings, then the evil would be clearly identifiable and contained. In this regard, Proctor is undoubtedly the hero, the rebel against a repressive system. But Miller asks us to see another, more subtle, and profound drama, in which the protagonist is fighting personal betrayal as well. To believe in his heroism we must also believe in the gravity of his offense against others and his own values, or else the moral victory rings hollow. Miller attempts to make the guilt credible. Indeed, as Christopher Bigsby observes, it is Proctor's "guilt that creates the conditions for self-betrayal."[24]

Bolt presents historical narrative in the form of polished melodrama; Miller transforms historical narrative into modern tragedy. The distinction is important, for as Eric Bentley reminds us, although "there is melodrama in every tragedy," tragedy "is melodrama plus something."[25] Miller's play is not hospitable to historical or Marxian determinism because it insists that human beings choose and so must accept responsibility. Miller declares in the Massey Lecture that *The Crucible* taught him "that a kind of built-in pestilence was nestled in the human mind, a fatality forever awaiting the right conditions for its always unique, forever unprecedented outbreak of alarm, suspicion and murder" (*E*, 295). If characters are victims, they are the victims of themselves, not simply of class or economic forces or social imperatives or political oppression. Yet Miller also insists on a paradoxical, but not contradictory, belief in destiny, in the inevitability of the meeting at the crossroads where once more his modern Oedipus must face his fate and yet claim that, although Apollo has brought him to his place, he has been his own criminal and his own judge.

A View from the Bridge

A View from the Bridge germinated from a story Miller's friend Vinny Longhi heard about a longshoreman's betrayal of two brothers to immigration authorities. He wrote the play several years after hearing the tale, when Martin Ritt asked Miller if he had a one-act he might stage at the Cornet Theater with a group of talented young

---

24. Bigsby, *Critical Introduction*, 197.
25. Eric Bentley, *The Life of the Drama*, 218.

actors. One-acts were then virtually never performed in New York and Miller had none on hand, so he responded by transforming the story into a one-act play, which he first called *An Italian Tragedy*, in a period of only one or two weeks; he added to this offering *A Memory of Two Mondays*, a one-act autobiographical play he considered "a kind of elegy for my years in [an] auto parts warehouse" (*T*, 353). *A View* instinctively seemed to him especially appropriate for the genre—"it always seemed to me to be a one-act play" (AMC, 366). He clearly considered it a tragedy in the tradition of classic Greek dramas, which he noted were always one-acts:

> [E]verything that is said in the Greek classic play is going to advance the order, the theme, in manifest ways. There is no time for the character to reveal himself apart from thematic considerations. . . . So I began *A View From the Bridge* in its first version with a feeling that it would make a single, constantly rising trajectory, until the fall, rather like an arrow shot from a bow. . . . I wanted to reveal the method nakedly to everyone so that from the beginning of the play we are to know that this man can't make it, and yet might reveal himself somehow in the struggle. (*Conv.*, 366–67)

Intent upon avoiding "the spectacle of still another misunderstood victim" and the "psycho-romanticism" that he felt produced "mere sympathy" on stage (*TE*, 219), as he wrote in the introduction to the 1960 republication of the play, Miller wanted to construct a play stripped of any extraneous material that might retard the protagonist's inexorable movement to his fated end. The opening New York production failed, however, only to be successfully restaged in London scarcely a year later. The young English director Peter Brook told Miller that the original play was "too relentless in the sense that some of the life of the family, the neighborhood, had been squeezed out." Convinced that Brook was right, Miller modified the play, slightly expanding it to two acts, letting "that life back in, especially the dilemma as seen by the wife. . . . I could see on the stage that I could give those actors more meat, and let the structure take care of itself a little" (*Conv.*, 367).[26]

26. Part of the inspiration for writing *A View* may have stemmed from Miller's collaboration with Elia Kazan on a film script concerning the Red Hook district,

The revisions in the two-act version (reducing or altering some of the free verse into prose, especially in Alfieri's speeches; incorporating more of the Red Hook environment; amplifying the characterization of Beatrice and Catherine; using the boxing scene between Eddie and Rodolpho to climax the first act; intensifying the triangles of Eddie-Catherine-Beatrice and Eddie-Catherine-Rodolpho; and revising the ending) have inevitably created disagreement among critics about which text is better, although Miller chose the two-act version for the *Collected Plays*. It subsequently has been the essential text performed on stage, and so it is the basis of my discussion here.[27]

Although *A View* seems to extend Miller's already established themes—the quest for identity, the conflict between society and the individual, the loss of innocence, the theme of betrayal—some feel it marks a departure from his earlier work. According to Robert Heilman, Miller "deliberately made a turn away from victims . . . who can never be tragic, to the story of self-injuring personality," though Heilman goes on to say that because Eddie "never knows himself, [he] falls away from the tragic magnitude that he has when . . . he is doubly caught between an imperative and a destructive passion." John Orr goes so far as to call Eddie "unconditionally tragic," unlike Willy Loman and John Proctor, and claims the play possesses "the power of tragedy" lacking in *Death of a Salesman* and *The Crucible*. Alan Stambusky, on the other hand, labels it "a final abortive attempt to display the tragedy of the common man in classical terms. . . . Eddie lacks true nobility of motive." And John Styan contends that the revised text, with its emphasis on Beatrice and Catherine's awareness of the sexual crisis in Eddie, moves *A View* "away from the Greeks" and as well "away from the social drama, away from the Ibsen of the social plays—perhaps toward Chekhov."

The Hook. The collaboration ended when Miller refused to make labor racketeers in his script into communists to satisfy the desires of Hollywood producers bent on pleasing politicians caught up in the anticommunist movement. Kazan went on to make *On the Waterfront*, which some contend may have triggered *A View* in response, though others disagree. See Gerald C. Weales, "Arthur Miller and the 1950s," 648–50.

27. For example, in addition to Gerald C. Weales, Sheila Huftel deems the original more "majestic in its simplicity" (*Arthur Miller: The Burning Glass*, 158), whereas Nelson sees the one-act version as implausible and too "rarefied . . . a neo-Grecian bubble machine" (Nelson, *Arthur Miller*, 211).

Clinton W. Trowbridge insists, though, that the play "shows a profound change in Miller's concept of fate," in that Eddie's "struggle is within, with a person that he can neither understand nor control," whereas in the earlier plays fate surfaces in the guise "of the social, economic or political forces in society."[28]

But in fact the drama's juxtaposing of counterforces operating within Eddie resembles the internal conflicts endured by Willy Loman and John Proctor in *Death of a Salesman* and *The Crucible*. Eddie's struggle to claim his name mirrors Willy's attempt to leave a thumbprint in the world and Proctor's effort to preserve his name; and it even echoes Mark Donegal's more simplistic quest for self-integrity in *The Half-Bridge*. Miller explores the psychological dimension with more intensity, perhaps, but the existential issue of self-identity had always been the driving motivation in his work. *A View* seemed to him inherently tragic in the Greek sense in its unwavering trajectory and inevitability, but he conceived of it, especially in the two-act version, as inextricably bound with a psychological and social determinism that seals Eddie's fate the more.

Miller has never considered his plays as narrowly deterministic, however. "Determinism," he has written, "is a contradiction of the idea of drama itself as drama has come down to us in its fullest development. . . . It is a process inconceivable without the existence of the will of man. His will is as much a fact as his defeat" (*TE*, 168). The two-act version, first performed in London in October of 1958, enhanced both the mythological thrust of the play and the psychosexual drama. As he writes in the 1960 introduction to the play, "The importance of [Eddie's] interior psychological drama was magnified to the size it would have in life. What had seemed like a mere aberration had now risen to a fatal violation of ancient law" (*TE*, 221). The three-storied tenement buildings in the London staging and the evocation of the Sicilian community of Red Hook established a closed and elementally threatening world. "On those fire escapes the neighbors appeared at the end like a chorus, and Eddie could call up

---

28. Heilman, *Iceman, Arsonist, and Troubled Agent*, 324, 150; John Orr, *Tragic Drama and Modern Society: Studies in the Social and Literary Theory of Drama from 1870 to the Present*, 229–30; Stambusky, "Arthur Miller: Aristotelian Canons," 408–9; J. L. Styan, "Why *A View from the Bridge* Went Down Well in London: A Story of a Revision," 148; Clinton W. Trowbridge, "Arthur Miller: Between Pathos and Tragedy," 229.

to them, to his society and his conscience. . . . The splitting in half of the whole three story tenement . . . opened the mind to the size of the mythic story" (*T*, 431). Here, unlike in the New York opening, members of the tight-knit society walked the streets and stared down from fire escapes, and interrelationships formed rigid societal bounds. More mythical and symbolic than naturalistic, the environment spoke of undeniable forces against which Eddie vainly attempts to exist. Writes Miller, "once Eddie had been placed squarely in his social context, among his people, the mythlike feeling of the story emerged of itself, and he could be made more human and less a figure, a force" (*TE*, 222). Internally driven by the unrelenting impulse to possess his niece, Eddie pays ironic allegiance to the ancient code of the polis that ultimately denies him. Euripidean in its passionate intensity, the drama retains a Sophoclean nature as well. Hopelessly divided, Eddie acts under the insistence of incestuous desire while futilely trying to maintain order. As Steven Centola observes in his essay "Compromise as Bad Faith," the play reflects the Freudian dialectic between order and chaos, between "civilization and its discontents." Recognizing Eddie's inability to articulate his crisis, Miller employs a stage narrator as chorus to provide the moral perspective and interpret events for the audience, much like the Greek chorus served as liaison between stage and audience. A "minor" but "crucial" character, in Miller's words, Alfieri, the lawyer-narrator, "represents common sense in the way that Greek choruses did. That is, common sense in relation to excess" (*Conv.*, 262–63).[29] Yet as he well knows, Alfieri is as helpless to avert the pending tragedy as the chorus in *Oedipus the King* or Linda in *Death of a Salesman*. Alfieri compares himself to "another lawyer" in ancient times who "heard the same complaint and sat there as powerless as I, and watched it run its bloody course" (*VB*, 5). Possibly modeled on a young lawyer from a Neapolitan family Miller knew, Alfieri stands outside the action and yet gives us an "objective" view in language that Miller intended to be "above mere everyday language without giving him

29. He remarks elsewhere, "I wanted to eliminate all the usual machinery. . . . so I introduced a narrator who would set up what I call the moral situation" (*AMC*, 111). In William Bolcom's successful 1999 operatic version of the play, premiered by the Lyric Opera of Chicago with Arnold Weinstein as colibrettist, a full Greek chorus serves the traditional functions of commenting on and interpreting the action.

too stiff a quality" (*Conv.*, 158). Alfieri's often elevated and dignified tone contrasts with the harsh colloquialisms of the blue-collar community and provides a more dispassionate view that transforms the psychological and social realism into myth. In Donald Costello's words, Alfieri "mythologizes the tale" by expanding it beyond the personal, familial, and social into the "universal . . . beyond time and space."[30] Lawyers, of course, figure prominently in Miller's works, which so often center on literal or symbolic trials. In *A View* the contest between the legal system and the ancient code of the Sicilian community of Red Hook, and even more elementally between illicit impulse and communal imperative within Eddie himself, constitutes a universal and timeless moral conflict that Eddie Carbone can neither evade nor resolve. The title alludes to the bridge linking the view of contemporary culture with the past, Miller has noted; from this vantage point, Alfieri senses that in "a little neighborhood an ancient tragedy is being worked out. . . . The narrator's view . . . is looking at it all from the point of view of American civilization and that ancient one that is really down there" (*AMC*, 111).

Like Willy Loman, Eddie Carbone possesses an innocence born of self-ignorance, what Christopher Bigsby describes as a yearning for "a kind of adolescency"—and such a "yearning for innocence is not merely a symptom of its loss but the beginning of an implacable evil."[31] Once again, nothing is so potentially destructive as the temptation of innocence, and Eddie's vain attempt to secure his innocence provides the impetus for the tragedy he brings upon himself. Yet ironically, even Catherine unwittingly preys on his innocence, acquiring a measure of complicity in his destruction.

The stage directions often show Catherine as a seductive figure, bound by her own naive innocence. But Catherine projects an innocence that Iskar Alter rightly calls "the innocence that unwittingly kills,"[32] and consequently assumes a degree of responsibility for the tragic consequences, however unaware she may be. When she first appears before Eddie to show off a new dress, she runs her

30. Donald P. Costello, "Arthur Miller's Circles of Responsibility: *A View from the Bridge* and Beyond," 449.
31. Bigsby, *Critical Introduction*, 206.
32. Iska Alter, "Betrayal and Blessedness: Exploitation of Feminine Power in *The Crucible, A View from the Bridge,* and *After the Fall*," 133.

hands down her skirt, *"turns for him,"* walks *"him to the armchair"* and *"sits on her heels before him"* (VB, 5–6). Later she lights Eddie's cigar, nearly burning her hand because she is so focused on him (20). When toward the end of the play Rodolpho asks, "Why are you so afraid of him?" (60), her long pause hints at something she fears to acknowledge. Her admission that "I can tell when he's hungry or wants a beer before he ever says anything. I know when his feet hurt, I mean I *know* him . . ." (61) constitutes a deeper confession than she intends or perhaps even understands. According to Albert Rothenberg and Eugene Shapiro, both Eddie *and* Catherine employ "projection, rationalization and repression" as defense mechanisms, and their "defensive patterns remain basically the same throughout the play, and they complement and intensify each other."[33] At one point Beatrice reminds Catherine, "You still walk around in front of him in your slip [and] . . . sit at the edge of the bathtub talkin' to him when he's shavin' in his underwear," and "when he comes home you sometimes throw yourself at him like you was twelve years old" (40). When she concludes "You're a grown woman, and you're in the same house with a grown man" (40–41) and insists that Catherine say good-bye, Catherine's naïveté finally gives way to self-knowledge, and she *"turns with some fear, with a discovery, to Beatrice"* (41). Ignorance is not synonymous with genuine innocence for Miller, and in his view no one can ultimately claim innocence. We all live after the Fall. Even at the end, when Eddie's need to protest his innocence leads him to violate the communal code by reporting Rodolpho and Marco, Beatrice sounds the chord: "Whatever happened we all done it, and don't you ever forget it, Catherine" (82),[34] anticipating Dr. Hyman's remark in *Broken Glass* that "we get sick in twos and threes, not alone as individuals" (BG, 27). And even Beatrice's innocence is compromised by her urging Eddie to forget what has happened and her assuring him that he is not responsible for his actions. Her complicity of accommodation, of ignoring the truth and evading responsibility, cannot be excused. But as Steven Centola concludes,

33. Albert Rothenberg and Eugene D. Shapiro, "The Defense of Psychoanalysis in Literature: *Long Day's Journey into Night* and *A View from the Bridge*," 66.

34. Henry Popkin calls Beatrice's speech "no more than a plea for pity" that divides responsibility for the tragedy ("Arthur Miller: The Strange Encounter," 44), but it is Eddie's guilt that ultimately concerns Miller.

"Beatrice and Catherine's culpability does not mitigate Eddie's responsibility" even though "Miller does seem to suggest that Beatrice and Catherine cannot be excused for their insincerity."[35]

It is of course Eddie's need for innocence that propels the play to its tragic end, and his guilt cannot be diminished by making it somehow communal. Unwilling or unable to see his own culpability, he displaces it by targeting Rodolpho. But it remains uncertain whether or not even Rodolpho is blameless. To be sure, Eddie's accusation of Rodolpho as a homosexual is a ruse to conceal his own unacknowledged love for Catherine.[36] He tells Alfieri that Rodolpho "give me the heeby-jeebies the first moment I seen him" (VB, 69). Noting his effeminate traits and actions—his blond hair and too-high tenor voice,[37] his cooking and sewing, his "pointy" shoes—he tells Beatrice that Rodolpho is taunted by the other longshoremen who work with him. Eddie must believe in his rival's guilt to displace his own; yet we do not know that Rodolpho's intentions *are* totally innocent, not because of supposed homosexuality but because he may be using Catherine. Given the immigrant experience, there may be some credibility in Eddie's claim that Rodolpho wants to marry Catherine to secure his citizenship even if the accusation that Rodolpho is gay is totally spurious.

Nevertheless, from the beginning Eddie reveals a powerful sense of guilt even as he claims the role of defender of the communal code. When Beatrice first warns him to "leave [Catherine] alone," he responds with *"open fright"* and *"in guilt walks out of the house"* (VB,

35. Steven R. Centola, "Compromise as Bad Faith: Arthur Miller's *A View from the Bridge* and William Inge's *Come Back, Little Sheba*," 107.

36. Arthur D. Epstein (in "A Look at *A View from the Bridge*") and others note that it is highly possible that Eddie and others consider Rodolpho gay, especially in the macho world of Red Hook. Henry I. Schvey argues that Eddie in fact exposes his own "latent homosexuality" in his attention to Rodolpho ("Arthur Miller: Songs of Innocence and Experience," 78), a claim shared by Myles R. Hurd ("Angels and Anxieties in Miller's *A View from the Bridge*," 5–6). We might add that the Lord Chamberlain's office at first denied the British production because of Eddie's grabbing and kissing Rodolpho, so the play was performed at the Comedy Theater, a designated private theater club, to escape the prohibition.

37. Zeineddine notes Rodolpho's singing of "Paper Doll" and the longshoremen's taunting him with the name, but she relates Rodolpho's "paper doll" to Eddie. "Catherine is Eddie's paper doll. That the singer wants to buy a paper doll parallels Eddie's insistence on his right [as breadwinner] to claim Catherine's actions due to the fatherly sacrifices he has made to raise her" (*Because It Is My Name*, 186).

38). Confidently judging his seventy-four-year-old Sicilian neighbor Vinny Bolzano for fingering his own uncle to immigration authorities (". . . a guy do a thing like that? How's he gonna show his face?" [18]), he seems horrified by Beatrice's insistence that he wants "somethin' . . . and you can never have her!" (83). Yet, as Miller states, "There is a sexual guilt operating" that is "combined with, and threaded through, the social situation" (AMC, 112). In fact the real crime for which he feels subconsciously guilty is not for the betrayal of Rodolpho and Marco, but a crime he never consummates. His love for Catherine turns from innocence as she grows up. It is not Catherine's innocence that is lost as she becomes Rodolpho's woman, of course, but Eddie's; and his struggle to retain that lost innocence leads him to tragic choice. If his guilty love for Catherine is a matter of pathos in that he is driven by forces beyond his control, his violation of the communal code is tragic in its implications. Eddie, some say, never acknowledges his culpability, never arrives at the self-recognition of a tragic hero, never chooses, and so lacks tragic stature. But when he informs on Rodolpho and Marco, he in fact does choose, translating the passive and private "sin" of his illicit love for Catherine into a wholly conscious and social act. When he tries to protect his innocence by imposing upon others the cost of violating his personal morality, he acts willfully. Trying to demand that others pay the price for his own offense, however unconsciously and, indeed, inevitably, he commits his real crime. Eddie is *not*, as Alan Stambusky argues, "a perfectly blameless character" any more than Oedipus can be excused because he fulfilled the destiny already marked out for him by fate.[38] Like Oedipus, he is the agent of his own destruction.

Christopher Bigsby, among others, argues that Eddie "has no choice," and "[w]here there is no choice there can be no culpability." In this sense, Eddie is a victim beyond judgment, "a psychological study of an individual who displaces his sexual passion into a concern with honor and family responsibility."[39] But, as Miller contends, the personal and social drama are so "threaded" that neither the impulse nor imperative can displace the other. Rather, the counterdemands placed on Eddie constitute tragic division and propel him to act, to

38. Stambusky, "Arthur Miller: Aristotelian Canons," 109.
39. Bigsby, *Critical Introduction*, 202, 204.

choose. As Miller explained in his introduction, he did not intend A View as "another revelation of a pathetic victim" but a tragic story rooted in an ancient code, played out in the arena of the modern age.

The end of the play, like the endings of other Miller texts, has raised vigorous debate about the "tragic" implication of the play, as well as questions regarding the lack of choice and self-knowledge. The controversy mostly concerns the way Eddie dies and the effectiveness of Alfieri's final speech, which has generated as vigorous a debate as Linda's final speech in the requiem at the end of Death of a Salesman. In the original version, as Eddie transfers his passion from Catherine to Marco in a desperate attempt to recover his honor, Marco fatally wounds him, and he crawls across the stage to die in Catherine's arms, seemingly oblivious to the true nature of his relationship with his niece, and a mere victim of inexorable forces. In a version first performed in Paris (and later in the 1962 Sidney Lumet film), Eddie kills himself, seemingly moving the play closer to tragedy, suggesting in Eddie's act a moment of self-judgment reminiscent of the ending of Othello. Such an ending, like that in Shakespeare's play, borders between melodrama, in which case suicide is a last act of pathetic self-aggrandizement, and tragedy, in which case the protagonist truly judges himself and inflicts self-punishment for his "crime." But in the revised text for the London production directed by Peter Brook that Miller chose for the Collected Plays, Eddie struggles with Marco, is mortally wounded, and dies in Beatrice's arms calling out, "My B.!" (VB, 85). To Miller this ending moved Eddie's death closer to being a suicide, but it fails fully to resolve the question of whether or not Eddie acts in self-awareness. Although it hints at Eddie's reconciliation with Beatrice, it offers no testament of responsibility or self-analysis.[40] Donald Costello considers this ending a "brilliant stroke" combining murder and suicide—and one might add, a fusion of imperative and impulse. "It is thematically appropriate that both Eddie and Marco have their hands, together, on the knife that kills Eddie," Costello explains. "Eddie's own actions

---

40. Murray claims that the ending's ironic depiction of a reconciliation between Eddie and Beatrice shows Eddie to be more "normal" than before, but it is difficult to draw such a conclusion when Eddie acts with such irrational passion (Arthur Miller, Dramatist, 109).

killed him, of course, but so did Marco, keeper of the codes."[41] Eddie's responsibility for his death, however, does not make the case that he acts in tragic knowledge. Alfieri had already said that "his eyes were like tunnels," devoid of light and understanding; and when just before his fight with Marco, Beatrice accuses him of wanting to possess Catherine, he is unable to believe himself capable of such offense. He is *shocked, horrified* (83), even to the end. Like Willy Loman, he lacks the capacity to comprehend his own potential for evil, utterly convinced that he has acted properly in protecting Catherine. Just as Willy never recognizes that the imperative that drives him is specious, Eddie never can understand the deviant impulse that compels him to act. As much his own executioner as Willy is, he apparently dies believing in the innocence that ironically seals his tragic fate despite his unacknowledged feelings of guilt. No more the victim of simple neurosis than Willy is, he, like Willy, acts in total commitment to a specious concept of his own innocence and worth. In reference to a recurrent theme in the early plays, Miller essentially characterizes Eddie Carbone as one who expresses "an aspiration to an innocence that when defeated or frustrated can turn quite murderous" (*Conv.*, 362). As Miller remarks in his introduction, "like Willy Loman [Eddie Carbone] . . . can be driven to what in the last analysis is a sacrifice of himself for his conception, however misguided, of right, dignity, and justice" (*TE*, 166).

Furthermore, just as Biff has to articulate the tragic awareness of *Death of a Salesman* because Willy lacks the ability to understand the tragic nature of his fate, Alfieri gives voice to the tragic import of Eddie's destiny in his controversial "alarm" speech at the conclusion of the play:

> Most of the time now we settle for half and I like it better. But the truth is holy, and even as I knew how wrong he was, and death useless, I tremble, for I confess that something perversely pure calls to me from his memory—not purely good, but himself purely, for he allowed himself to be wholly known and for that I think that I will love him more than all my sensible clients. And yet, it is better to settle for half, it must be! And so I mourn him —I admit it—with a certain . . . alarm. (*VB*, 86)

41. Costello, "Arthur Miller's Circles," 453.

Although, as Nada Zeineddine warns us, Alfieri's claim that Eddie "allowed himself to be wholly known" should be taken "with reservation,"[42] especially given Eddie's sustained self-ignorance, Alfieri's speech draws tragic meaning from the protagonist's fate. Neither the product simply of social determinism nor of mere psychological imbalance, Eddie's violation of social and moral taboo assumes mythic proportion in its consuming force. It is of course ironic that, although allowing himself to be "wholly known," Eddie did not know himself. But in near-Euripidean power, he embodies the universal, mythic passion, "perversely pure," of human potential. In this he exposes the "sacred truth" to which Alfieri alludes, a truth nonetheless "natural" and destructive in its assertion. Eddie is a fully realized human being, at once lesser than others, and, as Alfieri concludes, more—so we "mourn him with a certain . . . alarm."

Comparing the earlier and later versions of the play, Miller argues that the revised text frees the "original, friezelike character" and moves the play "closer toward realism," while at the same time sustaining Eddie's mythic nature. Again, like Willy Loman, Eddie "possesses or exemplifies the wondrous and human fact that he too can be driven to what in the last analysis is a sacrifice of himself for his conception" (TE, 166). As Vincent Canby wrote in response to Anthony LaPaglia's Tony-winning performance as Eddie in the Roundabout's revival in 1998, Eddie Carbone "aggressively invites his doom and invites it with a desperation that only increases as an awful self-awareness becomes inevitable. . . . [This is] as close as the skeptical contemporary theater will ever get to a classical tragic hero."[43]

It is perhaps symptomatic of Miller's risky argument for his plays as tragedy that he has shifted the weight of critical discussion from the virtues of the plays themselves to a continuing debate about the viability of tragedy in the modern age. It is hardly surprising,

42. Zeineddine, Because It Is My Name, 190.
43. Vincent Canby, "A Classically Riveting 'View from the Bridge.'" To the contrary, Driver, long a Miller critic, contends that in an age lacking "universal moral sanction," the theme of a man who destroys all his family because of jealousy has "no level of meaning, law, providence, or fate, upon which an action that transcends character can act" ("Strength and Weakness," 20). Driver echoes the sweeping contention of George Steiner and others that "the death of tragedy" occurred with the emergence of scientific determinism in the nineteenth century, a claim Miller has vigorously rejected.

then, that alongside Canby's high praise of A View we might place Edith Oliver's qualified response to Ulu Grosbard's successful 1965 off-Broadway revival: "If the play never attains the stature of classical tragedy, it is still an effective and exciting melodrama."[44] Like many responses to All My Sons, Death of a Salesman, and The Crucible, it seems faint praise indeed—good melodrama but short of tragic greatness. Yet the fact is that Miller's commentaries have enjoined the debate and largely determined the course of Miller criticism for good or ill.

A Memory of Two Mondays

Miller has called A Memory of Two Mondays "an exploration of a mood, the mood of the thirties and the pathos of people forever locked into a working day," a "pathetic comedy," and a "moral romance" in which "the warehouse is our world—a world where things are endlessly sent and endlessly received; only time never comes back" (TE, 260, 263, 65). Although the play has generated sparse criticism and has been seldom performed, in the introduction to the Collected Plays Miller declares that he wrote it "in part out of a desire to relive a sort of reality where necessity was open and bare," and he "hoped to define for [himself] the value of hope." Despite its limited recognition since its first production along with the one-act version of A View, Miller declares in the introduction to the Collected Plays, "Nothing in this book was written with greater love, and for myself, I have nothing printed here better than this play" (TE, 164). Although few would agree with Miller's assertion or with Albert Wertheim's assessment that it is "perhaps Miller's best . . . and most neglected play," nevertheless, as Robert Hogan asserts, it is "a considerable achievement . . . moving, technically adroit . . . one of the rare instances of a one-act tragicomedy."[45]

Miller began working at an auto parts warehouse when he was eighteen. He stayed until August 1934, when he had saved the five hundred dollars he needed to enroll at the University of Michigan

44. Edith Oliver, "The Theatre: Off Broadway."
45. Albert Wertheim, "Arthur Miller: After the Fall and After," 24; Robert Hogan, Arthur Miller, 32.

in September. Fictionalized as Bert in the play written some twenty years later, Miller projects his experiences onto the stage, peopling it with the men and women he worked with for nearly two years and recreating the grim setting of the warehouse filled with "filthy windows" looking out onto "a newly installed five-story bordello" (*T*, 218).[46] Feeling very much an outsider, an ambitious Jewish boy among Irishmen trapped in their economic and social cage, Miller came to gain a deep affection for the characters he saw bound to "serve an industrial apparatus which feeds them in body and leaves them to find sustenance for their souls as they may" (*TE*, 65). The story's Marxian quality emphasizes pathos, as all the characters, except for Bert, fall prey to a socioeconomic imperative they cannot escape, doomed forever to live in a purgatory of endless repetition.

Miller later admitted that the play was something of a departure from his earlier work, despite its heavy Marxian elements: "I have since come to believe we have a lot more to do with our fate than that play implies. But at the time . . . there seemed no conceivable way of escaping it" (*Conv.*, 309). Yet the play is not a simplistic social melodrama. Despite "the endless, timeless, will-less environment a boy emerges who will not accept its defeat or its mood as final. . . . The play speaks not of obsession but of rent and hunger and the need for a little poetry in life" (*TE*, 164).

Raymond, the manager, twice sounds the central theme: "It's the same circus every Monday morning" (*MTM*, 10, 37), and the others repeat it. Gus laments, "Oh, boy. Oh, goddam boy. Monday morning. Ach" (10), and the proper Kenneth echoes, "Oh here's another grand Monday! . . . It's the sight of Monday, that's all, is got me down" (31, 34). Monday represents the repetitious cycle of aimless existence in their sordid world that provokes Bert's poetic evocation at the end of the play as he is leaving:

> Every morning and every morning,
> And no end in sight.

46. In *Timebends*, Miller describes specific people at the warehouse who emerged as fictional characters in the play: Gus is modeled on the sixty-five-year-old packing boss at the warehouse; the new immigrant, Dennis MacMahon, appears as Kenneth; one of the three female bookkeepers, Dora, becomes Agnes; one of the stock clerks, Huey, surfaces as Larry; and the unnamed boss at the actual warehouse is fictionalized as Mr. Eagle in the drama.

That's the thing—there's no end!
Oh there ought to be a statue in the park—
"To All the Ones That Stay." (42–43)

Miller's sympathetic identification with the characters is obvious: Kenneth, the moralistic poet "fresh off the boat"; the gruff Gus, veteran of twenty-two years in servitude, who fails even to make it to his wife's funeral; Gus's drinking buddy Tommy Kelly, who manages to defeat his alcoholism by the time Bert leaves but remains trapped after sixteen years at the job; Larry, whose dream to buy an Auburn because he "loves the valves" shatters when familial demands force him to sell the car; and Agnes, the spinster in her late forties who always tries to ease the tension in the little community—all are portrayed with compassion and dignity, however flawed they may be. As a sort of central consciousness, Bert, like Alfieri in A View from the Bridge, gains an appreciation for their worthiness and leaves with a painful awareness of the fate that awaits them all. Not fully realized as a character, perhaps, and not tragic in any critical sense of the word, he nonetheless provides the critical focus into a community of the oppressed who somehow achieve a measure of victory in their stubborn survival.

Miller's adroit choreography of entrances and exits around the shipping table, juxtaposed with Kenneth's plaintive songs, Bert's poetic speeches, and the lyric laments of characters against the sounds of workers riffling through orders, the coarse sexual talk of Frank and Jerry and the truck drivers, and the cacophony of sounds in the "fiery furnace" (MTM, 13) interweave pathos and naturalistic detail. When Kenneth begins to quote "When lilacs last in the dooryard bloom'd," Gus asks pointedly, "What the hell you doin'?" Kenneth ironically replies, "Why, it's the poetry hour, Gus, don't you know that?" (12). Throughout the text, harsh realism and poetry surface in delicate equipoise.

In the setting we see "a place of dust" on the first stifling hot Monday, with long shadows cast across a vast, cavernous space marked with Kafkaesque alleys and bins. By the second Monday, when Bert is about to depart, the cold light of a winter day illuminates the sterile microcosm where "It's rainin' dust from the ceiling!" (MTM, 17). The first Monday ends when Kenneth and Bert wipe off one of the caked windows and let in the lurid light illuminating the reality of their subterranean home. All through the first Monday, Kenneth pleads that someone clean the windows to let in "God's light" (29). He asks Gus, "What do you suppose would happen, Gus, if a man took it in his head to wash these windows?" (13), and he proposes to Larry, "you suppose we could get these windows washed sometimes? I've often thought if we could see a bit of sky now and again it would help matters now and again" (20). Finally he convinces Bert to act when he queries, "How would you feel about washing these windows—you and I—once and for all?" (29). But the act ends ironically when they look on a five-story brothel out the window and the brutal light of reality floods the stage.

Despite their personal anguish and gruff nature, the characters remain loyal to each other. On the first Monday, even Raymond, the manager, tries desperately to save Tommy from being fired for drunkenness. Gus, Jim, Larry, Kenneth, Bert, and Agnes all provide cover for their drunken colleague. When Gus thinks Mr. Eagle, the boss, is going to fire Tommy, he vows to quit in protest. For all their resentments and their being symbolically impaled like the orders stuck on the large spindle on the back wall, they find this *"little world a home to which, unbelievably perhaps, [they] like to come every Monday morning"* (MTM, 6). Amid this communal setting, Bert sometimes stands off and speaks in soliloquy. Part of the circle, yet separate from it, at one point he stands to the side and thinks, "There's something so terrible here! There always was, and I don't know what," and he concludes:

> It's like a subway;
> Every day I see the same people getting on
> And the same people getting off,
> And all that happens is that they get older. God!
> Sometimes it scares me; like all of us in the world
> We're riding back and forth across a great big room,
> From wall to wall and back again,
> And no end ever! Just no end! (30–31)

At the end of his time at the warehouse, Bert has seen the debilitating effects of the life he observes around him. Kenneth succumbs to drink. Gus guiltily abandons his dying wife Lilly and even misses her funeral for a drunken binge with Jim. The brothel intrudes on the warehouse, setting the puritanical Kenneth against the "lot of sex maniacs" (MTM, 39) who leer out of the window. Larry sells his Auburn, recognizing "It's out of my class" (40). In a moment of high irony, Kenneth protests to Mr. Eagle, "There's got to be somethin' done" about the brothel, and Eagle replies, "Shouldn't have washed the windows, I guess" (41). Most dramatically, Gus, driven by guilt, wastes the money collected from insurance for his wife's death and dies in Dionysian abandon in the arms of a whore in a taxi, trying, as Jim says, to "do it right" (45). After their initial shock, the characters resume their work in another choreographed scene: Jim takes an order off the spindle, Raymond goes back to his office, men walk up and down with orders in their hands, Kenneth begins wrapping a part, and the truckers prepare to make a delivery to the Bronx. As the workers resume their meaningless lives in the purgatorial realm of the warehouse, Bert vainly tries to say his goodbyes, leaving with the promise, "So long as I live they'll never die, / And still I know that in a month or two / They'll forget my name" (43).[47]

Claiming to have written the play "to define for myself the value of hope" (TE, 164), Miller in fact offers relatively little hope, save for the stoic determination of the characters to survive in their grim world and Bert's unwillingness to "accept its defeat or its mood as final" (164). But Bert possesses a ticket out from the beginning, and his departure is less an earned victory over defeat than the completion of a predetermined end. Indeed, the play lacks a fully developed protagonist. Bert can scarcely serve as a divided hero who gains awareness as a result of choices he makes, and a strong argument can be made for Gus being the more central character. But of course Miller never thought of A Memory of Two Mondays as tragedy, which he did the other more famous one-act he offered Martin Ritt for the Cornet Theater productions. Never bound by the constraints of genre, he saw the play as a nostalgic panegyric to a community of oppressed workers struggling to survive the agony of the Depression, which has so strongly marked Miller's work. Miller's fondness for the play is understandable, given his long-standing commitments and compassion

---

47. Miller writes that when the other workers at the auto parts warehouse discovered he was going off to college, he, like Bert, felt alienation because "I was not only trying to escape their common fate but implicitly stating that I was better than they" (T, 218). He recalls that when he revisited the warehouse sometime later, he had indeed "vanished" from their minds even though "the whole crew . . . stayed fixed in mine" (222).

for the socially and economically deprived. It is no real surprise that he could write, "Is this, I wondered, why writing exists—as a proof against oblivion? And not only just for the writer himself but also for all the others who swim in the depths where the sun of the culture never penetrates?" (*T*, 222).

4   *The Misfits* and *After the Fall*

The next two major Miller texts, *The Misfits* and *After the Fall*, will be forever related to Marilyn Monroe. Although no true appreciation of the play will really come until it is out from under the shadow of the Monroe legend, neither it nor the movie can be fully separated from her biography or Miller's association with her. In a sense both these texts explore existence "after the Fall," both depict characters driven East of Eden, as conveyed in the dying myth of the American West, long a Miller theme, and in the more encompassing paradigm of the biblical myth so elementally a part of Miller's heritage. The film is interesting both as it looks back to works such as *Death of a Salesman*, which ends with Biff's embracing of the dream of the American West so utterly shattered in *The Misfits*, and forward to *After the Fall*, which transforms the hopeful Roslyn in the film into the self-destructive Maggie in the highly controversial drama, both reflections of Miller's failed relationship with Marilyn Monroe. More importantly, *After the Fall* is *The Misfits* only more so, an extension of the Fall myth, inherently interwoven in all Miller's plays, and the struggle somehow to live in a world of devastating self-knowledge and spiritual collapse.

The Misfits

By the midfifties Miller's twenty-five-year marriage to Mary Slattery was breaking up, and his relationship with Marilyn Monroe deepened. In 1957 he moved to Pyramid Lake northeast of Reno to establish temporary residence and secure a divorce. Through a neighbor he met two crusty cowboys at a house in the remote area of Quail Canyon. Sometimes assisted by a younger,

94

more innocent cowboy, they captured wild horses on their off times using a Piper Cub to round up the horses and weighted tires to anchor them when the men lassoed the horses from a moving truck.

Miller was fascinated by their tales but did not make use of the accounts until after he married Monroe in 1957 and was living in England while she finished making Terence Rattigan's light comedy *The Prince and the Show Girl* with Laurence Olivier. Miller had briefly met Monroe in Hollywood in 1950, and after reencountering her at a party in 1955, he and the film star began having a serious affair. Miller first wrote *The Misfits* as a long short story that was published in *Esquire* after it was edited down in size. The writing of the screenplay did not occur until later in 1957, after Marilyn Monroe suffered a miscarriage. Acting on the suggestion of New York photographer Sam Shaw, Miller began writing the screenplay as "a gift" for his suffering wife. "I felt an urgency about making something for her" (*T*, 458), he has written, "my gift of words" (*T*, 464). The autobiographical elements that infuse the text lie deeper than Miller's desire to offer "a gift" to his wife, however. As Miller came to realize after the marriage ended, underneath lay a specter of guilt as well: "reality worked the immortal worms of guilt, the guilt each of us felt at having been naive and foolish, or even worse, having misled the other" (*T*, 460–61). His marriage already on shaky ground, Miller sought a way to stabilize it and yet was exposed to his own complicity as well his famous wife's.

It is little wonder, then, that critics have attacked *The Misfits*, as they criticize *After the Fall*, on personal as well as aesthetic grounds. As David Savran notes, it has "been criticized more caustically by Miller's critics than any other work falling between *All My Sons* and *After the Fall*,"[1] and it is most often accused of being self-serving and sentimental, especially in the characterization of Monroe's character, the young divorcée Roslyn Taber.[2] Despite its occasional defenders,

---

1. Savran, *Communists, Cowboys, and Queers*, 43.
2. In a 1998 interview with Serge Toubiana, Miller acknowledged the association between Roslyn and Monroe. Asked if the film were "a documentary on Marilyn Monroe," Miller replied, "Actually, the character was based on a different woman, but that does not matter. I agree with you she was so much like Roslyn; but for that kind of person, who cannot get connected, Nevada was the perfect place, because people like that are all over the place" (Arthur Miller and Serge Toubiana, *The Misfits: Story of a Shoot*, 37).

Miller critics have generally dismissed the screenplay or found it seriously wanting. Leonard Moss calls it "Undoubtedly the poorest product of the dramatist's mature years." Arthur Ganz similarly ranks it as "blatantly bad" and "by far Miller's worst work." Miller's depiction of Monroe in the character of Roslyn has provided a particular target for detractors already antagonistic to Miller's portrayal of women, seeing in Roslyn the sweet but naive "earth mother," simply the inverse of Maggie, the vindictive "bitch" in *After the Fall*. To Dennis Welland, Roslyn is nothing more than an "idealized dream girl of romantic imagination,"[3] a criticism often echoed by others.

His first screenplay since his failed attempt *The Hook*, based on his exploration of the longshoremen culture of the Red Hook district in Brooklyn, *The Misfits* assumes a different shape from the dramas. Miller calls the published version "an unfamiliar form, neither novel, play, nor screenplay" (M, ix).[4] The written text "avowedly uses the perspective of film in order to create a fiction which might have the immediacy of image and the reflective possibilities of the written word" (x). Fully conscious of the distinction between play and film, Miller recognized that *The Misfits* "couldn't be a play . . . because one of the elements is a sense of wandering without any elaborate preparation or reason, a sense of wayward motion, which is manifestly a movie technique."[5] Moving from the more rigid causal structure of traditional tragedy and Ibsenian drama, Miller saw in the film a potential to capture the restless and aimless lives of "a few isolated, lost, and lonely people on the vast mythic plain of existence" (T, 463). The ability to employ the camera to scan the huge emptiness of the Nevada landscape, with its primal feel and scope, reinforced his sense that film rather than stage was his proper medium. Here, in such vastness, he recalls in *Timebends*, he could tell "a story of three men who cannot locate a home on earth for themselves . . . and a woman as homeless as they, but whose intact sense of life's sacredness suggests a meaning for existence" (438). The homeless woman is of course Marilyn Monroe, for whom, Miller claims, "I had given up any hope of writing" (466) until starting to write on the script—"for the first time since our marriage working from breakfast to dinner" (458).

3. Leonard Moss, *Arthur Miller*, 53; Ganz, "Silence of Arthur Miller," 226; Welland, *Miller the Playwright*, 84.
4. Throughout, I use Miller's published version rather than the actual screenplay.
5. James Goode, *The Story of* The Misfits, 106.

The making of the film, directed by John Huston, has entered film lore, not only as the last film of both Monroe and her costar Clark Gable, but as a revelation of the vagaries of the film industry.[6] The shoot ended on November 6, 1958, forty days over schedule and some half million dollars over budget. Bad fortune seemed to follow it with the unexpected death of Clark Gable shortly after the completion of the film and Marilyn Monroe's suicide in 1962 (Monty Clift was to die in 1966 and Thelma Ritter in 1969, leaving only Eli Wallach alive among the actors within seven years of the shooting of the film). Lesley Brill has observed that the deaths of the four stars within a short time of the filming "attach to it an aura of tragic richness as an avatar of its ill-fated cast . . . gritty characters, written and played by damaged human beings who were as brave in their professionalism as they were afflicted in their destinies."[7] Furthermore, soon after the filming, on Armistice Day, Marilyn Monroe announced her coming separation from Miller. And by the time of the film's belated premiere in 1961, to largely mediocre reviews and limited commercial success, Miller and Monroe had divorced. Yet despite all the personal and professional disappointments accumulated in the making of the film, Miller "felt proud we could create it."[8]

Miller's tale about "isolated, lost, and lonely people" was intended, he writes in *Timebends*, as "a story of indifference I had been feeling not only in Nevada but in the world now. We were being stunned by our powerlessness to control our lives, and Nevada was simply the perfection of a common loss" (*T*, 439). His characters all face an existential crisis that cripples their capacity to act. Guido's unfinished house serves as the main symbol of their homeless lives. Unfinished, dilapidated, and vacant, it "seems as terribly alone as a stranded boat" (M, 22), an apt mirror of the characters associated with it.

Displaced and restless, Guido has become "a naïve spender of time underneath cars" (M, 4), who periodically flies his decrepit plane to shoot eagles for rangers and occasionally help round up wild horses to sell for dog food. After Roslyn and Gay begin to live in his abandoned

6. In addition to Miller's accounts of the filming in *Timebends* and in various interviews and John Huston's in his autobiography, *An Open Book* (1980), see also the book-length studies *The Story of the Making of* The Misfits (1963, by James Goode, reissued as *The Making of* The Misfits in 1987), and the recently published *The Misfits: Story of a Shoot* (2000, by Miller and Serge Toubiana).

7. Lesley Brill, "*The Misfits* and the Idea of John Huston's Films," 10.

8. Goode, *Story of* The Misfits, 331.

house, Guido is even more displaced. Ironically, Gay asks him, "You think you could break away from paradise long enough to do some mustangin'?" (46)—but it is already a paradise lost. He admits to Roslyn, "I think most of us . . . are just looking for a place to hide and watch it all go by" (48). As Lesley Brill comments, Guido "wallows in misfortune," finally bitterly denouncing all women and resembling "the mendicant of the 'Church Auxillary' [at the rodeo] . . . in her preying on the living to support the dead."[9] Roslyn, who is unpersuaded by his argument that he did not send for a doctor for his dying wife because "She didn't seem that sick" (24), later gently tells him he could have taught his wife to dance if he really loved her: "Because we have to die, we're really dying right now, aren't we? All the husbands and all the wives are dying every minute, and they are not teaching one another what they really know" (31). She directs her bitterest denunciation at him at the end of the story when he suggestively offers to stop the roundup of the wild mustangs if she gives him "a reason": "You have to get something to be human? You were never sad for anybody in your life, Guido! You only know the sad words! You could blow up the whole world, and all you'd ever feel is sorry for yourself!" (116)

Gay, Brill contends, represents an opposite to Guido. Unlike Guido, he does not deny responsibility for his own failed marriage, and rather than turn cynical and bitter like Guido, he expresses no outrage at his wife's infidelity. Possessing a significant degree of self-irony, he never lapses into the morbid self-pity that Guido does. "Such contrasts embody fundamental dialectics in The Misfits," according to Brill, "between love and selfishness and between the energy of life and the entropy of a defended isolation." Christopher Bigsby sees Gay as a projection of Biff Loman, "an ageing cowboy reduced to rounding up wild horses to be turned into dog food while refusing to acknowledge the collapse of the dream" venerated by Biff of living without "wages" in the open West.[10] That is perhaps true to some extent, for Miller Gay assumes more dignity than Bigsby implies. "Most of us are just looking for a place to hide and watch

9. Brill, "Misfits and the Idea," 12.
10. Ibid., 15; Bigsby, Modern American Drama, 90. Bigsby also refers to Gay as "an ageing cowboy as bewildered by the collapse of his world as Willy Loman had been" (Critical Introduction, 185).

it all go by," he has said. "But one of Gay Langland's great mottoes is 'I'll teach you how to live.'" And it is Gay, flawed and blind as he is in most of *The Misfits*, who helps bring Roslyn to an awareness and who finally "has to find some means of coming to terms with a settled existence."[11] When Roslyn accuses him of killing mustangs, he illuminates her crisis as well as his own:

> Yes. Maybe we're all the same. Including you. . . . We start out doin' something, meaning no harm, something that's naturally in us to do. Like dancin' in a night club. You started out just wanting to dance, didn't you? And little by little it turns out people ain't interested in how good you dance, they're gawkin' at you with something different in their minds. And they turn it sour, don't they? (M, 94)

His willingness to try to make Guido's house a home, his assuming domestic chores and planting a garden, signals his effort to reconcile the opposing poles in an internal dialectic: the antisocial, hunter, macho instinct he tries to satisfy by his connection to the life of a "free" cowboy in the West and his need for union and acknowledgment that his mythic quest for a paradise lost is no more than a dream.

Miller's text follows a dialectical pattern, juxtaposing a large number of visual images and themes to generate a growing tension in the script. Although nearly half the scenes take place in the truck, symbolic of the "waywardness" of the homeless characters, the two prime locations, other than the ubiquitous Nevada landscape, are Guido's house and the rodeo. The irony attached to the house is obvious. The struggle to make it a home, a refuge against the pervasive loneliness of the physical and metaphysical landscape, constitutes the futile aim of the central characters. Guido had all but abandoned it after his wife's death. Unable to establish contact with anyone, he tells Roslyn, "I can't make a landing. And I can't get up to God either" (M, 83). Roslyn and Gay futilely try to transform the house into a home. As David Press comments, Miller casts "Gay and Ros in the roles of the American Adam and Eve,"[12] who struggle to secure not

11. Goode, *Story of* The Misfits, 78, 75.
12. David P. Press, "Arthur Miller's *The Misfits*: The Western Gunned Down," 43.

only their own private world but the illusory paradise of the American West. Placing a doorstep under the raised door, then growing a garden, fixing the rooms, removing the morbid wedding picture of Guido and his dead wife from above the bed, they begin to talk about a future together. But when the scene shifts to the rodeo, the setting inverts domestic images of harmony and growth into images of cruelty and violence. The jostling crowd, the cacophony of sounds and smells, the bloody brutality of the rodeo events, and Perce's injury all describe a "parliament of monsters."

Miller's focus falls heavily on Roslyn, whose lines, despite the charge of sentimentality, carry a poignancy in reference to Marilyn Monroe. Indeed, toward the end of the filming, the film's producer, Frank Taylor, called The Misfits "a spiritual autobiography" of Monroe: "This is who she is. This is why life is so painful for her and always will be."[13] To Miller, "Roslyn's dilemma was hers," and the role possessed "the womanly dignity that part of her longed for" (T, 466). As Laurence Goldstein points out, Miller adapted the short story by making Roslyn an "interpretive dancer" rather than a schoolteacher and introducing Isabelle (Iz) as an older friend well adapted to the Reno scene (most of the time she is even one-armed like the slot machines) and a foil to Roslyn's seeming innocence and naïveté. Although she represents the polar opposite of the macho ethic of the hearty Western cowboy, Roslyn, like the others, is isolated and orphaned, "like a little child in a new school" (M, 7). Seeking a divorce yet uncertain what to do, she tells Iz, "I suddenly miss my mother. Isn't that the stupidest thing?" (16). Throughout the narrative she defends the victims of cruelty and tries to rescue them from their suffering. Begging Gay not to kill the jackrabbits in the garden, she remarks, "I can't stand to kill anything, Gay" (43). As Goldstein notes, she is a "trope for Nature itself, an Earth Mother," who stands against male violence against nature, as reflected not only in the slaughter of the mustangs, jackrabbits, and eagles but also in such details as the brutality of using bucking straps on bucking horses. Roslyn's extreme sensitivity has provoked a lively critical response.

13. Taylor quoted in Goode, Story of The Misfits, 257. Brill suggests that "[m]uch of the screenplay and Monroe's lines in particular can be read as a melancholy meditation on the failing union of the playwright and the star and, perhaps, as a last plea to save it" ("Misfits and the Idea," 9).

To some, like Benjamin Nelson, she is little more than "the good Fairy," the mere shadow of a fully realized character, a view shared by Arthur Ganz, who finds her "vague sentimentality . . . singularly inadequate" and Miller's view of the world "as simpler than it is." And although calling *The Misfits* "a brilliant and disturbing piece of work—and an excoriating indictment of male brutality," and praising Roslyn's character as reversing "the binary opposites between 'nature' and 'culture' that *Death of a Salesman* and other plays work so zealously to sustain," David Savran goes on to accuse Miller of ultimately exploiting Monroe as a sexual object for the pleasure of "heterosexual male viewing." Yet Goldstein finds a larger dimension to Roslyn's character, who, he contends, "emerges . . . as the idealized figure of resistance to the American leaders who justify the slaughter of millions of Asians by turning them into nothing but data. . . . [T]hat Roslyn can embody such a range of moral imperatives . . . speaks well for the relevance of *The Misfits* in a feminist era." It would be difficult to argue that the screenplay is a feminist document, but it is worth noting that Miller does use Roslyn as the moral center of the work and the catalyst to Gay's epiphany at the climax of the tale.[14]

All the characters have suffered failed relationships: Roslyn's husband, Raymond, and her parents were "not there"; Iz lost both a husband and a cowboy lover; Perce's girlfriend abandoned him when he was in a coma, and his stepfather usurped the ranch he expected to inherit from his father; Gay's wife left him for another man, and his two children rarely see him; Guido's dead wife looks poignantly from an elaborately framed wedding picture. Brill cites the symbols of their

14. Laurence Goldstein, "The Fiction of Arthur Miller," 739–40; Nelson, *Arthur Miller*, 238; Ganz, "Silence of Arthur Miller," 225; Savran, *Communists, Cowboys, and Queers*, 47, 49 (Savran attributes Miller's treatment of Monroe to "psychological particulars" arising from the fact that Miller's "wife's career not only eclipsed but threatened his own" [54]); Goldstein, "Fiction of Arthur Miller," 741.

Hogan argues that "Miller saw in Miss Monroe a rare example of innocence in the modern world, and the growing disillusionment of his own thoughts certainly prompted him to grasp at innocence" (*Arthur Miller*, 37).

During the filming, Eli Wallach, commenting on his character, Guido, observed that "When he talks about dropping the bombs [ostensibly during the Korean War], this is a mere recitation of war deeds on a one-dimensional level. On another level, it is Miller's absolute brilliance in having him say this at the moment he wants something else, Roslyn" (Goode, *Story of* The Misfits, 69).

broken lives, such as Roslyn's dented Cadillac, Iz's shattered arm and the broken clocks in her house, Perce's shattered body, and of course Guido's uncompleted house and nearly grounded airplane.[15] To escape this realm of shattered lives and the debilitating capitalistic culture that is consuming them, Ros and Gay must, like Quentin and Holga in *After the Fall*, risk life East of Eden. Only truth can free them from their paralysis. By stripping each other of their self-deceptions, Ros and Gay create the possibility of choice, of freedom. Failing to stop the roundup of the stallion, mares, and colt (which symbolizes her and Gay's potential child), Roslyn bitterly tells the men, "You know everything except what it feels like to be alive. You're three dear, sweet dead men" (M, 118). Gay stands "as though he had been beaten in a fistfight in a cause he only half-believes" (119). Perce discovers "It's all a joke" (121). Only Guido persists in the illusion. Horrified by the men's brutal treatment of the "misfits" and unable to "buy" the horses from Gay to rescue them from death at the hands of dog-food processors, she at last cries out: "*Liar!* . . . Man! Big man! You're only living when you can watch something die! Kill everything, that's all you want! Why don't you kill yourselves and be happy?" (118). Yet, as Gay tells her, "We're all the same. Including you . . ."

The freedom to choose life "after the Fall" comes as a result of the climactic scene when, after Gay and Perce lasso the horses, Roslyn frees them. Without benefit of any mechanical tool, Gay wrestles to keep the stallion from escaping, in what Goldstein calls "ritual acts of violence"; in doing so, he successfully completes a test of his own integrity that matters far more than the mere recovery of the horse. In capturing and then cutting loose the stallion he has just reclaimed, he frees himself to choose Roslyn. As David Press writes, he relinquishes "his hold on the Western myth." In effect he gains knowledge that comes after the Fall, and forsaking his empty dream, he wills to walk from a spurious paradise with his Eve.[16] Roslyn, too, acquires the knowledge necessary to embrace the life she has always represented, not in a Pollyanna faith with which she could somehow

15. Brill, "*Misfits* and the Idea," 12.
16. Goldstein, "Fiction of Arthur Miller," 740; Press, "Arthur Miller's *The Misfits*," 44. Press proposes that Miller approaches tragedy in Gay's renunciation of the Western myth: "He had maintained, until he set the stallion free, a 'fanatic insistence upon his self-conceived role,' which is Miller's stated criterion for tragedy. Yet finally he is a committed man without a commitment" (44).

evade reality, but with cognizance of her own flawed humanity. "As for her," Miller concludes, "it's the end of the flight when she comes to see that violence in man, which is the violence in all of us, can exist side by side with love."[17] Good, she discovers, cannot exist apart from evil—the ultimate knowledge of the Fall. *After the Fall* could not be far behind.

It is not surprising that Miller rewrote the end of script four times during production of the film, no doubt realizing the difficulty of depicting the dramatic transformation of his characters. He admits that he wrestled with the conclusion because "I still could not concede that the ending had to be what I considered nihilistic, people simply walking away from one another. At the same time . . . I could not deny a certain indeterminacy of life was really all these characters had to rely on" (*T*, 473–74). The most common charge is that the ending is too contrived or "mawkish." Stanley Kauffman claims that "after all the candid confrontation of harsh facts in our world, it is suddenly and incredibly 'up beat' as anything by the late Oscar Hammerstein," and Gerald Weales calls the ending "a kind of twilight-of-the-Gods" that projects a trite "faith in love as an anodyne." Laurence Goldstein accuses Miller of violating the integrity of the original short story by yielding "to a happy ending in which he permits Roslyn and Perce to let the mustangs go, except for the stallion, which [Gay] wrestles . . . then frees to show that he is still in control." David Savran attacks the conclusion on other grounds as a sexist reflection of the "hegemonic masculinity" of the postwar society, arguing that although Miller "half-heartedly" attacks the sexist culture, at the end he "betrays the widespread anxiety generated by the employment of women outside the home" and, he concludes, the "domesticated Gay and reformed Roslyn, replete with the prospect of a child, promise to reclaim these misfits for a refurbished nuclear family that will complete Guido's house and take up residence behind its locked door." Benjamin Nelson contends that Gay and Roslyn "appear to recapture a kind of innocence. . . . They should not be returning to Eden, but trying to live in a world after the Fall."[18]

17. Goode, *Story of* The Misfits, 76.
18. Stanley Kauffmann, "Across the Great Divide," 26; Weales, "Arthur Miller: Man and His Image," 178; Goldstein, "Fiction of Arthur Miller," 740; Savran, *Communists, Cowboys, and Queers*, 5; Nelson, *Arthur Miller*, 236.

In truth, though, Miller does not return his characters to a lost paradise. They are now armed with knowledge:

> God damn them all! They changed it all around. They smeared it all over with blood, turned it into shit and money just like everything else. You know that. I know that. It's just ropin' a dream now. (M, 129)

Gay knows he lives outside paradise. And Roslyn's awareness that humanity cannot exist in a world free of violence and that even Gay possesses the potential look of hate denies her simplistic dream of an innocent world. Robert Corrigan properly concludes that Ros and Gay's choice "To live in a relationship is . . . the Kierkegaardian leap."[19] Noting that "*The Misfits* is the first work of mine in which the hero doesn't die," Miller confessed during the filming, "I am feeling my way toward a way to live."[20] Rather than being merely the account of what happens to Biff's dream of going West "against history," as Christopher Bigsby argues (DS, xix), *The Misfits* in large measure reflects Miller's growing existential vision. As early as the postwar period, he was introduced to existential thought and attended a "*réunion* of writers in a palais near the rue de Rivoli" in Paris with the French novelist and Resistance hero Jean Bruller Vercors, who was the French publisher of Miller's early novel *Focus* (T, 158). Although "tinged" with "Hollywood sentimentality," as David Press asserts, the movie essentially assumes an existential position. The "gift of life" emerges only when the characters will it against the knowledge of impermanence, uncertainty, and the potentiality of violence. No blind affirmation, it comes with the painful recognition that, as Brill writes, you can only act "without the promise or expectation of anything beyond the living itself."[21] For Ros and Gay to "Go home!" (as Ros cries out to the stallion) (M, 125) is not to return to the illusory Eden but to discover "home" in the risky reality East of Eden.

By the time the film ended, Miller realized that his life with Monroe was finished, that "I was almost completely out of her life" (T, 477). By 1961, when the film premiered, the divorce was final, and the next year Miller married Inge Morath and Marilyn Monroe took

19. Robert W. Corrigan, "The Achievement of Arthur Miller," 157.
20. Goode, *Story of* The Misfits, 77.
21. Press, "Arthur Miller's *The Misfits*," 44; Brill, "*Misfits* and the Idea," 13.

her own life. But when Miller wrote his next play, Monroe's shadow again haunted the text, however consciously or unconsciously, and for that very reason it has never received the critical appreciation it deserves as one of his most powerful works.

After the Fall

Asked which of his dramas he would like to see revived in New York in light of the highly successful reproductions of his plays in the late nineties, Miller responded, "Well . . . I have to say, 'After the Fall.' "[22] No wonder. No work of his has been more maligned and disregarded by American drama critics. Only with the award-winning revivals of Miller's established canon (*All My Sons, Death of a Salesman, A View from the Bridge,* and *The Price*) has Miller's reputation in the United States begun to recover from the intense attacks mounted on *After the Fall*, the drama that essentially drove Miller from the American stage and shifted his popularity and respect largely to Europe and other parts of world. Despite Miller's claim that two-thirds of the play was completed before Marilyn Monroe's death, critics widely accused him, and still do, of committing an unforgivable sin. In his infamous review, "Arthur Miller's *Mea Culpa*," the leading American theater critic Robert Brustein sounded the assault, accusing Miller of writing "a spiritual striptease while the band plays mea culpa" in "a three-and-a-half-hour breach of taste, a confessional of embarrassing explicitness." Echoing Brustein's vitriolic attack on the "shameless piece of blind gossip, an act of exhibitionism which makes us all voyeurs," Richard Gilman accused Miller of engaging "in a process of self-justification which at any time is repellant but which is truly monstrous in the absence of any intelligence, craft or art." And more recently, David Savran similarly condemns the play as "a self-serving construction designed by Miller to quell the gossip surrounding one of the most public marriages of the 1950s and to clear his name of responsibility for Monroe's suicide."[23] Although the play was produced some seventeen months after Monroe's death

22. Dan Hulbert, "Arthur Miller: A Dramatist for the Ages."
23. Robert Brustein, "Arthur Miller's *Mea Culpa*," 26, 27; Richard Gilman, *Common and Uncommon Masks*, 153–54; Savran, *Communists, Cowboys, and Queers*, 57. Stambusky calls it a failed effort that "could have been universalized into a modern parable of guilt and innocence" but collapses into "self-conscious pretense," as

and after Miller was settling into his life with Inge Morath, the furor it raised was immediate and has never fully abated.

Nonetheless, some American theater personalities and critics have recognized the play's stature. David Rabe, for one, has complained about Miller's mistreatment at the hands of American critics despite Miller's worldwide success; he adds, "The plays I most love are the ones that haven't done well here, like *The Price* and *After the Fall*, both of which are, I think, great plays." Rabe especially zeroes in on critics who accuse Miller of maltreating Marilyn Monroe in the character of Maggie: "he treats her with more dignity than anybody else has ever treated her in her career or life. Maggie is a character of great power and dignity—not the ditz Monroe was made into by the media, her directors, other writers and critics." He concludes "it's a mystery to me why it isn't recognized" (AMC, 145–46).[24]

A number of critics have noted that *After the Fall*, Miller's first play after a hiatus of some nine years, marks a change in his work. It essentially shifts focus from the devastating forces of society to the dark passages of the human psyche. In *After the Fall*, Julie Adams comments, "Miller's focus shifts from social abandonment to existential abandonment as he dramatizes Quentin's search for meaning and judgement." In moving the dramatic center from the tendency of social constructs to destroy moral perception, to the internal crisis of guilt and action, Miller centers less on exposing the source of guilt than on its ongoing consequences. Quentin must not redeem a crime that he is coerced to reenact but a series of crimes that force him to accept that he can "kill again." With consciousness comes the frightening awareness that morality has become so slippery that good and innocence may themselves be forms of evil and guilt. As Robert Corrigan notes, all Miller's characters are circumscribed by guilt, but his

Quentin "ingeniously preserves his innocence" by letting Maggie kill herself and absorb all the guilt ("Arthur Miller: Aristotelian Canons," 111).

24. Other theater people, such as Sidney Berger, the chairman of the Department of Theater at the University of Houston, have begun to come to the play's defense. In a 1998 interview, Berger claimed it was "his greatest" play (Lawson Taitte, "Productions Prove It's Miller's Time"). Some early critics did acknowledge *After the Fall* as a powerful work. In his early pamphlet on Miller, Robert Hogan considered it "very possibly a masterpiece" and Miller's "most intellectually probing play" (*Arthur Miller*, 44); while Trowbridge labeled it "not only his greatest triumph but one of the few genuinely tragic plays of our time" ("Arthur Miller: Between Pathos and Tragedy," 229).

early protagonists "could never acknowledge that the source of guilt was in themselves,"[25] whereas the dilemma confronting the later protagonists is that such knowledge can paralyze the will. Describing this change in his perception, Miller told Corrigan in a 1973 interview, "I take doom for granted [in the later plays] and look for some kind of life-line to hang onto," to "find some means in myself that would lay a hand on life and find a principle in man to counter the destructive force" (*Conv.*, 253–54).

In a sense, Miller begins to reject the reductive view that society carries the primary responsibility for evil and that man is somehow perfectible, and he moves closer to the concept that guilt is an inevitable consequence of human nature itself, that it is both corporate and personal. He moves closer to the idea that in a world devoid of moral certainty, the self becomes the sole repository of value and judgment and the only stay against chaos. In the plays beginning with *After the Fall*, good and evil begin to shift roles: Good even more than before easily aligns with innocence and becomes a source of evil, and guilt becomes a generative force of good. Hersh Zeifman perceptively sees Miller's growing consciousness in the contrast between Chris in *All My Sons* and Quentin in *After the Fall*. He argues that Chris embodies "the 'ghostly father' against whom the writer is rebelling in his own earlier self." Quentin, in short, is Chris grown up and on trial, a reflection of Miller's own rejection of Chris's easy moralism and the contrived conventional structure of tragic drama as a rigid Aristotelian construct. In *After the Fall*, he adopts a revisionist form to depict a "deliberately confusing, a fluid, seemingly illogical stream-of-consciousness that mimics not the objective patterning of divinity but the subjective free-for-all of the human psyche." The assumed inexorable order operating in *All My Sons* undergoes a test of conscience in Quentin's agonizing confession. Quentin, says Zeifman, is Chris on trial before himself—"Quentin represents himself for the identical crime that previously allowed Chris to become the prosecutor: the myth of innocence and goodness."[26] Put another way,

25. Julie Adams, *Versions of Heroism in Modern Drama: Redefinitions by Miller, Williams, O'Neill, and Anderson*, 156; Corrigan, "Achievement of Arthur Miller," 148.

26. Zeifman, "All My Sons After the Fall," 113–14. Zeifman points out that Chris served as Miller's alter ego when Miller was about thirty-two years old, Chris's

though stripped of its theological trappings, original sin carries enormous significance for Miller. Quite simply, human beings cannot *not* be guilty.

In *After the Fall* the allusion to the Fall pertains not only to the Holocaust and to the political injustices of the McCarthy era, but also to the particular spiritual condition of a man who must unequivocally face his own complicity in the evil of his age on a universal scale and in the sufferings of those lives he has directly touched. Like Camus's Jean-Baptiste Clamence in *The Fall*, Quentin begins his personal drama in crisis *after* the Fall, tottering between action and inaction, evasion and choice. Miller's adaptation of the Genesis story doubtless stems from his Jewish heritage and his deep roots in the American Puritan tradition. Leonard Moss has commented on Miller's "strong interest in the fall theme—the crisis of disillusionment—from the start of his career in the early nineteenforties." In particular, N. S. Prudhan links Miller's "re-evaluation of the myth of Eden" to his rebellion "against the innocent and righteous American Adam that history is supposed to have created out of his European experience."[27] In any case, depravity and guilt have been ultimate concerns in all his major works. Miller himself has commented in an interview with Philip Gelb, "I can't see

---

age in the play, and that Quentin reflects Miller seventeen years later. Miller "explores Chris's complicity and guilt, to expose his spurious order in *All My Sons*." Miller castigates Chris's "simplistic approach to moral issues," revealing an "idealism [that] can easily come off as smug self-righteousness, as nothing more than adolescent whining" (111–12). Christopher Bigsby sees Quentin as Willy Loman "made finally to admit to his egoism and to the cruelty which this imposes on those around him" ("The Fall and After—Arthur Miller's Confession," 129).

27. Leonard Moss, "Biography and Literary Allusion in *After the Fall*," 40; N. S. Prudhan, *Modern American Drama: A Study in Myth and Tradition*, 73. In *Arthur Miller*, Moss insists that "Miller reinterprets Old and New Testament ethical concepts in a wholly secular manner" (94). Reno goes further: "From *All My Sons* to *After the Fall*, Miller has been dismantling the Christian myth. However, to accomplish this he has had to use the myth, and so has been caught in a rhetorical trap. His symbolic figures . . . have forced on him questions he was perhaps not prepared to answer" ("Arthur Miller and the Death of God," 1084). See also Stephen Barker's argument that the play "intimates that the original fall, from Eden, is recapitulated by each individual through the fall into consciousness, and thus into choice" ("Critic, Criticism, Critics," 237), and Steven Centola's discussion of the play as "monomyth" that translates "the personal drama into a symbolic drama of universal significance" ("The Monomyth and Arthur Miller's *After the Fall*").

the problem of evil evolving fruitfully unless the existence of evil is taken into account" (*Conv.*, 48). *After the Fall* addresses the problem of evil, for it depicts man not only after his personal fall but also after the corporate fall that is the overwhelming fact of postwar Western culture.

A lawyer twice married, Quentin contemplates a third marriage, this time to a German-born archeologist named Holga. Like the narrator in Beckett's play *Krapp's Last Tape*, he plays back the reels of his past, giving voice to the various selves that compose the drama of his life and judging them before the bench of his own consciousness. Talking to an imaginary listener, he wonders aloud whether or not to risk love again after acquiring a record of failed relationships, including two shattered marriages. He begins a lengthy confessional narrative, which the play dramatizes on different levels of the stage, representing different times and associations. The scenes are patterned associatively rather than chronologically, taking the form of a memory play in which, as Paul Nolan notes, the memories hold meaning not for "what they are but for what they are *to the narrator.*"[28] The form projects action through consciousness, approaching a monodrama in which a single character talks to himself, reenacting events shared by others but only presented through the speaker's consciousness.

In employing the form of a memory play or extended soliloquy, Miller sets for himself an imposing artistic challenge. Because the play is strictly a personal interpretation of historical events from the point of view of the first-person narrator, the narrator himself is at once the condemned and the forgiven, the villain and the hero. There is no opportunity for the objective distance provided by an outside narrator like Alfieri in *A View from the Bridge:* the whole "case" rests on the central character's own perceptions of truth about himself. This poses a subtle irony, and we may be less inclined to accept his heroism. So brutally does he strip away the masks of his self-deceit that we wonder if there is an authentic self at all. Yet Miller pulls off the juggler's trick by forcing Quentin to earn his self-knowledge in the telling through horrific self-accusation. In a modern age given to cynicism, we are suspicious of any martyrdom,

28. Paul T. Nolan, "The Memory Plays: *The Glass Menagerie* and *After the Fall*," 31.

especially when the martyrdom is directed to affirming a self that postmodernism has made us doubt the more. But, old fashioned though it may be in its moral stance, *After the Fall* attests to a moral authority residing in the self by virtue of a sustained self-irony that denies the protagonist any escape from his own culpability. This gives extraordinary privilege to the narrator, but it also gives credibility to one who, without the presence of others to impress, willingly confronts his past—a confession before a mirror rather than merely a staged justification before a public jury.

Although Camus's *The Fall* was the obvious inspiration for the play,[29] and in it Miller tries to posit an alternative ending to the spiritual crisis confronting Camus's antihero, in many respects Miller's play recalls Dostoyevsky's *Notes from Underground.* He recalls believing Dostoyevsky and Tolstoy "the two greatest writers I knew of" while an undergraduate at the University of Michigan, and he concluded that in *All My Sons* "I had unknowingly picked up where my beloved Russians had left off, but without Tolstoy's and Dostoyevsky's privilege of a god" (*T*, 145). Like Quentin, the Underground Man experiences a crisis of self-awareness prosecuting himself before an empty bench; and like Dostoyevsky's antihero, Quentin keeps reliving a past he cannot escape, haunted above all by his memory of the woman who offered him his only escape from self-absorption and self-hate. Knowing himself too well, he cannot take himself seriously. Every time he finds himself lapsing into moral pronouncements or enacting the role of hero, or finds himself expressing compassion for anyone other than himself, he derisively exposes his egotistical motivation and cannot believe in his own image. But whereas the Underground Man rejects Liza's compassion, only to run desperately after her in the snow, Quentin chooses to risk embracing the person to whom he has revealed his darkest self, thus

---

29. Miller has admitted that the play is to some degree a response to Camus's novel. In fact, he once turned down a request by Walter Wanger to adapt *The Fall* for the stage (*T*, 483–85). Several critics have compared the Camus and Miller texts, most recently Derek Parker Royal in his essay "Camusian Existentialism in Arthur Miller's *After the Fall.*" Royal contends that Miller, contrary to the claims of Centola and others, adapts Camus's existential vision rather than Sartre's. Both Miller and Camus, he writes, "proposed a tempered reality of limits where the individual and community co-exist in a symbiotic relationship of mutual definition and responsibility" (201).

he is another of Miller's characters to take a Kierkegaardian leap of faith even in light of the absurdity he sees in himself and in human nature.

The first act can be roughly divided into scenes relating to Quentin's growing up and family life, his disastrous first marriage, his involvement in the political life of his friend Lou, and his first meeting with his second wife, Maggie. The structure, which Miller describes as "surging, flitting instantaneousness of a mind questing over its own surfaces and into its depths,"[30] vacillates across time—distant past, recent past, the immediate present. The openness of the structure permits Miller to bring together in the same scene characters from different periods in Quentin's life, implying thereby a unity of theme, a pattern of repetitive events and images that integrates the whole. Although Maggie, Quentin's second wife, dominates the second act, she appears significantly in the first to accentuate the meaning at certain points set earlier in time. The setting, according to Miller, is "monolithic, a lava-like supple geography in which, like pits and hollows found in lava, the scenes take place" (*AF*, 1). The multilayered stage represents levels of the mind, and the stone tower of a Nazi concentration camp provides further means of unity in the extended monologue.

In a foreword to the play, Miller explains the basis of his title. Eve, he says, opened up "the knowledge of good and evil" by presenting Adam with a choice. And "where choice begins, Paradise ends. Innocence ends, for what is Paradise but the absence of any need to choose . . . ?" (*TE*, 255).[31] Subsequently, he continues, humanity

---

30. I am using the published final stage version of 1964, although Miller did make other revisions for the 1984 off-Broadway revival with Frank Langella.

31. Several critics have commented on the play as a modern adaptation of the Fall parable. Schlueter and Flanagan conclude that Quentin learns that "guilt is an essential of human nature—not an impediment to healthy relationships" (*Arthur Miller*, 97). Clinton S. Burhans Jr., in "Eden and the 'Idiot Child': Arthur Miller's *After the Fall*," and John J. Stinson, in "Structure in *After the Fall*: The Relevance of the Maggie Episode to the Main Themes and Christian Symbolism," treat the play as a Fortunate Fall. Observing that Miller showed "a strong interest in the fall theme—the crisis of disillusionment—from the start of his career," Moss argues that he does so "in a fully secular manner" ("Biography and Literary Allusion," 39–40). In "Clichés in the Garden," Gerald Weales somewhat sarcastically calls Quentin's nagging sense of guilt "the post-Freudian variation on original sin." Miller himself told V. Rajakrishnan in a 1980 interview that Quentin "before the fall . . . was

has always had to choose—between war and peace, destruction and love. Like the late Romantics, Miller refers to the story of Cain and Abel as the quintessential embodiment of that choice, but he does not make Quentin a Byronic hero so much as the representative of humanity's destructive nature. In his essay "Our Guilt for the World's Evil," he contends that when the ancient rabbis selected Cain as "the first personage . . . who can be called human," they did so "not out of some interest in criminology, but because they understood that the sight of his crimes is the highest agony a man can know, and the hardest to relate to."[32] Miller's protagonist stands precisely in that position, a Cain surveying the record of his own criminality in the Kafkaesque arena of his own emerging consciousness. His guilt, he discovers, extends beyond the obvious murderous gestures of his life. "There are nonactions, and we have . . . a literal blood connection with the evil of the time," Miller has commented,[33] a culpability for what we allow as well as for what we do ourselves. In this respect, Quentin shares in the offense of Jean-Baptiste Clamence, Camus's cunning antihero, whose innocence is violated by the suicide of another, an act in which he participates by virtue of not acting, just as Quentin bears responsibility for Maggie's death. For Miller, as for Camus, the idea of original sin, even without its theological trappings, assumes genuine significance. As Paul Tillich proposes in his Christian existentialism, innocence is always "dreaming innocence," and the Fall is "a symbol for the human situation universally, not . . . the story of an event that happened 'once upon a time.'"[34]

Like Camus's antihero, Quentin rehearses his past in a quasi-confessional narrative; but whereas Clamence's Machiavellian strategy leads to truth only through ironic revelation, Quentin's earnest recitation is no trompe l'oeil. Ironic it certainly is, but it is a self-directed irony that stems from a shocking awareness of his own

---

struggling . . . against forces outside himself" but ultimately tries "to confront and define a world in which he is culpable" (Conv., 335). And in the foreword to the play Miller writes that Quentin "is faced . . . with what Eve brought to Adam—the terrifying fact of choice. And to choose, one must know oneself, but no man knows himself who cannot face the murderer in him, the sly and everlasting complicity with the forces of destruction" (TE, 256).

32. Arthur Miller, "Our Guilt for the World's Evil," 48.
33. Richard I. Evans, Psychology and Arthur Miller, 74.
34. Paul Tillich, Existence and the Christ, 29.

capacity for evil. It mitigates against our feeling too sympathetic for a character who cannot even take himself seriously.[35] The bitter irony surfaces throughout the repetitious patterns of events and gestures that belie the contexts of various staged events—for example, Quentin's twice-enacted cruciform pose, which he strikes when he reaches out for two light fixtures on the wall of his hotel room, portrays him as anything but a Christ—as he knows full well when he flirts with his own suicide. In watching the episodic scenes from Quentin's past we need to maintain aesthetic distance from the actors projected on the various levels of the stage. We cannot expect Quentin in his literal reenactments to provide either illumination or honesty. We must respect the gap between the Quentin that was, and is projected in the reenactments, and the Quentin who is watching himself after the Fall. The staged experiences reveal his ignorance before acquiring self-knowledge and exposing his potential for self-deception. In glossing over the critical distinction between Quentin past and Quentin present, critics have often missed a dimension of irony and have assumed that Quentin is simply Miller self-glorified or that Miller uses his narrator to exonerate himself after the suicide of Marilyn Monroe. In fact, Quentin's pomposity is most often a deliberately self-conscious revelation of the character he *was* and now fears. Quentin's moral failing authenticates all else in the play; to disbelieve it is to discredit all that takes place. Miller puts his early idealists, like Chris Keller and perhaps even John Proctor, on trial for their self-righteousness; but whereas Elizabeth provides the moral center in *The Crucible*, in *After the Fall* it resides in the consciousness of Quentin himself. In the tradition of the most significant Romantic literature, God has entered the psyche and assumed the role of judge. To be sure, we might question whether Quentin as narrator does not too easily vindicate himself in playing out his autobiography; however, Miller's artistic intention was to establish a dialectic between Quentin the narrator in the present and Quentin the actor of historical events, reenacting and judging his past self from the perspective of *after* the Fall.

35. Patricia Schroeder reminds us that "We cannot hope to understand *After the Fall* unless we accept Miller's basic assumption that 'this was a play which reflected the world as one man saw it.' Through the play the mounting awareness of this man was the issue" ("Arthur Miller: Illuminating Process," 288–89).

An extended conversation with an implied listener, *After the Fall* is in effect an interior monologue like *The Fall*, though Miller thought Camus's novel "ended too soon, before the worst of the pain began" (*T*, 484).[36] The listener to whom Quentin speaks throughout never interrupts nor directly challenges Quentin's interpretation of events. Although, as Miller says in the foreword, he may be a psychologist to some or God to others, he is "Quentin himself turned at the edge of the abyss to look at his experience, his nature and his time in order to bring light, to seize and—innocent no more—to forever guard against his own complicity with Cain, and the world's" (*TE*, 257). Perhaps in a larger sense we as listeners become coparticipants. We are privy to the most intimate revelations, listening as to a serpent's voice giving us knowledge, which makes us responsible not only for the knowledge Quentin gains but also its meaning for us individually. Critics who object to this stratagem argue that Miller "could have dispensed with the listener entirely";[37] to them the listener seems nothing more than an artificial device to gain pretended objectivity. The point of view being solely Quentin's, we are asked to accept the complete validity of his self-evaluation. Tom Prideaux warns that "in all voluntary public penitents there is a touch of ham. Self-castigation begins to give off an embarrassing hint of self-infatuation, especially when it is offered center stage."[38] But to what degree is

36. Leslie Epstein simply says that Quentin "lacks courage"—"first he expounds his own bad conscience until it becomes, and is lost in, the guilt of the world; second, he falsified—just barely—his relationship with those around him" ("The Unhappiness of Arthur Miller," 166). In large measure, *After the Fall* is an extension of *The Fall*, which Miller reread in the early sixties. Miller concluded that *The Fall* "is about trouble with women, although the theme is overshadowed by the male narrator's concentration on ethics, particularly the dilemma of how one can ever judge another person once one has committed the iniquitous act of indifference to a stranger's call for help. The anti-hero . . . has on his conscience his failure to come to the aid of a girl he saw jump off a bridge into a river" (*T*, 484). The parallels to Quentin's seeming "indifference" to Maggie's suicide can hardly be denied, though Quentin opts to embrace the "absurdity" by risking love again whereas Camus's Jean-Baptiste Clamence remains in his "little ease" like Dostoyevsky's Underground Man scurrying back to his underground mouse hole.

37. Murray, *Arthur Miller, Dramatist*, 138.

38. Tom Prideaux, "A Desperate Search by a Troubled Hero," 64B. See also Bigsby's thesis that "the man who strikes his chest in confession may derive his satisfaction not so much from his admission of guilt as from the exquisite nature of the blow" ("Fall and After," 134).

Quentin in the *process* of discovery? At times, he is pompous or arrogant or hypocritical; but so long as we see his monologue as a coming
to knowledge and a reenactment of the past done in order somehow
to be reconciled to the present—that is, so long as we accept Quentin
the actor and Quentin the narrator as parts of a divided self—we cannot legitimately dismiss the listener, to whom the present Quentin
acknowledges his growing awareness. He provides not only the motivation for telling the story, but also a distinction between what
Quentin was and what he is struggling to become. As the present
Quentin constantly derides his past self, he is his own prosecutor,
and what he reveals is undeniable guilt that freezes him and renders
him impotent to act. Though Quentin has undergone a Fall, though
he already "knows" something of his potential for evil, though he has
even gained a measure of self-understanding that exposes both past
failure and his still-deficient wisdom, the Quentin who sees and hears
vicariously through the listener—his other self—must be reconciled
to the Quentin who plays out the scenes of betrayal from the past.[39]

Quentin begins his recitation by bringing the supposed listener up
to date. He tells of having quit fourteen months ago the successful
law firm that he long served, acknowledges his mother's death five
months earlier, and recounts his meeting Holga, the German woman
about whom he must make a decision. Holga, an archeologist, has
survived the Second World War even though she had participated
indirectly in the plot to assassinate Hitler. Showing Quentin the
horror of the Nazi concentration camp, which is illuminated in the
back of the stage, she had admitted her profound sense of guilt—
"I don't know how I could not have known" (AF, 15). Having acknowledged and accommodated herself to her guilt, Holga presents
Quentin with a solution to his Kierkegaardian despair. But in light
of his two divorces and the undeniable testimony of a life full of betrayal, Quentin fears to act, experiencing the incapacitating "sickness unto death" that comes to those who know only too well the
dark passages of the self. Living with guilt before an empty bench,

39. Nolan insists that Miller "does not 'excuse or defend' his protagonist, but
rather he makes Quentin responsible for his memory, not that it was formed, but
responsible for what it will mean. When all is said and done, the audience for
After the Fall has more sympathy for Maggie than Quentin has—but the audience's
sympathy is a product of Miller's craftsmanship, not a denial of it" ("Two Memory
Plays," 37).

with no God to acquit or condemn him, Quentin inherits the most modern of modern ills, the prolonged ennui of "the endless argument with oneself." Unable to be the innocent boy who opens his eyes like Adam in the first morning of the world and unable to pass judgment on himself, he suffers a crisis of will at "the edge of the abyss." To act he must come to grips with what he has been and what he is. Holga's promise compels him to enter the "field of mirrors" that illuminate his past.

Quentin first recalls a few brief episodes with Felice, whom he had represented as lawyer in a divorce case and briefly desired. He had told her, in one of the many ironies that dot the text, that in divorce, "no one has to be to blame!" Quentin as narrator breaks into the recreated scene with Felice to say to the listener-other with obvious self-mockery: "God, what excellent advice I give!" (AF, 5). In direct contrast to Quentin's simplistic comment, Holga later tells him that indeed everyone is guilty. The distance between the Quentin talking to Felice in a recreated memory and the Quentin talking to the listener in the present of the play is terribly important; for in the first case he talks to Felice *before* receiving self-knowledge, in the second case to the listener *after* receiving it. Far from being without irony, Miller's play depends upon it. Furthermore, it extends into the present of the play; that is, it occurs in the midst of Quentin's "conversation" with the listener. At one point, when he is telling Felice, "You never stop loving whoever you loved" (4), his two wives, Louise and Maggie, suddenly appear before him, and he cries out, "These goddamned women have injured me! Have I learned nothing?" (5). Given what Quentin learns by the end of the play, Miller can only mean this self-pitying protest as high irony.

The brief encounter with Felice in the opening scene leads associatively to the first important cluster of scenes, those relating to his own family, chronologically the period of first betrayals. Felice fades into the darkness just after she blesses Quentin for rejuvenating her life, symbolized by the frivolous act of having her nose rebuilt. "I feel like a mirror in which she somehow sees herself as glorious," Quentin remarks. The image triggers the recollection of his mother's death five months before. He remembers that at her burial he saw "a field of buried mirrors in which the living merely saw themselves" (AF, 19).

The following scene reconstructs his meeting his brother Dan at a hospital where his father is recovering from an operation. The mother has died unexpectedly, and Quentin tells Dan they must give their father the news—"It belongs to him, as much as his wedding" (*AF*, 10). Quentin, as throughout, exposes his guilt in recalling the moments. Like an actor on stage, he poses as the successful young lawyer, mouthing high-sounding platitudes to his brother, but as self-judge in the present, he turns to his listener and admits, "Or is it that I am crueler than he?" (7). Realizing that he cannot grieve for his mother and that even his father returned to normal life "with all his tears," he senses that all is somehow related to the tower, which suddenly lights up in the background. Seemingly no one can escape the fact that he cannot totally give himself to another person, that there is a hint of betrayal even in his father, despite his extreme grief. The ultimate statement of the distance between human beings is the lighted tower, the consummate symbol of dehumanizing separation. After an intervening scene with Holga, who shows him through the concentration camp, Quentin returns to the record of offense in his family, thereby juxtaposing the tower, the macrocosm of human criminality, with family, the microcosm of universal guilt.

Quentin's mother appears at the end of a key address to the listener. As the tower "bores in on him" and changes color, he remarks, "Why do I *know* something here? . . . It's that I no longer see some final grace! . . . [S]ome final hope is gone that always saved before the end!" (*AF*, 15–16). When his mother breaks into the reverie, talking to him when he was a boy on the day of his uncle's marriage, he exclaims with surprise, "Mother! That's strange. And murder?" (16). Linking his mother with lost grace, he recalls her bitterness, viewing it not as the innocent boy enacting his past but as a man after the Fall. He remembers her guilt, her resentment at being forced into a marriage and losing a scholarship to Hunter College, her embarrassment over her husband's inability to read, her deep hostility over his bankruptcy. She had called Quentin's father a "moron" and "an idiot"—"I should have run the day I met you" (20), she says to him. Realizing that the boy Quentin had heard her remarks, she had denied saying them: "I didn't say anything! . . . Darling, I didn't say anything!" (21).[40]

40. Nelson notes that Esther Simon in *They Too Arise* "most clearly antedates . . . Quentin's mother in *After the Fall*" (*Arthur Miller*, 34). In Savran's view, Miller collapses all his misogynic stereotypes, "all the unruly women," into the

Edward Murray contends that Miller "whitewashes" Quentin in his relationship with his mother, "because the focus is almost wholly on *her* guilt and not on Quentin's 'complicity': this complicity, however, is rather passive, and not necessarily blameworthy in all respects."[41] Murray refers in part to the second act when Quentin recalls how his mother favored him over his brother Dan, trying to recover the lost promise of her own youth. When the father insisted that he needed Quentin to regain his lost fortune, the mother demanded that he be able to go to college rather than Dan, "because he's different!" (*AF*, 67). True, Quentin did act upon his mother's insistence rather than his own, but he hardly exonerates himself as he reenacts the moment. "Yes, I felt a power, in the going," he admits, "and the treason in it" (67). He could excuse the boy, perhaps, but not the man who sees the boy.

In a later scene with Maggie, he ironically *"turns out to the listener, with a dread joy"* and tells her how much he admires her "not pretending to be—innocent" (*AF*, 74). Dan, who sacrificed his own opportunities so that Quentin could go on to school, suddenly appears. "I came to like her," he says, as Dan's image disappears, just as he liked Dan, for her "goodness!" (75). He knows Dan's "goodness" was not "fraud." He also knows, therefore, that he cannot deny his share in his mother's betrayal. Miller hints at an Oedipal relationship between Quentin and his mother, as his strained encounters with Louise and Maggie suggest. The implication is not so much psychological as moral or religious, a manifestation of original sin; the association with his mother as coconspirator against his father and brother recalls the treason of Jacob and Rebecca against Isaac and Esau. In no sense can Quentin excuse his guilt, nor does he.

The second and third groups of scenes concern Quentin's personal and professional life with Louise and their friends Elsie, Lou, and Mickey. His life with Louise had been "some kind of paradise"—"I

"figure of the Mother," and "the Nazi commandant" becomes "a more efficient replacement for Mother" (*Communists, Cowboys, and Queers*, 70). Wertheim offers the more likely thesis that Quentin comes to discover that "his mother's love for him is in part based on hostility toward her husband . . . and that his love for his mother must be tempered by the remembrance of psychological betrayal" when she calls the father an "idiot" ("Arthur Miller: *After the Fall*," 23). In effect he must confront his own culpability, a complicity in his mother's betrayal.

41. Murray, *Arthur Miller, Dramatist*, 148–49.

had a dinner table and a wife . . . a child and the world so wonder-fully threatened by injustices I was born to correct! . . . There were good people and bad people. And how easy it was to tell! The worst son of a bitch, if he loved the Jews and hated Hitler, he was a buddy" (AF, 22). Yet, he confesses, when he began "to look at it" in con-sequence of his Fall, he found here, too, the evidence of his guilt. He visualizes the time Elsie changed from her wet bathing suit in front of him, and he could not deny his illicit desire. Seeing the relationships among his friends, he knows by hindsight that their apparently altruistic gestures were undercut by a selfish instinct for survival. Elsie's advice to Lou not to publish his textbook lest he further endanger himself before the House Un-American Activi-ties Committee seemed a gesture of genuine concern for Lou, but when he threatened to follow Quentin's suggestion to go ahead with publication, Elsie expressed her deep contempt for his naïveté. As she acts out her disgust, Quentin remembers the moment when his mother called his father an "idiot." At the point Mickey tells Lou he will tell the truth about his involvement with the Communist party and will name names, he almost seems noble. In the name of brotherhood "opposed to all the world's injustice" and for the sake of "truth," he urges Lou to go with him before the committee. But his nobility fades in light of his admission that he is testifying only because if he does not, "I'll be voted out of the firm" (33). And Lou fears dismissal as well, despite his high-blown rhetoric: "Everything kind of falls away excepting one's self. One's truth," Lou says. "Be-cause if everyone broke faith, there would be no civilization!" (36). Yet, as Mickey reminds him, he must acknowledge that at Elsie's prompting Lou himself once burned a book manuscript revealing the truth about the communist rule in Russia and rewrote "lies." As a bystander, Quentin shares in the guilt of betrayal. Had he recog-nized in himself the same impulse that drove Mickey to betrayal, Miller has said: "he could look at Mickey and say, 'This is beneath all contempt even,' you would have a big scene of arraignment. But he doesn't! He looks at it and it has resonances in his head . . . of all the other instances and of all the other experiences where people have acted just that way." In short, "he recognizes in himself some Mickey" (*Conv.*, 204). Mickey had told Quentin with overriding irony, "There is only one thing I can tell you for sure, kid—don't ever be guilty" (AF, 57). At one point, Quentin admits to Mickey that he never returned his calls because "I guess I—I didn't want to know," and as he turns to the listener in the present, he unmasks his true motive, "Yes, not to see! To be innocent!" (32).

Quentin exposes Louise's depravity in particular. From the day his Edenic world collapsed "and nobody was innocent again" (*AF*, 25), Quentin saw Louise's culpability as well as his own. He relives their painful confrontations when she always assumed her innocence. Even when he had once tried to tell the truth about refusing Maggie when he wanted to sleep with her, she turned his account into an admission of guilt. Feeling himself the victim of this Eve, Quentin sees her now alongside his mother, the first female betrayer in his experience. When Louise later discovered a letter Quentin received from another woman, she accused him again and refused to accept either his repentance or her own complicity. Finally, she claimed to be a "separate person" with her own right to be. Ironically, she proves to be right; but as Quentin discovers, it is precisely separateness that allows us to inflict our tyranny upon others.

The moments between Louise and Quentin seem at first to make him something of the victim of what he earlier called "[t]hese god-damned women . . . !"[42] Beyond question, Louise is an unrepentant Eve. But Quentin is not the passive victim of her cold-blooded puritanism; she provides a penetrating revelation of Quentin's guilt whether or not she herself is at fault. Significantly, Quentin says to the listener as he recalls her words, "Why do I believe she's right! . . . Why can't I be innocent?" And as the tower again is illuminated, he asks, "Even this slaughterhouse! Why does something in me bow its head like an accomplice in this place!" (*AF*, 30). The Quentin in the past, as Louise quite rightly tells us, keeps trying to defend himself, but Quentin the objective narrator, who speaks after the Fall, cannot evade responsibility for his actions. Not the least of Louise's

42. His cry has of course generated a strong response from feminist and other critics. Savran especially accuses Miller of "informing" in an attempt to "recuperate a desperate masculinity"—"the hatred of the misogynist beneath what is supposedly an inescapable network of universal guilt" (*Communists, Cowboys, and Queers*, 69). Ann Massa, however, declares that Miller "created a passionate man who is self-critical, not self-centered . . . who despairs of his failure to make his flawed practice match his high standard of perfectibility, who forces himself 'to face the worst thing I could imagine—that I could not love'" ("Some Kind of Love Story: Arthur Miller," 130).

perceptions is her comment that Quentin seeks his mother in his women—a truth even more apparent in his relationship with Maggie. But Quentin could not understand that truth and avoided it until he reached the climactic moment in his life with Maggie. Louise ironically calls Quentin "an idiot" at the conclusion of the restaged confrontations, a direct mimicking of his mother's condemnation of his father (Elsie also once called Lou a *"moral idiot!"*). For all her moral arrogance, Louise is no simple foil to Quentin's "goodness," and Quentin is no poor victim. The looming presence of the tower lends a certain credence to her revelation; and even Quentin is, as Miller writes, *"stopped by this truth"* (40). In fact, he wondered if he *invited* Louise's "suspicion in order to—to come down off some bench, to stop judging others so perfectly. Because I do judge . . ."—and he wondered if he left the recriminatory letter about Felice that Louise found "in order . . . somehow to join the condemned; in some way to start being real" (55).

After his first meeting with Maggie, Quentin meets Louise one last time. Critics especially point to this episode as "whitewashing," but it is more delicately balanced than that implies. Quentin's mind wanders from meeting Maggie to seeing Louise reading a book upon his belated return from the office: "How beautiful! A woman of my own! What a miracle!" (*AF*, 52). Although he tries to express affection for her, he again meets her disdain. He had forgotten a parent-teacher meeting he had promised to attend, and more importantly, he had apparently lied about working late; Louise had called the office and discovered that he was not there. Accidentally meeting Maggie, he had also forgotten a crucial meeting with the others in the law firm to discuss his intent to defend Lou before the congressional investigating committee. When he tries to explain his unexpected meeting with Maggie, Louise angrily tells him that she will not sleep with him. At this point the phone rings, and one of his partners tells him that Lou has killed himself by jumping in front of a subway train. Until now, the scene portrays Louise's guilt more than Quentin's, but the news about Lou's death destroys any illusion we—or Quentin— might hold of his innocence.

As the actor in the present recalling the event, Quentin ponders why Lou should have died. When Louise, in the reenactment, tells him that Lou could not have committed suicide—"Lou *knew* himself! He knew where he *stood!*" Quentin replies, in the present,

"Maybe it's not enough—to know yourself. Or maybe it's too much" (*AF*, 58). Resuming his role as narrator, he directly tells the listener that Lou died because he knew he had no friend left in the world; ironically, he was the "separate person" that Louise willed to be:

> It was dreadful because I was not his friend either, and he knew it. I'd have stuck it to the end, but I hated the danger in it for myself, and he saw through my faithfulness. . . . Because I wanted out, to be a good American again, kosher again—and proved it in the joy . . . the joy . . . the joy I felt now that my danger had spilled out over the subway track! (59)

Glancing at the blazing tower, he asks, "How can one understand that, if one is innocent? If somewhere in one's soul there is no accomplice—of that joy, that joy when a burden dies . . . and leaves you safe?" (59). Miller lays no small blame at his protagonist's feet. Camus's sarcastic antihero speaks of the joy we secretly feel over another's death because it lifts our burden of obligation to another human being. The full weight of that awful truth falls upon Quentin in the present as he rehearses the past.

The last encounter with Louise concludes not with Quentin's posturing virtue but with his own gesture of violence toward Louise. Angered by her self-righteousness, he had raised his clenched fist. At once "terrified" and animated by his own "aborted violence," he discovered a power not in innocence but denial: "Not to see one's evil—there's power! And rightness too!—so kill conscience. . . . Know all, admit nothing" (*AF*, 61). But Quentin the narrator knows that denial is impossible, and he acknowledges his own fraudulent goodness: "I bought the lie that she had to be 'saved'! From what? Except my own contempt!" (82). Hope resides not in escape from guilt but in the coequal belief in elemental decency, the remembrance that when he wakes, as to the first morning of the world, he opens his eyes "like a boy even now" (61). Salvation lies not in the ignorance of evil but in the belief in human goodness as well. Act 2 portrays both the full knowledge of that evil and its redeeming opposite, which ironically depends upon it. It makes clear that Quentin is not a static figure mouthing a moral stance long established before the play begins but a dynamic character whose moral victory is achieved only in the context of the present as Quentin contests his own claims of innocence. In short, this is a drama of becoming, not being.

Ostensibly, act 2 begins as Quentin talks to the listener while awaiting Holga's arrival from Frankfurt. The freedom of Miller's dramatic structure permits him to retard or accelerate the action as Quentin's thoughts dictate. Consequently, the act opens with Holga's greeting, which triggers a rapidly paced collection of scenes and characters, then focuses primarily on Quentin and Maggie, and finally returns to Holga's "Hello" and Quentin's symbolically affirmative response. Although various speeches by other characters and past events intersperse the lengthy account of Quentin's life with Maggie, the major portion of the plot is a direct rendering of their relationship. This most controversial portion of the play draws Miller's theme into focus and contains some of the best drama he has yet written.

Although Robert Hogan calls Maggie "the best character that Miller has drawn or attempted to draw since Willy Loman,"[43] no character he has created has been such a lightning rod for criticism. The association with Marilyn Monroe is unavoidable, a fact heightened in the New York premiere on January 23, 1964, by Elia Kazan's having Barbara Loden wear a blond wig in imitation of Monroe's hair. It seems implausible that Loden could claim, "It honestly never occurred to me that anyone was trying for a literal resemblance, or that the audience would see one, because I didn't see one" (Conv., 79).[44] Miller's denials notwithstanding, Maggie assuredly embodies the image of Marilyn Monroe. As a character in a play, however, she of course carries larger significance as well, and the real question is not so much whether Maggie really is Monroe as whether she acquires the stature and integrity as a character that Miller intended. In this, critics have also been vocal and contradictory. The controversy heightens in reference to the climactic scene in act 2 when Quentin walks away from Maggie's suicide.

The fragmented pattern at the beginning of the act weaves together the events recalled in the first act and both reinforces and recapitulates the central theme—the power of one human being over another. Quentin tells his listener that he "can be clearer, now" if he can just recover that second "somewhere along the line" when "I saw my life. . . . And that vision sometimes hangs behind my head, blind

43. Hogan, Arthur Miller, 44.
44. In the 1990 London production, Michael Blakemore cast Josette Simon, a black actress, as Maggie in an apparent attempt to diminish the resemblance.

now, bleached out like the moon in the mornings and if I could only let in some necessary darkness it would shine again. I think it had to do with power" (*AF*, 64). Power, the individual's or the system's, is the Cain potential that everyone and every social construct possesses. Struggling somehow to understand his own responsibility for "the death of love," Quentin now sees power as the essential weapon of destruction. Recalling the power he felt when he sided with his mother and left Dan and his father, the unwitting power he exercised over Felice in their fleeting encounter, and the power that he acquired over Maggie, he defines his own Cain-like nature. For this reason he justly fears loving Holga.

Holga appears amid the haunting images of those victimized by Quentin's destructive will. In effect, all his victims gave him license to destroy them. They all "adored" him, and his vanity in essence reinforced the tyranny of his will. A fraudulent self emerged, beginning with his mother's monumental claim that he was a born savior. "I saw a star" gone bright and fall at your birth, she had told him, "and you being pulled out of me to take his place, and be a light, a light in the world!" (*AF*, 67). Felice's constant blessing also legalizes that power. And above all, Maggie, who saw him "like a god," a surrogate father, granted him "the power" to murder her (72). Seen as a kind of god by the subservient women in his life, Quentin now knows himself to be a counterfeit savior. He recreates with unquestionable self-mockery the Christlike pose he struck the night Felice left him in his hotel room after he resisted sleeping with her.

Quentin's "vision of universal love, expressed in the context of the crucifixion, suggests his attraction to pre-lapsarian Innocence, redeemed through Christ's sacrifice," Schlueter and Flanagan contend; but if so, Miller undercuts the attempt by the "explicit reference to the Nazi death camp," John Stinson observes, making Quentin's gesture "all too easy cheap sensationalism." Aspiring to imitate Christ's love, Quentin's act becomes "a tragic kind of irony." And Hersh Zeifman, comparing Quentin to Chris in *All My Sons*, suggests that "Quentin is not Chris(t) . . . although many of those who loved him over the years tried to make him into one. . . . Quentin knows, however, that he is not a god, despite the temptation to play the part."[45]

45. Schlueter and Flanagan, *Arthur Miller*, 95; Stinson, "Structure in *After the Fall*," 238; Zeifman, "All My Sons After the Fall," 115.

We might qualify this by noting that it is Quentin *in the present* who obtains such self-knowledge in consequence of his fall. Miller himself has commented on Quentin's self-knowledge: "Well, he's quite aware when he does that, that it is an archaic reconciliation. That is, it doesn't work. He doesn't believe in God. But he's going through what is at the moment the only available gesture which men could go through in order to climb above their suffering. But . . . there's no cross and he doesn't deserve it. In other words, he hasn't earned that kind of glory" (*Conv.*, 202).

Quentin assumed the cruciform position in self-mockery after leaving Felice and courting his own death. And when he reassumes the position later, recalling his last encounter with Maggie, he acts with full consciousness. He knows his apparent virtue was in part a pretense, just as he is stung by the awareness that beneath all his seeming compassion for Maggie was an elemental tyranny. He lied to her, he tells the listener in a bitter outburst of self-blame: "I should have agreed she *was* a joke, a beautiful piece, trying to take herself seriously! Why did I lie to her, play this cheap benefactor, this—" (*AF*, 70). With her limited understanding, Louise had told him, when he tried to explain his first chance meeting with Maggie, that he really saw her as a tart—"But what did it matter as long as she praised you?" Although it is an unjust accusation, her remark points to a truth. The will to love never cancels out the will to wield power over the object of one's love; and when that power comes directly by means of another's adoration, it brings consummate temptation. Until experience proves otherwise, Quentin's mother, Felice, and Maggie conferred an innocence on him that he knew to be false. He knew his apparent goodness was in part a pretense, just as he is stung by the recognition that beneath all his seeming compassion for Maggie resided an elemental tyranny. He admits to the listenerself that he knew that barbiturates kill by suffocation and that her sighing was a sign of her diaphragm being paralyzed, yet he gambled her life willingly to secure his innocence. "What can be so important to gamble her life?" he asks. And he concludes, "My innocence, you see? To get that back you kill most easily. . . . Those deep, unnatural breaths, like footfalls of my coming peace—I know . . . I wanted them" (112).

What importance do we give to the autobiographical element of the play? To what extent does it reflect self-blame? Self-exoneration?

It is a serious charge to say that Miller excuses Quentin's guilt or per-haps his own by means of acknowledging the guilt of all—in other words, by suggesting, "If all have sinned, then I may not be better than the others, but I'm no worse." The problem is, if we cannot be-lieve in the profundity of the character's guilt, we cannot believe in the profundity of his recovery from the Fall. It is therefore important to examine carefully whether Miller really intends for us to believe in Quentin's fallen nature, or if he dilutes the guilt by abstracting it in some amorphous statement about the common condition of man in an imperfect world. Central to this pivotal question is the account of Quentin and Maggie's marriage and, by extension, quite possibly the marriage of Miller and Marilyn Monroe.

Miller's dramatic use of the memory play once again poses an artis-tic dilemma. To bring Quentin to the revelation that he is the author of his own criminality, we must allow him at first to depict Maggie's fallen state. That is, to achieve the dramatic reversal of the climax when Quentin fully knows *himself* to be Cain, he must first make himself the apparent victim of Maggie's destructive power. Other-wise, the climax would not present the epiphany needed to trigger the end of the action. In that only he is privy to Maggie's flawed condition, Quentin is once again in the uncomfortable position of being her accuser even while he poses as her savior. But it is not so much Maggie's guilt as Quentin's misconception of Maggie that Miller wants us to see. At first Quentin's speech is full of rhetorical flourish and sham sentiment—"But you're a victory, Maggie, you're like a flag to me, a kind of proof, somehow, that people can win" (*AF*, 88). In what Schlueter and Flanagan describe as "an expression of a temptation of Innocence," Quentin's love for Maggie disguises "a desire to return to a world before the Fall."[46] With remarkable naïveté, Quentin had endowed her with the same adoration that he himself received unjustly from others. When Maggie seemingly changed, then, ironically insisting on receiving his total devotion as he had received the devotion of others, he began to analyze her fault. In a sense, as she loses her innocence, he tries to reclaim his own. Once he had told her, "We want the same thing," that she

---

46. Schlueter and Flanagan, *Arthur Miller*, 99. They go on to note the irony that "in his attraction to her prelapsarian innocence, Quentin has imposed upon himself a postlapsarian responsibility for her life" (100).

should become a true artist. But he turns to the listener and admits that they both really wanted "power"—"to transform somebody, to save!" (95). In effect, they both sought innocence by manipulating someone else. Primarily because Quentin as lawyer possesses more verbal skills, he seems to argue the better case in the quest for innocence, but much of the time he seems exactly the arrogant "Judgey" that Maggie called him.

But Miller never intends for us to admire him for his pontificating. Invariably his rhetoric is undercut by action. Even when he seems the kindly victim of Maggie's viciousness—spending 40 percent of his time keeping her out of legal trouble, arguing for the rights of the poor people she runs over roughshod, suffering the abuse of her constant accusations—there is something dishonest in his long-suffering martyrdom. His most quotable, polished speeches (for example, "It's that if there is love, it must be limitless; a love not even of persons, but blind, blind to insult, blind to the spear in the flesh, like justice blind, like . . ." [AF, 100]) are framed by the mocking images of his betrayal. As he moves closer to recounting the climactic "last night" with Maggie, Quentin sees the lie of his own innocence. He had wanted to wash his hands of Maggie's self-destructive impulse, just as deep within he willed Lou's death to free him from obligation. Having twice rescued her from suicide, he wanted to free himself from the responsibility for her life, to force her "to look at what you're doing" (103). It all sounds noble—but just as the last scene with Maggie is being played out, Quentin introduces it by asking the listener, "But in whose name do you turn your back?" (100). The Quentin struggling to depict the story reluctantly reenacts his part in the suicide even as he ironically repeats his words to Maggie that she must be responsible for herself.

There is surely irony in the juxtaposition of scenes, and one form of irony is that as he introduces his last moments with Maggie, he recalls his mother's once betraying him, going to Atlantic City with his father and Dan, leaving him alone. He, too, threatened suicide by locking the door and running water in the bathtub. But if his mother had betrayed him, did he not betray Maggie? He rationalized his leaving her by ironically repeating Louise's claim: "We are all separate people." He told Maggie, "I have to survive too, honey." And that is precisely what Quentin was doing, trying to survive his fall and preserve his innocence, as Miller says in the foreword, "obliterating whatever stands in the way, thus destroying what is loved as well." To evade responsibility, Quentin had accused Maggie of making him the source of "all the evil in the world . . . [a]ll the betrayal, the broken hopes, the murderous revenge" (*AF*, 104).

Quentin's speech carries a measure of truth, as does his protestation to Maggie that "something in you has been setting me up for a murder" (*AF*, 106). Maggie did want to transfer responsibility for her life onto Quentin—but the play does not end here, and we cannot say on the basis of Quentin's past comments to Maggie that Miller makes a hero of him. In an ironic repetition of an earlier speech to Louise, when he had begged her to "say something, something important was your fault and that you were sorry" (42), Quentin urged Maggie to confess her own guilt, to say, " 'I have been kicked around, but I have been as inexcusably vicious to others, called my husband idiot in public, I have been utterly selfish despite my generosity, I have been hurt by a long line of men but I have cooperated with my persecutors—' " (107). Later, he tells Maggie, "Do the hardest thing of all!—see your own hatred and live!" (109). But Maggie cannot "see that like everyone else she had essentially made her own life," Miller writes—and such "Innocence kills" (*T*, 527).

But something rings hollow here, and it is precisely what Maggie said it was: "You're still playing God! That's what killed me, Quentin!" (*AF*, 109).[47] Referring to a note she had found in which Quentin had written, "The only one I will ever love is my daughter" (108), Maggie justly accused him of betraying her love. Coming close to the truth, he had to admit that he had written it when he had seen in her eyes "that I'd made you feel you didn't exist." And "it closed a circle for me," he told Maggie, because that was exactly what Louise had said to him—"And I wanted to face the worst thing I could imagine—that I could not love" (106). With near-truth, he concluded, "Maggie, we were born of many errors; a human being has to forgive himself! Neither of us is innocent" (109). But such an intellectual truth can only be attested to by experience, and that evidence of guilt came at the end, when, in his Cain-like anger, he grabbed the pills from Maggie's hand and, "transfixed," choked her as she suddenly assumed the person of his mother in the present, a repetition and extension of his violence toward Louise as well. At this moment

47. According to Nelson, Maggie senses "that the Savior is also the Destroyer" (*Arthur Miller*, 266).

Quentin realizes that in willing Maggie's death he is articulating his earlier desire to kill his mother and Louise as well, the women upon whom he tried vainly to place the blame for his own failure. The point is, he manifests his own destructive will to power, and so he comes to answer his own question: "In whose name do you ever turn your back—*he looks at the audience*—but in your own. In Quentin's name. Always in your own blood-covered name you turn your back!" (112). Such knowledge comes after the Fall when innocence can no longer be justly claimed. Quentin says this *to the audience;* he closes the circle once more. The seeds of the most monstrous atrocities grow in the individual soul. Miller elevates a personal tragedy to the level of public horror, for to believe in Quentin's potential for evil is to believe absolutely in the possibility of a holocaust.

The reconstruction of Quentin's attempt to strangle Maggie/his mother/Louise ends abruptly when Holga appears *"on the highest level"* of the stage. Her return brings a swift resolution to the action—so swift a resolution that it may strain credulity to accept it as a legitimate end. Allan Lewis defends Miller against the charge that "Quentin puts the blame on Adam . . . and goes off to marry Holga."[48] However, the general accusation that Holga's character is not adequately developed, given her significant role, is not without some merit; she appears only in two full scenes and otherwise in very abbreviated moments. Nonetheless, her function as a kind of Jungian anima seems clear enough, and she serves effectively as a symbol if not as a three-dimensional character. Once again, given the form of the play as the "memory" of a single character, Holga is after all only a projection of Quentin's consciousness.

After being introduced briefly by Quentin at the beginning, Holga figures prominently in only one scene in the first act. At the Nazi concentration camp, she surveys her life and explains to Quentin her near-obsession with visiting the camp. Although she had been imprisoned for two years by the Nazis, she had later found it difficult to enter the United States as a survivor until she had proven she was neither a Communist nor a Jew but the blood relative of several Nazis. As though spreading the net of culpability, Holga had come to the profound realization not just of her own guilt but of the common guilt of all. Finding that "survival can be hard to bear," she could

48. Allan Lewis, *American Plays and Playwrights of the Contemporary Theatre*, 40.

nevertheless proclaim her own guilt without, in Quentin's words, "looking for some goddamned . . . moral *victory*" (*AF*, 14, 15). But while Quentin admitted that he felt "an understanding with this slaughterhouse" (16), he felt neither "indignant" nor "angry" at the horror, as though the very enormity of the crime had swallowed up the moral outrage. The scene at the camp concludes just after Quentin relives his betrayal of his father when he went off to college. Sensing the pervasive evil of the place, Quentin had challenged Holga to race to the car—"The car will be all sweet inside!" But seeing the tower he recognizes that "*he had committed a sacrilege.*" As Holga had told him, "Quentin, dear—no one they didn't kill can be innocent again" (21).

Act 2 contains another short scene with Holga, set at a Salzburg café. She had expressed the fear that she was "boring" him, a reflection of Louise's observation that Quentin paid no attention to her. With Louise, Quentin had the altruistic idea that he needed somehow "to step between her and her suffering." He had known that she "didn't like her face" portrayed in the mirror, and "I felt guilty even for her face!" (*AF*, 66). With Holga, though, "there was some new permission" that would allow him to go from her without judgment until he could return her love. Having the freedom to leave her in order to recover the will to commit himself to her had triggered his long night's journey into day. Holga lends meaning to Quentin's long search and, at the end, validates his recovery, however tenuous, from the Fall.

Holga had told Quentin at the concentration camp about a recurring dream. She had given birth to an idiot child, which would run away but always return to her lap. She sensed that "if I could kiss it . . . perhaps I could sleep. I think one must finally take one's life in one's arms, Quentin" (*AF*, 22). The child figure personifies the absurdity and guilt to which everyone gives birth. Not to accept, not to embrace that child, would be to commit the unforgivable sin against life and against the self. In embracing the child, Iska Alter suggests, Holga "reconstitutes the significance of the term idiot, incorporating even the negative resonances, and permits Quentin to redeem both the paternal legacy and the maternal embrace."[49] Quentin knows at

49. Alter, "Betrayal and Blessedness," 143. Welland observes that the word *idiot* occurs fourteen times and is directly linked to the idiot child: "the idiot child image

the end of the play "that we are very dangerous!" (113). His "we" is not the "everyone and no one" that Camus's Jean-Baptiste Clamence subtly employs to shift responsibility from himself, but the recognition that Roslyn comes to in *The Misfits*, that not even love can exonerate guilt or cancel out the possibility of evil. Hope can be constructed only on the foundation of the knowledge itself—"To know, and even happily, that we meet unblessed; not in some garden of wax fruit and painted trees, that lie of Eden, but after, after the Fall, after many, many deaths" (113). Paradoxically, Quentin is able to greet Holga at the end of the play because of, not despite, the knowledge that "the wish to kill is never killed" (114). The moral victory is not solely in recognizing that he was guilty but in accepting the consequences of choice, not in exorcising the idiot child but in embracing it and assuming responsibility for it. As Iska Alter notes, "blessedness and betrayal emerge from the same psychic matrix; and . . . betrayal necessarily signifies blessedness because it removes the destructive expectation of deceiving innocence."[50] The only victory over evil is through evil, not with it; not despite but, paradoxically, because of it—it alone generates its opposite and so is necessary to moral wholeness. Saved from the incapacitating and deadly potential of self-knowledge, Quentin accepts "the validity of the evidence without resorting to 'the everlasting temptation of innocence.' Not to accept is to live a life of 'pointless litigation of existence before an empty bench.'"[51] The end challenges the existential nihilism of Camus's antihero by proposing a leap of faith in Quentin's union with Holga.[52] Miller moves his drama away from

---

haunts him, and Quentin, when he does something he regrets, almost always speaks of it as 'idiotic,' thus ambivalently evoking both motifs—the acceptance of the idiot child exorcizes the 'Idiot!' " (*Miller the Playwright*, 101). Nelson claims that Holga's child embodies the "absurdity" that "shows existence for what it is," devoid of "all hopes, illusions, and ideals" (*Arthur Miller*, 267).

50. Alter, "Betrayal and Blessedness," 119. Miller told Christopher Bigsby that "the idea of innocence" is "the enemy." "I can't begin to tell you how many letters I've gotten from psychoanalysts since that play was published who tell me that this probably is essentially the closest to a moral evaluation of psychoanalysis that they have ever come upon" (AMC, 140).

51. Robert Corrigan, introduction to *Arthur Miller: A Collection of Critical Essays*, 11.

52. Bigsby comments on Miller's "existential viewpoint" in that Quentin is "condemned to be free" in a world where he must take "total responsibility" for his

strict allegiance to the dictates of Greek tragedy that so shaped his vision in the earlier plays. For the first time, a protagonist does not find death the only alternative, and in Miller's view this disqualified his play as tragedy: "I can't, quite honestly, separate in my mind tragedy from death. . . . There is no possibility, it seems to me, of speaking of tragedy without it" (*Conv.*, 88–89). Yet he opts for no simplistic resolution. Rather, *After the Fall* finds hope—and that tenuously— only in embracing the absurdity and the knowledge that even in a world without God, human beings can assume the risk of love, commitment, and responsibility if only they can evade the temptation of innocence. As Allan Lewis asks, "Why condemn Miller for seeking moral values and admire Genet and Ionesco for tearing them down?"[53]

At the end of *After the Fall*, when Quentin turns to leave the stage and confronts all the people who have played roles in his past, he comes to Felice, who tries once more to bless him for his seeming goodness to her. When she *"is about to raise her hand in blessing— he shakes her hand, aborting her enslavement"* (*AF*, 114). His gesture summarizes the crucial message of the play, that nothing, nothing can enslave like innocence—that the greatest of crimes is the self-ignorance that fosters the tyranny of innocence and allows it to exert its annihilating power. Miller shows us that, after the Fall, the supreme temptation is innocence itself. Steven Centola describes Quentin's "descent into the dark fires of his psychic inferno" as a version of the monomyth of the hero, who "discovers that the original fall is perpetually reenacted with each hero's fall into consciousness, struggle with his egoism, conflict with others, and fundamental choice between good and evil, between Cain's and Abel's alternatives." Robert Hogan calls Quentin's recognition that no one "can be innocent again on this mountain of skulls" a "remarkable statement" from "the young Communist sympathizer of the 1940s holding aloft his white and unsullied banner." And he even argues, "It is a statement to file away with other hard-won verities like Stephen

---

life ("Fall and After," 132–33). Ruby Chatterji similarly explores Quentin's "existential position," contending that his "renewed effort at human relationships" is "founded on existentialist 'truths'" ("Existentialist Approach to Modern Drama," 95).
53. Lewis, *American Plays and Playwrights*, 50.

Dedalus's courage to be wrong and Faulkner's 'They will endure.' It is not precisely a *Reader's Digest* kind of sentiment, but it is probably one of the few mature remarks ever made in an American play." Audiences may resist Miller's conclusion because "he demands more of us than just love or sympathy; he calls for comprehension." What finally keeps Quentin from being a "separate person" is ironically the common guilt he shares with all others. In finding his "brotherhood" in the criminality of all (as Clamence calls the Nazis "our Nazi brethren"), he escapes the estrangement that threatens his relationship with Holga. And in Quentin's search we discover again both the dark possibilities and the hopes of the Romantics' belief in self as the repository of values. In Christopher Bigsby's words, "We are not the product of the past but of what we choose to make of that past, and that is the grace which this play offers and [Miller's] earlier works do not. . . . Quentin is redeemed not merely by acknowledging his own guilt but by accepting guilt itself or, more strictly, responsibility."[54] Says Miller, Quentin "refuses to settle with being guilty. This is where most people stop, because if you don't stop there then you've got to act" (*Conv.*, 356). Unlike Jean-Baptiste Clamence, he is able to emerge from the Erebus of his own soul with the slender but firm hope that truth can set him free from the consuming self-absorption that claims Camus's "empty prophet for shabby times."

54. Centola, "Monomyth," 53; Hogan, *Arthur Miller*, 253; Bigsby, *Modern American Drama*, 106.

5   Incident at Vichy to Creation of the World and Other Business

Although, as Christopher Bigsby perceptively observes, "in play after play, the longing for innocence is not merely a symptom of its loss, but the beginnings of an implacable evil. . . . It fails to break the surface as an issue until *After the Fall*."[1] The three plays following *After the Fall—Incident at Vichy*, *The Price*, and *Creation of the World and Other Business*—all directly extend the theme of lost innocence, exploring its psychological, social, and mythological dimensions. Indeed, virtually every Miller text, including his novel *Focus* and many of the short stories, turns on issues of innocence and guilt, choice and responsibility. Particularly in the later plays, moral issues arise from the inexorable reality that guilt can neither be evaded nor assuaged, that it must be borne and finally exploited as the source of moral responsibility. The three plays under discussion in this chapter present variations on the theme in works that create an ensemble of characters trapped in an absurdist world of no exit, a pair of brothers enjoined in battle over the consequences of past choices and the guilt they generate, and a cast of mythological figures embodying the ur-drama of the Fall and after.

Incident at Vichy

In the same year that *After the Fall* and *Incident at Vichy* premiered, Miller and his wife, Inge Morath, visited the Mauthausen death camp, and later in the year, Miller covered the Nazi trials in Frankfurt for the *New York*

1. Bigsby, *Critical Introduction*, 206.

Herald Tribune. Based on a true story,[2] a fact often ignored by critics who judge the play mere melodrama or trite sermonizing, *Incident at Vichy* extends Miller's conception of universal guilt after the Fall. The title signals a shift from the magnitude and mythic scope of *After the Fall*; and in it Miller forgoes the sprawling, multilayered stage of the earlier play to focus on the tightly closed arena of a detention center somewhere in Vichy in 1942.[3] The much more expansive earlier play moves circuitously to its climax, but the tautly constructed one-act play follows a much more direct path to its dramatic end. Schlueter and Flanagan pay apt tribute to the "exquisitely crafted" sonata form of this "quintessentially modern play."[4]

Coming on the heels of the ruckus raised by *After the Fall*, *Incident at Vichy* of course became a target of lively debate when it premiered. Always in the vanguard of Miller's detractors, Robert Brustein dismissed it as "a new entry in the Guilt sweepstakes," which offers "another solemn sermon on Human Responsibility." Calling it a throwback to the thirties, "a period the author never seems to have left," he accused Miller of stumbling "upon Pressing Questions long after more subtle minds have exhausted their possibilities" and trying "to pass them off as Powerful Revelations." Like some critics who accuse Miller of excusing Quentin's guilt by subsuming it in an indiscriminate claim of universal guilt, Philip Rahv attacked Miller's basic premise, declaring that "if all are responsible none are responsible. It is simply not true that we are all responsible for the Nazi horrors" (231). But Howard Taubman praised it in his *New York Times* review as "one of the most important plays of our time" and "a drama of towering moral passion."[5]

2. Leduc was based on a psychoanalyst Miller knew, and Von Berg was based on Prince Josef von Schwarzenberg, a friend of Miller's wife, Inge Morath, and descendant of an aristocratic Austrian line, who suffered as a result of his resistance to Nazi persecution.

3. In his notes on directing the play, Harold Clurman wrote of the set: "Something hard, mysterious, 'Kafka-like' desired. A 'no-man's land' enclosure" ("Director's Notes: *Incident at Vichy*," 78).

4. Schlueter and Flanagan, *Arthur Miller*, 106.

5. Robert Brustein, "Muddy Track at Lincoln Center," 26; Philip Rahv, *The Myth and the Powerhouse*, 231; Howard Taubman, "Theatre: *Incident at Vichy* Opens," 116. Among other detractors, Stambusky reduces the play to "a didactic moral lecture on guilt and responsibility" ("Arthur Miller," 113), and Mottram contends that in it "the structure of society goes uncondemned and unanalyzed" ("Arthur Miller:

In the play, nine men and a boy are brought in by authorities in Vichy as suspected Jews with false papers. Apparently, among the ensemble of diverse detainees only the Gypsy and Von Berg are non-Jews, though no one directly acknowledges his race. Even though the businessman, Marchand, secures a pass, perhaps because he works with the Ministry of Supply, Lebeau says, "I could have sworn he was a Jew!" (IV, 25). One of those who believes absolutely in the need for "order," Marchand rationalizes the roundup of suspected Jews: "There are thousands of people running around with false papers. . . . You can't permit such things in war time. . . . [Y]ou have to expect things to be more strict, it's inevitable" (4). Confident that "if your papers are all right" (5) all will be well, he naively rests his security on the efficiency of the political system and at least temporarily escapes.

The most openly anxious of the characters, Lebeau expresses the existential crisis of Kafka's protagonist in The Trial. Asking "Does anybody know anything?" he resists acknowledging that they have been detained as Jews and seeks some explanation of the "crime": "You begin wishing you committed a crime, you know? Something definite" (IV, 2, 3). Incredulous that such evil can exist "in the middle of Europe, the high peak of civilization" (6), he desperately holds to the fact that "There's nothing about Jew in my papers" (36). Yet even as he reaches for straws, finding faint hope in the detention of the Catholic nobleman Von Berg, his angst betrays his consciousness of the situation. While recognizing that "Whenever a people starts to work hard, watch out, they're going to kill somebody" (10), he whistles in the dark, taking comfort in Von Berg's nose looking "bigger than mine" and declaring, "I'm often taken for a gentile myself" (28). In his powerless defenses, he expresses a guilt for being a Jew, irrespective of a crime.

The communist electrician, Bayard, tries to convince himself that "this may all be routine," and asserts, "As far as I know, nobody here is Jewish" (IV, 5, 18). But he, too, knows, perhaps even more than the others, the fate that awaits the detainees. He had discovered that "They're working Jews in Polish camps" and fears the impending

Development," 23). Orm Överland sarcastically concludes that at least Incident at Vichy does not resort to " 'Requiem,' explanatory footnotes or narrator to express the play's dominantly public theme" ("The Action and Its Significance: Arthur Miller's Struggle with Dramatic Form," 10).

consequences. When Von Berg accuses the Nazis of being "vulgar," he protests, "You make it sound like they have bad table manners, that's all" (23). Pointing to the oppression of the workers as the true source of evil, he contends that "The bourgeoisie sold France; they let in the Nazis to destroy the French working class" (30). Banking on the future overthrow of the oppressing classes, he places his hope on the Socialist future, convinced that Marxian determinism will somehow redeem the situation. But another threat lurks in his consciousness. In the detention of the Gypsy, he fears the enactment of racial laws in Vichy that would certainly seal his fate. Furthermore, his naive faith in political salvation is shattered by the cynical psychiatrist Leduc, who notes that the "Communists refused to support France" when the Germans attacked but then changed when Russia was itself invaded by the Nazis. And even worse, Von Berg, an aristocrat, points out that "ninety-nine percent of the Nazis are ordinary working-class people" and that "My cook, my gardeners, the people who work in my forests, the chauffeur, the gamekeeper—they are *Nazis!* . . . That, that, is the dreadful fact" (33, 34).

Monceau's illusions are stripped away as well. Holding to the belief that art and depravity cannot coexist, the actor insists that "I happen to have played in Germany; I know the German people" (*IV*, 20). No audience "is as sensitive" as the German audience, he maintains, "And nobody listens to music like a German" (24). Like Marchand and Lebeau, he keeps finding rational explanations to evade the truth. He tells the others that rather than being enslaved labor, people "have been volunteering for work in Germany"; he tells them that his cousin was "sent" to Auschwitz and "he's fine"; he claims immunity from persecution "in the French Zone"; he expresses incredulity at the existence of death camps—"are you telling me all those people are dead? Is that really conceivable to you? . . . I mean Germans are still *people*" (19). But even if he does not acknowledge the ominous reality surrounding him, at least he recognizes it. He warns the others "not to look like a victim. Or even to feel like one. . . . One must create one's reality in the world. I'm an actor, we do it all the time" (29).

Other than the two main characters, Leduc and Von Berg, whose exchanges constitute the moral center of the play, the other, more minor, characters contribute to the general theme. The Waiter excuses the Major as "really not a bad fellow" and condemns the Gypsy as a thief who "steals everything," revealing both his own naïveté and his culpability. The seventy-year-old Jew, who alone makes no attempt to conceal his Jewishness, becomes the object of Von Berg's kindness when he collapses; but his bundle of treasure, a faint symbol of hope, proves to be nothing but feathers. According to Schlueter and Flanagan, "The Old Jew's willingness to be a victim" along with the others "converts innocent victims to guilty conspirators, extending culpability to all," perhaps a reflection of Hannah Arendt's thesis that the passiveness of Jewish victims made them corroborators in their fate. Accusing him of being "an accomplice," they find in his silence "as much oppressor as oppressed."[6] The most innocent and sentimentally drawn character is the Boy, whose only desire is to rescue his waiting mother. Opposite him stands the Major, a cynical soldier wounded at Amiens and coerced into "police duty" in Vichy to help with the roundup of suspected Jews. Though aware of the injustice, he tries to wash his hands, claiming "I'm not in charge of this procedure" (IV, 11) and complaining to the "Professor" in charge that "I am a line officer, I have no experience with things of this kind" (42). Ironically, he "plays a beautiful piano," the Waiter tells the others, "Gives himself French lessons," and "Always has a few nice words" (12)—but he remains the captive of the system he fails to resist, a "nice" Nazi.[7] So, too, the café owner, Ferrand, attempts to absolve himself of responsibility. Though he weeps when he tells them, "They have furnaces. It's not to work. They burn you up in Poland," he futilely pleads, "What can I do? I told you fifty times to get out of this city! Didn't I? . . . Didn't I?" (35). As for the Gypsy, he serves as the quintessential scapegoat, even of the Jews. A projection of Miller's theme that everyone participates in the persecution of the Other, the Gypsy becomes the object of everyone's scorn, illuminating Leduc's claim that "even Jews have their Jews" (66).

6. Schlueter and Flanagan, Arthur Miller, 103.

7. Dennis Welland says of the Major: "He condones the atrocities but does not initiate them, seeing himself as the victim of a kind of historical necessity in a world where 'There are no persons any more.' . . . The Major's argument is vitiated by its Monceau-like defeatism and by the drunkenness in which it is delivered; self-pity mingles contemptibly with a denial of responsibility and with the belief that love and respect are no longer possible, but he is not totally evil" (Miller the Playwright, 111).

The primary exchanges, however, pit the rationalistic realist Leduc and the aristocratic idealist Von Berg as counterforces engaged in a battle somehow to secure a moral and rational base in an absurd world. Like the others, both must confront the devastating truth that annihilates their assumptions. Leduc, who tries to reassure Lebeau that "I never heard of forced labor in the Vichy Zone" and that "It's still French territory, regardless of the Occupation" (*IV*, 15, 17), appears at first more self-assured than the others. Having studied for five years at the Psychoanalytic Institute in Vienna, he assesses and at times manipulates the others. When Bayard confidently states that "We're members of history" and "symbols" in a great class struggle, Leduc rhetorically challenges his Communist colleague, "So that in a sense . . . you aren't here. You personally." Asking "what can one be if not oneself?" (32), he poses the moral question of the play. If one abnegates personal responsibility by allegiance to any externally defined force, whether in the form of a sociopolitical authority or some abstract set of principles or beliefs, the capacity for moral choice is sacrificed as well and, with it, the potential to commit a truly moral act. While Leduc poses the seminal moral questions in the play and attempts to control the situation by analysis and considered action, he himself comes to stunning awareness when Von Berg commits his ultimate act of irrational choice, giving the psychiatrist his pass to freedom.

Like Holga in *After the Fall*, who wondered how she "could not have known," Von Berg tells the others he had "no idea" they were Jews—"I'm terribly sorry" (*IV*, 18). Freely admitting to his aristocratic past, he half defends himself when Leduc claims "I have taken for granted that the aristocracy is . . . always behind a reactionary regime," ironically remarking, "Oh, there are some certainly. But for the most part they never took any responsibility, in any case" (22). Judging the Nazis guilty of "an outburst of vulgarity" (23), he tells the others he left Germany because of their "table manners" and "their adoration of dreadful art" and wonders, "Can people with respect for art go about hounding Jews?" (24). Shocked and "*depressed*" by the cutting truth that confronts him, he comes to understand that "Art is perhaps no defense against this" (24), a theme Miller was to take up later in *The Archbishop's Ceiling*. Trying desperately to find a moral surety somewhere, he sadly tells Bayard that "I admire your faith; all faith is beautiful. And when I know it is based on something untrue—it's terribly disturbing. . . . I cannot glory in the facts; there is no assurance there" (34).

Not just naive, however, Von Berg is criminally "innocent" like the others. Countering his idealistic assertion that "There are people who would find it easier to die than stain one finger with this murder" (IV, 65), Leduc tells him, "I owe you the truth. . . . I have never analyzed a gentile who did not have . . . a dislike if not a hatred for the Jew" (66). Although Von Berg still believes that he could not "have something to do with this monstrousness," Leduc reminds him that his cousin, Baron Kessler, is a Nazi who helped dismiss Jewish doctors from the medical school in Vienna and that "You must have heard that at some time or other." Having to confess, "Yes. I heard it," Von Berg bears the full weight of his guilt. "When you said his name it was with love," Leduc goes on to say, and "Baron Kessler was in part, in some part, in some small and frightful part—doing your will" (67). By casting the net of responsibility over all the characters, as Janet Balakian perceptively concludes, Miller "sees the atrocity of Nazism as part of an ubiquitous social injustice, and in this play he translates that belief into an archetypal situation." "Like After the Fall," Kinereth Meyer remarks, "Incident at Vichy turns on a central axis of the 'complicity with Cain.'"[8] And like the brutality of the Holocaust casting its dark shadow over Quentin's private world or the terrors of McCarthyism reflected in the witch trials in Salem, it becomes an emblem of fallen humanity at large.

Finding no answer to the charge, Von Berg responds "in full horror," like Kurtz passing judgment on his own image in Conrad's Heart of Darkness; and he asks the ultimate question, "What can ever save us?" (IV, 68). Yet, for all his foresight, Leduc is not simply a moral spokesman for Miller. Benjamin Nelson notes that Leduc gives "very little" to the others in the way of help, largely detaches himself from them, and, despite his insistence that the others act, remains essentially passive.[9] The cynical Major's later interrogation of him exposes Leduc's own capacity for evil, and he remains an ambiguous figure even to the end. Striking the pose of a hero, he tries to compel the

8. Janet N. Balakian, "The Holocaust, the Depression, and McCarthyism: Miller in the Sixties," 126; Kinereth Meyer, "'A Jew Can Have a Jewish Face': Arthur Miller, Autobiography, and the Holocaust," 249.
9. Nelson, Arthur Miller, 287.

others to act by overcoming the guard, yet Leduc himself does not initiate action and only follows the Boy when he bravely bolts for the door guarded by a lone soldier. The others find reasons for not acting: Monceau reiterates his naive faith that there are no furnaces because "what good are dead Jews to them. . . . [T]he Germans are not illogical" (37); Lebeau declares hunger to excuse himself—"I'm so hungry I wouldn't do you much good"—and rationalizes that "if your papers are good, maybe that's it" and that "if it was all that serious, wouldn't they be guarding us more heavily?" (44, 46); Von Berg, who expresses some fear about his own vulnerability despite being an aristocratic gentile, apologetically tells Leduc, "I'm afraid I'd only get in your way. I have no strength in my hands" (37). And Von Berg goes on to explain why none of them seems able to act. The Nazis' capacity for evil, he tells them, is so "inconceivable" that "it paralyzes the rest of us" (38). And in a spectacular reversal of his earlier faith in the redemptive power of art, he goes on, "They are poets, they are striving for a new nobility, the nobility of the totally vulgar. . . . Their motives are musical, and people are merely the sounds they play" (39–40).

When the Major challenges Leduc's motives after he stops him and the Boy from escaping, he exposes the psychiatrist's culpability. Like the others, the Major stops short of commitment. He expresses obvious compassion for the detainees and tries to rescue the Boy and Leduc from certain death when they start to attack the guard. As he had earlier, he tries to exonerate himself by arguing that "this is all as inconceivable to me as it is to you" (IV, 53); he threatens the Professor and calls him a "civilian bastard"; he pleads with Leduc that "I am trying to understand why you are better for the world than me" (56). And yet despite his inability finally to commit himself for the others, he lays bare Leduc's own flawed humanity. When he asks Leduc, "Why do you deserve to live more than I do?" the psychiatrist answers confidently, "Because I am incapable of doing what you are doing" (54). As some critics have suggested, Leduc's constant analysis of others can be seen as a means of control—after all, he had studied at the Psychoanalytic Institute for five years. We begin to suspect his motives, especially when he declares himself "incapable" of committing acts of profound horror. Knowing this, we are left with serious questions at the end of the play, and most certainly with doubts about Leduc's innocence. We learn at the end that he asked Von Berg to tell his wife about the furnaces, but not his children. Yet he bitterly admits later that he did so only to pun-ish her: "God, at a time like this—to think of taking vengeance on her! What scum we are!" (63). Yet even his expression of "*great self-contempt*" is compromised by his willingness to sacrifice another to gain freedom. The Major pointedly asks him if he were released and the other kept "would you refuse?" When Leduc confesses "No," the Major extends the challenge, demanding, "Would you go out that door with a light heart . . . ?" Leduc answers evasively, "I have no duty to make a gift of myself to your sadism" (56–57).

All along, Leduc has been the inquiring analyst, questioning the others and denying them their illusions. "I am being as impersonal, as scientific as I know how to be" (*IV*, 49), he contends. And he arrives at the existential position that "one way or the other . . . we have been trained to die. The Jew and the gentile both" (51). Armed with such a vision, he judges Von Berg. His essential accusation is that "you'll survive," as though he were the victim speaking Holga's contention that "no one they didn't kill can be innocent again." According to Ruby Chatterji, Leduc's charge to Von Berg—that "It's not your guilt I want, it's your responsibility"—is "partly genuine and partly in 'bad faith,'" because at the end of the play, he willingly allows Von Berg to go to certain death by accepting the Baron's pass to freedom.[10] Some might even suspect that Leduc shames Von Berg into sacrificing himself as a means somehow of expiating his guilt, but the question remains open.[11] One thing we know for certain: Leduc

10. Chatterji, "Existentialist Approach," 96. Chatterji relates the play especially to Heidegger and Sartre in the conviction that "man exercises his greatest choice when confronted with death" (95). Lawrence Lowenthal also discusses the existen-tial elements in the play, concluding that "the presence of the Other [the Nazis] is Sartre's vision of the fall, since the Other cuts off man's freedom and renders him vulnerable to feelings of shame and ossification. . . . The Other freezes our possibilities for transcendence by imposing on us a 'Nature,' an outside, an objec-tive identity" ("Arthur Miller's *Incident at Vichy*: A Sartrean Interpretation," 179). Robert Martin Jr. sees the play as "pure Sartrean"; to him it asks, "'What is real-ity in the face of the absurd?'" ("Arthur Miller: Public Issues, Private Tensions," 103). Schvey also discusses Miller's "philosophical existentialism, that man must free himself from the dilemma of innocence" in order to be "free to choose, to act positively and with responsibility toward his fellow man and himself" ("Arthur Miller: Songs of Innocence and Experience," 86).

11. See especially Schlueter and Flanagan, *Arthur Miller*, 104–5, and Murray, *Arthur Miller, Dramatist*, 166. Bigsby sees Leduc as more authentic, claiming that

must bear responsibility for the Baron's fate; he must therefore accept guilt along with the others.

Leslie Epstein argues that Miller in effect undercuts the authority of the central theme that all are guilty by making Von Berg a plaster saint. The ending is "gratuitous, unmotivated, phony—a high school gesture, not an act," she judges—"Unable to judge men, Miller offers us a handkerchief." But Miller makes clear that Von Berg does not sacrifice himself without awareness of his own culpability. Indeed, Miller suggests that guilt provides the impetus for choice. Contrary to David Bronson's argument that the play returns to Miller's "pre-*After the Fall* view" that innocence is possible and that "It takes the way of giving awareness of evil to one character and sheer innocence to another," Miller shows that good does not exist apart from evil, that it is in some measure dependent upon it, for the capacity for evil makes moral choice possible. Von Berg acts not because he is inno-cent but precisely because he knows he is not. Miller told Steven Centola in an interview that "Guilt is not guilt if it is conscious. It is then something even more sinister . . . guilt is a sense of un-usable responsibility, it's responsibility that can't be expressed, that can't be utilized for one reason or another. On the other hand, it is a way of self-paralysis." If such awareness is potentially incapacitat-ing, however, it is also the trigger for moral action. Von Berg, like Quentin, "refuses to settle with being guilty," even though "it would have been far more palatable if he shot himself" as he threatened to do when he felt the burden of guilt for the death of his Jewish musicians—"if you don't stop there then you've got to act" (*Conv.*, 356). In another interview Miller told Matthew Roudané that "the play comes down to that, the step from guilt to responsibility and action" (*Conv.*, 372).[12]

_____

"having accepted the fact of his own guilt, Leduc accepts the responsibility and decides to live with it. By taking the pass from Von Berg, he endorses Quentin's refutation of those previous Miller heroes for whom guilt and the acknowledgment of it was only the prologue to the revolver or the speeding car" ("Fall and After," 135).

12. Epstein, "Unhappiness of Arthur Miller," 173; Bronson, "*Enemy of the People*," 245. Describing Von Berg as "apart from the rest of mankind," Miller adds, "that a saving act should come from . . . a decadent personality . . . might sound strange. And yet there it is—for some ironical reasons he is the one who can make this kind of gesture" (*Conv.*, 339). To those who argue that Von Berg's sacrificial

Incident at Vichy depicts a world no less absurd than that in a Beckett play, but it maintains a belief in the capacity to choose, even if the choice offers no escape from the human condition. We know, of course, that Von Berg will surely pay the price for his act and that other detainees are entering the detention center even as Leduc escapes, in all likelihood for a very brief time.[13] Robert Corrigan contends that Von Berg's sacrificial act in fact "makes our guilt unbearable by destroying that balance of quid pro quo which we have created in an effort to justify our guilt." Clearly, Miller insists that such choices are possible. Not "content with a world-picture which sees man as a victim of a hostile society," as Christopher Bigsby observes, Miller insists that one can commit an act of love if "aware of its limitations" and of the legacy of the Fall against which it occurs. The play operates with a dialectical pattern in which Leduc's near nihilism establishes the opposing pole to Von Berg's idealism and generates the Baron's triumphant act. Leduc's powerful truths are essential to free Von Berg from the stasis of his innocence. As Benjamin Nelson writes, the "inevitable climax" answers Von Berg's question "What can save us?"—"Not the lie of Eden, but also not the blanket acceptance of despair inherent in Leduc's final searing nihilism." Von Berg acts "in full knowledge of his separateness and his destructive potential." Miller does more than offer testimony of original sin. In this play, as in his earlier texts, as Janet Balakian notes, Miller depicts a tragic consequence—"it is about Von Berg's inability to walk away from the central conflict, and therefore, about his tragic existence."[14] What determines the action is not the question of

---

act strains credulity and resorts to melodrama, we might note again that the text is based on a true story. Meyer notes the irony that Von Berg assumes the role of "Christian savior" at the end. He "acts out Leduc's statement that 'each man has his Jew; it is the other. And the Jews have their Jews.' The self-sacrificing Christian, Von Berg, becomes Leduc's 'Jew' and, Christ-like, dies in his place—*imitatio Christi* taken to its logical conclusion" ("'Jew Can Have,'" 252).

13. To some, like Lawrence L. Langer, "the magnitude of the sorrow and the loss dwarfs the deed, however noble, of one man for one man" ("The Americanization of the Holocaust on Stage and Screen," 224). Brater notes that in an absurd world, because there are four more victims brought in, "even the heroes are victims. Martyrdom has become an anachronism" ("Ethics and Ethnicity," 132).

14. Corrigan, introduction to *Arthur Miller*, 14; Bigsby, *Confrontation and Commitment*, 41; Nelson, *Arthur Miller*, 288; Balakian, "Holocaust, Depression, and McCarthyism," 129. Miller told Steven Centola in an interview that an individual

innocence or guilt so much as how one chooses to act in consequence of the Fall. "There are actions that we call nonactions and we have what I won't call a moral responsibility for but rather a literal connection with the evil of the time," Miller has said in summation of the play: "we have an investment in evils that we manage to escape. . . . [W]hat happens is simply that by virtue of these circumstances, a man is faced with his own complicity with what he despises."[15] Because the Baron recognizes his love for his Nazi cousin Kessler,

> This partaking of evil is finally [Von Berg's] responsibility. . . . He wishes to expiate it because it implies a complicity with everything he despises, and he substitutes himself for the psychoanalyst. . . . But with the pass goes his guilt, and the doctor in accepting it, in accepting his own survival, is himself caught in complicity with the destruction of another man . . . and guilt goes on.[16]

However necessary his accusation of guilt may be, in accepting Von Berg's pass, as Albert Wertheim comments, Leduc "must acknowledge . . . Von Berg's positive concept of man."[17]

In *After the Fall*, *Incident at Vichy*, and the plays following through the seventies and beyond, Miller's characters, in their struggle to survive, must endure the guilt of a survivor. It cannot be denied, negated, or assuaged but must be borne—even as it threatens the self-annihilation of despair and offers the promise of a leap of faith.

The Price

Along with the major New York revivals of Miller's best-known dramas at the end of the century came a reassessment of the

---

"Absolutely . . . has the potential for the kind of self-determination" expressed by both Quentin and Von Berg (*Conv.*, 359).

15. Miller quoted in Evans, *Psychology and Arthur Miller*, 74. Edward R. Isser contends that in *Incident at Vichy*, Miller presents a "universalist" as opposed to a "particularistic" approach to the Holocaust. He violates historical accuracy, according to Isser, and blames "the French Jews . . . for their own fate because of their inability to face events and their failure to act decisively" (*Stages of Annihilation: Theatrical Representations of the Holocaust*, 68).

16. Evans, *Psychology and Arthur Miller*, 74–75.

17. Wertheim, "Arthur Miller: *After the Fall*," 26.

canon at large. The critically acclaimed revival of *Death of a Salesman*, with masterful performances by Brian Dennehy and Elizabeth Franz, confirmed the play's rank as, by most measures, the preeminent American drama; the 1998 Roundabout restaging of *A View from the Bridge*, with Anthony LaPaglia's Tony Award–winning portrayal of Eddie Carbone, secured the play's place as a major American tragedy. But perhaps the 1999 revival of *The Price*, directed by James Naughton, did more than any of the reproductions to enhance the critical reputation of a Miller text. Although successfully staged in London later in the same year, the play's 1968 premiere on Broadway had met with mixed response; however, acclaim for the 1999 revival was pretty much universal. The New York critics began to appreciate why a handful of critics had championed the play even over the years when Miller's stock on Broadway was at an all-time low.

As with *Incident at Vichy*, which compresses the stage setting and presents the action in a taut structure, *The Price* is constructed with extraordinary economy and directness. Intensely concentrated on four characters in a claustrophobic attic setting crammed with ten rooms' worth of furniture, a record of lives lived and lost, of choices made and consequences suffered, the play gives evidence of Miller's remarkable control of his craft. Once again pairing brothers, as he had done with Arnold and Ben Simon and Max and Harry Zabrinsky in his undergraduate plays *No Villain* and *Honors at Dawn*, David and Amos Beeves in *The Man Who Had All the Luck*, Chris and Larry Keller in *All My Sons*, Biff and Happy Loman in *Death of a Salesman*, and Quentin and Dan in *After the Fall*, Miller pits Victor and Walter Franz together to engage in a brutalizing vivisection of their pasts.[18] They, Victor's wife, Esther, and a Jewish Russian furniture dealer, Gregory Solomon, constitute the entire cast, though the absent father, dead some sixteen years, haunts the play as surely as General Gabler haunts Ibsen's *Hedda Gabler*; and the shadow of the absent mother surfaces in objects that embody her presence. As Alan Downer writes, the setting provides "The architectural envelope

18. Several critics note the parallels between *The Price* and earlier plays. For example, Carson, *Arthur Miller*, 126, and Welland, *Miller the Playwright*, 121, both speak of Victor and Walter Franz as Biff and Happy Loman twenty years later, and Qun Wang, in "The Tragedy of Ethical Bewilderment," relates them to the inner struggles of Joe Keller and Willy Loman.

that has caused and is to affect the life histories of the characters." Downer concludes that "The very locale is eloquent, expository; the action could occur nowhere else, no other action would justify it."[19] A pervasive symbol of the presentness of the past, the attic piles together an accumulation of objects, ruins from a paradise lost and what Miller himself calls "the architecture of sacrifice" (*Conv.*, 316). A sculling oar, a fencing foil and mask, emblazoned gauntlets, a cracked harp, a lap robe, an opera hat, an embroidered golden gown, all images of a dead but haunting past and of people gone but not forgotten; and the furniture, like the two chests representing the two brothers and the ubiquitous chair evoking the presence of the father at center stage—all give evidence of Miller's ability to speak poetry on stage even without benefit of language.

A major charge leveled at the play in its American premiere was that it avoided the issues of the day. "The nation's cities are in total disarray . . . our disgraceful involvement in the Vietnam conflict is making large numbers ashamed of being Americans," Robert Brustein complained in his caustic review entitled "The Unseriousness of Arthur Miller"—"Yet, Arthur Miller, the most public-spirited of dramatists, continues to write socio-psychological melodramas about Family Responsibility. . . . *The Price* is virtually divorced from concerns that any modern audience recognizes as its own."[20] But once again Brustein misunderstood and underappreciated Miller's artistic vision. It seems highly doubtful that someone as involved in the public debate as Miller could be justly accused of being "divorced from concerns that any modern audience recognizes as its own." In fact, just as he had assumed a public role and risked taking a moral stance during the McCarthy era, Miller was again embroiled in the politics of the day, directly participating in the antiwar movement, speaking out against the war even at West Point, contributing to the University of Michigan teach-ins on the war and defending student protests generally, and refusing an invitation to the White House in protest of President Johnson's Vietnam policy. In the year *The Price* opened, he was a delegate for Eugene McCarthy at the Democratic National Convention in Chicago, where he also again participated in sit-ins against the war. In roughly the same period, he served

19. Alan S. Downer, review of *The Price*, 156.
20. Brustein, "The Unseriousness of Arthur Miller," 39–40.

as president of PEN and visited Russia the year before the play's opening to petition the Soviet Union to end the ban on Aleksandr Solzhenitsyn's works. In the light of such efforts, Brustein's charge of "Unseriousness" seems petty at best and embarrassingly wrong at worst, given the play's social and political implications.

In fact, Miller comments in *Timebends* that *The Price* was "in part an exorcism" of the "paralyzing vision of repetition" represented by the Vietnam conflict, the American proclivity of "looking almost completely outside ourselves for salvation from ourselves" (*T*, 542). In an essay addressing why he wrote *The Price* that appeared in the *New York Times* the day before the play's 1999 revival opened, Miller stated that "it was a reaction to two big events. . . . [O]ne was the seemingly permanent and morally agonizing Vietnam war, the other a surge of avant garde plays that to some degree or another fit the absurd style. I was moved to write a play that might confront and confound both." In no way did Miller write a drama "divorced" from the realities of the age—"As corpses piled up," he explained, "We were fighting in a state of forgetfulness. . . . If the play does not utter the word Vietnam, it speaks to a spirit of unearthing the real that seemed to have very nearly gone out of our lives" (*E*, 298–99).

What Miller saw as a unifying theme linking the Vietnam War, avant-garde absurdist drama, and *The Price* was the human tendency to deny the reality of the past and subsequent claim of innocence that leads eventually to "the paralyzing vision of repetition." At the time he wrote the play, as he explained in his essay, "the very idea of an operating continuity between past and present in human behavior was démodé and close to a laughably old fashioned irrelevancy. . . . It was as though the culture had decreed amnesia as the ultimate mark of reality." For one deeply rooted in the tradition of Greek tragedy and Ibsen's dramas, with their extreme consciousness of the causal pattern of human existence, such a view was intolerable. "*The Price* grew out of a need to reconfirm the power of the past, the seedbed of current reality, and the way to possibly affirm cause and effect in an insane world" (*E*, 297–98). In other words, the play set out to reassert the elemental tragic theme interwoven into most of Miller's plays, a belief in the abiding presence of the past and the inevitable reality that, finally, "the birds come home to roost."

Far from being out of the mainstream, *The Price* submerges the issues of the sixties in a larger tragic vision that transcends the passing crises of the moment. Miller went on to declare in his essay that he wanted to show the cost of denying the past, a blindness that he believed created the war, by projecting into the play as emblem the crisis of the thirties "when we learned the fear of doom and had stopped being kids for a while . . . and that Depression cataclysm . . . seemed to teach that life indeed had beginnings, middle and a consequential end" (*E*, 298–99). The Depression became for him the symbol of denial just as the Vietnam War projected an evasion of the past that might have ended it. Miller translates the theme in the persons of two contesting brothers, whose meeting to sell off the remaining family furniture after a separation of sixteen years occasions "an exorcism of this paralyzing vision of repetition. . . . [I]t all comes back, the angry symbols evoke the old emotions of injustice, and they part unreconciled. Neither can accept that the world needs both of them—the dutiful man of order and the ambitious selfish creator who invents new cures" (*T*, 542).

Although even at eighty-four Miller was still reading Aristotle's *Poetics* and the Bible, as Douglas Feiden discovered when he interviewed him just before the opening of the revival of *The Price* at the Royale Theater in 1999, Miller goes beyond the restraints of Aristotelian tragedy in the play and transforms it and the Ibsenian "problem play" into a much more existential drama that, in Christopher Bigsby's view, asserts "the imperfection of human nature" but insists "on man's responsibility for his own fate." It reflects both the determinism of the past, which strikes a tragic chord, and, in the vein of Ibsen's later plays, projects an existential awareness of the dramatic tension between what is irrevocably given and what is consciously or unconsciously willed. Like the sisters Gunhild and Ella in Ibsen's *John Gabriel Borkman*, Victor and Walter Franz meet as victims both of themselves and of inexorable forces from the past; yet, as Alan Downer notes, "Like the later plays of O'Neill, [*The Price*] goes beyond the tragic catastrophe to the maturity of understanding and acceptance." The "no exit" attic carries with it an inexorable history that neither brother has been able to shake. It is the return to the crossroads once again, and they come as haunted figures trying one last time to still the memories of a past that has shaped and hounded them. As Morris Freedman notes, "The issue of the price of the furniture becomes enlarged to include the price of any transactions, of any bargain that is struck in the world, of any memory or other possession or attainment that we may have gathered and cherished."[21]

The family chronicle records yet another Depression tale, a history of family betrayal and defeat at the hands of unavoidable economic forces. Overwhelmed by the crash of 1929, the family begins to self-destruct, and the feeble alliances between members rapidly dissolve. The mother, who blames her husband for her unrealized musical career, vomits up her resentment and disgust when Franz tells her that they have nothing left—she just "kept on vomiting," Victor tells Walter, "like thirty-five years coming up" (P, 108). She dies soon after when her favorite son, Victor, is only twelve. Reduced to living in the attic of the once-prosperous house, Franz retreats with Victor from others, mostly sitting in his ubiquitous chair and eating food cooked on a hot plate. While Walter goes to medical school, largely ignoring the plight of his family, Victor begins school in 1934. At nineteen, he meets and marries Esther; and when Walter refuses to loan him five hundred dollars to finish college, he joins the police force, where he remains twenty-eight years despite his disdain of the work. When Franz dies in 1959, Victor unsuccessfully tries to contact Walter to dispose of the furniture; but now, in 1964, when the building is about to be demolished, Victor arranges to meet the dealer, Gregory Solomon, a remarkable Russian Jew of near ninety, and waits for him with Esther as the play opens. As the first act ends and Walter suddenly appears, the drama becomes another long day's journey into night as the brothers, meeting for the first time in sixteen years, confront years of growing recrimination and guilt.

Although Walter does not appear until the very end of the first act, Victor and Esther clearly make him the center of their conversation. The wise Solomon pointedly asks if there is a brother or sister involved in the sale, because "the average family they love each other like crazy, but the minute the parents die is all of a sudden a question who is going to get what and you're covered with cats and dogs" (P, 32). Clearly the price involves far more than the value of the furniture. Esther insists that "There's such a thing as a moral debt" (14) that Walter needs to account for. But if a "moral debt" exists at

21. Bigsby, Critical Introduction, 224; Downer, "Review of The Price," 156; Morris Freedman, American Drama in Social Context, 57.

all, it remains a question who is ultimately most responsible for it.[22] In his production notes to the play Miller seems to withhold judgment on both characters, contending that "As the world operates, the qualities of both brothers are necessary to it. . . . The production must therefore withhold judgment in favor of presenting both men in all their humanity and from their own viewpoints. . . . [E]ach has merely proved to the other what the other has known but dared not face" (117).[23]

At the beginning, before Solomon interrupts them, Esther and Victor rehearse the past that has brought them to this moment. Although she had resorted to drink to sustain her, Esther has remained with Victor despite her embarrassment at his job and resentment of his unwillingness to confront Walter. She prods him to secure a good price for the furniture because "we need the money" now that Victor is supposedly about to retire and their son Richard is at MIT. But her role exceeds that of long-suffering wife. Part referee and part accuser, she serves an essential function in the play. Alan Downer considers her "tritagonist; because of her the play remains a drama and never descends to debate."[24] She accuses both brothers and drives the action to its conclusion. Admitting her dissatisfaction with Victor's hesitancy to retire and lack of assertiveness, she insists that he take all the money from the sale when Walter tells them he has no interest in it. And when Walter later proposes that Solomon overestimate the value of the furniture so that he can declare a large tax deduction as a contribution and give all the proceeds to Victor (doubling the amount Solomon offered to pay in the first place), she demands that Victor accept. When he refuses, even after Solomon reluctantly agrees to the shady plot, she tells him with some justification that he "can't bear the thought that [Walter's] decent" (*P*, 78). Yet she, too,

---

22. Robert W. Corrigan declares that "the whole agon between the brothers hinges on the assumption that 'There is a moral debt.' Both men have justified everything that they have done, as well as everything that has or has not happened to them, in terms of this imperative" (introduction to *Arthur Miller*, 17).

23. Elsewhere, though, Miller appears to side with Victor: "I'd say that I wish he would win but I have my doubts. . . . [T]here are creatures like his brother Walter, a surgeon, who are cruel and destructive. But without them we are going to stand still. . . . We need that guy. But Victor is much more careful about life. . . . So there's a dialectic. There's a Ying and Yang in there" (*AMC*, 148).

24. Alan Downer, "Review of *The Price*," 157.

assumes a measure of responsibility for their lives, admitting to Victor that "I knew you'd never get out if you didn't during the war—I saw it happening, and I said nothing" (19).

Like the brothers, she, too, confronts an existential crisis. She asks Victor, "God, what's it all about? When I was coming up the stairs just now, all the doors hanging open . . ." (P, 8). Symbolic of the "theater in your head" that Miller first conceived of with *Death of a Salesman* and projected on levels of the stage in *After the Fall*, the set presents a psychic as well as a physical landscape, where once again past and present interweave and the characters all feel, as Miller says of Victor, "Caught by the impact of time" (11). "Time, you know," Solomon ironically declares, "is a terrible thing" (30). Esther's perspective prepares us for the revelation Walter is to give later on, that the house was always full of deceit and resentment. She recalls living in the house when she and Victor were first married, and "it always used to seem so pretentious to me, and kind of bourgeois" (7); she reminds Victor of how they laughed when he put on his first uniform—"It was like a masquerade. And we were right. That's when we were right" (21). She later pronounces the ultimate condemnation of Victor, even more than Walter, when she declares that Franz "was a calculating liar! And in you heart you knew it!" (106).

But having stayed on the police force for twenty-eight years, Victor seems unable to act even though he, too, recognizes the "masquerade" he has been living, and Esther seeks recompense for the life he has made her live as well. Victor's paralysis comes not only from a fear of failure, though, like the fear Walter expresses of being suddenly crushed like their father under the weight of financial collapse, but also from a deep residue of guilt. Somewhere deep inside, he knows that his claim of victimization is fraudulent, and he strikes the pose of martyr to ward off a truth he cannot confront without acknowledging the irony that Quentin sees in himself when he plays the crucified victim in *After the Fall*. Consequently, he "conspires to create his own irrelevance," Christopher Bigsby concludes, and "denies his freedom rather than accept the price that goes with it."[25] In Miller's own words, "he participated in his own alienation from himself and in so doing discovers himself in what he did."[26] In a way he accepts

25. Bigsby, *Critical Introduction*, 226.
26. Ronald Hayman, *Arthur Miller*, 18. Miller told Pat Hingle, who played Victor in the 1968 production in Philadelphia, "Victor knows the price he paid taking care

servitude *willfully*, just as Leduc in *Incident at Vichy* claims that Monceau left his names on books he sold because he really wanted to be caught by the Nazis.

Walter, on the other hand, "has made a lifetime practice of moral compromise," Morris Freedman observes, "a capacity not available to his more simple-minded brother,"[27] a distinction heightened by their differing vocations. Walter obviously seeks to alleviate his guilt by returning to the house and trying to help Victor financially. Lamenting the price he has paid for his selfish pursuit of a career—a failed marriage, estranged children, a mental breakdown—he proposes to make some kind of restitution. Neither he nor Victor is innocent, yet in their attempt somehow to heal their fractured relationship, they only expose the self-deceit of the other as they try to assert an innocence neither possesses.

It is Gregory Solomon, the unique, ninety-year-old furniture dealer, who strikes the balance and provides the moral perspective in the play. A replacement for the selfish and failed father, he assumes Franz's seat center stage. Solomon possesses the resilience that his predecessor lacked—having survived struggle in six countries, four periods of economic collapse (in 1898, 1904, 1923, and 1932), and four marriages (at ages nineteen, twenty-two, fifty-one, and even seventy-five), he is unlike Franz and can "bounce" back from defeat. Understandably declaring "I enjoy that character more than anybody I ever wrote" (AMC, 148), Miller traces him to his Jewish past: "Gregory Solomon in *The Price* has to be Jewish, for one thing because of the theme of survival, of a kind of acceptance of life, seemed to me to point directly to the Jewish experience through centuries of oppression" (*Conv.*, 183). A "wryly wise choral Kibitzer so common to American Jewish family life," according to Morris Freedman, Solomon is "rabbinical commentator on the point, the worth, the ends, the values of life itself." Solomon also reflects his namesake, as Albert Wertheim adds, the biblical "king who demonstrated his wisdom by presiding over the impossible division of the child," a point reinforced when Walter tells Victor at the end of the play that "we're really like two halves of the same guy" (P, 110).[28]

---

of his father, but he doesn't know what he got from it. And that's his main problem in the play" (AMC, 151).

27. Freedman, *American Drama*, 55.

28. Ibid., 56; Wertheim, "Arthur Miller: *After the Fall*," 28.

In a series of telling pronouncements, Solomon establishes the moral basis of the play. Claiming that "The price of furniture is nothing but a viewpoint" (*P*, 38), he explains the particular limitation of the heavy furniture he assesses—it lasts forever in an age when "shopping" has become a means of salvation: "With this kind of furniture the shopping is over, it's finished, there's no more possibilities" (41), a symbolic reference of course to the dead end of the brothers' past. When Victor laments the world of competition and crass capitalism, Solomon reminds him, "it's already in the Bible, the rat race. The minute she laid her hand on the apple—that's it. . . . [T]here's always a rat race, you can't stay out of it" (*P*, 50). Seeing life as existence after the Fall, Solomon has learned to transcend the guilt that can freeze action and that makes Victor hesitate to act. Although deeply moved by his daughter's suicide in 1916 and dreaming of her every night, he has gone beyond self-recrimination to accept her death as a consequence of life itself. As Miller explains to Steven Centola, Solomon says, in effect, " 'I was the way I am; she is the way she was; and what happened was the inevitable result of that. So what could have changed it?' . . . [Solomon has] a kind of cosmic acceptance of the situation" (*Conv.*, 353). His vision does not deny responsibility but neither does it bury the will to live under the weight of pointless nihilism. Repeating Quentin's hard-earned wisdom, Solomon advises Victor: "it's not that you can't believe nothing, that's not hard—it's that you still got to believe. *That's* hard. And if you can't do that, my friend—you are a dead man!" (37). Miller claims that Solomon's pronouncement emerged from his own reaction to the nihilistic tendency in the sixties and early seventies when "the whole question arose in the States as to whether any kind of life was possible that wasn't totally self-serving, totally cynical, that wasn't truly false and unsupportable" (AMC, 148).

The play crescendos to the climax as the brothers both cling to the illusion of their innocence in contrast to the other's guilt. At first trying to heal the schism with Victor by telling him "it never dawned on me until I got sick—that you'd made a choice," Walter tries to compliment his other: "You haven't hurt other people to defend yourself" (*P*, 83–84). But when Victor denies Walter's attempt at reconciliation, accusing him of merely wanting "the old handshake" to relieve his guilt, his brother explodes in judgment. It "was your decision, not mine," he insists, even though "[I warned you] not to allow him to strangle your life. . . . He exploited you!" (90–91). Victor's ironic reply that "I am nobody's victim" (92) speaks a truth he himself does not yet fathom, and he slips back in the self-defensive pose of innocence. "You want to make up for things," he tells Walter, but "I didn't invent my life. Not altogether. You had a responsibility and you walked out on it" (101). But his defensive posture fades when Walter reveals that Franz all along had four thousand dollars stashed away that could have paid for Victor's schooling. As Esther forces Victor to admit, "You certainly knew he had *something*" (104). With "*A shame flooding into him*," the younger brother begins to expose a measure of guilt, an undeniable awareness of his fraudulent role as martyr. Walter pointedly claims that their mother's harp alone would have paid for Victor's college. The object significantly stroked by all the characters as they attempt to recover a dead past and "the heart and soul of the deal" (57) to Solomon, the harp symbolizes the mother's estrangement from their father and the guilt by association Victor feels as her favorite. Walter half accusingly had told Esther that his and Victor's mother "would run all the way to school with his galoshes" if it rained—"Her Victor—my God! By the time he could light a match he was already Louis Pasteur" (76).

When Esther realizes that Victor must have known of the father's hidden funds all along, she bitterly cries, "It's all a goddamn farce! . . . No wonder you're paralyzed—you haven't believed a word you've said all these years" (*P*, 105–6). Victor tries to explain that when he confronted his father with the fact that Walter offered to send money for his education, Franz simply laughed; and he recounts going to the park, which was "a battlefield; a big open-air flophouse" peopled by other victims of the Depression. "He loved me Esther!" he protests. "He just didn't want to end up in the grass! It's not that you don't love somebody, it's that you've got to survive" (107). He admits now, with genuine understanding, that "We do what we have to do" (107), an echo of his cry to Walter that "I am nobody's victim" (92). Although Esther angrily protests, Victor refuses Walter's offer of a job at the hospital, not to protect his illusion of self-worth and innocence, like Willy Loman does in rejecting Charley's offer, but to affirm his freedom.

Victor, despite his "shame" at making Esther pay the price for his loyalty to his father, comes to accept the truth that, far from being a victim of fate and others, he *did* indeed choose. Ironically, when

Walter insists "You made those choices, Victor! And that's what you have to face. . . . You don't want the truth you want a monster!" Victor realizes that he acted, quite simply, because "I didn't want him to end up on the grass" (*P*, 111, 112). He had been crippled all these years not because of resentment so much as guilt for trying to foist responsibility for his life onto Walter; as with Chris Keller, his self-righteousness enchained him. Now, though, rather than deny what Walter had told him earlier, "That you'd made a choice" (83), Victor embraces it, accepting both the responsibility and consequences. Esther laments to Solomon, "The one thing he wanted most was to talk to his brother. . . . It always seems to me that one little step more and some crazy kind of forgiveness will come and lift up everybody. When do you stop being so . . . foolish?" (114). But she comes to appreciate the integrity of Victor's choices at the end, when she tells him to wear his uniform rather than civilian clothes to dinner, transforming them from a symbol of embarrassment, "a masquerade," to a badge of honor.

There is an existential victory in Victor's acceptance of his choices: In the face of absurdity, he had acted to preserve his father's dignity, knowing full well that, looking back, "all I can see is a long brainless walk in the street" (*P*, 48). As Gerald Weales declares, this is a confrontation of Victor with himself more than with Walter.[29] At the end, when Walter washes his hands of the family, accusing Victor of trying "to destroy me with this saintly self-sacrifice, this mockery of sacrifice" (112), and flinging his mother's gold gown at his brother, he, too, survives impotence by guilt; but he does not achieve Victor's deeper epiphany. Like Victor, as Miller writes, he "is left touching the structure of his life" (17). Yet despite his insistence that the production of the play should "withhold judgment in favor of presenting both men in all their humanity and from their own viewpoints," Miller gives Victor larger stature. Not only does he alone appear in all but the very end of the first act, he has the last say of the two brothers, and it is he whom Solomon defends against Walter and even Esther at times. As he leaves, he symbolically "*buckles on his gun belt*" and puts on his uniform (115), reaffirming his choice, and he tells Solomon that he will return for the fencing foil, mask, and gauntlets, realigning himself with the family Walter abandons.

29. Gerald C. Weales, "All about Talk: Arthur Miller's *The Price*," 199.

When he stops indicting Walter, Victor, who like Quentin is true to the existential ethic, takes his own life in his hands. He forgoes martyrdom for self-knowledge—and with such knowledge comes the loss of innocence. He knows and must acknowledge that his self-sacrifice served no real purpose and that such self-denial meant nothing in a family Walter reminds him was devoid of love or loyalty: "there was no love in this house. There was no loyalty. There was nothing here but a straight financial arrangement" (109). Yet Victor realizes that he acted with free will and in accord with his own sense of values. It is this that Esther understands when she declares, "Nothing was sacrificed" (112).[30]

It is fittingly Solomon who speaks the benediction to the play, telling Victor *"with a glance at the furniture:* Well. . . . Who would ever have believed I would start such a thing again . . . ?" (*P*, 115), repeating the act of survival he had enacted after his economic defeats and failed marriages. When he at last plays on the old hand-cranked phonograph the "laughing record" Victor plays at the beginning of the play, and joins in the laughter, he transforms Franz's cynical laughter at Victor by laughing at the vagaries of existence instead, one who yet again "bounces back," a survivor once more in the face of an absurd world. Like "the 'Dybbuk' of Jewish folklore, a spirit who inhabits human bodies until he is exorcised. . . . Solomon takes title to the Franz brothers' past," according to Schlueter and Flanagan. Clearly, in him Miller challenges the nihilism he heard expressed in the late sixties, staged in absurdist theater, and voiced in the agonizing context of the Vietnam War. In his continuing exploration of the presentness of the past and the consequences of choice, Miller again evokes tragic rhythm without writing a conventional tragedy. Among others, Santosh Bhatia sees such a tragic vision in Miller's text. He notes that unlike Beckett and Pinter, whose characters cannot recover a past grown dim, "Miller's social commitment as a playwright forced him to tell the story in terms of cause and effect. . . .

30. Anthony S. Abbott writes that "Victor is not guilty in the sense that Joe Keller or Willy or Eddie is guilty, but he has destroyed his life for an illusion, the illusion that human beings are better than they are, and his final triumph is to turn that illusion into truth. He brings Gregory Solomon back to life, and just as he must remain true to the idealized memory of his father, he must remain true to his bargain with Solomon. And for this we love him, as we cannot love Walter" (*The Vital Lie: Reality and Illusion in Modern Drama*, 139).

The tragic feeling is aroused by the irrevocability of certain deeds and actions accomplished in the past." He claims that *The Price* is more of "an existential tragedy. Existentialists claim that man is surrounded by objective uncertainties and that in a world full of possibilities man has to make a choice."[31] Miller, however, refers to the plays of Beckett, Ionesco, and other absurdist dramatists in the existential tradition as "parody tragedy," which he could not imitate. "I felt that there was enough dissociation in life, without my adding it to the theater" (*Conv.*, 341).

The ending exposes the high risk and promise of fully confronting the truth. Victor—and to some degree Walter—survives not only because he has faced the truth, but also because he has gained a moral integrity by eschewing innocence. In a way, nothing is resolved other than the sale, but ghosts are exorcised, and the characters are at last freed from the shackles of innocence. As Walter destroys the myth of Victor's victimization, he allows his brother to act "without illusions from the dream of martyrdom," Benjamin Nelson argues. The brothers are "neither condemned nor redeemed, only a little wiser."[32] The encounter has stripped away the lies and self-deceit and triggered the self-awareness each brother finds as a consequence. No longer in the "plastic Eden" that Quentin also escapes in *After the Fall*, they must assume responsibility for their lives as the cost of their freedom.

Creation of the World and Other Business

In response to the opening of *Creation of the World and Other Business*, Miller confessed to Josh Greenfield that his later work is "getting more and more mythological. . . . Characters in all my other plays are also mythological. . . . I mean, the most psychological of my characters was probably Willy Loman. And I've become aware now that I was dealing with something much more than Willy Loman" (*Conv.*, 243). In fact, as we have discussed, the Fall myth is the substratum of virtually all his texts. In a revealing 1982 interview with Steven Centola, Miller admits that although he "was never a

---

31. Schlueter and Flanagan, *Arthur Miller*, 114–15; Bhatia, *Arthur Miller*, 110, 103.
32. Nelson, *Arthur Miller*, 311–12.

religious person in the conventional sense. . . . [A]ll the ideas" that permeate his plays "are stemming from the Old Testament. The more I live the more I think that somewhere down the line it poured into my ear. . . . I am reading it again now, and I'm amazed at how embedded it is in me" (*Conv.*, 355).[33] He describes the genesis of *Creation* as a product of his involvement in the effort to free an eighteen-year-old Connecticut youth, Peter Reilly, who confessed to brutally murdering his mother and sexually abusing her with a bottle. Convinced that the confession was forced and that the case rested on the interrogator's "horrifyingly cold and perfectly cynical misuse of Freudian psychology," Miller spent five years working to free the young man, who was subsequently released when the confession was thrown out. As a reaction to the case, *Creation* depicts "the fratricidal enigma, but seen now as a given of man's nature. . . . The play seeks in fratricide, the first dilemma and the Bible's opening event, for a sign of hope for man" (*T*, 555, 558).

To be sure, Miller took a real risk in attempting to dramatize biblical myth without the constraints of realism, which had long anchored his earlier dramas. In an interview with Harry Brandon in *Harper's*, he himself had declared, while discussing Graham Greene's plays, that "God escapes realism," and that you cannot have realism and a transcendent spiritual play at the same time because you work on a different "form of consciousness. I don't see how that leap is possible within . . . realistic form. To make it you would have to create an inspired world from the beginning; I could believe in that. I don't think I could explain it, but I could believe in it" (*TE*, 228). Now attempting to create such a fictive world, he only partially succeeded. As a result, the play closed after only twenty performances, by far the quickest close of any opening production of his plays, with the exception of *The Man Who Had All the Luck*. Almost unanimously rejected by theater reviewers, who were by now used to dismissing Miller's newer plays, it garnered some of his harshest reviews. Speaking for many, Jack Kroll caustically concluded in a *Newsweek* review, "quite

---

33. In *Timebends* Miller writes that "It was only in college that I discovered the Bible." At first ridiculing it as a "manmade collection" of fantasy and mocking its authenticity with sophomoric questions, he gradually recognized its authority. "Slowly . . . it began to matter less that humans had authored the Bible, for what remained was hypnotic" (*T*, 558–59).

simply, his pastiche of the book of Genesis deserves no comment or any attempt to unravel its stupifyingly boring muddleheadedness and I hereby order my fingers to stop typing about it."[34] Miller certainly was aware of the risk he was taking. Abandoning the elements of realism for fantasy and myth, he lapses into philosophical rhetoric and manipulation of characters as agents of discourse. Nonetheless, *Creation* examines the ancient question of how a just God could allow "such monstrous acts" as Abel's murder and why he "has apparently designed mankind so as to perpetuate them" (*T*, 558). Though a slight piece and at times obscure, the play confronts the paradox that surfaces so often in Miller's plays: Although no moral victory can be gained without escaping the tyranny of innocence, such self-awareness can produce paralyzing self-judgment.

Comic elements are certainly not absent in many Miller texts, and he admits that even in writing *The Crucible*, "I often wished I'd had the temperament to have done an absurd comedy, since that is what the situation often deserved" (*E*, 290). *Creation*, however, marks his first sustained effort to write a comedy. At times whimsical and often bordering on the irreverent or near obscene, it nonetheless treats with growing seriousness the metaphysical and existential questions he poses in his earlier plays of the sixties. The story of the Fall is "the first tragedy in our religious mythology," Miller told Janet Balakian, "but I treated it comically as man's groping his way to his own human nature with no instruction" (*TE*, 485). To Ann Massa, however, "The issue of the fall into good and evil is only sketchily addressed, and sin is treated perfunctorily. The fall is into potency; the question is what to do with that power."[35] Yet Miller clearly intended the play as a dramatization of the loss of innocence, the seminal theme in all his major works and the basis of his tragic vision, which presupposes the capacity to choose, accept responsibility, and bear consequences: "The fall is the fall from the arms of God, the right to live, to eat, to be conscious that there exists all the world. It's the fall from unconscious existence and from the pleasant and unconscious slavery of childhood. . . . [T]he fall is the threat of freedom, of having to make choices instead of having them made for

34. Jack Kroll, "Double Trouble." Weales called *Creation* "The most vulgar reworking of the biblical material that I can recall" ("Clichés in the Garden").
35. Massa, "Some Kind of Love Story," 128.

you" (*Conv.*, 354). Elementally grounded in Miller's conception of tragedy despite its comic tone, *Creation* moves from near farce to the dark moment when Cain kills Abel, and reaffirms the tragic nature of human existence. As we have discussed, those who claim innocence, in Miller's view, prevent the redemptive, if potentially destructive, power of self-consciousness. This pattern of drama, in which action moves climactically to a moment of self-awareness, parallels what Miller sees as the rhythmic progression of tragedy. Once again, he distinguishes between pathos, which can produce "sadness, sympathy, identification and even fear," and tragedy, which in addition "brings us to knowledge or enlightenment" (*TE*, 9).

God and Lucifer establish the dialectical struggle in the play, not between good and evil but, as Schlueter and Flanagan note, between the "Good of Evil" and the "Good of Good," a juxtaposition of opposites.[36] In many respects the debate between them embodies the Romantics' conception of the Fall, especially as expressed in Blake, Shelley, and Byron. On one hand Lucifer represents the good of evil as he plays a sort of Blakean rebel shaking the chains of a god of moral absolutism. Lucifer psychoanalyzes the deity, claiming that God put the Tree of Knowledge in the garden "to tempt Himself" and that "He's not of one mind about innocence" (*CWOB*, 19). As the unacknowledged Other, he utters the Faustian cry, "Now Evil be my good" (19), and contends that only through his disobedience "was Eve made pregnant with mankind" (36), fathered not by Adam but by Lucifer himself. He rebels against the tyranny of innocence and tells God, "You've got to thin out the innocence down there" (14), because without some opposite to innocence, some capacity for free will, there is no escape from stasis. Claiming to be God's agent, his own unsuspected Other, he insists, "I am God's corrected symmetry, that festering embrace which keeps the world from impotent virtue" (36). And the somewhat befuddled God must confess to his ambivalence: "I have never before been in conflict with Myself"

36. Schlueter and Flanagan, *Arthur Miller*, 123. Moss compares the debate between God and Lucifer to the "recurring father-son situation" in Miller's dramas and the "prosecution-defense interplay" between Walter and Victor, Joe Keller and Chris, the witch-hunters and Proctor, Alfieri and Eddie, Leduc and Von Berg—both sides expressing the extreme positions of "realism versus idealism, survival or success versus respect or love, disillusioned detachment versus innocent faith" (*Arthur Miller*, 86).

(32).[37] Even though God rejects Lucifer's offer to corule the world and resists the more subtle suggestion that Lucifer be "the God of what-they-are and you in charge of improvements" (87), he must ask of his Other, "Why do I miss him?" (42). He appears to need his Lucifer as Faust needs his Mephistopheles.

But Miller implies that though Lucifer's disobedience frees humanity from "impotent virtue," it also poses a greater threat in the scheme of human history—a world without moral distinctions and so without choice or responsibility. At the climax of the drama, when he tries to stop Abel's sacrifice to God, Lucifer, throwing off his mask and identifying with human freedom, pronounces that "Nobody's guilty anymore! / . . . I declare one massive, eternal, continuous parole! / From here on out there is no sin or innocence / But only Man" (CWOB, 86). He really offers the modern accommodation of good and evil, an easy neutrality that dissolves away any responsibility for action as well as guilt. In other words, he attempts to reconstruct Eden, where "people would never come to hate themselves, and there's an end of guilt. Another Eden, and everybody innocent again" (39). He reiterates what Miller saw as the morally degrading invasion of a cynical realism in art and the modern temperament when "along came psychology to tell us that we were again victims . . . and we are essentially irresponsible" (TE, 212).

Ironically, having failed to convince Cain not to murder Abel because "if man will not kill man, God is unnecessary" (CWOB, 94), Lucifer accuses God of arranging Abel's murder. God admits that he did, hoping that Cain, "remembering his love for Abel and for me, even in his fury[, would] lay down his arms" (98). He wanted Cain to choose good. Yet God discovers that "love . . . is not enough" and that human beings "love, and with love, kill brothers" (103), a theme that runs through much of Miller's work, especially echoing Quentin's query: "But love, is love enough? What love, what wave of pity will ever reach this knowledge—I know how to kill. . . . And what is the cure? . . . No, not love" (AF, 113). Even in this

37. Miller's discussion here is reminiscent of Jung's discussion of ontological and theological issues in Answer to Job, although Miller has not to my knowledge mentioned Jung as a possible source or inspiration. He was familiar with Jung's works, however, once telling Robert Corrigan that discoveries attributed to "Freud, Adler and the rest of them, and Jung" were in fact already part of the "old literature" of the Greeks, biblical writers, and other ancient literatures (Conv., 257).

despair, though, Eve finds a basis of hope: "If [Cain] loved his brother, maybe now he feels . . ." (*CWOB*, 102). Because humankind is born "not of dust alone, but [of] dust and love," guilt and responsibility may emerge after innocence. "But what about Cain?" Eve asks. "How do I hand him his breakfast tomorrow: How do I call him to dinner? 'Come, mankiller, I have meat for thee?'" (101). And even as he disappears offstage, God replies, "what did you say to me a moment ago—'Why can't we just live?' Why can't you do it? Take your unrepentant son and start living" (101). As in Thorton Wilder's *Skin of Our Teeth*, Cain remains part of the human family, the agent of the ubiquitous potential for human violence. It is, of course, Quentin's awareness as well, that even knowing—indeed, because of knowing—that we are all potential Cains, we must opt for life "not in some garden of wax fruit and painted trees, that lie of Eden, but after, after the Fall . . ." (*AF*, 113).

Creation is highly untypical of Miller's work in its rather flat characterizations, fantastical elements, and sometimes obscure dialogue. Its themes nonetheless interfuse the rest of the canon, and the conclusion defines what Miller describes as the essential human predicament. Adam, who finally affirms human existence divorced from "the lie of God, the false tears of a killer repenting!" cries out, "Cain, we are surrounded by the beasts! And God's not coming any more. . . . Boy, we are all that's left responsible!" (*CWOB*, 101, 106). It is in this world East of Eden that Miller's protagonists live, in a landscape without metaphysical certainties, where good and evil yet reside in the self and where choices must therefore be made and consequences borne.

At the end of the play, as God walks off like a strolling deity, he leaves the first family its "just desserts"—paradoxically, simultaneously in guilt and in rebellion against the paralyzing power of guilt, and in harsh self-judgment potentially redeemed by action, by acts of compassion, and by forgiveness, like those of a Holga or Von Berg, who choose to live even at the price of innocence. As Jacques Huisman of the *Théâtre National de Belgique* has commented, "*Creation* is as dark in its existential content as any of its predecessors" (*AMC*, 230); but it nonetheless offers the painful hope of tragedy as well. Like the other plays of the sixties and seventies, *Creation* expresses what Henry Schvey calls "the problematical nature of our perception of reality."[38] In this play, Miller evokes a moral as well as existential crisis, for if nothing is certain—if we cannot distinguish reality from illusion—then how can good and evil not be equally elusive and chameleonic in their nature? And yet it is this paradoxical nature that presents the dynamic of good ever becoming evil and evil that begets good, and so generates moral actions and choices. Temporarily abandoning the New York stage after the failure of *Creation* and its musical adaptation, *Up from Paradise*,[39] performed at Ann Arbor two years later in 1974, Miller did not desert the theater itself or his continuing search for a moral center in the human drama. In his plays of the last quarter of the century he has continued to hold fast to his central themes and concerns in the light of a growing cynicism and his own gradual accommodation of postmodern themes.

38. Schvey, "Arthur Miller: Songs of Innocence and Experience," 92.

39. As the title implies, the musical version of *Creation* emphasizes the positive meaning of the play. Miller made a number of significant changes in the new text, especially diminishing the debates between God and Lucifer and Lucifer's importance generally. More importantly, he dropped the branding of Cain and showed Angels covering Abel's body as Adam and Eve come to the awareness that life must continue. For an excellent comparison of the two texts, see Welland, who concludes that "*Up from Paradise* is more of a piece but less of a challenge" (*Miller the Playwright*, 132).

6   Other Plays of the 1970s and 1980s

After the failure of *Creation of the World and Other Business* in 1972, Miller waited for five years before attempting to stage a new play, excluding the unsuccessful musical adaptation of *Creation* in 1974 (and television productions of *Incident at Vichy* and *After the Fall*). Originally intended to premiere at the Long Wharf Theater in New Haven, preparatory to staging a New York production, *The Archbishop's Ceiling* eventually premiered at the Kennedy Center in Washington, D.C., when Miller could not complete the script in time for the scheduled Connecticut production. Published with *The American Clock* in a 1989 reissue with an introduction by Miller,[1] *The Archbishop's Ceiling*, like *The American Clock*, explores a given historical moment, though very differently from the second work. *The Archbishop's Ceiling* traces the profound effect of a possibly bugged ceiling on a group of writers meeting in the seventies in an unnamed Iron Curtain country under tight state control. The other play returns to the Great Depression, which informs so much of Miller's writing, and employs the form of what Miller called "A Vaudeville," a sprawling epic partially based on Studs Terkel's *Hard Times*. The first work confronts the "present" of the late seventies when, Miller remarks in the introduction, "Power everywhere seemed to have transformed itself from a forbidding line of troops into an ectoplasmic lump that simply swallowed up the righteous sword as it struck" (*AC/ACl*, vii); the later text recounts

1. Miller modified the initial stage version of *The Archbishop's Ceiling* in time for the successful Bristol Theatre Royal production in 1985. He deleted a character named Martin to focus on the four principal players: Adrian, Maya, Marcus, and Sigmund. For a comparison of the earlier and later versions, see Welland, *Miller the Playwright*, 156–64.

the tragic, at times humorous, consequences of the Great Depression. One describes a world after the Fall, the other the American Eden in the act of falling.

The Archbishop's Ceiling

Doubtlessly, *The Archbishop's Ceiling* is in part a reflection of Miller's years of service as president of PEN, the international writers' association, from 1965 to 1969, during which time he visited several East European countries, including Czechoslovakia, where he met with Václav Havel and expressed his support of dissident writers. It was a decade when "The very notion of thinking, conceptualizing, theorizing—the mind itself—went up the flue," he wrote in an essay entitled "Miracles" (*E*, 132). And yet despite the power of tyrannical forces "to distort and falsify the structure of reality," the determination of writers in countries like Czechoslovakia expressed "something like love . . . a prophetic yearning and demand" (174).[2] Despite the largely negative press that closed the show and aborted a New York production, Miller kept his faith in the play. He told a *Washington Post* critic, "I'm far from giving up on the play. . . . I think of the play as a string quartet, yet not unlike 'The Price,' which also had four voices." And he began to interpret the play as a kind of religious allegory, telling the interviewer, "Your man who saw God in the play is quite right, though I certainly didn't know it while working on it. . . . I think of the play as a widening, lateral movement of how we all are affected by things, powers, beyond us, circumstances and people of which we have not only no control but no knowledge." And he extended the religious interpretation, even commenting that Sigmund, the dissident writer whose fate constitutes the central plot in the play, is "Christ. He knows that the time will come when he must openly, actively oppose Marcus," the "state" author who may or may not be a spy for the regime. And he even

2. An interesting 1974 essay by Miller, "What's Wrong with This Picture?" reproduces the photograph of a banned Czech writer and his wife knee-deep in water—"A couple that has learned how to live without illusions and thus without severe disappointment" in waters that may go up or down. Like Sigmund in *The Archbishop's Ceiling*, they refuse to emigrate even though the regime acts as though they do not exist (*E*, 139–44).

says of Maya—a former mistress of both the visiting American author Adrian Wallace and Marcus—"you might think of [her] as Mag-
dalene," who knows that "Sigmund has retreated to the bedroom,
needing to be alone to gather his forces, his nerves. This is the time
when Sigmund must have his apartness in a desert, a garden . . . a
quiet time."[3] But as sometimes happens when Miller explains his
plays, he provides as much obscurity as clarity. It would be highly
reductive to see the play in such bald terms as Miller's comments
suggest, and it is doubtful that he really intended them to be taken
too literally.

Nonetheless, the play does describe a world that raises elemental
religious issues, even as it portrays a locale where God is only a faint
shimmer in a "palace" claimed by the secular state. Here the writers
and artists play out roles before an absent God, who may or may not
be listening in, an image not unlike that evoked by the naturalist
Loren Eiseley in *The Firmament of Time*, who asks,

> What if we are not playing on the center stage? What if the
> Great Spectacle has no terminus and no meaning? What if there
> is no audience beyond the footlights, and the play, in spite of
> bold villains and posturing heroes, is a shabby repeat perfor-
> mance in an echoing vacuity?[4]

It is such a frightening and ambiguous arena in which the play occurs.
The cavernous space of the archbishop's palace, long deserted by any
spiritual powers that may have once possessed it, provides a setting
of sustained ambiguity and tension, where, as June Schlueter comments, the characters become "performers, uncertain of their scripts.
Each . . . creates, interprets, and revises the truth, collapsing fiction
and reality into one indistinguishable line."[5] Miller confronts a postmodern world, one in which God in any conventional sense has ab-
sented himself from the stage, leaving only the enclosed remains of
a failing structure, symbolized by ineffectual light absorbed by dark

3. Richard L. Coe, "What Happened to Miller's Play?"
4. Loren Eiseley, *The Firmament of Time*, 118–19. Bigsby writes that Miller acts
as "a kind of god who observes the characters he creates" in a world devoid of God.
"Remove that heavenly audience, deny the hearing ear and the seeing eye and
what would remain? A text with no author" (*Modern American Drama*, 113–14).
5. June Schlueter, *Dramatic Closure: Reading the End*, 62.

walls, dimly lit corridors "of large unsurfaced stones," and a ceiling "darkened unevenly by soot and age" (AC, 3). "Wherever you put a lamp it makes the rest seem darker" (5); the four central characters meet here, searching for truth and leaving the audience, finally, to perform as a substitute God who can somehow sort truth from fiction and arrive at judgment. As audience, we assume, willingly or not, the God's-eye view, seeing and overhearing, in ironic mimicry of the supposed microphones hidden in the ceiling.

The room has been usurped by the new order, reducing the once-vast palace to a sitting room and a bedroom we never see—"But the rest of it's never used" (AC, 5), Maya tells Adrian. Contemporary culture partly invades the space (a contemporary lamp that looks "like an electrified hookah," "A Bauhaus chair in chrome and black leather," and current books), but it is absorbed in the two-foot-thick walls that lend "weight and power" to the room. The juxtaposition of old and new, religious and secular, seen and unseen, frames the action and underscores the ambiguity posed by the constant question of whether or not microphones are in fact concealed in the ceiling. Miller creates an empty space in which illusion and truth coexist but cannot be distinguished, an enclosed garden defined by an absent God who nonetheless exerts his presence and compels characters to respond in the fear that he exists and overhears. The supposed microphones disarm all the characters as they become unwitting actors in an absurdist plot.

In relationship to the earlier plays, this play signals a major shift in Miller's evolving dramatic vision. Asked by Christopher Bigsby if the play reveals a growing sense that "the moral world has begun to disappear slightly," Miller responded, "Oh yes, very much so. I think that it's been doing that in my work for a long time" (AMC, 165). He acknowledged in a 1989 interview with Janet Balakian that his later plays focus on the "necessity to reconstruct a moral world in the ethical void left by the death of God," that they are "an extension of [my] earlier plays" but "more apocalyptic. . . . After this is truly the void." On this deserted stage, characters must, as Miller remarked to Steven Centola, "talk themselves into positions."[6] Rather than assuming prescriptive positions reflecting a fixed moral stance

6. Janet N. Balakian, "An Interview with Arthur Miller," 39–40; Centola, " 'Just Looking,' " 94.

and established set of values against which a character is measured and defined, as in the tradition of conventional tragedy and Miller's earlier plays, on this stage without God, moral certitude or even a clearly defined political presence, characters all struggle to locate a moral center. As critics have suggested, this no doubt represents Miller's struggle to accommodate the seeming relativity of the absurdist drama of the sixties and seventies and its major proponents, especially Beckett, Pinter, and Albee. As George asks Nick in *Who's Afraid of Virginia Woolf?* "Truth and illusion. Who knows the difference, eh toots? Eh?"[7]

In the lengthy opening scene of the play the American writer, Adrian, after an absence of four years from the country, converses with Maya in the great room at the archbishop's residence. Ostensibly, he has come to escape the boredom of a conference on modern writers in Paris, but a different motivation compels him. Under Maya's persistent question, "Why have you come back?" he confesses that he has returned to learn more about her and the country because he has written a novel about her. When he reassures her that "nobody'll recognize you" (AC, 13), she senses a deeper motive, a desire to expose the tyranny of the state and to determine the validity of another writer's claim that she and Marcus organize "orgies" for young writers at the palace in order to expose and endanger their efforts to write against the regime. The truth becomes ever more ambiguous in a convoluted web of discourse.

Even at the beginning, Adrian describes the view looking down on the city as "a dream" (AC, 4). And a whole series of topics keeps raising the question of truth and illusion. Maya declares that she has reconstructed herself to match the figures in *Vogue* magazine, "the only modern art that excites me," modeling herself after the "beautiful, stupid, everlasting" fashion goddesses that people the magazine (9). Claiming to embrace the images in *Vogue* where "everyone is

---

7. Edward Albee, *Who's Afraid of Virginia Woolf? A Play*, 201. Miller has expressed qualified praise for Albee in interviews, though he has claimed that Albee differs from Beckett and other absurdist dramatists because he "is essentially much more concrete in terms of behavior and is much more realistic and is much closer to the realistic tradition of this country" (*Conv.*, 151). Albee has expressed appreciation for Miller's "serious writing" and claims that "He and I have been to the barricades together often and I am never surprised to see him. His plays and his conscience are a cold burning force" (AMC, 1).

successful" and "No one has apologized because she was beautiful and happy," she insists, "I believe this magazine" (12). Having discovered when her pet bird, Lulu, died that "she" was in fact a male, she has apparently accommodated the illusory nature of reality. Indeed, her own name means "illusion."

Adrian, too, lives in a world of make-believe. Even his marriage to Ruth proves a mirage. Having never married, he and Ruth feign that they are married—"We're apart together" (AC, 9). More importantly, like Miller's protagonist in his short-story-turned-screenplay *Fame*, Adrian doubts his own authenticity as a writer. Reflecting the writer-protagonist of Miller's short story and Quentin in *After the Fall*, Adrian stands in judgment of himself and of his art. "Here I'm laying out motives, characterizations, secret impulses—the whole psychological chess game—when the truth is I'm not sure anymore that I believe in psychology. That anything really determines what we're going to do" (9). His fictive world, ironically, is elementally fictitious, raising profound doubt about not only his own work but also the very function and nature of art itself. Placing himself before the bar in a stance of self-judgment—certainly a familiar pose in Miller's work—he may well articulate Miller's growing uncertainty about the value of art, even his own, in a world without some metaphysical core.

Adrian tells Maya that Ruth "cured" her fits of depression by taking a pill that "plugged her in to some . . . some power" (AC, 10). Yet she is not really aware of her true self, he argues—"The interior landscape has not been lit up. What has changed is her reaction to power. Before she feared it, now she enjoys it" (10). Thinking of himself and of his art, he wonders aloud what would have happened if Hamlet and Socrates had possessed such a miracle cure. What would have been lost? "Some wisdom, some knowledge found in suffering" (11), he surmises, but little else. Miller appears to voice his own growing sense of the demise of tragedy that critics like George Steiner had already announced (Steiner's famous critical study *The Death of Tragedy* came out in 1961).[8] Miller seemingly confronts the full force of postmodern cynicism more in this play than ever before: the denial

---

8. George Steiner concludes that "tragedy is that form of art which requires the intolerable burden of God's presence. It is now dead because His shadow no longer falls upon us as it fell on Agamemnon or Macbeth or Athalie" (*The Death of Tragedy*, 353).

of permanence, meaning, or even truth in art; and art's replacement by an oppressive will to power. "It's hard for anyone to know what to believe in this country" (17), Adrian suggestively remarks; and yet, for Adrian, the search for truth provides the impetus for action. "[I]t's like some Jerusalem for me" (13), he tells Maya of this illusory land of truth and deception, a kind of religious quest to find a surety in which he can believe.

Throughout the scene, we are unable as audience to discern with any assurance what is true about the characters or their motives. On one hand, Adrian reveals his doubt of Marcus's integrity, implying that his former friend is "a bit of an operator" (AC, 14) who has sold out to the power structure. Maya, however, counters his suspicion, noting that Marcus spent six years in state imprisonment for his beliefs. Furthermore, she challenges Adrian's holier-than-thou attitude, just as Miller's earlier work seemed to undermine the claims of his fiercest idealists, like the self-righteous Chris Keller and the self-congratulatory Quentin standing in judgment of Maggie. When Adrian tells Maya about Sigmund's new manuscript's being concealed behind his chimney, Maya stiffens and draws him into the hall where "We can talk" (21), all but admitting to the hidden microphones. When she interrogates Adrian, though, we wonder if it is to help Sigmund or to pump more information for the unseen government. Finally, reentering the sitting room, Adrian responds to Maya's request that he protect Sigmund's work by speaking a retraction for the benefit of the microphones. He tells Maya that he gave the manuscript to a second cousin who took it to Paris. We as viewers, concealed like the microphones, cannot know whether it is Maya or Adrian who speaks the full truth or even why they say what they do. "[T]his is what I never got into my book," Adrian finally concludes: "—this doubleness. This density with angels overhead. Like power always with you in a room. Like God, in a way" (23). As the scene ends, he asks Maya, "Is it always like a performance? Like we're quoting ourselves?" (24). The questions remain unanswered, and so when Adrian blurts out, "You're a government agent?" Maya aptly responds, "What can I say? Will you believe me?" (25). As Martha tells George in Albee's play, "Truth and illusion . . . you don't know the difference."[9]

9. Albee, *Who's Afraid of Virginia Woolf?* 202.

Even as Adrian claims his abiding faith in Maya, desperately want-ing to believe that she is in reality as he has portrayed her in his book—"that deep inside you're a rebel and you hate this goddamn government," she protests, "Wait a minute . . ." (AC, 26)—and Marcus suddenly enters with his apparent current mistress, Irina, a "beautiful, very young" Danish woman, wife of the head of Danish programming for the BBC. With the appearance of Sigmund, whom Marcus claims to have met accidentally at the airport and brought to the palace, the quartet of main characters is complete, and the extraordinary conversation that ensues for the remainder of the play charts a circuitous journey to an uncertain end.

In a sense, *The Archbishop's Ceiling* treats innocence as a kind of naïveté. The characters lack full self-awareness and vacillate from one opinion to another, at times seemingly betraying others and be-ing betrayed—at times betraying themselves, acting heroically and being rescued by the heroism of others. They do not know who they themselves are, much less the others. In this arena of shifting truths the sustaining metaphor is art itself, the capacity of writers or actors to create and recreate the characters others see as the embodiment of their own creations. The drama moves through constant mutations, and characters assume a protean capacity to evolve and reconstruct their identities as they define, and are defined by, other characters. As they assume new roles, they come to see themselves as some-how a construction of the others—and all of them in some measure creations of the power source embedded in the ceiling. Here stark cynicism butts up against hopeful idealism. The ultimate tyranny, fi-nally, is the presence of power itself, which at once determines each character's actions as an expression of the will to power and makes each subject to the tyranny of others' perceptions.

Discovering that Sigmund's manuscript has already been taken by the authorities, who possibly discovered it from Adrian's own re-marks to Maya, the American author threatens to publicize the theft; and Marcus, cognizant of the bugged ceiling, instructs him to "*con-tinue speaking, to amplify*" his threat to assure that the microphones pick it up. Ironically—perhaps cynically—he concludes that "the government spends a lot keeping [the ceilings] in repair." And Sig-mund confirms that "This is true. They are repairing all the angels. It is very good to be an angel in our country. Yes, we shall have the most perfect angels in the whole world" (AC, 39). But even when

Marcus hints at the state's transparent attempt to project innocence, he remains suspect. Sigmund noted earlier that Marcus secured permission to carry a weapon on the airplane despite the law against it. Furthermore, when Adrian starts to go with Maya to get supplies for a party, Marcus stops him, apparently to maintain control of his movement. And when he runs outside to rescue Maya and protect Sigmund from hoodlums out for revenge against the dissident writer, "the traitor to the motherland," his intentions remain unclear. Even Maya is "alarmed and angry" at Marcus, blaming him for betraying Sigmund, even though she, too, is apparently an agent of the state. Marcus also announces that he has invited Alexandra, daughter of the minister of the interior, whose reputation as a writer soared following her father's rise to power. Sigmund immediately sees this as evidence that "I am to be arrested" and that Alexandra "is collecting the dead for her father" and will try to force him to go on television to apologize to the government—"Mea culpa . . . kissing their ass" (48).

Adrian, too, accuses Marcus of betrayal, telling Sigmund that Marcus is "envious of you" as the writer who has replaced him in prominence and that "he's trying to destroy you" (AC, 51). Yet even as he seems to judge Marcus, Sigmund as suddenly defends him, claiming in his broken English that "Is possible to believe he is trying to help me," forcing Adrian to wonder, "Could he have simply wanted to do something decent. . . . [M]aybe he figures your only chance is actually to make peace with the government" (52). But when Marcus tells the others that the government program is to drive Sigmund out of the country or "to make it impossible for him to function" and proposes "he must emigrate" (54), it remains uncertain what motivates him. Taking Adrian into the hall, Marcus responds to Adrian's charge that he is a government agent, contending that contrary to bringing writers to the palace to expose them, "I have always warned people to be careful what they say in here" (58). To test him, Adrian insists that he repeat his remarks in the bugged room. Echoing Miller's own efforts on behalf of censored writers, he tells Marcus, "Level with him, Marcus . . . this is your Hemingway, your Faulkner, for Christ's sake—help him!" (59).

The lengthy first act ends with Adrian's challenge and Marcus's anger at the American author's accusations. With rich irony, Marcus reminds Adrian that the regime has "a right to be terrified" by Sigmund's "fiction," a bold affirmation of the transforming power of art that Adrian himself began to doubt when he first expressed to Maya his fear that "the whole psychological chess game" of his fiction is pure illusion. Even as he struggles to discern Marcus's motivation, Adrian exposes his own duplicity, his capacity to betray, and his self-righteousness. Marcus, June Schlueter has commented, "suggests that Adrian's concern for Sigmund's manuscript is really a concern for the story he is recording and creating."[10]

In the extraordinarily complex second act, the turns, surprises, and recriminations continue as the action revolves around whether or not Sigmund will flee the country. The characters all incriminate one other, and the action crescendos to a conclusion, if not a resolution. Telling the others that Sigmund is to be put on trial, the protean Marcus continues vigorously to protest his innocence: "Break off my trip, fly across Europe, and now I'm asked . . . to justify myself?" (AC, 61). Reestablishing the theme of truth and illusion, he claims that a government agent in the London embassy told him to tell Sigmund "to get out this month or he will eat his own shit for five or six years. . . . It was quite an act" (63)—of course we are not certain who is the real actor, though a number of revelations suggest that Marcus may be more authentic than he might seem to be. We discover that not only did he spend time in prison for his political protests but also that he served in the American army against the Nazis for three years and was nearly a U.S. citizen. As importantly, he edited a liberal magazine that was "like some sort of Bible" to reformers, which "every week" published "a new prophecy" and was the first to dare to publish W. H. Auden's poetry (70). When Adrian charges "I think you've accepted something" in return for supporting the government, Marcus aptly quips to the spoiled American writer, "And you haven't?" (82).

Wrestling with the nature of truth after the collapse of the deity and a moral center, Sigmund describes their lives as a "bad" play

10. June Schlueter, "Power Play: Arthur Miller's *The Archbishop's Ceiling*," 137. Miller told Janet Balakian that Adrian is "doing the same thing as the bugged ceiling," snooping, but that "the purpose is something else." Though "exploitive" of the others, Adrian "has to do that in order to create his image" ("An Interview," 41). Bigsby concludes that, as an artist, Adrian is involved in making fictions just like the new power brokers in this realm of "competing fictions." The dilemma becomes how to discover some center of truth and "some basis for moral action" amid such seeming relativity (*Critical Introduction*, 236–37).

within a play: "Our country is now a theatre, where no one is permitted to walk out and everyone is obliged to applaud"; he later alludes
to their metaphysical crisis as "some sort of theatre, no? Very bad
theatre—our emotions have no connection with the event" (AC,
78, 90). Similarly, Marcus looks to the heavens emblazoned on the
archbishop's ceiling and comments that it "was never anything but a
sentimental metaphor; a God which now is simply a form of art" (83).
Power becomes aligned with art, and the essential question becomes
who is writing the script and, more elementally, who constructs and
controls the self. Bigsby and others are surely right in claiming that
Miller ventures into the dark world of the absurd, if not entirely
succumbing to its cynical vision.

The thin plot accelerates when Alexandra calls to inform them
that Sigmund's manuscript will be returned. To the others, this provides impetus for Sigmund's departure: Adrian vows to take him to
Paris and force his publisher to give Sigmund a large advance on
his book, and Maya insists that he must "get out" before a trial.
But despite his immediate joy, Sigmund begins to feel he has been
given a part to play in a government-scripted text. Sensing that he
is being fated to play "some sort of . . . comical Jesus Christ" (94),
he wonders if Marcus's story about the government agent in London is true and doubts that his trial is really being planned, convinced that Marcus was brought back "to make sure my departure"
(98). Sensing that the regime returned his manuscript only to secure his gratitude, corrupt his moral protest, and assure his exile,
knowing that he "will not be able to write in some other country,"
Sigmund asks, "How will I support this silence I have brought on
myself?" (96).

The climax occurs when Sigmund poses the ultimate question,
which applies to all the characters. In the absence of God, he asks,
who has scripted his part? "Who is commanding me? Who is this
voice? *Who is speaking to me?*" (AC, 97); and Maya gestures upward to
the ceiling and replies, "It is there. . . . [T]hey have heard it all. . . .
Who else have we been speaking to all evening[?]" (97). Although
Marcus insists "It isn't true, there's nothing" (97), it really does not
matter whether or not the microphones exist. The characters act
and react as though they do, and so they must struggle somehow to
maintain the integrity of a self distorted by being forced to perform
before an unseen power.

As Sigmund wonders who he really is and who the others really are (he asks Maya, "I know your name. Who is this woman?" [AC, 98]), Marcus calls him a "moral blackmailer" and imposes moral choice on Sigmund: "We have taken all the responsibility and left you all the freedom to call us morally bankrupt. . . . [T]he responsibility moves to you. Now it's yours. All yours. We have done what was possible; now you will do what is necessary, or turn out the lights" (99). To this, Maya charges Sigmund with not being able to write without hatred of the state: "They are your life, your partner in this dance that cannot stop or you will die of silence. . . . [T]hey are in you, darling. And if you stay . . . it is also for your profit . . . as it is for ours to tell you to go" (101).

The price of freedom is precisely what Marcus tells Sigmund it is: moral responsibility. It is the central theme in all of Miller's work, but here the issue of choice remains richly complicated and ambiguous. Although the play ends with Sigmund's vow not to leave and admonishment to Adrian that he give "certain letters" to writers throughout the world (writers Miller himself knew as the president of PEN), nagging issues still remain. Even after he asks Maya to "forgive me" and she gives her blessing, stroking his face and saying "Thank you," the moral dilemma does not disappear, not even when Sigmund cries out, "Oh, my god! Thank you Maya" (AC, 102). There seems no doubt that Sigmund takes a heroic stand and embodies the moral courage Miller has defended in all his political and artistic life, but the struggle of reconstructing a moral world finds no simple affirmation. After all, Marcus, too, can claim a certain integrity and moral courage. And there may be a bit of self-parody in the role of Adrian, the outsider who ostensibly comes to rescue Sigmund but is motivated as well by the "profit" he can gain by exposing his friends and former lover. Yet, despite his perhaps unconscious selfishness and naïveté, "there's something precious" about Adrian as well, Miller has said. "If the world loses what he's demanding, it's all gone. We would simply end up a beehive."[11] To be sure, the moral center of the play does seem to shift from much of Miller's earlier works. In them, the plays tend to move toward a moral resolution reflecting an established code of morality.

11. Centola, "'Just Looking,'" 93.

The moral vision in John Proctor's world confirms a single moral stance, whereas in *The Archbishop's Ceiling* the focus shifts from *the* moral end to the *search for* a moral position and the affirmation of self. In a way, Miller attempts to accommodate the relativity of postmodernism without abandoning the idea of moral choice and responsibility.

It is easy enough to argue that in this play Miller rejects outdated causal dramaturgy and the constrictions of Ibsenian drama or classical tragedy. The trope of the bugged ceiling challenges the very concept of causality and moral certainty and moves the play closer to modern metatheater. And Adrian's inability to believe in the transcendence of his art, a possible reflection of Miller's own growing uncertainty, constitutes a commentary on the nature of art itself and a fading faith in the concept of a linear plot with a defined beginning, middle, and end, and even of character as the personalities all dissolve in the presence of the unidentifiable power mounted in the ceiling, a power that has usurped not only God but also the essential role of the artist to create reality and construct a self. But even if the play represents Miller's later attempts to probe deeply into metaphysical questions, it would be a mistake to consider his work a complete departure from the earlier texts. Though no doubt tempered by absurdist drama and postmodern concerns, the play retains much that marks it as a Miller text. Rather than forgoing Ibsen, the play in fact seems to follow the later Ibsen as he moved closer to symbolic drama and explored profoundly the very nature of art and the integrity of the artist in late plays like *The Master Builder, John Gabriel Borkman*, and especially *When We Dead Awaken*—even the missing manuscript, an echo of *Hedda Gabler*, recalls Ibsen. And the unresolved ending echoes the rich ambiguity of Ibsen as much as it does the nihilism of much of the modern theater. Moving undeniably closer to the postmodern stage and accommodating many of its concerns, Miller in his later plays provides a link to the earlier canon as much as he rejects it.[12]

12. Even in his 1989 interview with Janet Balakian, Miller repeated his unwillingness to succumb totally to the absurdist position. He expressed discomfort with those who "celebrate the meaningless. It ends up with fascism. When they get too comfortable with the inevitable defeat of human hope, with man as a creature who

The American Clock

Although written after Miller's screenplay *Playing for Time*, based on Fania Fenelon's account of her survival at Auschwitz while singing with the concentration camp's Jewish orchestra, *The American Clock* was published in its most widely recognized version jointly with *The Archbishop's Ceiling* in 1989.[13] First successfully premiered at the Spoleto Festival in 1980, it was revised and staged unsuccessfully later the same year at the Harold Clurman Theater in New York, where it closed after only twelve performances. The production was so unsuccessful that some critics considered it evidence that Miller was no longer a force to be reckoned with on the contemporary stage. Nonetheless, the play continued to be performed in various revised versions, most notably at the Mark Taper Forum in Los Angeles and in London in 1986, first at the Cotterhoe Studio and then in a major production at the Olivier that resulted in its being nominated as best new drama of the year. It returned to the American stage in 1988 at the Williamstown Theater Festival, and it was the opening play in New York for the 1997 Signature season devoted to producing Miller texts.

A panoramic string of vignettes of the Depression under the direct influence of Studs Terkel's *Hard Times*, the play seems to break new territory in Miller's canon. Injecting more humor than appears in most of his plays, Miller's restaging of one of the two major shaping events in his, and he would argue the nation's, life takes the form of what he calls a "mural" or "vaudeville." Arranged in a series of quick-paced scenes, the play's structure seems a far departure from the early Miller. Employing a series of recitations interspersed with period songs by Gershwin, Berlin, and Kerns, the play portrays

---

is doomed to slip on a banana peel, I smell dictatorship around the corner" ("A Conversation with Arthur Miller," 163).

13. Miller himself has noted the major difference between the earlier and later versions of the text. He points out that "the first emphasizes the family, whereas the second emphasizes the society." The Grove edition, used in this discussion, is favored by Miller because it more clearly reflects his initial conception of the play as staged at the Spoleto Festival, which he feels he violated when he revised it for the Broadway production in 1980. The later version, upon which the London and Signature productions were based, returns the play to its earlier focus on society. "The family is there in order to illuminate the social crisis" (Balakian, "Interview," 32).

both the personal and public consequences of the economic catas-trophe in comic and tragic form, not unlike the tradition of Yiddish vaudeville, "a vaudeville at the end of the cliff" (E, 310). It is a juxtaposition of the comic and tragic, the epic and the private, the good and the bad.

The play seemingly abandons depth for breadth in its epic sweep. Although the demise of the Baum family serves as the central story, a reflection of Miller's own experiences, the drama forgoes much of character development to erect a wide mosaic of the national crisis, peopled with a large cast of characters from high-stake financiers to a vast assortment of common people scattered across the national landscape: a shoeshine man, a chauffeur, a farm family, a number of blacks, a prostitute, a federal relief supervisor, a seaman, a butcher, law enforcement figures and soldiers, a welfare worker—in all, more than three dozen representatives of America's multicultural melting pot of the twenties.

Although sometimes accused of putting his dramas in structural straitjackets, Miller in this play appears to adapt the openness of the musical stage; but with *The American Clock*, as with *The Archbishop's Ceiling*, it would be a mistake to see the drama as a great departure from the essential Miller. Most obviously, the text conveys Miller's autobiography. The Baum family resembles Miller's own to the de-gree that the Baum son, Lee, directly corresponds to Miller, who was himself trapped in the Depression as an adolescent (Miller was four-teen in 1929) and who also was educated at Michigan and made early attempts to write for the WPA. Miller has of course often spoken of the impact the Crash had on him as a young man, "because I was so convinced of the authority of the system that I lived in and in which my father was a great success" (AMC, 15). More importantly, even though the drama moves closer to Brecht's theater of alienation than any other Miller work—in the way characters are allowed to intrude upon scenes, skits and musical texts are likewise interjected, and Lee and the savvy financier Robertson narrate directly to the audience—it still carries Miller's signature.

Like the rest of Miller's work, even beginning with *The Man Who Had All the Luck*, *The American Clock* is both experimental and a re-iteration of seminal Miller themes. Dennis Welland accurately lists the "big themes of personal responsibility, guilt, the relation between the microcosm of the family and the macrocosm of modern society, the effect of the passing in time on memory and on perspective, the moral stance and value of protest, public and private integrity" as undeniable signature themes.[14] More specifically, we see the continuing saga of the family disrupted by economic and social threat—the Kellers, the Lomans, the Franzes, all bearing witness. Once again Miller dramatizes the inevitable need of the son to be reconciled with his father, a theme introduced even in Miller's apprentice plays at the University of Michigan. Of course the overriding sense of pending fate that lies at the heart of Greek tragedy and Ibsen's plays overshadows the text. Miller has said that "there is a fundamental insecurity in Americans, a fear of falling."[15] And here, as in the established tragedies of the earlier period of Miller's career, the Fall assumes metaphysical and mythic dimensions. A fear that "the whole system would simply stop working" transforms the Depression into "a mythic event" (AMC, 198). And with the sense of a Fall arises a Puritan consciousness of guilt, a consciousness that the economic disaster is a consequence not of accident but judgment. Rather than being uncharacteristic of Miller's early imitations of Greek tragedy and Ibsen's dramatization of a rootless modernity, *The American Clock* retains Miller's shaping vision. As he has remarked to Christopher Bigsby,

> The idea is that there is a clock running on every civilisation. . . . I've gotten obsessed with the idea that we are literally creating our history. . . . I've come out of that playwrighting [sic] tradition which is Greek and Ibsen where the past is the burden of man and it's got to be placed on stage so that he can grapple with it. That's the way those plays are built. It's *now* grappling with *then*, it's the story of how the birds come home to roost. Every play. (AMC, 200–201)

For all the suffering it created, the Depression developed in its survivors a capacity to survive, despite the individuals who jumped from skyscrapers and the disintegration of characters like Rose Baum. It reestablished and generated other values as well, and bestowed a kind of grace or blessing, like the paradoxical nature of tragedy. Above all, a sense of community emerged, as the economic crisis acted as a leveler in the society, producing an ironic democracy of suffering. In

14. Welland, *Miller the Playwright*, 149.
15. Balakian, "Interview," 31.

the play, these changes are presented in images of married children with their own families returning to their parent's homes; families gathering to sing "We gather together to ask the Lord's blessing . . ." (*ACl*, 130); friends circling around a farm family in Iowa to protect the property against the bank's repossessing it; the black Marxist, Irene, rescuing a starving man at the welfare office, insisting "Time has come to say brother" (180); the Baums offering to help the Iowa farmer Taylor when he comes begging after he loses his farm; Rose continuing to assist vagrants, giving the desperate seaman, Stanislaus, a place to stay in the basement; and the senior executive, Theodore Quinn, resigning as president of GE to assist small businesses because the monster company is buying up failing independent businesses and "[it is] haunting me" (145). For many, a transforming guilt produces a sense of responsibility for the larger community. Even the clairvoyant Arthur Robertson, who dreams of the coming Crash and pulls his money out of the stock market in time to escape the disaster, is shocked into consciousness and compassion as he looks down with understanding and even admiration on the thousands living in cardboard boxes below the window of his wealthy Riverside Drive apartment—"Remarkable, the humor they still have, but of course people blame themselves rather than the government" (154).

The very need to survive both ennobles and diminishes the characters who scramble to make it by whatever means. Like the others, Lee's friends adopt any strategies they can to keep from drowning. His college buddy Ralph vows to stay in college another semester solely to get a root canal free from the health service. Another college chum, Joe, a would-be dentist, plots to marry his girlfriend so he can live in her father's house. He ironically gives his prostitute, Isabel, Engels's *The Origin of the Family* so she can understand "that underneath our ideals it's all economics between people, and it shouldn't be" (*ACl*, 163). Meanwhile, Lee's cousin, Sidney, succumbs to his mother's plan that he propose to the landlady's daughter, Doris, so the family can live in their apartment for free.

Using the wide canvas of America—from the Mississippi River, where Lee escapes to work on the river, to an Iowa farm about to be repossessed, and to a speakeasy where a group of ruined financiers gather to cynically assess their fate—Miller paints a portrait of communal disaster. The integrating focus, however, remains on the Baum family and especially on the gradual collapse of Rose Baum, whose defeat, as others have observed, mirrors the nation's spiraling descent. As always in Miller, the fish is in the sea, and the sea is in the fish—"society was in the bedroom, it was in the living room, it was in the kitchen" (AMC, 206). The American clock is a "menacing image," Miller told Studs Terkel; "I was fascinated by the ideal of having an objective view of society and running through it, as a counter-motif, the story of a family" (Conv., 309).

The parallels between Moe Baum and Willy Loman are apparent; though, as Miller has claimed, Moe is "the opposite of Willy Loman" in his unwillingness to "surrender to his defeat" (Conv., 312). Guarded by an unbounded optimism and faith, Moe can endure the most humiliating experiences, borrowing a quarter from Lee to get downtown and pretending to have thrown his son out of the house so Lee can gain a job with the WPA. Despite his blind faith in the future, Moe is "a practical man, a realist," according to Miller. No "romantic" like Willy, he holds "few illusions,"[16] but he can only watch the demise of his fortunes and the dismantling of his family. When Lee returns home to gain his father's approval, he has already accommodated his father's failure and, unlike Biff, has already endured a rite of passage and found himself. It is Rose, though, whose story charts the essential movement of the text.

Although she is used to the luxury of her eleven-room New York apartment and the city's cultural life, Rose at first endures the financial crisis with considerable grace and strength. She willingly pawns the diamond bracelet Moe bought her for her birthday and defends his not declaring bankruptcy because he wanted to protect his reputation and "be honorable." She comforts Lee when his bike is stolen by some desperate thief and stubbornly holds to her faith that "This is going to be a good day—I know it!" (ACl, 154). As the first act concludes, Lee, secure in his mother's reassurances, directly tells the audience, "we pretended that nothing had happened" (156). But when the family settles into a crammed Brooklyn home and Rose must finally give up her beloved piano, she begins to lose control. "How stupid it all is. How Stupid!" she cries out to her absent son: "Oh my dear Lee, wherever you are—believe in something. Anything. But believe" (164). At last trapped in her house with all

16. Ibid., 33.

the windows closed on a hot summer day lest the mortgage collector think the family home, she spills out her bitterness at Moe for not asking his mother for help and wonders, "What is left to believe. The bathroom. I lock myself in and hold on to the faucets so I shouldn't scream" (192). Dreaming of "a young man's death," she fears Lee's fate; and when the doorbell ominously rings, she prays, "Oh, my god, help our dear country . . . and the people!" (200). As Lee reminisces about her for the audience at the conclusion of the play, Rose slips into insanity singing "Life Is Just a Bowl of Cherries," a further reflection of Miller's constant ironic juxtaposition of the tragic and comic throughout the play. "She was so like the country," Lee eulogizes for the audience; "money obsessed her, but what she really longed for was some kind of height where she could stand and see out and around and breathe in the air of her own free life" (203), a longing not unlike Willy Loman's desire to recover the lost world of innocence he once knew before the woods in Brooklyn were replaced by apartment buildings and concrete. Despite her painful end, Lee finds in her a victory in defeat as well: "[A]ll I know for sure is that whenever I think of her, I always end up—with this headful of life!" (203).

The play ends in a certain ambiguity, just as the entire text both affirms human values ironically generated by the Depression and exposes the Crash as a consequence of guilt. Although self-delusion proves destructive in most Miller plays, he argues here that "the dream for a better world does not necessarily have to be an illusion";[17] "You can't be an American without a future" (AMC, 204). The image of the American clock foreshadows a coming doom, perhaps, but also a sense that it continues to beat—"my play should be left with the clock still ticking. We still don't know where we are going, and time is not standing still."[18]

Rather than denying tragic vision in the play, Miller incorporates it in his sprawling structure as an essential interweaving thread. However much the characters seem to be victims, they are also suffering the consequences of their own crass materialism, indifference, and naïveté. The excesses of the twenties sowed the seeds

17. Centola, "'Just Looking,'" 90.
18. Balakian, "Interview," 33. Miller told Bigsby, "I'm not a fatalist. I don't believe there is no hope for man, but I do believe we stand on a very thin edge and that it is liable to go down at any moment" (AMC, 20).

of destruction, so it is no accident that the characters feel some sense of guilt and responsibility despite the comic tone and residual optimism. Miller aligns the sense of guilt with the Puritan tradition in American culture. He told Studs Terkel that "in order to believe they were real Americans," people "believed they were responsible for their own fate." Such belief constituted "part of our theology," that God was punishing us for our sins. "Now, when something goes wrong, you'd have to be an idiot to really blame yourself altogether" (Conv., 307–8). The end of the play affirms that there is a price to be paid for choices made—the birds again come home to roost. Furthermore, when Miller projects the drama into the future by having Lee and his friends in the present allude to subsequent wars in Korea and Vietnam, which Miller so vigorously protested, and the whole company takes up singing "Life Is Just a Bowl of Cherries" as Quinn breaks into a soft-shoe dance and invites the audience to join in, he signals a return to the naive innocence that surely portends another Fall. For the Depression taught us again "that life indeed had beginnings, middles and a consequential end" (E, 298–99).

Playing for Time

First a teleplay shown on CBS television in 1980, Playing for Time was subsequently published as a two-act stage drama in 1985.[19] Based on Fania Fenelon's autobiography of the same name, it dramatizes Fenelon's experiences as singer with the women's orchestra at the infamous Auschwitz-Birkenau concentration camp. Although viewed by an audience of some forty million viewers, the television show drew criticism from a number of Jewish groups and from Fenelon herself for casting Vanessa Redgrave in the main role, especially given the actress's highly vocal support of the Palestinian Liberation Front and advocacy of a Palestinian homeland. Appearing

19. Critics have noted the aesthetic problems occurring when changing the genre from film script to stage play, especially the loss of a camera to focus on given characters, the difficulty in managing constantly shifting locales and episodes in the confines of a rigidly defined stage space, and the limitations imposed on characterization when handling such a large cast without the benefit of the visual techniques afforded in film.

between *The Archbishop's Ceiling* and *The American Clock*, the television drama (later, a play) appears to be distinctly at odds with the comic tone of the latter play. But in fact it is elementally similar in its essential theme of survival, which produces a moral crisis of tragic paradox. The appearance of the text first as teleplay demonstrates, as Susan C. W. Abbotson writes, Miller's "growing despair of his plays receiving proper attention in what he sees as an increasingly unserious theatrical arena, and his awareness that the important message which his script contains demands that it be viewed by the sheer numbers a television airing can draw."[20]

Miraculously saved from the gas chamber when one of the orchestra members recognizes her as an acclaimed Parisian singer, Fenelon is "invited" to sing with the orchestra of thirteen women, whose survival depends solely on the pleasure of the German command and especially the infamous Doctor Mengele. The group, consisting of a few Polish and mostly Jewish women, is directed by Alma Rosè, niece of Gustav Mahler and daughter of the concertmaster of the Vienna Philharmonic who, like the others, finds herself trapped in moral ambiguity.[21] On one hand, her fierce devotion to art protects the women from certain death. When Paulette, the cellist, falls ill with fever and is taken away ostensibly to the hospital to face the inevitable fate of the weak and dying at the camp, Alma demands that she be spared for the sake of the orchestra. She also conceals Greta's deficiencies as a player to keep her alive. But she is also driven by something other than moral commitment.

She tells Fania that she needs her support despite her severity with the others because displeasing Mengele would seal their fate; "If it weren't for my name, they'd have burned them up long ago" (*PT*, 47). Arrested as a Jew despite being "so . . . German" that they did not shave her hair, she survives by total commitment to her art. "You must back up my demands" on the others, she pleads with Fania. But if her salvation is art, art is also a return to innocence. When Fania declares that "one wants to keep *something* in reserve. . . . [W]e can't

20. Susan C. W. Abbotson, "Revisiting the Holocaust for 1980s Television: Arthur Miller's *Playing for Time*," 62.

21. Fenelon and Miller's depictions of Alma Rosè are to some extent fictionalized. For an accurate biography, see Richard Newman with Karen Kirtley, *Alma Rosé: Vienna to Auschwitz*.

really and truly wish to please them" (45), because sooner or later "one looks out the window" at the prisoners being marched to the death chambers, Alma says she has *"refused* to see."[22] For Alma, art becomes a shield against the truth rather than a moral weapon. She tells Fania she "will have to be an artist, and only an artist" (49). For her, art expresses the temptation of innocence that we have seen as an integral theme in virtually every Miller text.

It is also a temptation to the others as well. Etalina protests her innocence by declaring the Polish women "monsters" and asserting her own Jewish blood. When the Polish violinist Elzvieta claims "we're not all like that," Etalina accuses her of merely adopting "a pet Jew. You like Fania" (*PT*, 29). Etalina again asserts her innocence when she condemns Marianne and Fania of the act of cutting the Star of David in two to show that they are only half Jewish. But Fania tells her, "Your contempt doesn't impress me. Not when you've accepted every humiliation without one peep" (53). Even more, the Zionist Esther dismisses Lagerführerin Mandel, the beautiful commander of all women at the camp, as "nothing but a killer" when she tries to rescue a child whose mother is sent to the death chamber. "Don't try to make her ugly," Fania tells Esther. "She's beautiful and human. . . . We are the same species" (42). With cutting insight she shatters any claims of innocence. She knows of course that Mandel sanctioned the death of the child's parent, despite her maternal instinct to embrace the child, and yet she tells Esther, "She *is* human. . . . Like you. And me. You don't think that's a problem?" (42).[23] At another point, when Esther condemns the waiflike Marianne because she prostitutes herself to gain food and privileges and boasts that she is "keeping herself for Jerusalem," Fania sarcastically retorts, "it's good you can keep yourself so apart from all this . . . so clean." And she voices the moral theme of the play: "All I mean is that we may be

22. Earlier, the imprisoned electrician Shmuel tells Fania she must look out the window and confront the horrors of the camp because "Someone has to remember" (*PT*, 39). Ironically, Fania tells Marianne early in the play that "We must have an aim. And I think that the aim is to try to remember everything" (17). Later, when Allied troops close in on the camp, Shmuel informs Fania that the Germans are accelerating the killings to twelve thousand a day, and he reminds her, "You mustn't stop looking, Fania!" (54).

23. Later, Esther wonders, "How can you still call them human?" and Fania responds, "Then what are they, Esther?" (*PT*, 78)

innocent, but we have changed. I mean we know a little something about the human race that we did not know before. And it's not good news" (78). Having gained knowledge, the characters have in fact moved beyond innocence, where a common humanity links prisoner and tyrant, good and evil.

As in *The Archbishop's Ceiling* and other later plays, Miller clearly explores the nature of art and perhaps the efficacy of his own work. *Playing for Time* celebrates "the power of art to sustain the individual," according to Neil Carson, not its capacity to redeem society; "In this respect the playwright has moved a considerable way from the position of his earlier plays."[24] To be sure, what Kinereth Meyer calls "the obscene conjunction of music, culture, and suffering" poses disturbing and persistent questions as one ironic juxtaposition follows another.[25] The music that Alma considers "the holiest activity of mankind" (*PT*, 24) is used to march the doomed to their deaths. When Fania sings "Un bel di" from *Madame Butterfly*, Doctor Mengele ironically responds, "I have rarely felt so totally . . . moved." Architect of one of the most horrific crimes in history, he finds music "a consolation that feeds the spirit" (40). Even while playing to preserve lives, Fania recognizes "the ultimate horror—their love for music" (40), an echo of Von Berg's illumination in *Incident at Vichy* that the German people "with respect for art go about hounding Jews" (*IV*, 24). As the first act ends, Alma divorces herself from the horror around her by escaping to her art—she plays "in an extraordinarily beautiful way" (*PT*, 50). And the ironies persist to the end. In the second act Paulette escapes from the hospital to announce that all the patients will be killed the next day as the orchestra plays. Then, when the sadistic Frau Schmidt poisons Alma to keep her from leaving to "entertain" German troops, the bestial Doctor Mengele not only allows the artist-musician the rare privilege of being buried in a coffin but respectfully places her baton on it to honor her. The last ironic juxtaposition of art and evil occurs when Mandel orders Fania and Marianne to sing the duet from *Madame Butterfly* to console her

24. Carson, *Arthur Miller*, 146. Zeineddine argues to the contrary that music in the play transcends the "ugliness, horror and contradictions" and that the drama reveals a progression in Miller's work "toward emphasizing the role of women and de-emphasizing that of men" (*Because It Is My Name*, 209).

25. Meyer, " 'Jew Can Have,' " 252.

for the horror of having to send to his death the Polish child she had taken from the condemned Polish woman.

Caught in this frightening paradox, Fania moves from stoic toughness to despair. As some have observed, Marianne, whom Fania first protects on the train to Auschwitz, seems the opposite of the singer. Astonishing the others, Fania dares to save Marianne by making her survival a condition for joining the orchestra. When Marianne undergoes a moral descent, thieving from the others and prostituting herself, Fania accuses her of being "a little child" unwilling to accept that "*this is where you are* . . . and it's a hell of lot better than most people!" and she boasts that she herself would not "turn into an animal for a gram of margarine or a potato peel!" (*PT*, 28–29). But while Marianne's guilt is obvious, Fania, too, feels culpable on a deeper, more subtle level.

Bothered even from the beginning by the privileges she receives for singing and orchestrating music for the orchestra, Fania finds it "harder and harder to look out the window" (*PT*, 32) and is "ashamed" to play for prisoners being marched to do slave labor. More "horrified and feeling guilty" as time passes, she realizes how the other prisoners "must hate us" (33, 35). Yet even with her high-minded morality and condemnation of Marianne, she succumbs to eating some sausage Marianne has purchased from a guard with her body. While Fania appears more willing than the others to recognize her guilt, she also tries to rationalize it as well: " . . . I prefer to think that I am saving my life rather than trying to please the SS" (27). Although her "eyes are tortured" with conflict, "she sings fully, beautifully to the finish" for "the music lover," Doctor Mengele (28). Yet she seems to understand the temptation of innocence. When Elzvieta asks her forgiveness for judging her a traitor to her Jewishness, Fania replies,

> Why? What did you ever do to me? You were in the Resistance, you tried to fight against this. Why should you feel such guilt? It's the other ones who are destroying us . . . and they only feel innocent! . . . You will survive, and everyone around you will be innocent, from one end of Europe to the other. (*PT*, 65–66)

But no one can claim innocence in Miller's moral universe. Although Edward Isser and some other Holocaust critics complain that

Miller blames "the victims" in plays like *Incident at Vichy* and *Playing for Time*, Miller addresses a larger guilt: However noble we may be, we all live after the Fall. As in *The American Clock*, survival comes at an enormous price at the end of the drama, and it carries with it guilt and responsibility. Like the earlier plays, this one asks if the self can ever acquire integrity in the specious garden of innocence—and the answer is a resounding no.

Yet, however dark, the play carries a paradoxical hope as well. The signs become ever more ominous in the second act as the Germans speed up the executions, take away the orchestra's piano, order the immediate slaughter of the sick and the insane, and finally order the orchestra members into trucks to be deported and killed so they cannot tell the Russian soldiers "what went on there." The nadir is reached when the orchestra is dumped at a barn where they are to be killed. Marianne, at this point nicknamed "Kapo," having seduced the trooper in charge, exercises power without moral consciousness, forcing the desperately ill Fania to "walk like anybody else" and striking her one-time savior with a club as the others try to restrain her and help Fania. Even here, the duplicity remains; as Marianne descends to the moral abyss, the others act to save the woman who had rescued them. The light in this dark landscape is indeed faint, but nonetheless present.

In the final analysis the slight moral victory that occurs comes finally from "seeing out the window," seeing not only the evil existent in the world, but the human capacity for unreserved brutishness and murder. In 1964 Miller reported on the Nazi trials in Frankfurt after visiting the Mauthausen death camp. In his essay "The Nazi Trials and the German Heart," he captures the human capacity to eliminate the past and reclaim illusory innocence: "And while the testimony fills the silent courtroom . . . German industry will pour out its excellent automobiles, machine tools, electronic equipment, German theater will excellently produce and open plays, German publishers will put out beautifully designed books—all the visible tokens of civilization will multiply . . ." (*E*, 66). But the moral victory of *Playing for Time* speaks of another, more painful, but authentic moral restoration. As Christopher Bigsby aptly puts it, "Redemption here does not rely either on love or self-sacrifice but on the acknowledgment of a guilt which implies the persistence of values which if abrogated still exert their pressure on the psyche. Under stress, betrayal, it seems, is a natural instinct, a survival mechanism; but beneath that is some residual moral sense which may be suppressed but not eliminated."[26] Miller reiterates Quentin's discovery in *After the Fall* that, armed with the knowledge that "we are very dangerous" and that "no man lives who would not rather be the sole survivor of this place than all its finest victims," we may yet escape the most insidious of evils, "that lie of Eden" (*AF*, 113).

One Act Plays: *Two-Way Mirror* and *Danger: Memory!*

In addition to producing the longer texts discussed thus far, Miller wrote four one-act plays in the 1980s that investigate his growing fascination with what he has called "the ultimate mystery" —time—and with the difficulty in differentiating between truth and illusion, which he explores as well in *The Archbishop's Ceiling*. The four short but complex dramas were published in two collections: *Two-Way Mirror*, published in 1984 and including *Elegy for a Lady* and *Some Kind of Love Story*, and *Danger: Memory!* published in 1986 and including *I Can't Remember Anything* and *Clara*. As Miller told Steven Centola in a 1990 interview, in his later plays he has "turned more to a consideration of the question what is real and what is illusion" from his earlier "intent on reaching a tragic form for our time."[27] In these four thin but by no means simple texts, Miller once again wrestles with the complexities, paradoxes, and ironies commonly expressed in postmodern literature without betraying his long-held optimism about the human condition.

Elegy for a Lady opened along with *Some Kind of Love Story* at the Long Wharf Theater in New Haven in October 1982 under the title *2 by A.M.* The plot is stripped of virtually all action; an unidentified Man and the Proprietress of a boutique where the Man seeks a gift for his dying mistress engage in a dialogue that is also a monologue— we are not certain that the Proprietress really exists or is a creation of the Man's psyche. He and the Proprietress are the sole characters, and the whole drama consists of their conversation. The play "concerns the question of how we believe in truth," Miller comments,

26. Bigsby, *Modern American Drama*, 107–8.
27. Centola, "'Just Looking,'" 86.

"how one is forced by circumstances to believe what you are only sure is not too easily demonstrated as false" (*Conv.*, 368). As the drama unfolds, the Man attempts to understand the meaning of his relationship with his mistress as the Proprietress begins to give voice and shape to her presence and challenge the Man's assumptions of truth by countering it with *her* truth. As with the second play on the bill, *Some Kind of Love Story*, *Elegy*, as Dennis Welland concludes, offers "a new credibility, as well as a new twist, to themes of guilt and responsibility, illusion and reality, and the human capacity for love and suffering."[28]

To achieve his end, Miller adopts "a different form than I've ever tried before," a drama "that takes place in the space between the mind and what it imagines, and sort of turns itself out" (*Conv.*, 368). In *Timebends* he refers to the form as "like an Escher drawing in which water runs uphill, defying the eye's effort to trace the ordinary pull of gravity, a reminder of how our brains have created the 'objective' physics of our lives." He goes on to remark that "the objective world grows dim and distant as reality seems to consist solely or partly on what the characters' needs require it to be, leaving them with the anguish of having to make decisions they know are based on illusion and the power of desire" (*T*, 590).

Miller insists that the form is not that of a dream but of "revery," in which a character "creates an arena in which to be free to say any-thing." The Man at first stares into the shop searching for "some-thing" for his mistress, and the glass window becomes a two-way mirror that he enters and in which he performs what Miller calls "a monologue. . . . He's trying to figure himself out and what his nature is."[29] The Proprietress may be real or not, and she may or may not be his mistress. Christopher Bigsby observes that we wonder if the characters "exist only in the mind of the other," if this is only "an elaborate charade, played out for their mutual satisfaction or per-haps for the author's pleasure in constructing character, language and story only to dissolve them again with equal arbitrariness? The questions proliferate."[30]

28. Welland, *Miller the Playwright*, 167.
29. Centola, "'Just Looking,'" 94.
30. Bigsby, *Modern American Drama*, 118. Chris Banfield adds that "it is not immediately clear which character creates the other" ("Arthur Miller," 86).

At base, the Man's search for a gift is a quest for self and for meaning in the shadow of death. Here in the fragmented world of the boutique, staged *"without walls, the fragments seeming to be suspended in space,"* he attempts to sum up who he is in light not only of his mistress's pending death but also of his own. Constantly alluding to his being older than she, he strikes a theme that Miller engages with increasing urgency in his later plays, the coming of old age in a world seemingly devoid of meaning, certainty, and transcendence. The sound of a violin playing with *"unresolved grief"* in a *"fine distant fragility"* accompanies the drama, which Miller describes as "a play of shadows under the tree of death" (*T*, 590) bound only by "the feeling of grief for a loved one. *That* is the play . . . a passionate voyage through the masks of illusion to an ultimate reality."[31]

The fragmentary nature of the self is projected in the set itself, which consists of disjointed body parts and the mannequin-like figure of the Proprietress, who remains passive and static, moving only to speak. Objects evoke the presence of the absent mistress—a sweater, a necklace, a garter, a scarf, a cap, and a muffler; also, her body is present in "a heap of broken images"—busts, a plastic thigh, an upturned arm, parts seemingly dangling from the ceiling. The dialogue imitates the fragmentation. It is filled with pauses, ellipses, unfinished sentences, broken short exchanges, and constant shifts of subject, violating, as Maria Kurdi puts it, "verbal linearity"—as chaotic as life itself.[32] Miller contends that the characters struggle "to define themselves because the moral situation is so nebulous and few people can ever know what side they're on, if there are sides. So they talk themselves into positions."[33]

As they consider the possibilities of a gift, the Proprietress begins to create the Man through the point of view of the mistress, exposing his sense of guilt and vulnerability. What seems a therapy session becomes a confessional as well. As the Man "creates" the other self, he becomes responsible for her. The man admits, "I've never really bought her anything. It struck me this afternoon. Nothing at all" (*TWM*, 5). He tells the Proprietress that he is married, and she responds "Yes," as though she, as the mistress, already knows this.

31. Balakian, "Interview," 44–45.
32. Maria Kurdi, "The Deceptive Nature of Reality in Arthur Miller's *Two-Way Mirror*," 268.
33. Centola, "'Just Looking,'" 94.

As she gets closer to forcing him to confront the truth of the relationship, he diverts his eyes and changes the subject to elude her, yet
he comes to a series of epiphanies: that he cannot even remember if
he met his mistress two or three years ago, that they "met only for
pleasure," that the relationship tended "to float pretty much on the
surface" (11) (and later, "it *is* all pretty superficial, isn't it?" [15]),
that he feels "a sort of contradiction" in both caring and not caring,
that my wife "is who I should be married to" (16), and, finally, that
he finds himself "being pulled under myself and suffocated" by her
death when he always thought of death ("even my mother's and father's") as a "feeling of release; an obligation removed" (11). Driven
by guilt he is coerced to accept the reality of the relationship, that it
was purely superficial, that "There is really nothing between us. . . .
[N]othing but an . . . uncommitment" (17).[34]

The Man craves innocence, but the Proprietress forces him to be
responsible and ultimately allows him to relinquish a paralyzing guilt
by accepting reality. As the two contemplate what to give the dying mistress, the Proprietress becomes more passionately involved
as she takes on the persona of the lover; in so doing, she frees the
Man to speak with uncompromising honesty within the frame of a
revery. She merges her identity with the mistress, confessing her desire for a baby like the one the Man denied his mistress because he
was too old. "A baby would be better" than her successful business,
the Proprietress confesses—"Often, actually" there is "[s]omething
appalling about business, something totally pointless—like empty-
ing a pail and filling it again every day" (*TWM*, 14). As she plays
the role of the lover, she places a silk scarf on her shoulders, then
wears it as a bandanna, and finally places it on the shoulders again
as the mistress might die "in bed, like this." The Man comes to see
her as his lover: "You have her coloring," he remarks, and "You're
just about her age" (9). As Chris Banfield observes, in modeling the
scarf the Proprietress "hints at her slide into the lover's role."[35] The
Proprietress speaks the lover's thoughts, insisting in *"personal rebellion"* that "everyone does not die" of cancer—"Not every case!" (10).
Unnerved by the Man's assumption that she is dying, she asks, "Why
do you go on assuming it has to be the end!" (15), forcing him to

34. Miller comments that *Elegy* is about the "mourning for a lack of [commit-
ment] in the face of death" (Balakian, "Interview," 45).
35. Banfield, "Arthur Miller," 86.

admit that the lover only literally talked about the "big day" of her operation and not her death. Furthermore, the Proprietress expresses the lover's motive in not allowing the Man to see her—because she wanted to look good for him, knowing that their relationship was only superficial anyway, based on appearance and without depth. As the Man repeats his incredulity that he is admitting to the Proprietress what he could not say to his mistress ("I never dreamed I'd have such a conversation! . . . I had no idea this was in me" [12]), she offers him a cup of tea, becoming the image of his lover seated by him at a café table, literally imitating the lover's near "vulgar" laugh, slapping her thigh in mimicry of the mistress's actions, and kissing him passionately. And having played the role of a kind of priest, hearing his extraordinary confession, she concludes on behalf of the lover, "I'm helpless not to forgive everything, finally." Unwilling to play a spurious romantic role in a melodrama, she remains detached and totally honest: "If you couldn't bring yourself to share her life, you can't expect to share her dying" (18). The lover only wanted him to be a "friend," after all, and "it's perfect, just as it is. . . . That is all it could have become" (19).

As the cathartic conversation moves to a climax, the Man admits he was painfully blunt to his mistress now that he sees through her eyes the true nature of the relationship, and he accepts that "she wouldn't be good to be married to" because of her own ambition and youth—"she needs the dangerous mountains not the marriage in the valley" (TWM, 16). So the Proprietress tells him at last that "you will survive this" (17) precisely because the relationship is meaningless. The lover, she remarks, refuses to see him because "She wants to make it stay exactly as it is . . . forever" (20). This truth leads to the Man's inspired selection of a gift—a watch on a gold chain, a gift of "time"—because "she wants to make it last forever." The gift signals his understanding. He gains empathy by having glimpsed the relationship through the lover/Proprietress's eyes. The watch marks the passing of time, but with it the acceptance of truth and the paradoxical death of an empty relationship—a freedom from illusion and the painful self-awareness that gives birth to a hope generated by truth.[36]

36. Bob Peck, who played the Man opposite Helen Mirren in the 1989 Young Vic production, simplifies the ending. Declaring the Man "healed or cured" when "a blight, or weight of conscience, has been lifted off him," he concludes that Miller

The revery ended, the man *"strolls away alone"* as *"The woman and the boutique go dark, vanishing"* (20).

If anything, the second play, *Some Kind of Love Story* (which Miller adapted as a screenplay for the 1990 film *Everybody Wins*) complicates the theme of truth and illusion by introducing as the female character a schizophrenic with multiple personalities, all of whom seem to illuminate something of reality without ever allowing the truth fully to emerge. As in most Miller texts, the private and the public intersect. The plot involves a detective who comes to see his former mistress, a prostitute now married to an abusive pimp. At issue is the innocence of a man unjustly imprisoned for murdering his uncle, a crime the detective has been devoted to solving for five years.[37] Convinced that the woman, Angela, knows information that would free the imprisoned victim, Tom O'Toole has periodically interrogated his one-time lover in hopes of uncovering the truth. Each time, though, she frustrates his efforts (the last time after meeting with her for over seven hours), leaving him in perpetual uncertainty; he remarks, "I always leave here with more questions than I came with" (*TWM*, 26). Desperate to believe that she will at last unlock the key to the case, he comes to her room once more, determined to discover the truth or to end the relationship forever.

Beneath the public drama lies the deeper personal one. Tom is driven by more than moral principles. Still in love with Angela, he, consciously or not, comes partly out of desire as well as moral responsibility. Angela, too, is caught in a similar paradox, compelled to try

---

"says it's alright, it's human" to enter into an adulterous relationship—"there's no need to carry a burden of guilt about it" (*AMC*, 173). Schlueter and Flanagan offer the far more convincing reading that the ending reflects on the Man's own coming death rather than his lover's. "When the Man comes to understand that his quest may be a meditation on a loss having nothing to do with cancer claiming his lady," they contend, the Proprietress embraces him and "maybe the woman, the meeting their farewell" (*Arthur Miller*, 137).

37. As noted earlier, in the seventies Miller was directly involved in such a case, working with others to secure a new trial for Peter Reilly, a Connecticut boy falsely accused of murdering his mother. Miller helped reverse the decision to convict Reilly by proving that the police had violated Reilly's rights and coerced him into a confession. In the screenplay for *Everybody Wins*, Miller allows Tom to pursue the case until it is reopened with the consent of an added character, Judge Murdoch, who pointedly tells the detective, "Just remember, kid—the human race ate the apple. Reversing this case is not going to hang it back on the tree!" (Arthur Miller, *Everybody Wins: A Screenplay*, 90).

to save a man she knows is innocent but also by a "desperate need" to retain Tom's love. As Christopher Bigsby accurately observes in the play's afterword, "both perhaps have a vested interest in the game which they play, a game in which truth is pursued in the understanding that it must never be discovered" (*TWM*, 68). For clearly, the truth would dissolve the nearly symbiotic dependence with which the characters survive. Elementally dependent on each other, they must know that so long as the truth remains hidden amidst illusion and self-deceit, they draw life from each other, staring again into a "two-way mirror."

Miller describes his later plays as attempts "to try to capture some of the smell and sense of this very vagrant thing we call existence,"[38] and in this subtle piece he again experiments with form, once more breaking from the arcing structure of tragedy to employ a more fragmentary design of abruptly ending scenes, rapid character transformations, and circularity. As Maria Kurdi notes, scenes end in a "cul-de-sac again and again," and "every newly introduced point is questioned or dropped as irrelevant."[39] Driven by doubt and trust alike, Tom remains trapped in irresolution to the end. Even though it frustrates him to reengage in "the same schizophrenic conversation we had fifteen times" (*TWM*, 31), he is seduced by Angela's stories, clearly mixtures of truth and delusion. In three calls to Angela's one-time psychiatrist, Josh Levy, he tries to convince himself that "everything factual she's told me has stacked up with my own information," that "she's got some terrific perceptions" and ironically "sees right through to your spinal cord" (36). "The reason you're sick is that you lie" (45), he tells Angela at one point, only to confess at the end that "I guess . . . I still believe you" (66).

If reality remains relative, a fiction created by the characters in their perceptions of each other and themselves, then memory surfaces in the present not in sharp illumination but in chimerical images and displaced fragments. Miller evokes such a world when the curtain opens on a "darkened room" filled with articles of clothing, another panoply of body parts, and Angela "barely visible sitting on the bed." From the opening, Tom presents a public and private self in tension. Morally committed to rescuing the accused killer Felix Epstein from false incarceration, he struggles against an escalating

38. Centola, " 'Just Looking,' " 94.
39. Kurdi, "Deceptive Nature," 270–71.

sexual desire triggered by the woman who "woke me from the dead, sexually" (*TWM*, 65). He is aware of the moral crisis, admitting that "I can't be concentrating on this case and banging you at the same time. It's all wrong" (27), yet he seems powerless to resist his love for Angela, however hard he tries. He acknowledges "I'm still in love with you" (29) even though his wife threatens separation because of his involvement with his former mistress. By the conclusion of the play he has not resolved the conflict. Even as he cries out "Oh, Darlin' . . . Oh, Ange . . . I can't help it, I love you!" (64), he *strides about, full of self-hatred*" as the play ends, like a Quentin passing judgment on his own image. And when he does claim nobility of purpose, Angela strips him of the illusion of innocence.

At one point, when she is especially threatened by Tom's persistence, she assumes the personality of the vulgar whore Leontine, who calls him a "jerked-off choir boy. . . . [Y]ou think you're better than anybody else?" (*TWM*, 34–35). When at another point he tries to comfort her by stroking her hair, she becomes Emily, a manifestation of herself as an eight-year-old child, when she was raped by her father, whom she apparently resurrects in Tom. She forces him to admit that he is driven as much by revenge against those who want to destroy his career as by principle in trying to free Felix. And as the aristocratic Renata Marshall, another of her multiple personalities, she declares that "what astounds *me* is how you get to think *you're* such a high grade individual and such a great Catholic" (59). But while she depicts the "fiction" of Tom as a moral hypocrite, she paradoxically constructs a character of seeming goodness. She credits him with saving her; she insists "You've still got a lot of priest in you" (30), compares him to Jimmy Cagney—"You got the same sweet-and-sour thing" (40), and repeatedly praises him for trying to free Felix.

In their mutually dependent relationship, each is a creation of the other, and each challenges the self the other generates. Angela, too, contends with her competing selves. "I've done more for Felix Epstein than you or anybody," she protests to Tom, and he tells her, "I always said you had class, darling, you know why?—'Cause of your conscience, most people would just sign out and butter their own potatoes, but not you. You suffer" (*TWM*, 45–46). Horrified that Felix is still falsely imprisoned after five years, she ostensibly calls Tom to reveal what she knows to free the prisoner: that Felix was framed by Charley Callaghan, the prosecutor, and the corrupt head of detectives Bellanca; that the murdered uncle ran drugs with the collusion of the police; and that the whole criminal justice system is involved in corruption. The "truth," however, surfaces only when Tom threatens to leave, and Angela withholds the essential evidence needed to prove the case: nine letters written to her by a remorseful Charley Callaghan acknowledging his self-judgment for succumbing to the mob pressure to persecute an innocent man. As Tom struggles to separate truth from fantasy, he ironically imitates the conflicted figure of the prosecutor that Angela paints for him. Callaghan, she tells him, was hounded by such self-condemnation. Tom suffers the same self-hatred that his rival endures when he tries to assuage his conscience. His verbal confession matches Callaghan's letters of self-condemnation.

At the core of this moral morass Miller introduces recurrent references to the Catholic Church, which links the characters and defines the larger metaphysical crisis they represent. Ironically, Angela feels drawn to Tom for much the same reason she is drawn to Charley Callaghan, with whom she has a continuing affair, because both wanted to be a priest. The Catholic Church represents a spiritual refuge no longer valid for either character. Yet Angela begs Tom to "Talk about the Communion Breakfasts" he used to attend, "And how important the Church was." But the Church has lost all meaning, and Tom shatters Angela's illusion when he tells her, "The Church was really important in the Department in those days. Like any cop who took money from whores . . . or like dope money . . . the priest lay his head open" (TWM, 41). The allusions to the Church, "God," "Christ," and "Jesus" that pepper the dialogue are tinged with irony. Denied the metaphysical preserve of the Church, Angela cannot attend confession or confess to a priest that Tom cannot become. Like the characters in the later plays, these two, as quoted earlier from Miller, are "trying to name themselves; they're trying to define themselves because the moral situation is so nebulous." As Miller remarks to Janet Balakian, Catholicism is "what she is and what he is, but I suppose you could say it's the lost order that has crumpled. They're left high and dry. They can only find reassurance in each other, if that."[40] As Tom remarks, they speak as "one ex-Catholic to another" (32) in a spiritual vacuum.

40. Centola, "'Just Looking,'" 94; Balakian, "Interview," 46.

Ultimately, rather than negating personal responsibility, the annihilation of a metaphysical surety in fact increases it. The absence of God does not abort the need to relocate a metaphysical center; indeed, as Christopher Bigsby concludes, "the need to do so . . . remains—a phantom, a lure, an illusion, but in some critical and inescapable sense, a necessity" (TWM, 70).[41] Angela wants Tom to come back, and he wills to do so, though pleading, "dear God . . . make it only one last time!" (66). So long as the characters talk their way to some kind of truth and self-understanding, however illusory, they remain morally viable and responsible, even if truth itself remains an illusion. Memory does not march inexorably forward into the present in the linear pattern of a tragedy in these short plays, but the line that blurs the present and the past also links the characters in a common humanity. "Their plight," Maria Kurdi writes, "is not tragic, as there is no other choice but to go on being aware of the tension" between past and present, truth and illusion, though unable to resolve it.[42] Trapped in "this goddam dream," Tom laments, "I mean I've got to stop looking for some red tag that says 'Real' on it"—but this is no option; Tom can only hope, "If it's real for me then that's the last question I can ask, right?" (62). Imprisoned by their perceptions, the two characters are caught in the act of forever reconstructing themselves and so redeeming themselves from the death of existential paralysis.

Although mostly slighted by critics, as is 2 by A.M., the one-acts performed as Danger: Memory! at Lincoln Center in February 1987 in important ways extend Miller's growing uncertainty about the causality and moral clarity of traditional tragedy. I Can't Remember Anything, like Elegy for a Lady and Some Kind of Love Story, is a twilight piece played at the margin of darkness, against which two characters engage in a kind of reckoning, a summing up of who they are in the shadow of death. Yet the play is spared from morbidity by its sometimes gallows humor and by a celebratory ritual dance at the end of the drama.

41. To Welland, the conclusion of the drama " 'begins responsibility,' for by the end the man has recognized that the relationship with his lover is such that 'she doesn't want it spoiled, you see, by deepening.' . . . For him this is the ultimate reality at the end of the passionate voyage" (Miller the Playwright, 166).
42. Kurdi, "Deceptive Nature," 271.

Once again stripped to a taut dialogue between two characters, the drama virtually unfolds without an external plot. Miller describes it as "looking at the phenomenon of time dying."[43] Indeed, the theme of death and dying permeates the text; an arthritic old man and the aging widow of his former employer and best friend meet in "another one of those conversations" (DM, 7), a ritualized daily encounter in which she visits his sparse rural home a few hundred yards from her own house. Speaking in point/counterpoint, they reenact a long, ongoing debate about the validity of the past and the crisis of the present, one a lifelong communist and the other the somewhat aristocratic widow of a highly successful capitalist. On one hand she attempts to erase memory, to exercise a willed amnesia, and barely survives in the beauty she finds in nature and in the moment. Yet subconsciously she is drawn to Leo's house to be prodded into remembering a past she claims does not matter. Her name, Leonora, and his, Leo, imply, as Chris Banfield comments, "that they might be two sides of the same human coin,"[44] a divided self and another reflection in a two-way mirror. Like the other pairs in the one-acts, they depend on each other for mutual support. Their verbal combat keeps them alive and vital, a stay against the chaos that clearly casts its lengthening shadow across the stage.[45]

The dialogue is interwoven with a darkly comic tone, especially in Leo's frequent references to wanting to donate his organs to Yale–New Haven Hospital. If you find me dead, he tells Leonora, "my eyes crossed and my tongue hanging out" (DM, 7), be certain to phone the number on the cardboard sign. Repulsed, Leonora later asks, "Will they take out your brains too?" and Leo responds with flippant sarcasm, "I guess so. For sweetbread. . . . And my liver with onions" (13). Ironically, the morbid theme resurfaces when Leonora tells Leo that she herself "felt ashamed" when she frightened a young deer earlier in the day—"And we full of dead chickens and rotting cow meat" (18).

43. Balakian, "Conversation," 165.
44. Banfield, "Arthur Miller," 90.
45. Miller writes in *Timebends* that the play "expresses my love" for Sandy and Louisa Calders, a decade older couple who befriended him "in the bad time I lost my passport and was being pushed around" (T, 503).

The conflict posits Leonora's depression against Leo's hopefulness, her litany of despair against his active participation in life. Leonora laments the present—"it's all too horrible"—and reflects the loss of an unrecoverable past when "I used to believe, as a girl—I mean we were taught to believe—that everything has its purpose" (*DM*, 7, 8). Drinking Leo's bourbon to evade reality, she finds nothing to give meaning to her life. "But what purpose have I got?" she remarks. "I am totally useless, to myself, to my children, my grandchildren, and the one or two people I suppose I can call my friends who aren't dead" (8). She even resents Leo's doing the crossword puzzles in the paper because "They do nothing but add triviality to the boredom of existence" (16).

In contrast, Leo's constant action challenges her debilitating depression. A lifelong bridge builder for Leonora's dead husband, Frederick, he first works on making a cardboard sign to hang by his phone with the number of the Yale–New Haven hospital, begins doing the crossword as soon as he finishes, and informs Leonora "I have work to do tonight," checking some calculations for a young engineer building a new bridge for the town. He keeps encouraging her to act as well—"Why don't you take up the piano again?" (*DM*, 8), he proposes, recalling how she used to play Mozart and Chopin. When she refuses, he jokes that she might take up the accordion. He then suggests seriously that she begin randomly calling names in the telephone book to ask strangers to donate their organs as he intends to do. He even tries to engage her in the crossword puzzle, asking her who was president of France when World War I started.

And although she spurns his attempts to break her stasis and remains secure in her indifference to his efforts, she gradually begins to respond despite herself. All along she declares her ignorance of the past. Sounding the chord announced in the title, she keeps repeating her supposed loss of meaning: "Sometimes . . . . I think I remember something, but then I wonder if I just imagined it. My whole life often seems imaginary. . . . Sometimes I wonder if *I'm* imaginary" (*DM*, 9); "I can't remember anything" (10); "I simply cannot remember anything at all" (11); "I can't remember anything political" (12); and "When I do think of anything . . . it's like some page in a book I once read" (14). But as the conversation evolves, Leo compels her to confront the past, revealing that it is not some vacant memory, "not a book, it's your life, kiddo" (14). And despite the play's seeming departure from Miller's earlier work, the past still becomes the present here, and it still remains the force the characters must confront to gain a present. As Leonora recovers memory, she finds a release, however temporary, from her despair.

As Leo provides glimpses of memory, he helps the reluctant Leonora find her lost self. He reminds her that she just ate three slices of bread last week when she claims not to have eaten bread in years. When she declares she cannot "remember anything political," he triggers her memory that Poincaré was the president of France when World War I broke out. Proclaiming, "it's a damn shame to forget all that," he tells her she used to use a lot of rosemary in cooking and "had a wonderful touch with any kind of lamb" (*DM*, 13). Remembering, she begins to recover lost values and faith. Recalling that her own son, Lawrence, sent her a record three years ago, she comments, "Yes, I remember now. . . . It was wonderful for a certain mood." And when Leo reads a comment in Lawrence's recent letter about separating from Moira and suggests that Moira must be "somebody he married," Leonora's *"eyes moisten with tears"* (15) as she remembers. Later, when Leo reminds her that tomorrow is the birthday of her dead husband, Frederick, she looks at him *"with faint guilt in her eyes"* (18). On her own, she remembers a visit to Russia with Frederick at a time when she, Leo, and Frederick espoused liberal causes like supporting the Spanish Republicans, and in so doing she brings the past against the present and defines her values against current society. "But what do they have to *believe?*" she asks about the present generation represented by Lawrence and by a young girl at the nearby nature store who is ironically writing a thesis on recurrence—"wasn't there something more precious about human life before?" (19). Even as she pours another drink, she resurrects the values of the past.

Symbolically, Leo reminds Leonora, "It's your birthday too," and he admits he "still misses" Frederick, whose persona he comes in some measure to represent. In an ironic reversal, Leonora now embraces the past, recalling how she first met Frederick. And holding to the past, she begins to exorcise her depression by finally exploding in anger to Leo because "you go right on thinking there is hope somewhere" when "The country is being ruined by greed and mendacity and narrow-minded ignorance" (*DM*, 24–25). Yet she keeps returning to Leo's precisely to find some hope. And he finally tells her, "if you're wondering why you're alive . . . maybe it's because you *are*, that's all, and that's the whole goddamn reason" (26). Claiming he is "going back to be a chemical; all we are is a lot of nitrogen," he tells her "Maybe you're so nervous because you keep looking for some other reason and there isn't any" (25). He brings her to a moment of epiphany: "Frederick was your life, and now there's nothing" (26).

Yet even with all the revelations ended, the two characters appear to go nowhere. She remarks, "I don't even remember why we started talking about this"; and he replies, "that's better than me—I don't remember what we were talking about" (*DM*, 26). Having undergone an intense exorcism of her evasion of her past, Leonora asks if she could play the record Lawrence has just sent with his current letter. "Didn't you and I dance once?" she recalls. In a reenactment of the past, the two begin to dance as the record plays a samba. Leonora becomes her past self as *"her sensuality provokes and embarrasses him,"* and he *"struggles to his feet"* until they both collapse laughing. Leonora pronounces a benediction of sorts. Lawrence, she claims, "does what is in him to do. Just like you. And everyone else. Until it all comes to an end" (27). Avoiding sentimentality or some resolution manufactured by a deus ex machina, Miller ends the play in "an acceptance of life"; as he told Steven Centola, "Yes. . . . That's exactly what should have happened." And he goes on to say, "we learn from Leo . . . that life is what it is; we just simply have to live it." The play ends in a duet (in contrast to the beginning when Leonora first enters and, solo, *"sits some distance"* from Leo), the samba becoming at once a recovery of the past erupted in the present and an embracing of the here and now.[46]

Miller has said that the other play, *Clara*, marks his continued fascination with what he calls "a kind of imploding of time—moments when a buried layer of experience suddenly surges upward to become the new surface of one's attention and flashes news from below" (*T*, 590). On one hand, it appears a further qualification of the playwright's belief in certitude and his continued experimentation with

46. Centola, "'Just Looking,'" 91. It is not without significance that the second record from Lawrence marks his own progression. The first record, which Leo thought sounded "like a bunch of cats locked in a toilet" (*DM*, 15), reflects his attempt to find spiritual solace in Eastern religion. In the second record, Leo surmises, "he decided to stop wasting his time and start playing human music" (27).

new form as well as matter. Yet the play reflects much of the earlier Miller as well. It consists of dialogue between a Jewish detective, Lew Fine, and Albert Kroll, the father of Clara, who has been
viciously murdered and decapitated. Once again, Miller establishes
a courtroom environment as Fine aggressively interrogates Kroll to
discover the name of Clara's Hispanic lover, the prime suspect in
the case. Like earlier Miller protagonists, Kroll must confront his
own culpability in "a very strong tragic sense." Miller labels the play
"a perfectly traditional tragic play. It's just that its way of unveiling
itself . . . is somewhat untraditional."[47] Kroll, in the fashion of other
Miller tragic figures, can only recover his lost values and sense of
self by encountering the past and his own guilt. The conflict, writes
Miller, posits "the voice of realism and the flesh against the immortal
spirit that transcends gain and loss; the death-in-life, and the life-
in-death" (T, 591). Nonetheless, the drama does treat "memory" in
inventive ways. Kroll, having "dropped out of time," is shocked by
his daughter's murder into recovering memory, driven by Fine's relentless pursuit to recover his own lost self and admit to his personal
responsibility for the tragic murder.

To dramatize the subjective tension, Miller employs a variety of expressionistic techniques to violate superficial realism. He fragments
the text, abruptly shifting dialogue and sometimes suspending incomplete sentences in midair. Concentrating the action in the living room of Clara's apartment *"swiftly lost in the surrounding darkness"*
(DM, 33), he punctuates the action with the popping of flashbulbs
from Clara's bedroom, where a police photographer takes photos
of the grisly crime scene. To this visual effect he adds screen pro-
jections of the horrific scene projected from Kroll's mind after he
gradually gets up from the floor, where he lies in shock. One projection depicts a shot of Clara's bloodied body and another shows
her bloody wounded hand. The device is extended as the drama
progresses and Kroll begins to visualize the past—later, the name
of Clara's lesbian lover flashes on the screen, and ultimately so does
the murderer's name.

Miller also makes use of other expressionistic techniques. Three
times Clara walks on the stage carrying a bird cage, another time
she appears on stage dressed in outdoor clothing, and finally she

47. Centola, " 'Just Looking,' " 86.

enters as a girl reenacting her crucial encounter with her father.[48] These visual "flashes . . . from below" are underscored by bits of music that suddenly link past and present: A John Coltrane saxophone solo suddenly "*splits the air*" when a young cop accidentally hits a tape recorder; at another point, piano keys sound; and the play ends with a twenty-five-year-old record of Kroll singing the song "Shenandoah." To these Miller introduces other surrealistic elements. Kroll notices, for example, the uncanny parallels between Lieutenant Fine and Kroll's one-time closest friend, Bert. Both are named Fine, suffer from back problems, say "okay" the same way, are missing toes on their left foot, and have a child who committed suicide. Indeed, Fine seems the persona of Kroll's one-time friend, who betrayed him after he worked for him ten years and consequently sapped Kroll's ability to trust others. The combination of unrealistic features converts realism into symbolic drama as Kroll unwillingly passes down the corridor of time while the past intersects the present and compels him to reenact his crime.

Stunned into disbelief by the shock of Clara's brutal death, Kroll resists its reality. He tells Fine that he does not "see the necessity" of the interrogation because he doubts the event really occurred, and he tries to evade the insistent detective—"I'm just wondering, maybe I should wait before I answer any more questions" (*DM*, 44). But Fine's hold on him is far greater than that of a police investigator, and their relationship drives the action inexorably forward. Not only does Fine mirror Kroll's former friend Bert, he seems to be part of Kroll as well. He is able to enter the grieving father's consciousness and articulate his thoughts, often with astounding clarity. Again and again, he gives words to Kroll's unspoken thoughts, exposing his unacknowledged guilt. Clara had embodied her father's commitment to social justice and reform, and when she was endangered as a hostage in a prison revolt, "deep down you were proud of her," Fine interprets. When Kroll resists Fine's questions, the detective explains why he does so as though he were Kroll's Freudian psychoanalyst: "[W]e block things

48. According to Savran, the appearances mark the progression of the plot and show Clara's evolving role as "metaphorical being . . . and the 'medal' her convicted murderer-boyfriend wears 'on his chest,'" and as a kind of divine sorceress with the power to stop a 'snarling, snapping' dog 'in his tracks'" (*Communists, Cowboys, and Queers*, 74).

we're ashamed to remember. . . . Things that make us feel guilty, you know what I mean?" (49). He hints at Kroll's feelings about Clara's bringing her convicted murderer-lover home and sleeping with him, and he expresses the question Kroll is reluctant to speak: "[A]re you guilty because you didn't put your foot down right then and there?" (52). Increasingly conscious of his failure to warn his daughter about the killer and to break up the relationship, Kroll attempts to skirt the truth; but Fine zeroes in on his evasions; "You're blocking this off . . . because you refuse to remember what you were feeling" (53). Not only did Kroll not warn his daughter, Fine charges, "you actually encouraged Clara" because she was reinforcing Kroll's once firm belief in people. When Kroll evasively complains "Not *encouraged*" (54), Fine coerces him to probe deeper into his memory. Kroll recalls accidentally seeing Clara walk to a car with her friend, Eleanor— and as though he *were* Kroll, Fine adds "They kissed?" With Kroll's own vision, he pronounces self-judgment: "it was such a relief to see her involved with a man. . . . [E]ven a Puerto Rican murderer wearing a mackinaw, that you . . ."—and Kroll completes the sentence as though he mirrors Fine's thoughts: "I think so" (59).

As the investigator gives voice to Kroll's thoughts, the real guilt the pained father feels surfaces. Warning Clara, his own best self, would have compromised his own position as an advocate for minorities and the poor as the director of the zoning board. It is of course an essential Miller theme that however noble, all choices involve consequences and moral responsibility, that we all live after the Fall. An essentially good person who lost his faith in the goodness of humanity when his former friend betrayed him, Kroll has tried to retain his idealism through Clara's work in the Peace Corps and involvement in social issues, and in his own efforts to speak on behalf of the oppressed as chairman of the zoning board; but, as Lew Fine reveals, he has sold out to the oppressors by working for a shady construction company and, however unintentionally, was responsible for Clara's death. With stark lucidity, the detective summarizes the litany of his guilt:

> You didn't level with Jean [Kroll's wife] about this lady friend; you didn't put your foot down when you know you never believed that this man was adjusted; and you've gone public in favor of these people coming into the community when you

know they're liable to do anything comes into their heads. . . .
[Y]ou can't stop telling your lies. You're not protecting a name,
are you? You'd like this man caught and killed, right? It's not
him, it's your lies you can't let go of. It's ten, twenty, thirty years
of shit you told your daughter, to the point she sacrificed her life,
for what—To uphold what you don't believe in yourself. (61)

Fine enjoins the battle, claiming that Kroll is unlike Clara, and, as
disillusioned as he is, "you're one of us" (63), he insists.

Now at last brought to the point of choice, Kroll must either confirm the values he prized in Clara or deny them—and her. Ironically, she became his agent, enacting his own will to believe in the
social good. In a sense she died for him. The choice falls between
his ideal and Fine's starkly realistic assessment of the human condition. As one who has accepted "my limitation," Fine rejects any
moral ambiguity. "Jewish or not Jewish, I think a man who cuts off
a human's head is a criminal" (*DM*, 53). Although Fine claims that
he never took "an illegitimate nickel" and declares his innocence,
he sees all humanity as motivated by "Greed. Greed and race . . .
blacks for blacks, and whites for whites. Gentile for Gentile and the
Jew for the Jew" (62). Once a believer like Kroll, he claims to have
lost his naïveté when he saw "those pictures of the piles of bones" in
Holocaust prisons. "That's the day I was born again," he tells Albert:
"and I've never let myself forget it.—'Do it to them before they can
do it to you. Period'" (63). Faced with such devastating cynicism,
the father, like all tragic figures, goes back to the point of offense,
however ironic it proves to be.

As the play climaxes, the detective's undeniable challenge im-
plodes time again, as Kroll relives the defining moment in his life—
the past "flashes news from below," resurrected from "a buried level of
experience" that surges into the present. As Clara once more enters
the stage, this time as a girl,[49] Kroll replays the moment when he re-
counted to her the story that gave her the uncompromising idealism
that led to her death.

49. Miller recalls that for the Lincoln Center production, at the suggestion of
the director Gregory Mosher, he deleted Clara's appearance on stage and instead
allowed Kroll to talk to her even though she was not present. However, he returned
to his original script for the London and later productions, convinced that she
needed to be seen on stage (Balakian, "Conversation," 165).

The conflict enjoins competing points of view. Fine's cynicism is that of a lapsed liberal, whose denial of his early idealism in part reflects Kroll's violation of his own high principles over the past twenty-five years. Yet Kroll retains a countering faith vested in and represented by Clara. Although Kroll, as Miller notes in *Timebends*, "becomes like others," he is not "a bad man but simply . . . the ideal has flown, along with his youthful hopes for himself and his faith in people" (*T*, 591). By recovering Clara through memory, he resurrects his own lost faith. As he reconstructs Clara from bits of memory (first introduced by the flash pictures of Clara's bloody body, her wounded hand, and decapitated head), he reconstructs his own former self, a point Miller emphasizes by paralleling Clara's mutilation and Kroll's being slit in the gut by a Japanese soldier in the Philippines. Ironically, Fine tells Kroll, "You know, Albert, a wound that deep up the belly will stay with a man right into the grave" (*DM*, 56).

Erupting from memory as a young girl with a ribbon in her hair, Clara forces her father to recount in the present his greatest moment of moral courage and conviction. As Miller stages the scene, the young assistant cop plays the recording of Kroll singing "Shenandoah" at the time he devoted himself to helping minorities and serving the common good. The record triggers "news from below" when Kroll, at Clara's pleading, tells her of his commanding a black troop in Biloxi when a half dozen of his men were nearly lynched by a mob. When the colonel refused to help save them, he made a daring rescue, driving a jeep into town, firing his .45 into the air and demanding that the mob "untie my men and hand them over right now." In response to his reenacted narration, Clara kisses his hand in admiration, calling "Oh, my dear Papa . . . !" as she fades "*toward the darkness*" (*DM*, 67). In his joyful declaration "Oh, my wonderful Clara. . . . I am so proud of you!" (67), he reasserts his own lost faith, Clara becoming the image of his own best self.

Earlier Kroll tells Fine he is "a little ashamed" he "didn't tell Clara how strongly I felt" about her lover, and he wonders "if I should ever have told her that story" (*DM*, 56) about saving the black soldiers. The answer comes when he relives the memory and embraces his youthful faith through Clara's eyes. Writes Miller, "The play ends on his affirmation; in her catastrophe he has rediscovered himself and glimpsed the tragic collapse of values that he finally cannot bring himself to renounce" (*T*, 591).

As the play ends Kroll finally pronounces the murderer's name: "Luis Hernandez." In speaking it, he acknowledges his complicity in not warning Clara (Fine had said he would remember the name if he faced "the truth") and, more deeply, his denial of the idealism that gave meaning to her life. Pronouncing the name, he both admits his failure and reclaims Clara as the projection of his own moral and socially responsible self.[50]

The varied and experimental nature of plot construction and dialogue in *Two-Way Mirror* and *Danger: Memory!* as well as in *The American Clock* and *The Archbishop's Ceiling*, a growing intrigue with the theme of illusion and reality, and an increased attention to the nature of art itself all give witness to Miller's continuously evolving art in the 1970s and 1980s. The plays of the 1990s continue to incorporate these elements as well as facets of the changing cultural scene and the emerging issues of the late century—as always, a reflection of Miller's long-held dictum that "the fish is in the sea and the sea is in the fish" (*TE*, 143). Perhaps more subtly, these latest dramas begin to explore both implicitly and explicitly a growing consciousness of the reality of age and of the need somehow to define one's self in the twilight of a long career.

50. In his vitriolic attack on Miller's supposed "hegemonic masculinity," Savran argues that Luis Hernandez is Kroll's "fantasmatic double"—"the intersection of remembrance and confession configures the murderer not as a distinct entity but as an Other within the self, as a man who, despite his superficial differences from Kroll, becomes his fantasmatic double" (*Communists, Cowboys, and Queers*, 74). To be sure, Kroll is paired with the Hispanic lover as murderer, as he himself must acknowledge, but to conclude that he thereby reveals a "jealous and violent ownership of women and the past" that Miller "strives so desperately to conceal" (75) is by any fair consideration an extreme exaggeration.

7   Last Plays of the Century

More than one reviewer quipped that the nineties proved to be "Miller time" because all the playwright's established early plays (with the notable exception of *After the Fall*) received major and highly acclaimed new productions. Although the performances reconfirmed his already secure place in the canon of American drama, they did not include some of the lesser-known works yet to be fully appreciated and analyzed. These and Miller's continuing dramatic experiments have provided an as yet untapped resource for further critical exploration. Four new plays premiered in the decade and a drama scheduled to open in England sometime in 2002 testify to the vitality and endurance of Miller's skills even after more than fifty years as the major voice in American drama. The four plays of the decade again illustrate the persistence of his themes and the dramatist's sensitivity to current issues and questions.

The Ride down Mount Morgan

One is tempted to see the plays of the nineties as significant departures from the early works, as qualified or even contradictory explorations of moral issues at the heart of the early plays, and as highly experimental attempts at inventing new dramatic form. To be sure, moral certainty blurs in these later texts, and they tend to be open-ended rather than resolved. The line between reality and illusion grows fainter, and a sustained ambiguity characterizes the whole. Miller's frequent revisions to *Ride down Mount Morgan*,[1] *The Last Yankee,* and *Broken Glass*

1. Miller revised the play after its premiere in London in 1991 and after it was published by Methuen in the same year and by Penguin in

suggest something of his own tentativeness. Yet the last plays are in remarkable ways very much related to his early works. *The Ride down Mount Morgan* is especially reflective of *Death of a Salesman*, not only in its dramatic situation but in its form. Like a financially successful Willy Loman, Lyman Felt betrays his family, suffers estrangement from his children, runs up against the limits of mortality, endures the anguish of guilt, contemplates suicide, and attempts vainly to rationalize his innocence. He drifts in the shady border between truth and illusion, dream and reality, past and present. Miller comments that "time is rather plastic" in the drama. "While the story is moving forward, it's also moving sideways and out."[2] Past and present collapse upon one another as Lyman mentally plays scenes of self-judgment in the manner of Quentin rehearsing his past in a psychic courtroom of the mind. Summoning as witnesses from memory his complementary wives, the self-indulgent bigamist futilely pleads his case before an implied audience and himself, trapped in a morass of moral ambiguity and tension. Memory, real time, and contrary points of view establish contrasting constructions of Lyman, in a pattern Miller describes as "an investigation into the morality of deceit,"[3] not least the moral complexity of self-deceit. It should be played, he has commented, "like a lyric rather than a drama."[4]

As the play opens, Lyman lies in a hospital bed after crashing his Porsche in a snowstorm on Mount Morgan. Until then a secret bigamist, he undergoes a crisis when his two wives are summoned to his bedside, one an older, cultured, seemingly puritanical and fashionable Episcopalian lady living with him in a fashionable New York home, and the other a sexy, aggressive businesswoman, twenty-four years younger, also intelligent and sophisticated, and living with him in Elmira. They have each given birth to Lyman's children: Theo, the elder wife, to Bessie; and Leah, his wife of the past nine years, to Benjamin. At the end of the play, Lyman asks his black nurse, Logan,

---

1992. Most notably, Miller deleted the character of Lyman's father, who appears to Lyman as a death figure in the original text. Changes in the 1991 Methuen and 1992 Penguin versions are discussed in Steven R. Centola's essay " 'How to Contain the Impulse of Betrayal': A Sartrean Reading of *The Ride down Mount Morgan*."

2. Balakian, "Conversation," 162.

3. Roy Hattersley, "The Guardian Profile: Arthur Miller: A View from the Barricades," 6.

4. Susan C. W. Abbotson, "An Afternoon with Arthur Miller."

"Hate me?" and she speaks for perhaps the audience at large when she responds, "I don't know. I got to think about it" (*RDMM*, 115). We see in the highly successful and totally self-serving businessman a character difficult to judge. Just as he can neither accept nor deny his guilt, we find ourselves drawn to him at times as a kind of seer revealing the moral condition of the age and yet also judging him, like Camus's Jean Baptiste Clamence in *The Fall*, "a shabby prophet for a shabby time."

In many respects Lyman embodies the ethos of the Reagan years in his unabashed self-gratification. In his first speech, he imagines himself speaking to his large staff about "the whole economic system" being "one enormous tit" (*RDMM*, 1), and his expressions of appetite persist throughout the play. Yet he culls from memory another self he proudly constructs for Nurse Logan. "I've got the biggest training program of any company for you guys," he tells her. "And the first one to ever put them in sales" (2). Ironically heading a large insurance company, he presents himself as a one-time socially conscious idealist, reminding his lawyer friend Tom Wilson that he created forty-two hundred jobs and raised sixty ghetto blacks to office positions (25). He proudly recalls his youthful days as a writer when "Jimmy Baldwin" told him, "Lyman, you're a nigger underneath" (3).[5] His total egocentrism and appetite seem at times to coexist with a contradictory sense of responsibility, as when he tells Tom, even as he plots to commit bigamy with the unaware Leah, that he wants to begin writing bigamy policies to protect women, and especially minority women. Social consciousness and unrelenting greed, love of family and profound betrayal expose a conflicted conscience that Lyman futilely denies in his attempt to have it all. "His crime," concludes Dianne Greene Mahony, "is that he refuses to say 'no' to himself,

---

5. As in *The Archbishop's Ceiling* Miller uses art as metaphor here. Schlueter presents a sensitive reading of Lyman's assumption of "authorial control" in creating the fictional Lyman of the past and his fictionalizing of characters and scenes in *Dramatic Closure*, 78–85. As readers, we ask, Who is creating the script; whose truth do we see? Lyman considered himself a writer in his youth and published poems in the *New Yorker* and a story in *Harper's*. When his father disparaged his success, he turned to business and ironically built a successful insurance company. Having sought immortality in art, he turned to insurance, which he tells Leah has become the contemporary means to immortality: "The soul was once immortal, now we've got an insurance policy" (*RDMM*, 43).

regardless of whom he destroys along the way"—it is "the tragedy of the 1990s. Or was that the 1980s?"[6]

The cause of the "accident" on Mount Morgan poses a central question in the play. Apparently Lyman removed a barrier to drive his car on the icy mountain, but under what motivation? On one hand it may indicate the love of risk, the exhilaration he felt nine years ago on the safari to Africa he took with Theo and Bessie when he stared down a charging lion. At moments when the play moves from the present to memory, Lyman achieves the transition by leaving his bed to reenact the past. The safari scene is triggered when Theo, toward the end of the play, begins to prick his conscience. "Theo, please!—now you are making me guilty!" (RDMM, 83). In a reflex action to avoid accusation, he slips from his bed and into his dream state, replaying the scene when he experienced his great epiphany—"it was so clear"—that "I've lost my guilt!" (84). Convincing himself that staring down the lion gave him the courage to reject all social and moral restraints and lay claim to total freedom, he shouts, " . . . I don't sacrifice one day to things I don't believe in—including monogamy, yes!—*arms thrown out, terror-inspired*—I love my life, I am not guilty! I dare you to eat me, son of a bitch!" (84). Pointing to his victorious encounter as justification for the way he has decided to live his life, he declares himself guilt-free and absolved of all responsibility for the consequences of his action—"I am all new!" (86). To admit to suicide, as June Schlueter observes, "would be agreeing to the judgment that he fears other would have of him."[7]

In the present, though, Lyman confronts the presence of death again, this time in the form of his aging body and growing awareness of failing power, a response to male menopause at the least and to a metaphysical and spiritual crisis at its deepest level. As surely as

6. Dianne Greene Mahony, "Arthur Miller, *Ride down Mt. Morgan.*" Bigsby describes it as "a diagnosis and perhaps a prognosis of a culture itself appropriating moral rhetoric to disguise a moral decay" (*Modern American Drama*, 123).

7. Schlueter, *Dramatic Closure*, 79. When he later lies to Theo about flying in a small plane from Elmira just to see her, she expresses shock that he could overcome his fear of flying (as she also expresses shock that he drives race cars). Ironically, he tells her, "The whole fear was guilt, Theo—I thought I *deserved* to crash. But I deserve to live because I'm not a bad guy and I love you" (RDMM, 96). As throughout, the claim of innocence always accompanies his actions.

in any tragedy, the ride down Mount Morgan marks "the fulness of time." It is time for a summing up, for a self-reckoning that beneath all his protests and rationalizations he cannot evade. In this sense the willful ride is paradoxically an attempt to taunt death and a form of self-judgment. Tom tells Theo that he hopes Lyman removed the barrier to commit suicide because "it would indicate a moral conscience" (*RDMM*, 55). And despite the constant denials, Lyman's too-insistent self-justification betrays a deep residue of guilt. In the shadow of death, he feels the need to justify his actions to others and to himself. Facing the possibility of death, he admits that "sometimes I feel I'm going to vanish without a trace, Theo" (47). Even at the end Theo wonders, "Why must death always sit on your shoulder" (97). Struggling like Willy Loman to "leave his thumbprint somewhere in the world," he rescues Benjamin from Leah's planned abortion to secure immortality and validate his life, telling her that their son will bear his own father's name and that of Alexander, his great grandmother, thereby ironically perpetuating the family obligations he ostensibly claims to be freed from.

As he drifts between consciousness and unconsciousness and envisions the first meeting between Leah and Theo, he is *"Terrified of self-betrayal"* (*RDMM*, 4–5). He ironically thinks, "Thank God I'm only imagining this to torture myself" (11), admitting the need to "torture himself" by confronting the consequences of his actions. He subconsciously willed the encounter and, as Steven Centola writes, "proceeds to investigate the past because he knows that only by doing so will he learn how to face his fear of death."[8] He finds it necessary to confess his unfaithfulness to Tom, even though the lawyer already knows. He naively proposes a Faustian compact to Leah in which they will have ten years together until he is rich, and then she completes the thought, " . . . walk away into the sunset" (30); but he cannot look into his daughter Bessie's "innocent face" without suffering. Conflicted whether or not he admits it, he weeps at the anguish he causes the others and keeps assuring himself that "nobody's any better, goddammit!" (65). He confesses only to excuse himself, telling Tom, "I'm a selfish son of a bitch. But I have loved the truth. . . . We're all ego, kid" (66–67). As though rejecting his own earlier self, he asserts, "I was a righteous young man; but I am

8. Centola, " 'How to Contain,' " 18.

an unrighteous middle-aged man" (67); yet he finds it necessary to lay claim to the earlier self when he proudly tells Nurse Logan about his assisting blacks and building a socially responsible company. He lays claim to innocence by virtue of being "no worse than anybody else!" and living truthfully for himself somewhere beyond good and evil like a god because "Gods are never guilty" (67, 98). But then he comically tries to leap out the window unaware that the room is on the first floor. This most deceptive of characters ironically announces that "deception has become my Nazi, my worst horror—I want nothing now but to wear my own face on my face every day till the day I die" (24). All the protestations and evasions prove futile, however, nor do they dissolve the moral questions or existential anguish he suffers in the knowledge that he is "as opaque and unknowable as some line of statues in a church wall. . . . We're all in a cave" (47).

The dialectical forces in the play, personified most clearly by the two wives, reflect themselves in Lyman's Jewish mother and Albanian father. Lyman associated his mother's Jewishness with law and judgment, whereas he identified his father with the bandit in the Albanian heart (the "two pieces of wisdom" he offered Lyman were "never trust anybody, and never forgive" [RDMM, 44]). The two wives embody the tragic dilemma the parents pose, for the legitimate claims of one inevitably violate those of the other, as Lyman recognizes, and defines the tragic fact of human nature. Trying to have both, he wills to escape the tragic consequences of existence; but having both, he is true to neither. According to him, Theo, the "godlike" wife of "girlish faith" and "idealism" also represents a "boredom" characterized by "awkward tenderness," "incurably Protestant cooking," "sexual inexperience," "sensible shoes," "intolerant former radicalism," and "stalwart love of country." Leah stands opposite as "an anarchist," "pleasure," "intensity," and "bare live wires." "I'd have no problem defending both of you to the death!" he cries as he imagines them together in bed with him: "Oh the double heat of two blessed wives—This is heaven!" (40). He needs both, he says. It is only human, and those who declare otherwise are hypocrites, like his business associate Tom Huddleston, who wants him fired for moral improprieties but "has more outside ass than a Nevada whorehouse" (70). Even Tom, he reminds his moralistic lawyer friend, has loved Theo and lusted after other women despite his moral protestations. In his ultimate defense, he echoes lines from After the Fall: "the first law of life is betrayal; why else did those rabbis pick Cain and Abel to open the Bible? Cain felt betrayed by God, so he betrayed Him and killed his brother" (66). Having betrayed Theo, ironically named after God, "Lie Man" declares himself "human" and therefore not responsible. In fact, life demands "choice," and Lyman's attempt not to choose but to possess both wives *is* tragic choice, nonetheless.

The second act contains key encounters with Leah and Theo in which the confident hero Lyman constructs out of selected memory and rationalization the conflicted Lyman in the present who wills the "ride" down Mount Morgan in the shadow of death to expose his duplicity and at last arrive at some kind of authenticity and perhaps even judgment. The two selves continue to compete in the haunted battleground between memory and the present. As he envisions his wives, he sees them not only as women he imprisons in his rapacious desire but also as judges who condemn him. In scene two of the act, they appear to him in highly sexist images, first wearing "kitchen aprons, with wifely ribbons tying up their hair" and then "dressed in sexy black tight-fitting body stockings and high heels . . . slithering" (*RDMM*, 61). Yet he dreams of judgment as well, as his unconscious keeps breaking into the illusory innocence he struggles to maintain. He sees the women in their *"deathly stillness as the sepulchral dream-light finds them"* and hears in their speech something *"godlike, deathly"* (61). Giving credence to the theory that the "ride" was a suicidal act, he cries out, "What dreams. God, how I'd like to be dead" (63). And when the two women come to confront him one by one for the final time, he seems unable to conceal his consciousness of guilt, as witnessed by his ubiquitous need to plead his case.

In the last meeting with Leah after she knows the truth of the bigamy and has already plotted divorce and repossession of her business, the house, and Benjamin, he reveals his guilt by *"Turning away from her"* and lamenting, "Jesus, what have I done to you." He tells her "it's sitting on my chest like a bag of cement. . . . My character" (*RDMM*, 90–91). Yet when she asks "do you feel responsibility or not?" he hedges and shifts the blame onto her: "You knew I was married, and you tried to make me love you, so I'm not entirely . . ." (92). He had told Tom he was "no worse than anybody else," and even here he cannot bear to utter the word "responsible" or "guilty." Furthermore, he brutally tells Leah that he is responsible for her becoming "the woman you want to be" after "all the those lonely postcoital showerbaths, and the pointless pillow talk and the boxes of heartless condoms beside your bed" (108). Giving her Benjamin, he goes on, he has given meaning to her life. Challenged by her accusations, he transforms them into innocence and near heroism.

With Theo as well, he exonerates himself. Leah accused him of hatred for Theo when he took her by the house in New York to see the pained older wife "haunted" at the window—"You had murder in you and you still do!" But Lyman insists "it hadn't felt like murder at all. I was on the high wire" (RDMM, 93). Here, too, he converts cruelty to daring risk-taking. He deflects Theo's condemnations with equal vigor. He counters them by repeating that his "betrayal" actually gave her "an interesting life" and made him and Theo closer. In Africa, when he stared down the lion and determined to marry Leah, he tells Theo, "We were never so close in our lives" (17). And when she calls him "a vulgar, unfeeling man," he cruelly mocks her, "But I made a good living" (72). Rejecting any charge against him, he boasts that because of his secret life with Leah as counterbalance, "I was never bored being with you." Denying that Theo was a victim of his betrayal, he explains, "Theo, you were bored—it's no sin." It was no "moral dilemma" but "just common domestic tedium, dear, it is life" (77). Outrageously telling her that she had been "happier" during the past nine years because *he* was content, he neatly washes his hands of guilt.

In contrast, Theo and Leah, who begin to refer to each other as "Mrs. Felt," achieve a higher moral consciousness by coming to accept their own culpability. Although much that Lyman says is true (that the impulse toward betrayal is a condition of human existence, that Thanatos and Eros battle in each person, and that the wives have gained something from his deceit), he stops short of confronting the sickness unto death and taking a leap of faith, retreating instead into a twilight zone of unresolved shadows. Unable to accept the consequences of his actions or to pass judgment on himself, he is left in total alienation at the end as the two wives come to accommodate their grief. Both women acknowledge their willing participation in the deceit that has bound all three. The truth is that Benjamin *has* helped make Leah "the woman you want to be." Aware of his past infidelities, she was a willing coconspirator in the illicit relationship and confesses, "I never really trusted him! Not really! I always knew there was something dreadful wriggling around underneath" (RDMM, 108). Even more painfully, Theo comes to the epiphany that she, too, bears responsibility. Seemingly suffering from a sudden stroke at the end of the play, she enters Lyman's room skirtless and disoriented and admits to Bessie, "I think I've always pretty well known what he was doing. Somewhere inside we all really know everything, don't we? But one has to live, darling— one has to live" (107). She had earlier remarked to Tom, "Maybe I've gone on because I'm corrupt. . . . He's rich, isn't he? And vastly respected, and what would I do with myself alone?" (59). In a brilliantly structured, if potentially melodramatic, moment, the women surround Lyman. As Bessie *"burst into tears. . . . A helpless wave of grief . . . now overflows to sweep up Lyman; then Leah is carried away by a wave of weeping . . . finally Theo is infected. . . . It is a veritable mass keening"* (110). Though all suffer, Steven Centola draws the important distinction that Leah and Theo's "ability to accept some of the blame for their crisis is what ultimately separates these women from their self-centered husband."[9] He weeps but cannot admit to his shame. He fails to confront his moral failure, which Tom describes in utterly simple terms: " . . . the problem is not honesty but how much you hurt others with it" (24). Even at this climactic moment Lyman declares innocence. While Bessie weeps, he asserts in utter egotism that "She wants her father back!" (109). Yet it is Bessie who most succinctly pronounces Lyman's guilt: "Will you once in your life think of another human being!" (103).

As the stage begins to empty, Lyman explains that he rode down Mount Morgan after he kept getting busy signals at Leah's home, where he was heading on the night of the storm. Fearing betrayal, "on my back in that room" in the motel, he tells her, "I started to die." As the storm increased, he goes on, "this whole nine-year commute suddenly seemed so ludicrous." On the verge of confession he instead boasts that "I can't leave you with a lie—the truth is that in some miserable, dark corner of my soul I still don't see why I am condemned" (RDMM, 113). Theo earlier announces her sense of a spiritual void because "Christianity is finished" (104), and at the end Leah concludes, "I don't know if I'll ever believe anything . . . or anybody again" (114). Lyman's response is as close as he comes to an admission of guilt: "Leah! Leah! Don't say I've done that!" (114).

9. Ibid., 23.

Ironically, Lyman needs the approval of those he betrays in order to secure self-approval. He tries desperately one last time to convert betrayal into victory. "I am not worthy. . . . But I am human and proud of it!—yes of the glory and the shit! The truth is holy, the truth is holy!" (*RDMM*, 111). But to know the truth of human existence, even if it is the first law of betrayal enacted in the Cain and Abel story, is not enough. The tragic condition of life does not exonerate one from responsibility for others in Miller's moral universe. To excuse Lyman would be a violation of Miller's long-expressed belief that guilt is potentially redemptive because it spurs moral responsibility for others. "Shame," Tom tells Lyman, "is the best part of you" (111). Lyman is "paralyzed" rather than freed by the truth, June Schlueter concludes, and so remains "alone and unshrived."[10] At the end everyone abandons him to face the void he has created for himself. All he can claim is his "loneliness . . . you earned it, kid, all by yourself. Yes. You have found Lyman at last!" (116).

Even in 1989, after working on the play for eleven years, and some two years before its premiere in London in 1991, Miller told Janet Balakian that "I'm not sure whether this will end up a tragedy or a comedy." He describes it as "viewing people at a tragic distance again, but with a certain forbearance, even a comic despair." Yet even with its twists, turns, and frets, its comic situations and eruptions of humor, the drama moves to a tragic rhythm. It "is still asserting that while we are weak the rules of life are powerful," Miller continues, "and they exist. And that's a tragic view, and therefore hopeful."[11] Caught in the web of memory, Lyman cannot escape the presentness of the past any more than Willy Loman can. To use Toni Morrison's phrase, his constant "rememory" of betrayal frustrates his declarations of freedom and authenticity and, above all, the spurious claim of innocence. In striking ways *The Ride down Mount Morgan* is another coming to the crossroads, another insistence that a price must be paid for the wages of sin, a confirmation that there is inevitably a judgment to be faced. If Lyman Felt never fully gains tragic awareness, the same can be said of Willy Loman. But there is no Biff to complete the tragic pattern for Lyman; and Miller's use of an open ending reveals the evolution of his art and especially the influence of

10. Schlueter, *Dramatic Closure*, 85.
11. Balakian, "A Conversation," 162.

absurdist drama on his thinking. At the end Miller does not carry out the death sentence that awaits his tragic figures in the early plays— Joe Keller, Willy Loman, John Proctor, Eddie Carbone. He denies closure, perhaps leaving Lyman an even more anguished fate, living with a truth he can no longer deny but is unable to act upon, a kind of Kierkegaardian figure living on the edge of the abyss but afforded no possible leap of faith in an absurd universe. Causality and consequences still exist as strongly as they do in any early Miller text, but no discernible metaphysical force can preserve a tragic victory in defeat. Lyman seems destined to remain unredeemed in a psychological inferno, forever pleading his case in vain before himself, a total narcissist self-absorbed in the prison of his own psyche.[12] The only "hopeful" sign comes at the end when Lyman asks Nurse Logan what she and her husband and son talk about when they go ice fishing. Their new shoes, she tells him; and he sees in their absurd gesture something to celebrate. "Imagine . . . three of them sitting out there together on that lake, talking about their shoes!" (RDMM, 116). Projecting his shared humanity onto them, he ends with his weeping at their absurd action and vows to "learn loneliness." In weeping for a lost innocence he sees projected in the family on the ice, there may yet be a faint glimmer of tragic hope.[13]

The Last Yankee

Though begun after The Ride down Mount Morgan, The Last Yankee was performed initially as a brief one-scene drama in 1991 in a festival of one-act plays in New York and subsequently in its final acting version as an extended two-scene play in 1993, when it received world premieres in both New York at the Manhattan Theater Club and in London at the Young Vic Theatre (it was also performed along with I Can't Remember Anything in 1998 during the Signature Theater season devoted to staging Miller plays). Miller describes it

12. Steven Centola writes, "Miller does not absolve 'Lyman'—a revealing name —of responsibility, for . . . even though everything in life is clouded with ambiguity, that fact does not mitigate Lyman's culpability for his betrayal of his families' trust" (" 'How to Contain,' " 18–19).

13. Miller's deletion of the father in the final acting version also implies a victory of sorts, as Lyman is no longer consciously bound by the destructive male legacy that represents death in the figure of the father.

in terms that might as well be applied to many of the later plays, such as the one-acts written in the eighties, *The Ride down Mount Morgan*, and *Mr. Peters' Connections*: "I have called this play a comedy, a comedy about a tragedy, and I'm frankly not sure why" ("About Theatre Language," *LY*, 94). A delicate balance of the humorous and the poignantly tragic, it employs the same intense concentration of the shorter plays in its tight focus on a very limited set of characters in a highly contained structure.

As the plot develops, two men of opposing values and economic status meet in the waiting room of a psychiatric hospital in New England where their wives are patients. Leroy Hamilton, a direct descendant of Alexander Hamilton, is a barely surviving forty-four-year-old carpenter with seven children, and John Frick is a childless but very successful older businessman. The opening scene stages a verbal duet by the two men, followed by a longer second scene in which two other carefully modulated duets follow, one between the two wives, Patricia Hamilton and Karen Frick, and the other between Leroy and Patricia, ending finally in a brief but moving quartet.

Yet another play about the disillusionment of family life, the drama once again pits American materialism against the need for more enduring human and spiritual values. The characters are all in some measure victims of the same specious mythology, the same perverted ethos that corrupts Joe Keller and Willy Loman. As Miller writes of the central couple, the Hamiltons, "these people are supremely the prey of the culture"; "they are bedrock, aspiring not to greatness but to other gratifications—successful parenthood, decent children, and a decent house and a decent car and an occasional nice evening with family or friends, and above all, of course, some financial security. . . . They are people who can be inspired to great and noble sacrifice, but also to bitter hatreds" (*LY*, 96, 92, 96). In the course of the drama, they struggle to retain the essential beliefs that have preserved them against the onslaught of cultural forces assaulting their core values— a love for each other, for family, and for the land. In a larger sense, this is a play that addresses the psychic wound that still festers in the American psyche—once more, "the fish is in the water, and the water is in the fish."[14]

14. In the essay appended to the text Miller, identifies the "split vision" that "has informed all the plays I have written. I have tried to make things seen in their social context and simultaneously felt as intimate testimony" (*LY*, 94).

Ostensibly the two men embody the opposing poles we have seen operating from the earliest Miller texts. The sixty-year-old John Frick has colonized his wife in his unrelenting quest of the American Dream. Incapable of understanding Karen's mental distress when she has "not a trouble in the world" (LY, 13), he is blind to his own crass possessiveness and indifference. Desperately trying to find the cause of her illness, he reflects the worst aspects of American culture, wondering if "it's the Negroes, you know?" and refusing to put Karen in a more expensive private hospital, the Rogers Pavilion, where he admits she would receive "absolutely first class" care, because "I could afford it, but what are we paying taxes for?" (15). Protesting having to pay a plumber seventeen dollars to fix a showerhead, he unwittingly offends Leroy, who later divulges his reluctance to charge the same seventeen dollars per hour as a carpenter despite being in economic straits. Frick naively assumes Leroy "must be doing all right" financially because he recently rebuilt the altar at the stately Presbyterian church. Shocked by the carpenter's indifference to money and to being from "an old family like that," he is stunned by Leroy's unwillingness to capitalize on his famous family's financial resources. Incapable of understanding either his victimized wife or Leroy's apparent lack of interest in making money, he unintentionally continues to offend Leroy until the carpenter explodes in anger at the end of the scene: "One minute my altar is terrific and the next moment I'm some kind of shit bucket" (34).

Whatever his self-righteous indignation, though, Leroy exposes another kind of insensitivity and blindness, though he seems the archetype of the self-reliant New Englander. If Frick introduces the central question, "Who are you going to blame?" (LY, 64), it is directed to the younger man as well. Though he has seen Patricia through two previous hospitalizations, taken on the major responsibility for raising their seven children, and remained faithful to her over the many years of her depression, Leroy is almost too glib in his refusal to seek financial gain, too smug in his insistence that he is "not competing" with everyone else, too defensive in his hostile pride in being "only a dumb swamp Yankee" (24).

Indeed, "depression" assumes metaphoric significance in the play. It attacks not only the women but their husbands as well. A modern version of the ennui that torments Ibsen's characters, depression is a manifestation of a universal disease Patricia comes to define.

"My problem is spiritual" (LY, 59), she tells Leroy. Miller remarks in a 1993 interview, "It's all over the world, in all advanced countries. . . . Depression has become the major disease of a technological society," which he goes on to attribute to unrealistic expectations: "People have been sold on some symphonic grandeur. . . . [A]n important part of the ethos now is the idea that we all have infinite possibilities."[15] Not just Patricia and Karen but the whole society falls prey to "the moral and social myths feeding the disease," characterized by the vast parking space behind the hospital where "crowds of stricken citizens converge on the place to visit mothers, fathers, brothers, and sisters" (94). In ironic ways the asylum provides an area of temporary relief from the devastating demands of the social myths that coerce the characters to measure the "disappointment" in their lives; the asylum opens the possibility, however slightly, of escape from the paralyzing weight of our societal oppression.

The exchange between Patricia and Karen that opens the second scene lays bare the suffering of both wives. Miller acknowledges to Robert Simonson in an interview that Patricia suffers from the same essential depression as Willy Loman,[16] because she accepts, despite her struggle against it, the ethos of the American myth. Driven by the financial successes of her immigrant Swedish family, she holds Leroy up to the expectation that he also acquire financial security. She identifies Leroy as the cause of her suffering, and she ironically blames him for not suing the doctor for incompetence because he failed to cure her after long years of treatment. Although she claims, "I know I have to stop blaming him," she adds, "It's just that he's got really well-to-do relatives and he simply will not accept anybody's help" (LY, 53). She resents his spending money on his banjo lessons, is irritated at his plot to donate his valuable saw-and-chisel collection to a museum, and is embarrassed by his nine-year-old car.

Yet in the same discussion with Karen she exposes her own sense of guilt. "Dear God," she laments, "when I think of him hanging in there all these years . . . I'm so ashamed"—but then she adds that "he absolutely refuses to make any money. . . . I can't be expected to applaud exactly" (LY, 32). Still, she keeps repeating to herself,

15. Robert Simonson, "Values, Old and New: Arthur Miller and John Tillinger on The Last Yankee," 15–16.
16. Ibid., 16.

"It's just not his fault. I have to remember that" (38). And she con-fesses to Karen that her brothers, Buzz and Charles, against whom she measures Leroy's failure as a provider, both committed suicide— "We were all brought up expecting to be wonderful and . . . *breaks off with a shrug* . . . just wasn't" (42). Caught between being a judge and a lover to her husband, she, like other Miller characters, suffers an incapacity to act.

For her part, Karen is rendered even more incapacitated by "disap-pointment." Drifting in and out of reality, she responds to Patricia's questions long after they pass and keeps interrupting her sympathetic fellow patient's comments with a string of non sequiturs. From the beginning she exposes the sense of intimidation she feels with her husband. He "doesn't like being kept waiting" (*LY*, 28), she keeps repeating, until she finally goes out to meet him. A number of reve-lations surface in the brief conversation that expose her fragile sense of self, among them that she "can't stand dead animals" (30), yet ac-companies her husband on hunting trips; that she goes unwillingly on Frick's fishing trips, even though "the sight of a catfish makes me want to vomit" (36); that she was a rejected only child whose mother left the farm to her cousin instead of her (another example of materialism turned to betrayal); and that she always wanted a gar-den (a parallel to Leroy's love of the land). All but oblivious of her husband's wealth, the center of his values, she remarks tentatively to Patricia that "We're rich, I think" (36). Like Patricia, she feels "so ashamed" of being here and seeks explanations for her depression, at one point repeating the cliché of modern psychology that "it's quite common when a woman is at home all day" (39). For all her lack of awareness and dazed condition, she serves as a kind of therapist for Patricia, whom she keeps saying is beautiful, looks to for support, and encourages. And Patricia more assertively becomes a therapist of sorts for her. She keeps trying to reassure her older friend, telling her not to put herself down or allow her husband to.

With nerves exposed in their conversations with Karen and Frick, Patricia and Leroy meet in their climactic duet in the second scene. Both characters, equally crippled by disappointment and under the paralyzing power of depression, undergo a sustained catharsis that compels the play to its end. Despite their resistance to the economic pressures of the social myth, they evaluate each other against the pervasive ethos. Agreeing not to argue, they soon lapse into a series of recriminations, caught up in a language peppered with economics: expenses and debts, wages and bills, survival and economic security, economic dependence and financial need. Even while looking to Leroy for emotional support so she can leave the hospital, Patricia cannot refrain from denouncing her husband's financial incompetency. "I can't bear it when you can't pay the bills" (LY, 59), she concludes. She uses his lack of success as a more subtle weapon against him as well. Their daughter, Amelia, "hears only disappointment in your voice," she declares, which she attributes to his unadmitted consciousness of failure. Accusing him of being part of a Yankee tradition that paid "fifty cents a week and called us dumb Swedes with strong backs and weak minds and did nothing but make us ridiculous" (53), she applies standards of economic justice to accuse him. Leroy responds with an equal claim of economic oppression. He bitterly reminds Patricia that her father had told him, "No Yankee will ever be good enough for a Swedish girl" (52), and he betrays his jealousy of her family's wealth and the Swedes' current power—"there isn't a good piece of property that isn't owned by Swedes" (53).

Ironically, both expose their susceptibility to the materialism they claim to resist. Despite himself, Leroy tries to convert failure into a mark of pride. "I'll get a bumper sticker printed up—'The driver of this car is a failure.' . . . Or maybe I should just drive out on a tractor and shoot myself!" (LY, 51). Patricia senses self-judgment behind his histrionics—"Your eyes are full of disappointment" (59), she tells him. Defensive in the extreme, Leroy knows he has been found wanting on the scales of economic success, though he insists it does not matter to him. Even if he self-righteously condemns the criterion of material success, he cannot escape the consequences of the "disappointment" it generates, even in himself. In light of Frick's essential question,—"Who you going to blame?"—he cannot dismiss the force of Patricia's penetrating accusations.

In counterpoint to their condemnations of each other, both characters express a sense of guilt as well. In the midst of her accusations, Patricia remorsefully comments, "You've had no life at all, have you?" (LY, 49); she confesses, "I've been very bad to you sometimes, Leroy, I really see that now" (55). Leroy's compassion surfaces as strongly as his resentment. "It's a long time since I blamed you," he remarks (49). As they shift from expressions of affection to outbursts of anger and accusation, the scene intensifies. It is difficult to know which character suffers most from the weight of depression. They see in each other their own "disappointment." Their "problem," as Patricia recognizes, is "spiritual." Secretly not having taken her medicine for three weeks, Patricia speaks with a new clarity as she tries to discover in Leroy the support she requires to return home and resume life. She comes to a point of tragic choice, rendered capable for the moment of choosing, of risking life outside what Quentin calls "that lie of Eden" and illusory innocence. Both she and Leroy are hesitant. She warns, "I don't want you to think I have no problems any more" (47). "I'm trying to find myself!" she blurts out, but "I'm not sure I could hold up. Not when I hear your sadness all the time and your eyes are full of disappointment" (57, 59). Seeing the anguish in Leroy, she questions how he could have been faithful to her during the twenty long years of her illness, knowing "There's lots of women would love having you" (57). She exacts his admission that "if it wasn't for the kids I probably *would* have gone" (58).

Leroy finally proposes the same solution Quentin comes to in *After the Fall*—and Patricia "*seems to be receiving him,*" despite her befuddled state when Leroy cries out: "We are in the world and you're going to have to find some way to love it! . . . [Y]ou just have to love this world" (*LY*, 59–60). The climax matches the redemptive vision of the earlier play. Risking life, however absurd, and risking love, however flawed, provide the only existence possible "after the Fall." As Leroy seems to embrace the absurd by preparing to go to his banjo lesson to learn a new song to play for Patricia, she "*hesitates, then kisses him,*" as the play moves into the final quartet when the Fricks reenter.

The ending juxtaposes possible outcomes to the condition of "disappointment" or despair in the human condition that both pairs confront. Though clearly compassionate, Frick cannot provide Karen with the understanding she needs to reclaim her life. In the comically poignant scene—indeed "a comedy about tragedy," we discover that Karen has evaded reality and tried to assert her worth by tap-dancing in the middle of the night. With Patricia's encouragement, she again puts on her costume to dance; as Patricia tells Frick, "She's got to feel treasured" (*LY*, 64). Reflecting her earlier charge against Leroy, she tells the elder man, "You're sounding disappointed to her," "She's terrified of your criticism," and "she's trying to get you interested" (65–66). But Frick cannot let go of his embarrassment. "I think it's kinda silly at her age" he comments (63), and it is "not normal" to get up at two or three in the morning to dance before a mirror. Offering the feeble excuse that his fueling business is "too complicated" to allow him to spend time with Karen, he tries to retreat from responsibility for his wife's depression. She draws him into the action, though, co-ercing him to sing "Swanee River" while she dances with increasing sensuousness. Finally, he explodes when Patricia tells him to look at her, *"I am looking at her, goddammit!"* (69). Karen's confidence is shattered; as her movement ebbs like that of a wind-up doll, Frick guiltily tries to erase his outburst: "I hope you don't feel I'm . . . dis-appointed or something, you hear . . . ?" (70). It is too late, though, and Karen finally *"stands perfectly still, staring at nothing"* (71).

Set against the drama played out by the older couple, Leroy and Patricia achieve a measure of hope. In Leroy's expressions of concern for the pathetic Karen, Patricia sees in her husband the compassion and understanding she needs to recover her life. In the earlier scene with him, she tells him he "can't bear to work with other human beings," but in his obvious compassion for Karen, Patricia now finds the "two ounces of trust" Leroy tells her she needs so "we could still have a life" (*LY*, 50, 52). She discovers in his empathy for Karen his capacity to support her. As the scene begins, Leroy tunes his banjo, and as Karen dances he shouts his encouragement: "Hey, she's great!" (69). Then when Frick's outburst of anger ends the dance, he begins to pluck out the song on the banjo to start it up again; but as he speeds up the rhythm at Karen's feeble request, the spirit goes out of her until she stops *"With an unrelieved sadness"* (72). It is as though the buoyant singing of "Life Is Just a Bowl of Cherries" that ends *The American Clock* fades in the light of painful reality.

Finding in Leroy's compassion the motivation to act, Patricia chooses to go, assuming responsibility for her life as all true Miller heroes must. Reaching out her hand to touch Leroy's face with *"a muted gratitude in her gesture,"* she gets her overnight bag to leave with him. Jokingly asking if "that car" is "going to get us home," she speaks symbolically of the depth of his love for her: "Once you believe in something you just never know when to stop, do you? . . . Between the banjo and that car I've certainly got a whole lot to look forward to" (*LY*, 73). Yet, though Leroy declares the end "a miracle," the play does not lapse into simple melodrama. As early as a 1973 interview with Robert Corrigan, Miller remarks that in his dramas written after the early tragedies, "I take the doom for granted . . . and look for some kind of life-line to hang onto" (*Conv.*, 254). In most of the late plays, with the possible exception of *Broken Glass*, he veers from the finality of tragedy. There is a cost to existence that is neither the absolute price that tragedy exacts nor the naive evasion of reality that melodrama invites. The play has no "sense of tying all the loose strings" characteristic of the tragedies of the forties and fifties, "nor should the play, which simply sets the boundaries of the possible. . . . For the theme is hope rather than completion or achievement, and hope is tentative always" (*LY*, 95). Writing in the twilight of his career, Miller deduces in the pattern of existence that the conclusion is that the conclusion cannot be written; and this is no more equivocal, after all, than in the endings of Ibsen's last great plays—artistic ambiguity being no literary offense.

Broken Glass

In his 1994 "Platform Lecture" at the Royal National Theatre where *Broken Glass* was being staged, Miller stated, "This is a story I have known and thought about for fifty years. . . . But I haven't written it before because it seemed to be part of the past."[17] Indeed, in many respects the play reverts to Miller's work a half century before. No play following *After the Fall* seems so clearly to embody the tragic rhythm that characterizes texts like *All My Sons* or *Death of a Salesman*. It became an easy target for Miller critics in New York, who found in it increasing evidence that Miller was long since passé. In his typically caustic tone, Robert Brustein called the 1994 Broadway production "just another spiral in a stumbling career." This "shaky piece of stagecraft," he continued, "is made of fragments from a more shatterproof phase of Miller's career," when his often "plodding, pedestrian, predictable and a little pompous" plays somehow "passed for modern tragedies." And David Richards's review in the *New York Times* branded the play "Ibsenism by the book," a rehash of Ibsen's preoccupation "with the impact of long ago deeds in the present."[18]

17. Quoted in Alice Griffin, *Understanding Arthur Miller*, 82.
18. Robert Brustein, "Separated by a Common Playwright"; David Richards, "A Paralysis Points to Spiritual and Social Ills," C11.

There is some truth to these charges, for some forty-seven years after *All My Sons* initiated his successful career on the American stage, Miller does indeed invoke the rhythms of modern tragedy sounded in Ibsen. The negative responses in New York led to the drama's closing within a relatively short time of its opening, yet it proved an overwhelming success in London, where it sold out at the National Theatre and was transferred to the West End to continue the run, eventually winning the Olivier Award for best new play. While Broadway critics tended to find a dull repetition of "creaky" nineteenth-century dramaturgy and overworked themes, British audiences found absorbing contemporary theater. In his lecture, Miller commented that "when ethnic cleansing came into the news," the as-yet-unwritten, fifty-year-old drama in his head "suddenly became part of the present."[19]

The direction of ever more positive current criticism of Miller has tended to rescue him from the Greeks and Ibsen and move him more securely into the twentieth century and toward postmodernism; but even if this critical tendency has allowed us to discover the currency and richness of Miller as a whole, *Broken Glass* stands as a reminder that Miller has retained a powerful and enduring sense of the conventions of more traditional drama.[20] To be sure, the play reflects Miller's growing uncertainty in the late plays about the shape of his drama (he continually revised it, during productions and after), and it certainly possesses contemporary elements; but in elemental ways it holds to the conventions of tragedy he employed in his very first successes. If *Broken Glass* "is a kind of coda to much of Miller's earlier writing," as Christopher Morley wrote in his review of the National Theatre opening, it "is in fact a breathtakingly brilliant exploration of the paralysis that overtook America in November 1938 as news of the Nazi persecution of the Jews just after Kristallnacht reached their Brooklyn cousins." A few years before the play reached the stage, Miller admitted to Steven Centola that his later plays in fact "may seem even more tragic" than his early dramas, in which "the characters' inability to face themselves gives rise to

19. Quoted in Griffin, *Understanding Arthur Miller*, 82.
20. Susan C. W. Abbotson argues that *Broken Glass* illustrates Miller's "efforts to redefine the postmodernist trend toward disjunction and otherness into a culture of connection and self" ("Issues of Identity in *Broken Glass*," 68).

tragic consequences."[21] Precisely because these later characters do "face themselves" at the culmination of a circuitous but inevitable movement through memory, they endure the full consequences of tragic choices glimpsed through shifting lenses of truth and illusion.

Like Willy Loman's inability to make it to New England, the crisis that triggers the action in the play—the unexplained paralysis of Sylvia Gellburg in 1938—parallels the coming of the plague in *Oedipus the King* or the appearance of ghosts in Ibsen's *Ghosts*. It marks the assertion of the *x*-factor in Aristotelian terms, which necessitates an unavoidable confrontation with the past. And like *Oedipus the King*, *Broken Glass*, as some critics have observed, becomes a psychological or spiritual detective story, a quest to resolve the mystery and a return to the "crossroads" where past and present intersect. In the rhythmic structure of the play, every step forward is a step backwards, a confrontation with past failures that erupt in true tragic rhythm in the presentness of the drama. The debilitating paralysis embodies the composite guilt shared by the characters. It represents both public and private, corporate and individual betrayals. Both Phillip Gellburg, her husband, and Dr. Harry Hyman, her analyst-doctor, suspect that Sylvia's condition is related to her obsession with the news of Nazi atrocities during Kristallnacht. It is worth noting that Miller alludes to his Jewishness and to biblical themes perhaps more than any other contemporary Jewish playwright, including Pinter and Mamet. He of course wrote about the Jewish experience in America in his novel *Focus* in 1945, and, as discussed, he expressly treats the horrors of the Holocaust in *Incident at Vichy* and especially in *Playing for Time*. Here he employs the theme more implicitly in the manner of *After the Fall*, in which he links the tyrannies of state terror with personal crimes. As Hyman tells Phillip, "we get sick in twos and threes and fours, not alone as individuals" (*BG*, 504). We "go into a state of oblivion" to avoid guilt, Miller comments to V. Rajakrishnan in an interview, and "continuously re-arrive at yet another state of innocence. . . . [W]e continually lapse into a state of innocence—which brings on the next cycle of our murderousness, since the innocent are permitted to defend themselves" (*Conv.*, 334). The only release from the cycle of criminality, *Broken Glass* reminds us, is to be freed from "the temptation of innocence"; that can only come, as Susan

---

21. Christopher Morley, "Miller's Crossing"; Centola, "'Just Looking,'" 86.

Abbotson observes, when we recognize that "denial, resignation, or ignorance . . . is tantamount to complicity."[22]

Paralysis symbolizes the moral impotency that arrests all the characters in the play. Phillip's twenty-year sexual impotency in particular represents both his incapacity to enact his love for Sylvia and his retreat to innocence, a point ironically underscored at the beginning of the play when Margaret, Hyman's "shiksa" wife, ironically assumes that he is the patient rather than Sylvia. Having denied his Jewishness in order to escape the judgment of the dominant society, he willingly humiliates himself as head of the Mortgage Department of Brooklyn Guarantee and Trust by doing the dirty work of the business and ingratiating himself to his anti-Semitic boss. Sending his son, Jerome, to West Point because "I wanted people to see that a Jew doesn't have to be a lawyer or a doctor or a businessman" (BG, 511), he wears a symbolic black suit, tie, and hat. Like everyone else in the play except for Sylvia, he ignores the suffering of the Jews in Europe, and he cannot tolerate his own Jewishness. He tells Hyman, "German Jews can be pretty . . . you know . . . *Pushes up his nose with his forefinger*" (496). Seeing his Jewishness as a source of guilt and shame, he acquires innocence by trying not to be a Jew and consequently victimizes others around him. To conceal his divided nature even from himself, he not only allows himself to be co-opted by the dominant WASP system that rejects him as Jew, but he warps his son's future and betrays his genuine love for Sylvia. He complains that Sylvia "does not like to hear about the other side"—German Jews "who won't take an ordinary good job you know; it's got to be pretty high up in the firm or they're insulted. . . . . [T]hey're supposed to be *refugees*" (496). Margaret quite rightly calls him "one miserable little pisser" and "a dictator," like Hitler (505). His self-hatred is a kind of self-death, projected in his black dress, and a tacit approval of the slaughter of the Jews in Europe. Tyrannizing Sylvia because of his self-detestation and self-defensiveness, he surfaces in her recurring nightmare in the guise of a Nazi who starts to cut off her breasts.

But Phillip alone is not guilty. Even the minor characters wash their hands of any criminality and are blinded by their "innocence." Sylvia's sister, Harriet, is willingly unaware of why the Nazis make old Jewish men scrub the street with toothbrushes; she also tells

22. Abbotson, "Issues of Identity," 70.

Sylvia that her obsession over the accounts of Kristallnacht "is not normal" (*BG*, 508). Margaret, who resents Hyman's insistence on living in the Jewish area in Brooklyn rather than in Manhattan, dismisses Sylvia's extreme empathy with the Jewish victims in Europe as "crazy" (538). Miller implicitly condemns not only the American government for its indifferent response to the horrors of the war, but also the Jewish community for its own blind retreat into innocence. The paralysis depicts the moral stasis on a corporate level, crossing race and rank and revealing a culpability shared by everyone. As Holga remarks about the victims of the Holocaust in *After the Fall*, "no one they didn't kill can be innocent again" (*AF*, 21). The criminal innocence is not only public or corporate, however; it extends, as always in Miller, to the private realm and to personal relationships where it leads to betrayal and another kind of Nazism.

All characters carry personal guilt with them buried somewhere in the unconscious. The play, John Lahr has written, is "an anatomy of denial," a tragic web of "the evasions and hostilities by which the soul contrives to hide its emptiness from itself."[23] Although he acts as something of the moral spokesman in the play and ironically acts as chief investigator of the cause of Sylvia's paralysis, as well as uncovering Phillip's criminality, even Hyman shares in the guilt. Margaret reveals personal betrayal in his relationship with her, as she exposes her handsome and jaunty husband's past infidelities. Seemingly opposite Phillip in his virility, Hyman, himself a lapsed Jew, cannot resist the temptation of betrayal. Margaret taunts him about taking on Sylvia's case. "Why not?" she asks—"She's a very beautiful woman" (*BG*, 505). Drawn to Sylvia, Hyman nearly makes love to her and admits, "I haven't been this moved by a woman in a very long time" (525). To persuade Sylvia to open up "things that are way down deep in your heart," he all but seduces her, telling her to "pretend" they have just made love. "And now it's over and we're lying together. And you begin to tell me some secret things" (529). When he fails to conceal his guilt and tries to evade Margaret's accusations, pleading that he has been faithful for the past six or seven years, she tells him, "You don't realize how transparent you are. You're a pane of glass, Harry" (537), an obvious evocation of the title and another linking of private and public guilt. "What is it—just new ass all the time?"

23. John Lahr, "Dead Souls," 96.

she continues. Hyman wonders why he takes Margaret's "suspicions seriously," and she responds with painful honesty, "Oh that's easy.— You love the truth, Harry" (538). Just as Hyman searches out Phillip's guilt, Margaret plays analyst in assessing Hyman's moral choices—a hopeless case, she ironically concludes. His near complacency about Kristallnacht, detached scientific determinism, and easy dismissal of religion as the opiate of the masses, suggest another kind of paralysis.

Nor can Sylvia retreat to a spurious innocence, despite her Cassandra-like vision. Although she sees in the Jewish victims a projection of her own suffering at the hands of a "Nazi" husband, she also must acknowledge her own culpability. Phillip attributes his symbolic and literal impotence to her not wanting him "to be the man here" (*BG*, 554), citing her refusal to give birth to a second child, perhaps an oblique reference as well to the children killed in Germany. In truth Sylvia is victim of her own choices and is responsible for them. Both she and Phillip have accommodated themselves to personal failure, accepted their roles as victim and scapegoat, and thereby assured their own defeat. Even as they incriminate one another, they reveal their own offenses. Like the characters we have noted in some of the one-acts and even in *The Last Yankee*, they share a symbiotic relationship in which they survive by feeding off each other. True to the tragic rhythm, whether in Greek drama or in Ibsen's pattern of retroactive illumination, characters are stripped of their masks; their illusive attempts to preserve innocence ultimately prove futile once again. David Richards has concluded that "Sylvia Gellburg is unable to walk because her husband is a cripple," but this is too neat and too simplistic. The tragic knowledge she possesses is also about herself, her self-consciousness of personal choices, and her willing acceptance of an unauthentic self. Like all tragic figures, she is as much a victim of herself as of others. Faced with "the mores of that time and society, and her amenable personality, and the influence of her mother," Miller has commented, she turns "against herself."[24]

Sylvia appears to be tormented only by others, especially by Phillip. Yet she stayed in a failed marriage because, as Harriet tells Hyman, "it would have killed our mother, she worships Phillip, she'd never outlive it" (*BG*, 518), an interesting parallel to Mrs. Alving in Ibsen's

24. Richards, "Paralysis Points," C11; Miller quoted in Griffin, *Understanding Arthur Miller*, 186.

Ghosts, who marries Captain Alving at her mother and aunts' insistence. She tolerates her role as a long-suffering wife, giving up her fulfilling career in business and remaining with Phillip even though he twice physically abuses her, once by striking her with a steak and once by throwing her up a set of stairs. Trying to explain her lost life to Harriet, whose son is determined to turn down a college scholarship, she declares, "If I'd had a chance to go to college, I'd have led a whole different life" (509). More poignantly, for twenty years she has lived with Phillip's impotency because she did not want to further embarrass him after her failed attempt to gain their rabbi's help distanced her permanently from her husband.

Yet her paralysis empowers her to exorcise her long-held hostility toward him. In a way it shifts the balance of power in the relationship and temporarily frees her from guilt and moral stasis, allowing her to respond when others seem powerless to act in response to the horrors of Kristallnacht. The baffled Phillip tells Hyman, "It's like she's almost . . . I don't know . . . enjoying herself" (*BG*, 503), because of her identity with the suffering Jews that Phillip remains largely indifferent to. And Harriet also remarks to Hyman that she is "more like . . . I don't know . . . like this is how she wants to be. I mean since the collapse" (517). Hyman himself tells her, "I'm afraid you're getting comfortable in this condition . . ." (525). Emboldened, she reacts sarcastically to Phillip's suggestion that the two of them seek Hyman's help in resolving his impotency and again try to make love. "It's too late for that . . . it doesn't matter anymore," she tells him as she "*draws back her hand*" (514). She openly taunts him when he tries to confess that he once thought about separating from her but has not "felt that way for years now." "I've been here a long time," she retorts; "Well I'm here. . . . Here I am, Phillip! . . . I'm here for my mother's sake, for Jerome's sake, and everybody's sake except mine, but I'm here and here I am and you want to talk about it, now when I'm turning into an old woman?" (515). As the scene climaxes, he desperately tries to force her out of her chair, until she collapses, looking "*at him in terror at the mystery before her*" (516), faced at last with the brutal truth of both his and her own self-betrayal.

Despite her bitter condemnation of Phillip and her fierce exposure of his failures, she comes to tragic *self*-knowledge as well. As John Lahr has written, "Sylvia can't face her disgust at herself any more than she can face down her husband."[25] "What I did with my life!" she cries out in anguish to Phillip. "Out of ignorance. Out of not wanting to shame you in front of other people. A whole life. Gave it away like a couple of pennies—I took better care of my shoes" (*BG*, 553–54). To find some resolve, she must, like Esther Franz or Theo or Leah Felt, stop blaming others and find the resources in herself. Ironically, she describes herself as suffering a form of birth trauma, a reflection of the death and rebirth motif tied to the seasons so elemental in traditional tragedy: "It's like I was just born and I . . . didn't want to come out yet. Like a deep, terrible aching . . ." (508). She later tells Hyman, " . . . it's almost like there's something in me . . . it's like . . . *She presses her chest*—something alive, like a child almost, except it's a very dark thing . . . and it frightens me!" (529), reminiscent of the symbolic ugly child Holga tells Quentin they must love at the end of *After the Fall*. In a mock birth scene later with Hyman, the doctor tries to force her to walk, instructing her to "send your thoughts into your hips. Tense your hips. . . . Come on now. The strongest muscles in your body are right there, you have tremendous power there" (528). In another striking allusion to the theme of birth, Phillip confesses to Hyman that "years ago . . . when I used to make love to her, I would feel almost like a small baby on top of her, like she was giving me birth. That's some idea? In bed next to her she was like a . . . a marble god" (565). As Hyman tells Phillip in their last conversation, "If you're alive you're afraid; we're born afraid—a newborn baby is not a picture of confidence" (563). These and other birth references suggest the frightening birth of an authentic self, frightening because such a birth can occur only through suffering, at the cost of the public self behind which the characters hide. Frozen by fear and an incapacitating guilt, Sylvia and Phillip have betrayed their true selves, and consequently each other. Only at a tremendous price can they achieve a tragic victory in defeat by looking into the mirror.

Phillip reenacts Sylvia's near welcoming of her paralysis after he himself collapses in his boss's office when he is fired, a scene clearly imitative of the one between Willy Loman and Howard in *Death of a Salesman*. Like Sylvia he finds something paradoxically freeing in the attack, "Like I suddenly had something to tell her that would

25. Lahr, "Dead Souls," 95.

change everything. . . . God, I always thought there'd be a time to get to the bottom of myself!" (*BG*, 560). Suffering a shock of recognition, he is forced to admit what he always knew, that his boss's real accusation is that he is a Jew. "I can't get to the bottom of myself," he pleads with Hyman: "It's unbelievable—I don't have a job anymore. I just can't believe it" (561). Up against an existential crisis, he begins "choking" on his thoughts, having to rediscover himself by reclaiming his Jewishness and admitting his love for and dependency on Sylvia. "I don't know where I am. . . . My thoughts keep flying around—everything from years ago coming back like it was last week" (562). Faced with the past like the traditional tragic figure, he confesses, "I feel like there's nothing inside me, I feel empty" (562). Paradoxically, it is a moment of truth he invites, yet it is only through painful self-confrontation that Phillip can somehow be redeemed from the past. Only by acknowledging his offenses against Sylvia and against himself can he achieve what Miller calls "tragic dimension." He tells Hyman he wants to "talk about being Jews" (562), struggling to embrace what he betrayed in himself, and he wants desperately to heal the breach between him and Sylvia by admitting his own self-denial of his Jewishness and cooperation with the "Nazis." As Kinereth Meyer concludes, the paralysis "is the displaced image of silence,"[26] a silence engaged in by everyone—Phillip, Harriet, Hyman, the government—in the presence of Kristallnacht and a silence of betrayal in the Gellburg house.

After an extended discussion of self-defensiveness and recrimination, Hyman offers Phillip the only solution to the tragic dilemma, though of course nothing can either rescue the characters from the price tragedy exacts or alter the past. "Look in the mirror sometime!" (*BG*, 565), he tells Phillip, not without irony given his own seeming indifference to the plight of the Jews in Germany. "I don't see any solution" to the crisis, "Except the mirror" (566). Only by confronting his own image can Phillip gain freedom, he insists, and "forgive yourself. . . . And the Jews. And while you're at it you can throw in the goyim" (566). Wanting to be the victim while at the same time denying the victims of tyranny the sympathy he himself wants, Phillip faces his complicity. What if Jews are "*not* different," Hyman asks, "who are you going to blame then?" "*Everybody's* persecuted," he

26. Meyer, "Jew Can Have," 245.

sarcastically continues, "It's really amazing—you can't find anybody who's persecuting anybody else" (566). He of course speaks from experience, as he reveals his own betrayals and conspiracy of silence.

As Phillip pleads, "Sylvia, forgive me!" (BG, 568), Sylvia acknowledges her own responsibility for the tragedy of their lives. She knows that her crime of silence, like the silence that denies the persecution of the Jews, has partly precipitated the tragedy. When the apparently dying Phillip falls back in the chair at the end of the drama, she *takes a faltering step.* Urging him to "Wait, wait," she releases the compassion for him she had earlier told Hyman she still feels but has been unable to express. The first time she stands after her paralysis is in a moment of intense anxiety over the events of Kristallnacht when she cries out to Hyman, "This is an *emergency!* What if they kill those children! . . . Somebody should do something before they murder us all!" (551).[27] Miller calls this "the first time she is taking her life into her own hands."[28] This communal gesture of compassion extends to all Jews and symbolically to all the oppressed. But it is not until the very end, when she stands a second time after her painful journey of self-awareness, that she can fully reach out to Phillip, forgiving him with whom she is inexorably bound in guilt.

If a central moment of truth occurs when Hyman tells Phillip, "you can't find anybody who's persecuting anybody else" because all find innocence in victimization, it is transformed into tragic resolve at the end when Phillip begs Sylvia's forgiveness, an admission of his Nazi self, his debilitating persona. It is an accounting for Phillip, an act of self-judgment that affirms a moral viability, even if it comes too late. And even as Hyman insists that she cannot blame herself, Sylvia knows that she, too, has been a conspirator in the silence, an ironic parallel to the public denial of events in Germany. She had already confessed to Harriet, "There is nothing I know now that I didn't know twenty years ago. I just didn't say it. . . . After a while you can't find a true word to put in your mouth" (BG, 599). And she informs Phillip, "I'm not blaming you, Phillip. The years I wasted

27. Miller uses the pronoun *us* to link the private and collective in the play. Here Sylvia obviously alludes to "us" Jews, a theme Phillip echoes in his question to Hyman, "Why must we be different?" (BG, 565); but *we* also alludes to the personal relationships that betrayal always threatens among the characters.

28. Quoted in Griffin, *Understanding Arthur Miller*, 186.

I knew I threw myself away. I think I always knew I was doing it" (567). Rejecting a truly crippling innocence, she passes judgment on herself: "I hate it all now. Everything I did is stupid and ridiculous. I can't find myself in my life." Striking her legs, the symbol of her false self, she insists, "I am not this thing" (567). Her painful recognition, like Phillip's, leads to a paradoxical victory in defeat.

Almost no one, not even Miller, was happy with the ending of the play at its premiere performance in New Haven or even later in New York and London at the world premieres. And despite Miller's alterations it remains a problem for many. Phillip's sudden illness and Sylvia's dramatic recovery certainly smack of Hollywood. But Miller describes *Broken Glass* as "tragedy,"[29] and whatever its artistic problems, the conclusion conforms to his concept of tragic action. Even in the sixties, as noted, Miller recognized that "it is unlikely, to say the least, that since so many other kinds of human consciousness have changed that [tragedy] would remain unchanged," yet he sees the end of tragedy as consistent, "still basically the same," and traceable back to the biblical Fall and "the earliest western literature" (*Conv.*, 200). However dramatically (or overdramatically), the ending of *Broken Glass* reasserts Miller's belief that "the rules of life are powerful and they exist. And that's a tragic view, and therefore hopeful" (*TE*, 489). As in the other late plays, "Miller is no more ready to give up on the future of the race now than he has ever been," Christopher Bigsby accurately writes. "But neither is he ready to retract his demand that we acknowledge our responsibility for the world that we have made."[30]

To be sure, Miller leaves open the question of divine judgment and leaves unanswered Phillip's penetrating question, "how can there be Jews if there's no God?" (*BG*, 564), as well as the full meaning of Sylvia's *"inward seeing"* at Phillip's death. Miller's mission as artist, he has claimed, "my effort, my aesthetic, is to find the chain of moral being in the world, somehow. It's moving in its hidden way through all my work" (*AMC*, 178)—and nowhere more assertively than here. *Broken Glass* "is not 'about' Kristallnacht. . . . [I]t is about men and women who struggle with their own contending impulses."[31] If so, it

29. Ibid., 186.
30. Bigsby, introduction to *The Portable Arthur Miller*, xxxvi.
31. Ibid.

mirrors the conflict between forces always at war in Miller's view of the human psyche. In the rhythm of the 1994 restaging of the play, Clive Barnes discovers Ibsen's sense of "the betrayed and unalterable past . . . the revelation of earlier sins and the ongoing follies of the present"[32]—which is to say, the play's insistent tragic impulse.

Mr. Peters' Connections

To gain a new perspective on Arthur Miller's long stage career, we might recall London in the summer of 2000, fifty-six years after his first play premiered on Broadway. The National Theatre in south London was staging a revival of *All My Sons* to sold-out houses, while in its north London stage the Almeida Theatre Company was performing the London premiere of Miller's last play of the century, *Mr. Peters' Connections*, which had been first produced at the Signature Theater in New York in 1998. Keeping in mind the original title of *All My Sons*—*The Sign of the Archer*—imagine an arc, a time bridge spanning more than a half century, linking the dramas; for Miller's last work is at once another bold experiment in his evolving dramaturgy and a play woven of the same threads interlacing his whole canon. It contains many of the essential themes we have observed from the very beginning—the irrepressible persistence of memory, the collapse of the American dream, betrayal and guilt, the nexus of the inner and outer world, the social and the personal—and it is infused with the muted "echoes down the corridor" of more than fifty years of playwriting.

Read next to *Broken Glass*, *Mr. Peters' Connections* is anything but "Ibsen by the book." It is far more akin to the late, expressionistic Strindberg or even to James Joyce than to Ibsen, and closer still to Beckett's absurdist vision. If Beckett's characters sit in the middle of a desolate landscape posing unanswerable existential questions, Miller's protagonist finds himself in the murky remains of a debunked New York nightclub facing questions of equal import. Like *Krapp's Last Tape*, the drama presents a man trying to discover some residue of meaning in the borderland between dreaming and waking, life and death.

32. Clive Barnes, "Fear and Self-Loathing amid *Broken Glass*."

Here, as in *Elegy for a Lady*, *I Can't Remember Anything*, or *The Ride down Mount Morgan*, the character moves to the margins of existence where he seeks understanding the only way he can, in reverie. Speculating about the play's autobiographical significance proves irresistible, for it doubtlessly records the thoughts of a man like Miller in the twilight of his life wondering what it all means, what is "the subject" of existence. It is "a poem," Christopher Bigsby eloquently writes, and "an elegy for an individual but also, in some sense, for a culture, for a century, indeed for human existence."[33] A near gloss of Miller's life and work, it is a text about aging, about a man looking back, thinking about his pending death and legacy—"based on a man," Miller explained in a telephone interview, "trying to discover some central significance to his life . . . trying to find some theme, some satisfying consequence, to his life by virtue of his memory, of his reflections."[34]

Peter Falk, who played the lead in the play's premiere, reportedly called it "a very funny non-comedy," which indeed it is. It contains no dramatic action to speak of, leads to no formal resolution or closure, and denies the linear development and causality of tragedy. Here the past appears not to move inexorably across some architectonic structure but rather dissolves into a circuitous set of fleeting encounters and images, conversations that dwell on the seemingly trivial (the powder room, bananas, boiling sheets, vacuum cleaners, laundry, and a new pair of cheap, squeaky shoes) and characters that rise from and then fade back into the underside of consciousness. The play moves in fits and starts, in disjointed, disconnected flights, as a dusty piano occasionally plays tunes ("a tinkle of Mozart," "Just One of Those Things," "I've got a crush on you, Sweetie-pie . . . ," "My Blue Heaven," "If You Knew Suzie") that sound and rapidly fade out. The dialogue follows suit, moving in improvisation, shot through with witty one-liners, sharp turns, elliptical questions, in an angular, jagged rhythm.

Yet glimpses of the earlier plays keep surfacing in brief and in more developed references,[35] such as the parallels between Cathy-May,

---

33. Christopher Bigsby, "Arthur Miller: Poet," 718.
34. Rohan Preston, "Miller Time."
35. One such earlier play, in particular, is "The Ryan Interview," a one-act in which a hundred-year-old man is interviewed by a young female reporter. With

Harry Peters's dead mistress, and Maggie in *After the Fall*, both reflective of Marilyn Monroe, even to the extent that at one point, Calvin,
the apparent ghost of Peters's dead brother Charley and seemingly
the owner of the decrepit nightclub, remarks, "All her underwear
has been sold, stolen or given away. And the phones don't ring that
deep" (*MPC*, 13).[36] When Peters discovered she was dead, he asked,
"Has she grown into herself at last?" (13), a central theme developed
in *After the Fall*, of course, and doubtlessly an allusion to Monroe,
whom Miller describes sensitively in *Timebends* as tragically unable
to find herself. Other less extensive images keep recalling earlier
plays, such as Leonard carrying his guitar like Leroy Hamilton in
The Last Yankee, or Peters talking about the virtues of flying in the
war, which echoes Chris Keller in *All My Sons*, or the black bag lady
Adele reading *Vogue* like Maya in *The Archbishop's Ceiling* and recalling the black nurse in *The Ride down Mount Morgan*. The dreamlike
structure goes all the way back to *Death of a Salesman*, which Miller
had considered calling *The Inside of His Head*. *Death of a Salesman*
is very much structured like *Mr. Peters' Connections* as "*a dream rising out of reality*" (*DS*, 1) The placing of the drama inside a single
self-exploring psyche directly imitates *After the Fall*. And the play
extends the central image of *The American Clock*, as revealed in
a striking passage by Peters about the winding down of American
culture. The founding fathers, he tells Leonard, his daughter Rose's
boyfriend, "were all Deists, you know; they believed that God had
wound up the world like a clock and then disappeared. We are winding down, the ticks are further and further apart. . . . And we get
bored between ticks, and boredom is a form of dying . . ." (39). Perhaps even more, Peters recalls the whole pattern of the Fall, which
underlies virtually the whole range of Miller's work. As he quips,
"things have been getting worse since Eden" (39).

The abandoned nightclub is something of a hospice, "a space
where the living and the dead may meet," Miller suggests in the
preface (*MPC*, viii). At one point, the frustrated Peters announces,

---

no military record, no tax record, and no social security registration, the old man
does not really exist for the government. Like *Mr. Peters' Connections*, the play is
concerned with the coming chill of death and the need to review life and sum up,
as Miller himself seems to be doing in the late plays.

36. Miller of course protested the "obscene" prices paid in the 1997 auction of
Monroe's underwear, clothes, and eyelashes.

"Oh, the hell with this, I'm leaving"; but Calvin, who is ostensibly his dead brother Charley in the guise of the nightclub owner and a likely reflection of the Calvinistic basis of American capitalism, informs him, "You can't!" (7). This is a termination point—an enclosed space like Lyman Felt's hospital room, the psychiatric hospital in *The Last Yankee,* and the gift shop in *Elegy for a Lady*—a psychic space framed by a void. It is a place where ultimate questions butt up against the most mundane and absurd of topics. Calvin keeps alluding to the elegant powder room as the crowning feature, especially to women, with its African mahogany toilet seats. Here "high class society ladies used to come to talk about their inheritance, and also . . . to have a pee" (15)—which is why Rose eventually enters the building. Adele, the black bag lady who keeps emerging and disappearing at the periphery of Peters's consciousness, ominously says the powder room is "like the silence of a cathedral where dead women linger. And the dusty oval mirrors still reflect the forgotten beauty of long-departed women in their satin gowns" (11).

In the confines of the set, Peters sits waiting for his wife, Charlotte, to come, for what reason he cannot recall. Haunted by ghosts drawn from his unconscious, the defunct nightclub becomes a corporate as well as a private symbol. It contains the collective memory of American culture, marking in its various incarnations the gradual decline of the nation as well as Peters's journey to old age. First it had been a bank, reflective of pre-Depression opulence; then it was a private library supported by a rubber-baron philanthropist; then it became a cafeteria and headquarters for Marxists; and finally it turned into a nightclub, always having been a money-winner, according to the capitalist Calvin—until the war in Vietnam (which Miller of course had protested) "Destroyed all the optimism. And the pessimism," leaving only "Vacillation, indecision, self-satisfaction, and religion—all enemies of nightclubs" (MPC, 19). On the edge of oblivion, Peters's first lines are a plea, a cry to find some reason to go on living: "To be moved. Yes. Even once more to feel that thunder, yes. Just once!" (1). As "*Something horrifying dawns on him,*" in the presence of ghosts, he wonders, "Say, you're not all dead here, are you?" (18), and he keeps asking, "You're all awake, aren't you?" (27)—"are you asleep?" (35). Surprised that he is "so fluent here," he is hounded by memory and loss, like "trying to paddle a canoe with a tennis racket" (3). Unable to remember why he is meeting Charlotte, why he bought new shoes, why he goes on living at all, he sees his life at a terminus: "I am older than everyone I ever knew. All my dogs are dead. Half a dozen cats, parakeets . . . all gone. Every pilot I ever flew with. Probably every woman I ever slept with, too. . . . I still pick up the phone to call some old friend until I realize . . ." (4). It is not Alzheimer's that will not let him find the connective thread to his life, he insists. Fearful that "There *is* no subject anymore!" (21), he still keeps repeating this most basic of postmodern questions— "What is the subject?"—some eighteen times in the short span of the play.

Desperately "in the hope of finding a . . . yes, a subject" (*MPC*, 30), he searches his past, recalling the times when both his life and the nation's seemed to possess meaning and value. Visited by shadows of the past, who, Bigsby observes, "As they die and withdraw from the stage . . . take incremental elements of meaning with them,"[37] Peters remarks, "I think what I'm trying to . . . to . . . find my connection with is a . . . what's the word . . . *continuity* . . . yes, with the past, perhaps . . . in the hope of finding a . . . yes, subject" (30). Baffled by a world whose values seem so twisted from those that charted his life, he reads ads in the newspaper and wonders, "WHY DON'T I UNDERSTAND THIS!" (22), and he looks back at a time when "we knew we were good and the Japs were evil" (8), when "old-time crooks were afraid of God" (17), when we were "saving the world" (20), when there were banana splits with four balls of ice cream—"That, my friend, was a country, huh! I mean *that was a country!*" (20). With sudden unexplained fits of weeping, he moves ever closer to the realm of shadows and darkness at the edge of the stage.

A modern-day Hamlet as an old man in an absurd world, he surmises, "I'm afraid one arrives at a sort of terminal indifference"; "I wonder if it's just a case of not wanting to be around anymore" (*MPC*, 39, 38). As memory slips from him, he tries vainly to recover it. He insists to Charley/Calvin that when they were growing up his brother would spend "whole *days*" with Marcia Levine down the street and would stare at the ceiling repeating "like a prayer, 'Marcia Levine's ass, Marcia Levine's ass . . . Marcia Levine has the most beautiful ass in America!'" (52), a close parallel to the conversations Biff and

37. Bigsby, "Arthur Miller: Poet," 719.

Happy shared in their bedroom at the Loman home years ago in a house in the same Brooklyn neighborhood as the nightclub. But, Calvin claims, "You're mistaking me for somebody else" and threatens Peters's very existence, making him wonder if he is indeed "embalmed": "If you forget me—who . . . *With a desperate cry.* Who the hell am I! . . . If no one remembers what I remember . . . if no one remembers what I . . . ." (53).

As the play nears its end, Charlotte arrives and voices a counterpoint to Peters in her unrelieved optimism. Claiming "I'm still everybody's mother" (MPC, 47), she declares the opaque, disheveled nightclub "marvelous . . . this is heaven!" and the infamous powder room "fantastic" (41, 45). She is a polar opposite to Peters. Whereas he concludes, "I feel I have lived my life and I eagerly look forward to a warm oblivion," she announces, "I'm feeling wonderful" (48, 45). Having fallen prey to a growing cynicism, Peters gives his account of the Fall, telling about his dream of a planet where "people were full of affection and respect," but then they "grabbed a few defectives and flung them into space. . . . They were full of avarice and greed. And they broke into thousands of pieces and fell to earth, and it is from their seed that we all descend" (51). When Leonard protests that "we usually assume that man is born good," and Rose places her hand defensively over her impregnated womb, Peters describes babies as reflective of all humanity: "the alpha and omega of their real nature is a five-letter word, g-r-e-e-d. The rest is gossip" (51).

As in other Miller plays, the question again is, At what cost life? The play reaches the same crisis that Miller portrays in *After the Fall*—looking back over a life and a nation exhausted and spiritually impotent, Peters knows that "they meet unblessed" after the Fall and that "God is precisely what is not there when you need him." Even faced with such nihilism, Peters tells Leonard "the main thing" is "Redemption" (MPC, 40). As in *After the Fall*, the only "redemption" possible is in the world and in union with others. He paradoxically announces near the beginning of the play that "facing reality is for the young who still have time to avoid it" (10), yet as he moves toward the darkness, "while breath still comes blessedly clear" (55), he finds in the shadow figures of his own memory the capacity for hope.

Peters retains a residue of hope that counters the nihilism of absurdity that surrounds him. "It's just that when you've flown into hundreds of gorgeous sunsets, you want them to go on forever and ever . . . and hold off the darkness . . ." (*MPC*, 31). Early in the play, Cathy-May first appears sexily dressed and dances with the *"Nearly weeping"* Peters; the second time, she enters from his unconscious and urges him to dance until "she's forgotten" (8); she next resurfaces as a middle-aged woman with glasses; and she reappears at the conclusion of the play. Trying to imagine what her husband was like, Peters projects him as the racist shoe salesman Larry in his reconstruction of memory, whom he envisions at the end of the play assaulting Cathy-May, ripping a shopping bag from her arm, accusing her of not wearing underwear in public, throwing her on her back, and shoving his hand up her legs.[38] Even as she suffers violation and betrayal, she cries, "You were loved, Harry!" (54), perhaps rewarding him with that brief moment of "redemption" he seeks. Yet she, too, fades from memory as Peters puts his ear to her chest and hears "Footsteps. And darkness. Oh, how terrible to go into darkness alone, alone!" (55). Although Cathy-May dissolves into memory like the others, Adele the bag lady, who lives in the ruined nightclub "with God's permission" (24), early remarks, "Something you forgot hasn't forgotten you" (9). Cathy-May's presence in memory allows Peters to recover something of meaning and value, even if fleetingly.

Charlotte's assertion of control also leads to some sense of affirmation in the play. Announcing her role as "mother" of four perhaps imaginary daughters, she "has powerful longings," Peters declares. She becomes the needed impetus to bring the drama to whatever resolution is possible. Symbolically dying, Peters cries out, "IF SHE DOESN'T COME DOES IT MEAN I CAN'T LEAVE! WHERE IS MY GODDAMNED WIFE!" (*MPC*, 36). When she enters, she immediately assumes her role as a kind of life force, claiming to be a gypsy who knows Rose is pregnant with a daughter, even though she is only six weeks along, and she tells Rose she should "let" Leonard be the father of the child. She encourages Leonard to "make up his mind" about entering the relationship, foreshadowing the ending, when Peters realizes that the only "connection" that really exists is that between people. In

38. Critics have been quick to note implicit allusions to Miller and Monroe: the Italian Larry resembles Joe Dimaggio, to whom Monroe was married before Miller, and it was commonly believed that Monroe did not wear underwear in public. There may also be a measure of self-guilt involved here as well.

answer to Peters's desire to keep flying into sunsets "and hold off darkness," Leonard admits "we're afraid" (32). Another absurd character in the surreal dream, Rose's investor friend and would-be composer Leonard excessively worries about picking up his laundry, and he is "not sure" about connecting with Rose or wanting a child. However, when he says at the end of the play "I want to be a father, Rose" (50), even as the American clock ticks with precarious slowness, he, too, speaks against the dying of the light. The play concludes with Larry's violation of Cathy-Rose being juxtaposed with the nearly mawkish scene of Rose begging her father, "Please stay. . . . I love you, Papa," at last providing Peters with the "connection" he has sought, a union with another person and an affirmation of life even "after the Fall" in the child carried in Rose's womb: "I love you, darling. I wonder . . . could that be the subject!" (56). The question remains unanswered as the light that illumines only Peters *"snaps out"*—but Miller, even in this most absurdist of his dramas, cannot let go of the hope that resides in all the dramas crossing the wide arc from the beginning of his career to its ending. The theme in *Mr. Peters' Connections* even recalls Miller's apprentice play *The Half-Bridge*, which employs the image of half a bridge to depict the same essential theme, the need for people to connect with one another to survive the human drama.

It seems almost premature to talk about these last plays as Arthur Miller's summing up, yet there seems little doubt that he is looking back and assessing the vast scope of his distinguished career. In differing ways these last dramas directly or obliquely survey as well the history of America's culture as Miller has experienced it, from the perspective at the turn of the millennium. Even here, Miller's confrontation with the present coexists with his continuing vision as he engages the cynicism of the postmodern era with a residue of hope long apparent in the range of his plays. In their themes and dramaturgy, even if in sometimes muted ways, they do indeed sum up a life, a career, a nation's history, forming an arc extending back to the forties when Miller's first play reached Broadway.

Across the wide range of his years, Miller has witnessed a stunning era of social change and national crisis—the Depression, the New Deal, the Second World War and the horrors of the Holocaust, the Cold War, McCarthyism, the New Frontier, the assassinations of John F. Kennedy and Martin Luther King, the Civil

Rights movement, Watergate, the Vietnam War, the collapse of Communism in Europe, the Persian Gulf War, and even the contested election of the first president of the new century and the War on Terrorism. But it is the past and the inevitable resurgence of memory that has always been the compelling force in his drama. With the voice of an Old Testament prophet, he has long repeated the moral dictum that only confrontation of the past can produce the promise of a future, however tenuous that may prove.

Tracing the evolution of his art from the earliest works, which struggle to reclaim the viability of tragedy near midcentury, to the late plays, which wrestle with the growing cynicism and ambiguities of the contemporary age, Miller maintains a core of basic beliefs and themes. Admitting to Janet Balakian in 1989 that his recent plays and Beckett's "end . . . the same," he adds the discriminating proviso that "the question is whether a work simply exploits chaos or strives to resist it for survival's sake." His end, he concludes, is "to achieve a coherency out of the chaos." The thrust of his art is "really illumination. It's the light. We strike it in life rarely. There's endless talk, and then suddenly somebody says something or does something and that's all that has to be said. It's to arrive at the point of illumination" (*TE*, 497–98). Time has always been the ultimate mystery for Miller. It is at once stable and relative, violating linearity yet moving inexorably to a "consequential end," fixed yet able to bend upon itself, making the present the past, and able to freeze yet always ticking toward an inevitable moment.

Miller has been seeking "illumination" for nearly sixty years in his plays. Still, he says, "I love the art. . . . I enjoy doing it, and if it's accepted, fine; and if it isn't—I can take it. Well, I can't: the work can. Because I believe in the work."[39] His faith is based on a set of essential beliefs. Chief among these is the conviction that we all live in paradise lost, and that the human will cannot evolve "fruitfully unless the existence of evil is taken into account" (*Conv.*, 48). Concomitant to this is his belief that innocence constitutes the ultimate source of evil, that it distorts right and wrong and freezes the moral will. He concurs with James Baldwin that "People who shut their eyes to reality simply invite their own destruction, and anyone who insists on remaining in a state of innocence long after that

39. Simonson, "Values, Old and New," 18.

innocence is dead turns himself into a monster."[40] From Joe Keller to
Harry Peters, Miller's characters can find redemption only by glimps-
ing their own criminal nature and risking commitment despite it,
or, as Quentin says, "knowing all . . . that we meet unblessed . . . after, after the Fall, after many, many deaths." Perhaps no writer in
twentieth-century literature has been more certain of original sin
than Miller, and more convinced that there is always a price to be
paid. When Christopher Bigsby ventured to suggest that "surely the
most terrible thought is that people do not actually have to pay for
their sins," Miller responded "But we do. Somebody has to. . . . You
rationalize in a way. You deny it and it keeps coming back in one
form or the other" (AMC, 202). What Stephen Barker says of *After
the Fall* might gloss the whole of his work: "that the original fall,
from Eden, is recapitulated by each individual through the fall into
consciousness, and thus into choice."[41]

Although the later plays seem more ambivalent in their resolve,
or lack of it, and in their recognition that an existential awareness
may be the best we can hope for, Miller never wavers in his conviction that the truth must be faced, even if it can prove as destructive
as the lie. If betrayal is the first law of human nature, there is also
potential reclamation in Miller's vision. Rather than a God-given
salvation, the capacity for redemption appears in the human gesture
of assuming responsibility for others in a world devoid of God but
not of a moral center, a capacity that resides somewhere deep inside
the self along with, and in large measure dependent upon, the guilt
than can generate moral action. From his early years, when Miller
declared on the first anniversary of *Death of a Salesman* that "We
ought to be struggling for a world in which it will be possible to
lay blame. Only then will the great tragedies be written" (TE, 14),
to Phillip Gellburg's acknowledgment that "I deserve it," Miller has
insisted that one must assume responsibility for his actions and for
the people around him. To the end, Miller has been true as well to
the dictum he set out in his 1958 essay "The Shadow of the Gods":
"The fish is in the water and the water is in the fish" (TE, 185).
The nexus of the social and the personal still constitutes the moral
center of Miller's work; he finds solace not in a god able to pardon the

---

40. James Baldwin, "Stranger in the Village," 129.
41. Barker, "Critic, Criticism, Critics," 237.

human condition, but in the realm of human experience with all its uncertainty and in the human capacity to assume responsibility for moral choice. "Ultimately," he writes, "every assault on the human mystery falls back to the ground, changing little, but the flight of the arrow continues claiming our attention over a longer time when its direction is toward the castle of reality rather than the wayward air" (E, 312).

Works Cited

Abbott, Anthony S. *The Vital Lie: Reality and Illusion in Modern Drama.* Tuscaloosa: University of Alabama Press, 1989.

Abbotson, Susan C. W. "An Afternoon with Arthur Miller." *Arthur Miller Society Newsletter* 1 (June 1999): 13.

———. "Issues of Identity in *Broken Glass*: A Humanist Response to a Postmodern World." *Journal of American Drama and Theatre* 11 (1999): 61–80.

———. "Revisiting the Holocaust for 1980s Television: Arthur Miller's *Playing for Time*." *American Drama* 8 (1999): 61–78.

Adams, Julie. *Versions of Heroism in Modern Drama: Redefinitions by Miller, Williams, O'Neill, and Anderson.* London: Macmillan, 1991.

Albee, Edward. *Who's Afraid of Virginia Woolf? A Play.* New York: Signet, 1962.

Alter, Iska. "Betrayal and Blessedness: Exploitation of Feminine Power in *The Crucible*, *A View from the Bridge*, and *After the Fall*." In *Feminist Rereadings of Modern American Drama*, ed. June Schlueter, 116–45. Rutherford, N.J.: Fairleigh Dickinson University Press, 1989.

August, Eugene R. "*Death of a Salesman*: A Men's Study Approach." *Western Ohio Journal* 7, no. 1 (1986): 53–71.

Austin, Gayle. "The Exchange of Women and Male Homosocial Desire in Arthur Miller's *Death of a Salesman* and Lillian Hellman's *Another Part of the Forest*." In *Feminist Rereadings of Modern American Drama*, ed. June Schlueter, 59–66. Rutherford, N.J.: Fairleigh Dickinson University Press, 1989.

Aymé, Marcel. "I Want to be Hanged Like a Witch." In *Arthur Miller: The Crucible: Text and Criticism*, ed. Gerald C. Weales, 239–41. New York: Viking, 1971.

Balakian, Janet N. "Beyond the Male Locker Room: *Death of a Salesman* from a Feminist Approach." In *Approaches to Teaching*

Miller's Death of a Salesman, ed. Matthew Roudané, 115–24. New York: Modern Language Association, 1995.

———. "A Conversation with Arthur Miller." *Michigan Quarterly Review* 29 (1990): 158–70.

———. "The Holocaust, the Depression, and McCarthyism: Miller in the Sixties." In *The Cambridge Companion to Arthur Miller*, ed. Christopher Bigsby, 115–38. New York: Cambridge University Press, 1997.

———. "An Interview with Arthur Miller." *Studies in American Drama: 1945–Present* 6 (1991): 29–47.

Baldwin, James. "Stranger in the Village." In *Collected Essays*, 117–29. New York: Library of America, 1998.

Banfield, Chris. "Arthur Miller." In *American Drama*, ed. Clive Bloom, 82–96. New York: St. Martin's, 1995.

Barker, Stephen. "The Crisis of Authenticity: *Death of a Salesman* and the Tragic Muse." In *Approaches to Teaching Miller's* Death of a Salesman, ed. Matthew Roudané, 82–101. New York: Modern Language Association, 1995.

———. "Critic, Criticism, Critics." In *The Cambridge Companion to Arthur Miller*, ed. Christopher Bigsby, 230–44. Cambridge: Cambridge University Press, 1997.

Barnes, Clive. "Fear and Self-Loathing amid *Broken Glass.*" *New York Post*, April 25, 1994, 123.

Bentley, Eric. *In Search of Theater*. New York: Vintage, 1959.

———. "Miller's Innocence." *New Republic*, February 16, 1953, 22–23.

———. *The Life of the Drama*. New York: Atheneum, 1964.

———. *The Playwright as Thinker*. New York: Reynal and Hitchcock, 1946.

Ben-Zvi, Linda. " 'Home Sweet Home': Deconstructing the Masculine Myth of the Frontier in Modern American Drama." In *The Frontier Experience and the American Drama*, ed. David Mogen, Mark Busby, and Paul Bryant, 217–25. College Station: Texas A & M University Press, 1989.

Bettina, Sister M., SSND. "Willy Loman's Brother Ben: Tragic Insight in *Death of a Salesman.*" In *The Merrill Studies in Death of a Salesman*, comp. Walter J. Meserve, 80–83. Columbus, Ohio: Charles E. Merrill, 1972.

Bhatia, Santosh K. *Arthur Miller: Social Drama as Tragedy*. New Delhi: Arnold-Heinemann, 1985.

Bierman, Judah, James Hart, and Stanley Johnson. "Arthur Miller: *Death of a Salesman.*" In *The Dramatic Experience*, 490–95. Englewood Cliffs, N.J.: Prentice-Hall, 1958.

Bigsby, Christopher. "Arthur Miller: Poet." *Michigan Quarterly Review (A Special Issue: Arthur Miller)* 37 (1998): 713–24.

———. "Arthur Miller: Time Traveller." In *"The Salesman Has a Birthday"*: *Essays Celebrating the Fiftieth Anniversary of Arthur Miller's* Death of a Salesman, ed. Stephen A. Marino, 1–17. Lanham, Md.: University Press of America, 2000.

———. *Confrontation and Commitment: A Study of Contemporary American Drama, 1959–66.* Columbia: University of Missouri Press, 1968.

———. *A Critical Introduction to Twentieth-Century American Drama 2: Tennessee Williams, Arthur Miller, Edward Albee.* Cambridge: Cambridge University Press, 1984.

———. "The Early Plays." In *The Cambridge Companion to Arthur Miller,* 21–47. New York: Cambridge University Press, 1997.

———. "The Fall and After—Arthur Miller's Confession." *Modern Drama* 10 (1967): 124–36.

———. *Modern American Drama, 1945–1990.* Cambridge: Cambridge University Press, 1992.

Bigsby, Christopher, ed. *Arthur Miller and Company: Arthur Miller Talks about His Work in the Company of Actors, Designers, Directors, Reviewers, and Writers.* London: Methuen Drama in association with the Arthur Miller Centre for American Studies, 1990.

———. *The Cambridge Companion to Arthur Miller.* Cambridge: Cambridge University Press, 1997.

Billman, Carol. "Women and the Family in American Drama." *Arizona Quarterly* 36 (1980): 35–49.

Blau, Herbert. *The Impossible Theater: A Manifesto.* New York: Macmillan, 1964.

Bliquez, Guerin. "Linda's Role in *Death of a Salesman.*" *Modern Drama* 10 (1968): 383–86.

Bloom, Harold. Introduction to *Willy Loman.* New York: Chelsea House, 1991.

Bolt, Robert. *A Man for All Seasons.* New York: Vintage, 1990.

Bouchard, Larry D. *Tragic Method and Tragic Theology: Evil in Contemporary Drama and Religious Thought.* University Park: Pennsylvania State University Press, 1989.

Brantley, Ben. "Arthur Miller Visits the Sins of the Fathers upon the Children." *New York Times*, May 5, 1997, C11, 13.

Brater, Enoch. "Ethics and Ethnicity in the Plays of Arthur Miller." In *From Hester Street to Hollywood: The Jewish-American Stage and Screen*, ed. Sarah Blacher Cohen, 123–35. Bloomington: Indiana University Press, 1983.

Brill, Lesley. "*The Misfits* and the Idea of John Huston's Films." *Proteus: A Journal of Ideas* 7, no. 2 (1990): 9–17.

Bronson, David. "*An Enemy of the People*: A Key to Arthur Miller's Art and Ethics." *Comparative Drama* 2 (1968–1969): 229–47.

Brustein, Robert. "Arthur Miller's *Mea Culpa*." *New Republic*, February 8, 1964, 26–28, 30.

———. "Muddy Track at Lincoln Center." *New Republic*, December 26, 1964, 26–27.

———. "Separated by a Common Playwright." *New Republic*, May 30, 1994, 29–30.

———. "The Unseriousness of Arthur Miller." *New Republic*, February 24, 1968, 39–41.

Budick, E. Miller. "History and Other Spectres in Arthur Miller's *The Crucible*." *Modern Drama* 28 (1985): 535–52.

Burhans, Clinton S., Jr. "Eden and the 'Idiot Child': Arthur Miller's *After the Fall*." *Ball State University Forum* 20, no. 2 (1977): 3–16.

Callow, Heather Cook. "Masculine and Feminine in *Death of a Salesman*." In *"The Salesman Has a Birthday": Essays Celebrating the Fiftieth Anniversary of Arthur Miller's* Death of a Salesman, ed. Steven A. Marino, 65–77. Lanham, Md.: University Press of America, 2000.

Canby, Vincent. "A Classically Riveting 'View from the Bridge.'" *New York Times*, January 4, 1998, sec. 2, p. 6.

Canning, Charlotte. "Is This Play about Women? A Feminist Reading of *Death of a Salesman*." In *The Achievement of Arthur Miller: New Essays*, ed. Steven R. Centola, 69–76. Dallas: Contemporary Research Press, 1995.

Carr, Jay. "*Crucible* Bewitches." *Boston Globe*, December 20, 1996, E1.

Carson, Neil. *Arthur Miller*. New York: Grove, 1982.

Centola, Steven R. "*All My Sons*." In *The Cambridge Companion to Arthur Miller*, ed. Christopher Bigsby, 48–59. New York: Cambridge University Press, 1997.

———. "Bad Faith and *All My Sons*." In *Arthur Miller's All My Sons*, ed. Harold Bloom, 123–33. New York: Chelsea House, 1988.

———. "Compromise as Bad Faith: Arthur Miller's *A View from the Bridge* and William Inge's *Come Back, Little Sheba*." *Midwestern Quarterly* 28, no. 1 (1986): 100–13.

———. " 'How to Contain the Impulse of Betrayal': A Sartrean Reading of *The Ride down Mount Morgan*." *American Drama* 6 (1996): 14–28.

———. " 'Just Looking for a Home': A Conversation with Arthur Miller." *American Drama* 1 (1991): 85–94.

———. "The Monomyth and Arthur Miller's *After the Fall*." *Studies in American Drama, 1945–Present* 1 (1986): 49–60.

Chatterji, Ruby. "Existentialist Approach to Modern Drama." In *Existentialism in American Literature*, 94–95. Atlantic Highlands, N.J. : Humanities Press, 1983.

Clark, Eleanor. "Old Glamour, New Gloom." *Partisan Review* 16 (1949): 631–35.

Clurman, Harold. "Director's Notes: *Incident at Vichy*." *Tulane Drama Review* 9, no. 4 (1985): 77–90.

———. *Lies Like Truth: Theatre Reviews and Essays*. New York: Macmillan, 1985.

Coe, Richard L. "What Happened to Miller's Play?" *Washington Post*, May 15, 1977, H1.

Cohn, Ruby. *Dialogue in American Drama*. Bloomington: Indiana University Press, 1971.

Corrigan, Robert W. "The Achievement of Arthur Miller." *Comparative Drama* 2 (1968): 141–60.

———. Introduction to *Arthur Miller: A Collection of Critical Essays*, ed. Robert W. Corrigan. Englewood Cliffs, N.J.: Prentice-Hall, 1969.

Costello, Donald P. "Arthur Miller's Circles of Responsibility: *A View from the Bridge* and Beyond." *Modern Drama* 36 (1993): 443–51.

Couchman, Gordon W. "Arthur Miller's Tragedy of Babbitt." In *The Merrill Studies in* Death of a Salesman, comp. Walter J. Meserve, 68–75. Columbus, Ohio: Charles E. Merrill, 1972.

Demastes, William W. "Miller's Use and Modification of the Realistic Tradition." In *Approaches to Teaching Miller's* Death of a Salesman, ed. Matthew Roudané, 74–81. New York: Modern Language Association, 1995.

Dickey, James. *Deliverance*. New York: Dell, 1970.

Di Giuseppe, Rita. "The Shadow of the Gods: Tragedy and Commitment in *Death of a Salesman*." *Quaderni di linque a letterature* 14 (1989): 109–28.

Dillingham, William B. "Arthur Miller and the Loss of Conscience." In *Arthur Miller, Death of a Salesman: Text and Criticism*, ed. Gerald C. Weales, 339–49. New York: Viking, 1967.

Downer, Alan S. Review of *The Price*. In *Critical Essays on Arthur Miller*, ed. James Martine Jr., 155–57. Boston: G. K. Hall, 1979.

Driver, Tom F. "Strength and Weakness in Arthur Miller." In *Discussions of Modern Drama*, ed. Walter J. Meserve, 105–13. Boston: D. C. Heath, 1965.

Dukore, Bernard F., ed. Death of a Salesman *and* The Crucible: *Text and Performance*. Atlantic Heights, N.J.: Humanities Press, 1989.

Eiseley, Loren. *The Firmament of Time*. New York: Antheum, 1966.

Eisinger, Chester E. "Focus on Arthur Miller's *Death of a Salesman*: The Wrong Dreams." In *American Dreams, American Nightmares*, ed. David Madden, 165–74. Carbondale: Southern Illinois University Press, 1970.

Eliot, T. S. *Murder in the Cathedral*. New York: Harcourt, Brace and World, 1963.

Epstein, Arthur D. "A Look at *A View from the Bridge*." *Texas Studies in Literature and Language* 7 (1965): 109–22.

Epstein, Leslie. "The Unhappiness of Arthur Miller." *Tri-Quarterly* 1 (spring 1965): 165–73.

Evans, Richard I. *Psychology and Arthur Miller*. New York: E. P. Dutton, 1969.

Feiden, Douglas. "Miller's Ongoing Drama: With Another Show Opening on Broadway, the Legendary Playwright Isn't Going Gently into his Third Act." *New York Daily News*, November 11, 1999, 56.

Feingold, Michael. "Post-Miller Time." *New York Theatre Critics' Reviews* 54, no. 2 (1993): 27.

Feldman, Robert Lee. "Arthur Miller on the Theme of Evil: An Interview." *Resources for American Literary Study* 17, no. 1 (1990): 87–93.

Field, B. S., Jr. "Hamartia in *Death of a Salesman*." *Twentieth Century Literature* 18 (1972): 19–24.

Foster, Richard J. "Confusion and Tragedy: The Failure of Arthur Miller's *Salesman*." In *Two Modern American Tragedies: Reviews and Criticism of* Death of a Salesman *and* A Streetcar Named Desire, 82–88. New York: Scribner's, 1961.

Free, William J. "Robert Bolt and the Marxist View of History." *Mosaic* 14 (1981): 51–59.

Freedman, Morris. *American Drama in Social Context.* Carbondale: Southern Illinois University Press, 1971.

Ganz, Arthur. "The Silence of Arthur Miller." *Drama Survey* 3 (1963): 224–37.

Gilman, Robert. *Common and Uncommon Masks.* New York: Random House, 1971.

Goldstein, Laurence. "The Fiction of Arthur Miller." *Michigan Quarterly Review (A Special Issue: Arthur Miller)* 37 (1998): 725–45.

Goode, James. *The Story of* The Misfits. New York: Bobbs-Merrill, 1963.

Goodman, Charlotte. "The Fox's Cubs: Lillian Hellman, Arthur Miller, and Tennessee Williams." In *Modern American Drama: The Female Canon*, ed. June Schlueter, 130–42. Rutherford, N.J.: Fairleigh Dickinson University Press, 1990.

Gordon, Lois. "*Death of a Salesman:* An Appreciation." In *Twentieth Century Interpretations of Death of a Salesman*, ed. Helene Wickham Koon, 98–108. Englewood Cliffs, N.J.: Prentice-Hall, 1983.

Griffin, Alice. *Understanding Arthur Miller.* Columbia: University of South Carolina Press, 1996.

Gussow, Mel. "A Rock of the Modern Age, Arthur Miller Is Everywhere." *New York Times*, November 30, 1996, sec. 1, p. 17.

Hagopian, John V. "Arthur Miller: The Salesman's Two Cases." *Modern Drama* 6 (1963): 117–25.

Harben, Niloufer. *Twentieth-Century English History Plays.* Totowa, N.J.: Barnes and Noble, 1988.

Harshbarger, Karl. *The Burning Jungle: An Analysis of Arthur Miller's Death of a Salesman.* Washington, D.C.: University Press of America, 1979.

Hattersley, Roy. "The Guardian Profile: Arthur Miller: A View from the Barricades." *Guardian*, October 24, 1998, 6.

Hayman, Ronald. *Arthur Miller.* New York: Frederick Ungar, 1972.

Heilman, Robert Bechtold. *The Iceman, the Arsonist, and the Troubled Agent: Tragedy and Melodrama on the Modern Stage*. Seattle: University of Washington Press, 1973.

―――. "Tragedy and Melodrama: Speculations on Generic Form." *Texas Quarterly* 3 (1960): 36–50.

―――. *Tragedy and Melodrama: Versions of Experience*. Seattle: University of Washington Press, 1968.

Hogan, Robert. *Arthur Miller*. University of Minnesota Pamphlets on American Writers no. 40. Minneapolis: University of Minnesota Press, 1964.

Huftel, Sheila. *Arthur Miller: The Burning Glass*. New York: Citadel Press, 1965.

Hulbert, Dan. "Arthur Miller: A Dramatist for the Ages." *Atlanta Journal and Constitution*, January 9, 2000, 4L.

Hume, Beverly. "Linda Loman as 'The Woman' in Miller's *Death of a Salesman*." *NMAL: Notes on Modern American Literature* 9, no. 3 (1985), item 4.

Hurd, Myles R. "Angels and Anxieties in Miller's *A View from the Bridge*." *Notes on Contemporary Literature* 13, no. 4 (1983): 4–6.

Hynes, Joseph A. "Arthur Miller and the Impasse of Naturalism." *South Atlantic Quarterly* 62 (1963): 327–34.

―――. "Attention Must Be Paid . . ." In *Arthur Miller, Death of a Salesman: Text and Criticism*, ed. Gerald C. Weales, 280–89. New York: Viking, 1967.

Isser, Edward R. *Stages of Annihilation: Theatrical Representations of the Holocaust*. Madison, N.J.: Fairleigh Dickinson University Press, 1997.

Jackson, Esther Merle. "*Death of a Salesman*: Tragic Myth in the Modern Theatre." *CLA Journal* 7 (1963): 63–76.

Kauffmann, Stanley. "Across the Great Divide." *New Republic*, February 20, 1961, 26, 28.

Kintz, Linda. "The Sociosymbolic Work of Family in *Death of a Salesman*." In *Approaches to Teaching Miller's* Death of a Salesman, ed. Matthew Roudané, 102–14. New York: Modern Language Association, 1995.

Kissel, Howard. "*Sons* Lacks Pop: Overacting Spoils Dated Miller Drama." *New York Daily News*, May 5, 1997, 33.

Koenig, Rhoda. "Seduced by *Salesman*'s Patter." *London Sunday Times*, October 20, 1996.

Kolin, Philip C. "*Death of a Salesman:* A Playwrights' Forum." *Michigan Quarterly Review (A Special Issue: Arthur Miller)* 37 (1998): 591–623.

Koon, Helene Wickham. Introduction to *Twentieth Century Interpretations of* Death of a Salesman. Englewood Cliffs, N.J.: Prentice-Hall, 1983.

Kroll, Jack. "Double Trouble." *Newsweek,* December 1, 1980, 71.

Kurdi, Maria. "The Deceptive Nature of Reality in Arthur Miller's *Two-Way Mirror.*" In *Cross-Cultural Studies: American, Canadian and European Literatures: 1945–1985,* ed. Mirko Jurak, 267–71. Ljubljana, Yugoslavia: English Department, Filozofska fakulteta, Edvard Kardelj University of Ljubljana, 1988.

Lahr, John. "Dead Souls." *New Yorker,* May 9, 1994, 94–96.

Langer, Lawrence L. "The Americanization of the Holocaust on Stage and Screen." In *From Hester Street to Hollywood: The Jewish-American Stage and Screen,* ed. Sarah Blacher Cohen, 213–30. Bloomington: University of Indiana Press, 1983.

Levin, David. "Salem Witchcraft and Recent Fiction and Drama." *New England Quarterly* 28 (1955): 537–46.

Lewis, Allan. *American Plays and Playwrights of the Contemporary Theatre.* New York: Crown, 1965.

Lindenberger, Herbert. *Historical Drama: The Relation of Literature and Reality.* Chicago: University of Chicago Press, 1975.

Lowenthal, Lawrence D. "Arthur Miller's *Incident at Vichy:* A Sartrean Interpretation." In *Critical Essays on Arthur Miller,* ed. James J. Martine, 173–87. Boston: G. K. Hall, 1979.

Mahony, Dianne Greene. "Arthur Miller, *Ride Down Mt. Morgan.*" *Library Journal,* September 1, 1992, 175.

Mandell, Jonathan. "Renaissance Man: At 82 Arthur Miller Is Pleasing a New Generation of Theatergoers." *Newsday,* October 28, 1997, sec. II, p. B03.

Mander, John. *The Writer and Commitment.* Philadelphia: Dufour Editions, 1962.

Martin, Robert, Jr. "Arthur Miller: Public Issues, Private Tensions." *Studies in the Literary Imagination* 21, no. 2 (1988): 97–106.

———. "Arthur Miller's *The Crucible:* Background and Sources." *Modern Drama* 20 (1977): 279–92.

Mason, Jeffrey D. "Paper Dolls: Melodrama and Sexual Politics in Arthur Miller's Early Plays." In *Feminist Rereadings of Modern*

American Drama, ed. June Schlueter, 103–15. Rutherford, N.J.: Fairleigh Dickinson University Press, 1989.

Massa, Ann. "Some Kind of Love Story: Arthur Miller." In *American Declarations of Love,* ed. Ann Massa, 122–36. New York: St. Martin's, 1990.

May, Rollo. *Love and Will.* New York: Norton, 1969.

McDonough, Carla J. *Staging Masculinity: Male Identity in Contemporary American Drama.* Jefferson, N.C.: McFarland, 1997.

McGill, William J., Jr. "*The Crucible* of History: Arthur Miller's John Proctor." *New England Quarterly* 54 (1981): 258–64.

Meyer, Kinereth. "'A Jew Can Have a Jewish Face': Arthur Miller, Autobiography, and the Holocaust." *Prooftexts* 18 (1998): 239–58.

Miller, Arthur. *After the Fall: A Play in Two Acts.* Final stage version. New York: Penguin, 1992.

———. *All My Sons: A Play in Three Acts.* With an introduction by Christopher Bigsby. New York: Penguin, 2000.

———. *The Archbishop's Ceiling; The American Clock: Two Plays.* New York: Grove, 1989.

———. *Arthur Miller's Playing for Time.* Woodstock, Ill.: Dramatic Publishing, 1985.

———. *Broken Glass: A Play in Two Acts.* Final acting version. In *The Portable Miller,* rev. ed., edited with an introduction by Christopher Bigsby. New York: Penguin, 1995.

———. *Conversations with Arthur Miller.* Ed. Matthew C. Roudané. Jackson: University Press of Mississippi, 1987.

———. *The Creation of the World and Other Business: A Play.* New York: Viking, 1972.

———. *The Crucible: A Play in Four Acts.* With an introduction by Christopher Bigsby. New York: Penguin, 1995.

———. *Danger: Memory! Two Plays:* I Can't Remember Anything; Clara. New York: Grove, 1986.

———. *Death of a Salesman: Certain Private Conversations in Two Acts and a Requiem.* With an introduction by Christopher Bigsby. New York: Penguin, 1998.

———. *Echoes Down the Corridor: Collected Essays 1944–2000.* Ed. Steven R. Centola. New York: Viking, 2000.

———. *Everybody Wins: A Screenplay.* New York: Grove Weidenfeld, 1990.

———. *The Golden Years* and *The Man Who Had All the Luck*. With an introduction by the author and an afterword by Christopher Bigsby. London: Methuen, 1989.

———. *The Great Disobedience*. Typescript. Harlan Hatcher Graduate Library, University of Michigan, 1937.

———. *Honors at Dawn*. Typescript. Harlan Hatcher Graduate Library, University of Michigan, 1936.

———. "Ibsen's Warning." *Index on Censorship* 18, nos. 6–7 (July–August 1989): 74–75.

———. *Incident at Vichy: A Play*. New York: Viking, 1964.

———. *The Last Yankee: With a New Essay "About Theatre Language."* New York: Penguin, 1994.

———. *The Misfits*. New York: Viking, 1961.

———. *Mr. Peters' Connections*. New York: Penguin, 1999.

———. *No Villain*. Typescript. Harlan Hatcher Graduate Library, University of Michigan, 1937.

———. "Our Guilt for the World's Evil." *New York Times Magazine*, January 3, 1965, sec. 6, pp. 10–11, 48.

———. *The Portable Arthur Miller*. Rev. ed. Ed. Christopher Bigsby. New York: Penguin, 1995.

———. *The Price: A Play*. New York: Penguin, 1985.

———. "Responses to an Audience Question and Answer Session." *Michigan Quarterly Review (A Special Issue: Arthur Miller)* 37 (1998): 817–27.

———. *The Ride down Mount Morgan*. New York: Penguin, 1999.

———. *Salesman in Beijing*. New York: Viking, 1984.

———. *Situation Normal*. New York: Reynal and Hitchcock, 1944.

———. *The Theater Essays of Arthur Miller*. Rev. ed. Ed. Robert A. Martin and Steven R. Centola. New York: Da Capo, 1996.

———. *Timebends: A Life*. New York: Penguin, 1995.

———. *Two-Way Mirror: A Double-Bill of* Elegy for a Lady *and* Some Kind of Love Story. With an afterword by Christopher Bigsby. London: Methuen, 1984.

———. *A View from the Bridge: A Play in Two Acts with a New Introduction*. New York: Penguin, 1977.

———. "Why I Wrote *The Crucible*: An Artist's Answer to Politics." *New Yorker*, October 21–28, 1996, 158–60, 162–64.

Miller, Arthur, and Serge Toubiana. The Misfits: *Story of a Shoot*. London: Phaidon, 2000.

Morley, Christopher. "Miller's Crossing." *Spectator,* August 13, 1994, 31.

Morse, David. "The 'Life Lie' in Three Plays by O'Neill, Williams, and Miller." In *Cross-Cultural Studies: American, Canadian, and European Literature, 1945–1985,* ed. Mirko Jurak Ljubljana, 273–77. Yugoslavia: English Department, Filozofska fakulteta, Edvard Kardelj University of Ljubljana, 1988.

Moss, Leonard. *Arthur Miller.* Rev. ed. Boston: Twayne, 1980.

———. "Biographical and Literary Allusion in *After the Fall.*" *Educational Theatre Journal* 18 (1966): 34–40.

Mottram, Eric. "Arthur Miller: The Development of a Political Dramatist in America." In *Arthur Miller: A Collection of Critical Essays,* ed. Robert W. Corrigan, 23–57. Englewood Cliffs, N.J.: Prentice-Hall, 1969.

Murphy, Brenda. "*The Man Who Had All the Luck:* Miller's Answer to *The Master Builder.*" *American Drama* 6 (1996): 29–41.

———. *Miller:* Death of a Salesman. Plays in Production Series. Cambridge: Cambridge University Press, 1995.

———. "The 1999 Revival of *Death of a Salesman:* A Critical Commentary." In *"The Salesman Has a Birthday": Essays Celebrating the Fiftieth Anniversary of Arthur Miller's* Death of a Salesman, ed. Stephen A. Marino, 29–43. Lanham, Md.: University Press of America, 2000.

———. "The Tradition of Social Drama: Miller and His Forebears." In *The Cambridge Companion to Arthur Miller,* ed. Christopher Bigsby, 10–20. New York: Cambridge University Press, 1997.

Murray, Edward. *Arthur Miller, Dramatist.* New York: Ungar, 1967.

Nathan, George Jean. "Review of *Death of a Salesman.*" In *The Theatre Book of the Year, 1948–49,* 279–85. New York: Knopf, 1949.

Nelson, Benjamin. *Arthur Miller: Portrait of a Playwright.* New York: McKay, 1970.

Newman, Richard, with Karen Kirtley. *Alma Rosé: Vienna to Auschwitz.* Portland, Oreg.: Amadeus Press, 2000.

Newman, William J. "Arthur Miller's Collected Plays." *Twentieth Century* 164 (1958): 491–96.

Nolan, Paul T. "Two Memory Plays: *The Glass Menagerie* and *After the Fall.*" *McNeese Review* 17 (1966): 27–38.

Oliver, Edith. "The Theatre: Off Broadway." *New Yorker,* February 6, 1965, 94.

O'Neal, Michael J. "History, Myth, and Name Magic in Arthur Miller's *The Crucible.*" *Clio* 12, no. 2 (1983): 111–22.

O'Neill, Eugene. *Selected Letters.* Ed. Travis Bogard and Jackson R. Bryer. New Haven, Conn.: Yale University Press, 1988.

Orr, John. *Tragic Drama and Modern Society: Studies in the Social and Literary Theory of Drama from 1870 to the Present.* Totowa, N.J.: Barnes and Noble, 1981.

Otten, Charlotte F. " 'Who Am I?': Re-investigation of Arthur Miller's *Death of a Salesman.*" In *Twentieth Century Interpretations of* Death of a Salesman, ed. Helene Wickham Koon, 85–91. Englewood Cliffs, N.J.: Prentice-Hall, 1983.

Överland, Orm. "The Action and Its Significance: Arthur Miller's Struggle with Dramatic Form." *Modern Drama* 18 (1975): 1–14.

Parker, Brian. "Point of View in Arthur Miller's *Death of a Salesman.*" In *Twentieth Century Interpretations of* Death of a Salesman, ed. Helene Wickham Koon, 41–55. Englewood Cliffs, N.J.: Prentice-Hall, 1983.

Poling, James. "Handy 'Gadget.' " *Collier's,* May 31, 1952, 56–61.

Popkin, Henry. "Arthur Miller: The Strange Encounter." *Sewanee Review* 68 (1960): 34–60.

———. "Historical Analogy and *The Crucible.*" In *Twentieth Century Interpretations of* The Crucible, ed. John H. Ferres, 77–85. Englewood Cliffs, N.J.: Prentice-Hall, 1972.

Porter, Thomas E. *Myth and Modern American Drama.* Detroit: Wayne State University Press, 1969.

Press, David P. "Arthur Miller's *The Misfits:* The Western Gunned Down." *Studies in the Humanities* 8, no. 1 (1980): 41–44.

Preston, Rohan. "Miller Time." *Minneapolis Star Tribune,* October 31, 1999, 1F.

Prideaux, Tom. "A Desperate Search by a Troubled Hero." *Life,* February 7, 1964, 64B-64D.

Prudhan, N. S. *Modern American Drama: A Study in Myth and Tradition.* New Delhi: Arnold-Heinemann, 1978.

Rahv, Philip. *The Myth and the Powerhouse.* New York: Farrar, Straus and Giroux, 1965.

Reno, Raymond H. "Arthur Miller and the Death of God." *Texas Studies in Literature and Language* 11 (1969): 1069–87.

Richards, David. "A Paralysis Points to Spiritual and Social Ills." *New York Times,* April 25, 1964, C11.

Rothenberg, Albert, and Eugene D. Shapiro. "The Defense of Psychoanalysis in Literature: *Long Day's Journey into Night* and *A View from the Bridge*." *Comparative Drama* 7 (1973): 51–67.

Roudané, Matthew. "*Death of a Salesman* and the Poetics of Arthur Miller." In *The Cambridge Companion to Arthur Miller*, ed. Christopher Bigsby, 60–85. New York: Cambridge University Press, 1997.

Rowe, Kenneth Thorpe. *A Theater in Your Head*. New York: Funk and Wagnalls, 1960.

Royal, Derek Parker. "Camusian Existentialism in Arthur Miller's *After the Fall*." *Modern Drama* 43 (2000): 192–203.

Savran, David. *Communists, Cowboys, and Queers: The Politics of Masculinity in the Work of Arthur Miller and Tennessee Williams*. Minneapolis: University of Minnesota Press, 1992.

Scanlon, Tom. *Family, Drama, and American Dreams*. Contributions in American Studies no. 35. Westport, Conn.: Greenwood, 1978.

Schissel, Wendy. "Re(dis)covering the Witches in Arthur Miller's *The Crucible*: A Feminist Reading." *Modern Drama* 37 (1994): 461–73.

Schlueter, June. *Dramatic Closure: Reading the End*. Madison, N.J.: Associated University Presses, 1995.

———. "Power Play: Arthur Miller's *The Archbishop's Ceiling*." *CEA Critic* 49, no. 2–4 (1986–87): 134–38.

———. "Re-membering Willy's Past: Introducing Postmodern Concerns through *Death of a Salesman*." In *Approaches to Teaching Miller's Death of a Salesman*, ed. Matthew Roudané, 142–54. New York: Modern Language Association, 1995.

Schlueter, June, and James K. Flanagan. *Arthur Miller*. New York: Ungar, 1987.

Schneider, Daniel E. *The Psychoanalyst and the Artist*. New York: International Universities Press, 1950.

Schroeder, Patricia. "Arthur Miller: Illuminating Process." *REAL: The Yearbook of Research in English and American Literature*. 3 (1985): 265–93.

Schvey, Henry I. "Arthur Miller: Songs of Innocence and Experience." In *New Essays on American Drama*, ed. Gilbert Debusscher and Henry I. Schvey, 75–97. Amsterdam: Rodopi, 1989.

Shaw, George Bernard. "How to Write a Popular Play." In *Playwrights on Playwriting: The Meaning and Making of Modern Drama from*

Ibsen to Ionesco, ed. Toby Cole, 53–57. New York: Hill and Wang, 1960.

Siegel, Paul N. "Willy Loman and King Lear." *College English* 17 (1956): 341–45.

Sievers, W. David. *Freud on Broadway: A History of Psychoanalysis and the American Drama*. New York: Hermitage House, 1955.

Simonson, Robert. "Values, Old and New: Arthur Miller and John Tillinger on *The Last Yankee*." *Theatre Week*, June 18, 1993, 13–18.

Stambusky, Alan A. "Arthur Miller: Aristotelian Canons in the Twentieth Century Drama." In *Modern American Drama: Essays in Criticism*, ed. William Taylor, 91–115. Deland, Fla.: Everett/Edwards, 1968.

Stanton, Kay. "Women and the American Dream of *Death of a Salesman*." In *Feminist Rereadings of Modern American Drama*, ed. June Schlueter, 67–102. Rutherford, N.J.: Fairleigh Dickinson University Press, 1989.

Steiner, George, *The Death of Tragedy*. London: Faber and Faber, 1961.

Stinson, John J. "Structure in *After the Fall*: The Relevance of the Maggie Episode to the Main Themes and Christian Symbolism." *Modern Drama* 10 (1967): 233–40.

Strout, Cushing. "Analogical History: *The Crucible*." In *The Veracious Imagination: Essays on American History, Literature, and Biography*, 139–56. Middlebury, Conn.: Wesleyan University Press, 1981.

Styan, J. L. "Why *A View from the Bridge* Went Down Well in London: A Story of a Revision." In *Arthur Miller: New Perspectives*, ed. Robert A. Martin, 139–48. Englewood Cliffs, N.J.: Prentice-Hall, 1982.

Taitte, Lawson. "Productions Prove It's Miller's Time." *Dallas Morning News*, February 15, 1998, Arts section, 1C.

Taubman, Howard, "Inquiry into Roots of Evil." *New York Times*, December 2, 1964, sec. 2, p. 3.

———. "Theatre: *Incident at Vichy* Opens." *New York Theatre Critics' Reviews* (1964): 116–17.

Tillich, Paul. *Existence and the Christ*. Vol. 2 of *Systematic Theology*. Chicago: University of Chicago Press, 1957.

Trowbridge, Clinton W. "Arthur Miller: Between Pathos and Tragedy." *Modern Drama* 10 (1967): 221–32.

Tynan, Kenneth. *Tynan Right and Left: Plays, Films, Places, and Events*. London: Davis-Poynter, 1975.

———. *A View of the English Stage, 1944–63*. London: Davis-Poynter, 1975.

Valente, Joseph. "Rehearsing the Witch Trials: Gender Injustice in *The Crucible*." *New Formations: A Journal of Culture/Theory/Politics* 32 (1997): 120–34.

Vogel, Dan. *The Three Masks of American Tragedy*. Baton Rouge: Louisiana State University Press, 1974.

Wang, Qun. "The Tragedy of Ethical Bewilderment." In *The Achievement of Arthur Miller: New Essays*, ed. Steven R. Centola, 95–100. Dallas: Contemporary Research Press, 1995.

Warshow, Robert. "The Liberal Conscience in *The Crucible*." *Commentary*, March 1953, 265–71.

Weales, Gerald C. "All about Talk: Arthur Miller's *The Price*." In *Arthur Miller: New Perspectives*, ed. Robert A. Miller, 188–99. Englewood Cliffs, N.J.: Prentice-Hall, 1982.

———. *American Drama since World War II*. New York: Harcourt, Brace and World, 1962.

———. "Arthur Miller: Man and His Image." *Tulane Drama Review* 7 (1962): 165–80.

———. "Arthur Miller and the 1950s." *Michigan Quarterly Review (A Special Issue: Arthur Miller)* 37 (1998): 635–51.

———. "Clichés in the Garden." *Commonweal*, December 22, 1972, 276.

Welland, Dennis. *Miller the Playwright*. 3d ed. New York: Methuen, 1985.

Wertheim, Albert. "Arthur Miller: *After the Fall* and After." In *Essays on Contemporary American Drama*, ed. Hedwig Bock and Albert Wertheim, 19–32. Munich: Hueber, 1981.

Whitley, Alvin. "Arthur Miller: An Attempt at Modern Tragedy." *Transactions of the Wisconsin Academy of Science, Arts, and Literature* 42 (1953): 257–62.

Williams, Raymond. "Arthur Miller: An Overview." In *Arthur Miller*, ed. Harold Bloom, 7–16. New York: Chelsea House, 1987.

———. *Modern Tragedy*. Stanford: Stanford University Press, 1966.

Zeifman, Hersh. "All My Sons After the Fall: Arthur Miller and the Rage for Order." In *The Theatrical Gamut: Notes for a Post-*

Beckettian Stage, ed. Enoch Brater, 107–20. Ann Arbor: University of Michigan Press, 1995.

Zeineddine, Nada. *Because It Is My Name: Problems of Identity Experienced by Women, Artists, and Breadwinners in the Plays of Henrik Ibsen, Tennessee Williams, and Arthur Miller.* Brauton Devon, England: Merlin Books, 1991.

Index

Abbotson, Susan C. W., 185, 229n20, 230–31

Abbott, Anthony S., 157n30

Abel and Cain. *See* Cain and Abel

"About Theatre Language" (Miller), 3

Absurdist drama, 109, 144, 157, 158, 169, 169n7, 177, 177–78n12, 220, 239

Adam and Eve. *See* Fall myth

Adams, Julie, 106

Adler, Alfred, 162n37

After the Fall (Miller): autobiographical element of, 105–6, 125–26; compared with other plays, 2, 3, 4, 95, 96, 102, 107–11, 110n29, 112, 114, 114n36, 124, 131, 133, 146, 197, 215–16, 230, 235, 240–41, 244; critics' responses to, ix, 105–6, 106n24, 120n42; Dan's role in, 116–17, 118, 124, 127; existential vision in, 106, 110–11, 110n29, 131–32n52; Felice's role in, 116, 121, 124, 125, 132; guilt and responsibility in, 105–6n23, 106–8, 111–12, 111–12n31, 114n38, 115–21, 124, 126, 126n46, 128–31, 131–32n52, 133; Holga's role in, 115–17, 123, 124, 129–31, 131n49, 139, 142, 163, 235; idiot/idiot child imagery in, 117, 118n40, 121, 130, 130–31n49, 131, 235; innocence/loss of innocence in, 105n23, 116, 119–22, 124–34, 126n46, 142, 226, 232; irony/self-irony in, 109–10, 112–13, 116, 119–20, 122, 124, 126, 127–28, 152; leap of faith in, 111, 131–32; Louise's role in, 116, 118–22, 125, 128, 130; Lou's suicide in, 121–22, 127; Maggie's role in, 20, 106, 111, 115n39, 116, 118, 121, 123–29, 123n44, 128n47; Maggie's suicide in, 106n23, 112, 114n36, 123, 125, 127; and Marilyn Monroe, 94; as memory play or extended soliloquy, 109–10, 113–15, 113n35; Miller on, 111, 114, 119, 121, 125; mother-son relationship in, 115, 116–18, 117–18n40, 120–21, 124, 125, 127, 128, 129; mythic allusions in, 108, 108n27, 111–12, 111n31, 114, 115, 126, 132, 190, 226, 248; New York premiere of, 123; Quentin's cruciform pose in, 113, 124, 125; Quentin's role in, 105–6n23, 106–33, 108n26, 112n31, 115n39, 120n42, 131–32n52, 163, 170, 171, 211, 226; Quentin's self-knowledge in, 125, 190, 197, 248; Quentin's violence in, 122, 128–29; revivals of, 111n30, 123n44; structure and setting of, 111, 123; television production of, 165

Aging. *See* Death and dying; Old age and aging

Albee, Edward, 169, 169n7, 171

Allen, Joan, 16n14, 71–72

All My Sons (Miller): awards for, 13; Chris's role in, 15–18, 19n19, 20–25, 24nn27–28, 107, 107–8n26, 113, 124, 156, 171, 241; compared

269

with other plays, 2, 10, 15, 17, 19, 21, 23, 61, 73, 107, 124, 146, 221, 241; guilt and responsibility in, 12, 15–25, 16n14, 107–8n26; innocence/loss of innocence in, 14–15, 19, 21–25, 22n24, 23n25; irony in, 17, 18; Joe's "all my sons" speech in, 18, 25; Joe's role in, 15–19, 23, 25; Joe's suicide in, 17, 18–19, 19n19, 21, 40; Kate's role in, 15–16, 16n14, 19–21, 19n21, 23; Larry's death in, 16, 17, 20–21; Miller on, 13–14, 110; original title of, 13, 239; revivals of, xn2, 16n14, 22n24, 25, 105, 239; set design for, 15; source of idea for, 13; symbolism and mythic allusions in, 14–15
Alter, Iska, 130, 131
American Clock (Miller), 165–66, 178–84, 178n13, 189, 209, 227, 241
American Dream/American culture, xiii, xiiin6, 35–37, 40–41, 53, 55, 222, 223, 239, 242–43
American West myth, 57, 94–105
Anderson, John, 12
Answer to Job (Jung), 162
Anticommunism. *See* McCarthyism
Antiwar movement. *See* Vietnam War
Archbishop's Ceiling (Miller), 139, 165–77, 165n1, 166n2, 179, 187, 190, 209, 212n5, 241
Arendt, Hannah, 138
Aristotle, 30, 30n10, 31n12, 37, 45, 59, 149, 230
Auden, W. H., 174
August, Eugene R., 45n38
Austin, Gayle, 44
Aymé, Marcel, 68n12

Balakian, Janet, 45–46, 140, 144, 160, 168, 174n10, 177n12, 198, 219, 247

Baldwin, James, 212, 247
Banfield, Chris, 191n30, 193, 200
Barker, Stephen, 29n8, 30n10, 35, 108n27, 248
Barnes, Clive, 239
Beaufort, John, 36
Becket, Thomas, 73
Beckett, Samuel, 109, 144, 157, 158, 169, 169n7, 239, 247
Bentley, Eric, 26, 33–34, 64, 76
Ben-Zvi, Linda, 44
Berger, Sidney, 106n24
Bettina, Sister M., 56n62
Bhatia, Santosh, 18, 24n28, 29n8, 157
Bible, 159–64, 159n33. *See also* Cain and Abel; Fall myth; Jacob and Rebecca
Bierman, Judah, 29n8
Bigamy, 211–12, 215–18
Bigsby, Christopher, xiiin6, 3, 4, 6–7, 21–23, 25, 29, 34, 35, 37, 39, 39n21, 46, 48, 55, 57, 57n64, 65, 74, 76, 81, 84, 98, 98n10, 104, 108n26, 114n38, 131n50, 131–32n52, 133, 142–43n11, 144, 149, 152, 167n4, 168, 174n10, 180, 183n18, 189–90, 196, 199, 213n6, 238, 240, 248
Blake, William, 161
Blakemore, Michael, 19, 123n44
Bliquez, Guerin, 43
Bloom, Harold, 30
Bolcom, William, 62, 80n29
Bolt, Robert, 63–70, 64n7, 72–76
Bouchard, Larry, xii
Brandon, Harry, 159
Brantley, Ben, 15, 22n24
Brater, Enoch, 14–15, 144n13
Brecht, Bertolt, 64, 64n7, 65, 179
Brill, Lesley, 97, 98, 100n13, 101–2, 104
Bristol Old Vic, 11
Broken Glass (Miller), x, 82, 210–11, 228–39, 237n27

Bronson, David, 61, 143
Brook, Peter, 77, 85
Browning, Robert, 37
Brustein, Robert, xn1, 105, 135, 147, 148, 228
Budick, E. Miller, 73
Burhans, Clinton S., Jr., 111n31
Byron, George Gordon, Lord, 161

Cagney, Jimmy, 197
Cain and Abel, 112, 114, 124, 126, 128, 132, 140, 160, 161, 162–63, 164n39, 216, 219
Calders, Sandy and Louisa, 200n45
Callow, Heather Cook, 45n36
Camus, Albert, 108, 110, 110n29, 112, 114, 114n36, 122, 131, 133
Canby, Vincent, 87, 88
Carlisle, Olga, 29n6
Carr, Jay, 71
Carson, Neil, xii, 146n18, 187
Catholic Church, 25, 197, 198
Centola, Steven R., 19n19, 24n27, 28, 75n23, 80, 82–83, 108n27, 110n29, 132–33, 143, 144–45n14, 154, 158–59, 168, 190, 203, 214, 220n12, 229–30
Chambers, R. W., 65
Chatterji, Ruby, 132n52, 142, 142n10
Chekhov, Anton, 78
Christian myth and Christ images, 5, 24, 108n27, 113, 124, 125, 144n12, 166, 175, 198, 218
Clara (Miller), 190, 203–9, 205n48, 207n49, 209n50
Clark, Eleanor, 30
Classical tragedy. See Greek tragedy
Clift, Monty, 97
Clurman, Harold, 19, 135n3
Cobb, Lee J., 58
Cohn, Ruby, 58
Collected Plays (Miller), 26, 78, 85, 88
Comedy and humor, 88, 160, 178–79,

183, 199, 200, 219, 221, 226–27, 240
Communism, 64, 78n26, 119, 132, 136–37, 247. See also McCarthyism
Concentration camps. See Holocaust
Conrad, Joseph, 140
Corrigan, Robert, 27n2, 32, 104, 106–7, 144, 151n22, 162n37, 227–28
Cortez, Hernando, 7–8
Costello, Donald, 81, 85
Couchman, Gordon, 47
Cowboys, 94–105
Creation of the World and Other Business (Miller), xii, 158–65, 164n39
Crime, 16–17, 16n15, 159, 195–98, 195n37, 204–9, 209n50. See also Prisons and prison imagery
Cromwell, Oliver, 67
Crucible (Miller), ix, xn2, xii, 2, 8, 12, 16n14, 61–76, 79, 113, 160, 177
Czechoslovakia, 166, 166n2

Danger: Memory! (Miller), 190, 199–209
Death and dying, 200–203. See also Old age and aging
Death of a Salesman (Miller): actors' portrayal of Linda and Willie, 46–47, 47n43, 58; awards for, 46; Beijing production of, 42, 43, 47; Ben's role in, 56, 56n62; Biff's role in, 42–43, 44n30, 46, 47–50, 49n49, 52–54, 56–57, 57n63, 86, 94, 98, 104; British response to, ix; Charley's salesman speech in, 57, 58n67; compared with other plays, 2, 10, 15, 17, 19, 21, 23, 57, 57n64, 79, 80, 81, 86, 87, 98, 98n10, 101, 146, 182, 183, 211, 214, 221, 223, 235, 241, 243–44; father-son relationships in, 41–43, 49–50, 53, 54; feminist criticism of, 44–46,

44n33, 45n36, 45n38; film version
of, 35, 37; Freudian readings of,
41–42, 41–42n26, 49, 49n49, 57,
57n63; guilt and responsibility in,
33n14, 39–40, 43, 46, 48, 50–51,
53; Hap's role in, 42, 43, 48–50;
irony in, 33, 36, 55, 57, 58; Kazan
as director of, 42, 46, 47, 47n43;
Linda's "Attention must be paid"
speech in, 46, 46n42, 59; Linda's
role in, 43–48, 43n28, 44n30,
46n42, 48n45, 57–58, 58n67;
Miller on, 26–27, 27nn2–3, 35–38,
40, 42–43, 42n27, 46–47, 46n42,
48n45, 51, 53–56, 55n57, 58n67;
mythic forces in, 41–42; requiem
in, 55–58, 58n67, 85; restaurant
scene in, 48–49; revisions of, by
Miller, 48, 49, 53–54; revivals of,
xn2, 16n14, 29n8, 36, 42–43, 46,
47, 105, 146; titles considered for,
38, 58, 241; as tragedy, 25, 26–38,
29–30nn8–10, 31n12, 41, 49,
51, 53, 54n56, 55, 58–59; Willy
as insane in, 37, 53n53; Willy's
choices in, 12, 39–41, 55; Willy's
commitment to American dream
in, 35–37, 40–41, 53, 55, 223;
Willy's self-knowledge in, 51–52;
Willy's sexual infidelity in, 39,
48, 49, 50; Willy's suicide in, 19,
21, 38, 40–41, 47, 53–57, 54n56,
55n57, 58–59
Deists, 241
Demastes, William, 41
Dennehy, Brian, xn2, 46, 58, 146
Depression (economic). See Great
Depression
Depression (emotional), 201–3,
222–27
Detectives, 195–99, 204–9
Devil in Massachusetts (Starkey), 62
Dickey, James, xi
Di Giuseppe, Rita, 30n10, 33, 56n62,
58

Dillingham, William B., 43n28
DiMaggio, Joe, 245n38
Dostoyevsky, Fyodor, 110, 114n36
Downer, Alan, 146–47, 149, 151
Driver, Tom F., 33n14, 64, 73, 87n43
Dukore, Bernard F., 37n18, 47,
48n46, 52, 57
Dunnock, Mildred, 46–47, 47n43
Dying. See Death and dying

Eastern Europe, 165, 166–77, 166n2
Eden. See Fall myth
Eiseley, Loren, 167
Eisinger, Chester E., 49n49, 56,
57n64
Eldridge, Florence, 60
Elegy for a Lady (Miller), 38, 190–95,
193n34, 199, 240, 242
Eliot, T. S., 73–74
Enemy of the People (Ibsen), 60–61
Engels, Friedrich, 181
Epstein, Arthur D., 83n36
Epstein, Leslie, 114n36, 143
Euripides, 80, 87
Eve and Adam. See Fall myth
Everybody Wins, 195, 195n37
Evil and goodness: in After the Fall,
107–9, 112–13, 115, 122, 128–31,
134; Bigsby on, 134; and Cain
and Abel, 112; in Creation of the
World and Other Business, 161–64;
in Incident at Vichy, 135–45;
innocence and evil, 24–25, 134,
247–48; and Lucifer, 161–62;
Miller on, 108–9, 112, 247–48. See
also Fall myth
Existentialism, 74–76, 75n23,
104, 106, 110–11, 110n29, 112,
131–32n52, 136, 142, 142n10,
149, 152, 156–58, 163–64, 236,
248
Expressionistic techniques, 39, 204–5

Falk, Peter, 240
Fall, Robert, 29n8, 46

Fall (Camus), 108, 110, 110n29, 112, 114, 114n36, 119–20, 122, 131, 133

Fall myth: in *After the Fall*, 94, 108–9, 108n27, 111–12, 111–12n31, 114, 115, 126, 132, 190, 226, 248; in *All My Sons*, 14–15; in *American Clock*, 180, 184; and *Broken Glass*, 238; in *Creation of the World and Other Business*, 158–64; in *Death of a Salesman*, 39; in *Everybody Wins*, 195n37; in *Incident at Vichy*, 145; in Miller's plays generally, xii–xiii, 134; in *Misfits*, 94, 131; in *Mr. Peters' Connections*, 241; in *Price*, 154. *See also* Innocence/loss of innocence theme

Fame (Miller), 170

Family: in *After the Fall*, 115, 116–18, 117–18n40, 120–21, 124, 125, 127, 128, 129; in *All My Sons*, 23–24; in *American Clock*, 178–84, 178n13; bigamy in *Ride down Mount Morgan*, 211–20; in *Death of a Salesman*, 41–43, 49–50, 53, 54; in *Last Yankee*, 221–28; Miller on, 41; in *Price*, 146–58; in *Ride down Mount Morgan*, 210–13

Fascism, 7, 11n9, 177–78n12

Father-son relationships, 23–24, 41–43, 49–50, 53, 54, 180

Faulkner, William, 133

Faust, 161, 162, 214

Federal Theater Project, 1, 7

Feiden, Douglas, 149

Feingold, Michael, x

Feldman, Robert Lee, 69

Female characters: in *After the Fall*, 96, 106, 115–32, 117–18n40; in *All My Sons*, 15–16, 16n14, 19–21, 19n21, 23; in *American Clock*, 182–83; in *Archbishop's Ceiling*, 167, 169–72, 176; in *Broken Glass*, 230–39; in *Clara*, 207–8; in *Crucible*, 70–71; in *Death of a Salesman*, 43–48, 43n28, 44n30, 46n42, 48n45; in *Elegy for a Lady*, 190–95; in *I Can't Remember Anything*, 200–203; in *Last Yankee*, 221–28; in Miller's plays generally, 16n14, 47n44; in *Misfits*, 95–96, 95n2, 99–104; in *Mr. Peters' Connections*, 244–46; in *Playing for Time*, 184–90, 187n24; in *Price*, 150–52, 155–57; in *Ride down Mount Morgan*, 215–18; in *Some Kind of Love Story*, 195–99; in *View from the Bridge*, 81–84, 82n34, 86. *See also* Feminist criticism

Feminist criticism, 16n14, 20, 44–46, 44n33, 45n36, 45n38, 70, 70–71n15, 120n42

Fenelon, Fania, 178, 184, 185–89, 186n22–23

Field, B. S., Jr., 49n49

Films, 16n14, 35, 37, 62, 71–72, 77–78n26, 85, 95–105, 195, 195n37

Firmament of Time (Eiseley), 167

Flanagan, James, 23, 51, 54, 111n31, 124, 126, 126n46, 135, 138, 157, 161, 195n36

Focus (Miller), 2, 12, 104, 134, 230

Foster, Richard J., 30, 33n14

Four Freedoms (Miller), 1

Franz, Elizabeth, xn2, 16n14, 46, 146

Free, William, 64

Freedman, Morris, 149–50, 153

Freud, Sigmund, 162n37

Freudianism and Freudian interpretation, 34n15, 41–42, 41–42n26, 49, 49n49, 57, 57n63, 80, 118, 205–6

Gable, Clark, 97

Galileo (Brecht), 64, 64n7

Ganz, Arthur, 68n12, 96, 101

Gelb, Philip, 108

Gender issues. *See* Feminist criticism; Hegemonic masculinity

Genesis story. *See* Fall myth

Genet, Jean, 132
Ghosts (Ibsen), 230, 234
Gilman, Richard, 105
Glengarry Glen Ross (Mamet), 46
God. See Fall myth
Golden Years (Miller), 1, 6–8, 7n7, 11n9, 62
Goldstein, Laurence, 100, 101, 102, 103
Good and evil. See Evil and goodness
Goode, James, 97n6
Gordon, Lois, 26, 51
Gorelik, Mordecai, 15
Grandpa and the Statue (Miller), 1
Grass Still Grows (Miller), 1, 2
Great Depression, 15, 92, 149, 150, 165, 166, 178–84, 246
Great Disobedience (Miller), 1, 3, 4–6, 5n6, 64
Greek tragedy, 12, 13, 25, 27–31, 28–29n6, 34, 35, 37, 38, 41, 43, 56, 59, 61, 77–80, 80n29, 87, 132, 149, 177, 180, 233
Greene, Graham, 159
Greenfield, Josh, 158
Grosbard, Ulu, 88
Guilt theme: in After the Fall, 106–8, 106–7n23, 111–12, 111–12n31, 114n38, 115–21, 126, 128–31, 133; in All My Sons, 15–25, 16n14, 107–8n26; in American Clock, 179, 180, 183–84; in Broken Glass, 230–33, 237; in Clara, 206–7; in Creation of the World and Other Business, 162; in Crucible, 69–76, 72n16; in Death of a Salesman, 33n14, 39–40, 43, 46, 48, 50, 53; in Elegy for a Lady, 191, 193; in Great Disobedience, 5; in Incident at Vichy, 135–45, 135n5, 142–43n11; in Last Yankee, 223–27; in Man Who Had All the Luck, 9–10; in Memory of Two Mondays, 92; Miller on, 230, 248; and Miller's marriage to Marilyn Monroe, 95;

in Miller's plays generally, xi, 106–8, 112, 134, 143, 143n11, 145; in No Villain, 3; in Playing for Time, 188–89; in Price, 150–58, 157n30; in Ride down Mount Morgan, 213–19, 213n7; in View from the Bridge, 82n34, 83–85, 86

Half-Bridge (Miller), 1, 6, 79, 246
Hamlet, 24n28, 30, 34, 36, 41, 170
Harben, Niloufer, 63
Hard Times (Terkel), 165, 178
Harris, Rosemary, 19
Harshbarger, Karl, 43–44, 44n30
Hart, James, 29n8
Havel, Václav, 166
Hayden, Michael, 22n24
Heart of Darkness (Conrad), 140
Hedda Gabler (Ibsen), 146, 177
Hegemonic masculinity, 44n33, 45n38, 46, 101, 103, 120n42, 209n50
Heidegger, Martin, 142n10
Heilman, Robert Bechtold, 18n17, 31, 31n12, 33, 37, 51, 66, 66n10, 68, 75, 78
Henry VIII, 63, 67, 72
Hingle, Pat, 152–53n26
Historical drama, 62, 63, 65, 68
Hitler, Adolf, 7, 8, 11n9, 115, 231. See also Nazism
Hoffman, Dustin, 58
Hogan, Robert, 88, 101n14, 106n24, 123, 132
Holocaust, 108, 111, 115, 117, 124, 129–30, 134–45, 145n15, 153, 178, 187–90, 207, 229–34, 236–38
Homosexuality, 83, 83n36
Honors at Dawn (Miller), 1, 3–4, 64, 146
Hook, 77–78n26, 96
Huftel, Sheila, 78n27
Huisman, Jacques, 163
Humor. See Comedy and humor
Huston, John, 97, 97n6
Hyman, Ronald, 29n6
Hynes, Joseph, 52–53, 53n53, 58n67

Ibsen, Henrik, xii, xiii, 11–14, 23, 25, 28, 28–29n6, 29, 30, 35, 38, 60–61, 78, 146, 148, 149, 177, 180, 222, 228–29, 230, 233–34, 239
"Ibsen's Warning" (Miller), 60
I Can't Remember Anything (Miller), 190, 199–203, 203n46, 220, 240
Iceman Cometh (O'Neill), 13, 25
Ignorance. See Innocence/loss of innocence theme
Illusion. See Truth and illusion theme
Incident at Vichy (Miller), 134–45, 153, 165, 187, 189, 230
Innocence/loss of innocence theme: in After the Fall, 106–7n23, 111–12, 116, 119–22, 124–34, 126n46, 142, 226, 232; in All My Sons, 14, 19, 21–25, 22n24, 23n25; in American Clock, 184; in Archbishop's Ceiling, 172–73; in Broken Glass, 230–33, 237, 238; in Creation of the World and Other Business, 158–64; in Crucible, 75–76; in Death of a Salesman, 183; in Elegy for a Lady, 193; evil and innocence, 24–25, 134, 247–48; in Honors at Dawn, 4; in Incident at Vichy, 140–45; Marilyn Monroe as symbol of, 101n14; Miller on, 24–25, 134, 148, 230, 247–48; in Miller's plays generally, xi, 2, 107, 108, 111–12, 131n50, 160, 162n36; in Misfits, 103–5; in No Villain, 3; in Price, 154–58; in Ride down Mount Morgan, 213–20, 213n7; in Some Kind of Love Story, 195–97; Tillich on, 112; in View from the Bridge, 81–83, 86. See also Fall myth
Ionesco, Eugène, 132, 158
Irony: in After the Fall, 109–10, 112–13, 116, 119–20, 122, 124, 126, 127–28, 152; in All My Sons, 17, 18; in American Clock, 183; in Archbishop's Ceiling, 172, 173–74; in Broken Glass, 236; in Clara, 207; in Crucible, 74; in

Death of a Salesman, 33, 36, 55, 57, 58; in Ibsen's plays, 61; in I Can't Remember Anything, 202; in Incident at Vichy, 144n12; in Last Yankee, 223, 225; in Playing for Time, 187–88; in Ride down Mount Morgan, 215, 219
Isaac and Esau, 118
Isser, Edward R., 145n15, 188–89
Italian Tragedy (Miller), 77. See also View from the Bridge (Miller)

Jackson, Esther Merle, 29n8, 37
Jacob and Rebecca, 118
Jews, 6, 135–45, 145n15, 153, 157, 178, 184–90, 204, 215, 229–39. See also Holocaust
John Gabriel Borkman (Ibsen), 149, 177
Johnson, Lyndon B., 147
Johnson, Stanley, 29n8
Josef von Schwarzenberg, Prince, 135n2
Joyce, James, 239
Jung, Carl, 162n37

Kafka, Franz, 90, 112, 136
Kauffman, Stanley, 103
Kazan, Elia, 38, 42, 46, 47, 47n43, 55, 77–78n26, 123
Kennedy, Arthur, 23n25
Kierkegaard, Sfren, 111, 220
King Lear (Shakespeare), 29, 29–30n8, 30
Kintz, Linda, 45
Kissel, Howard, 22n24
Koenig, Rhoda, 45n36
Koon, Helene Wickham, 36n17
Korean War, 184
Krapp's Last Tape (Beckett), 109, 239
Kroll, Jack, 159–60, 160n34
Krutch, Joseph Wood, 32
Kurdi, Maria, 192, 196, 199
Kushner, Tony, 54n56

Lahr, John, 232, 234–35
Lang, Fritz, 51n51

Langella, Frank, 111n30
Langer, Lawrence L., 144n13
LaPaglia, Anthony, 87, 146
Last Yankee (Miller), x, 3, 4, 38, 210–11, 220–28, 233, 241, 242
Law and lawyers, 16–17, 16n15, 80–81, 115, 117, 121, 127, 161n36, 212, 214
Leap of faith, 111, 131–32, 145, 217
Lear (Shakespeare). *See King Lear* (Shakespeare)
Lewis, Allan, 129, 132
Lewis, Robert, 60
Lillo, George, 29
Lindenberger, Herbert, 62
Listen My Children (Miller and Rosten), 1
Loden, Barbara, 123
London Merchant (Lillo), 29
Longhi, Vinny, 76
Loss of innocence. *See* Fall myth; Innocence/loss of innocence theme
Lowenthal, Lawrence, 142n10
Lucifer, 161–62
Lumet, Sidney, 85

Mahler, Gustav, 185
Mahony, Dianne Greene, 212–13
Mamet, David, 46, 230
Mander, John, 34n15
Man for All Seasons (Bolt), 63–70, 72–76
Man Who Had All the Luck (Miller), x, 1, 6–7, 7n7, 8–12, 11nn8–9, 13, 21, 146, 159, 179
March, Frederic, 37, 60
Mark Taper Forum, 178
Marron, Hanna, 19n21
Martin, Robert A., xii, 27, 28, 32, 142n10
Martine, James J., 28n6
Marxism and Marxist interpretation, 2–3, 34n15, 35, 64–65, 65n8, 75n23, 89, 137

Masculinity. *See* Hegemonic masculinity
Massa, Ann, 120n42, 160
Master Builder (Ibsen), 11, 177
May, Rollo, xi
McCarthy, Eugene, 147
McCarthyism, 61, 61n3, 62, 64, 68, 72, 108, 119, 140, 147, 246
Melodrama, 3, 31, 34, 55, 59, 66–67, 66n10, 69, 75, 76, 85, 88, 144n12
Memory: in *After the Fall,* 109–10, 113–15, 113n35; in *American Clock,* 180; in *Clara,* 203–9; in *I Can't Remember Anything,* 199–203; in *Mr. Peters' Connections,* 243–44; in *Price,* 151–53; in *Ride down Mount Morgan,* 211–13, 216, 219
Memory of Two Mondays (Miller), 26, 77, 88–93, 89n46
Mengele, Doctor, 185, 187, 188
Mental illness, 195–99, 221–28
Meyer, Kinereth, 140, 144n12, 187, 236
Miller, Arthur: awards for, 1, 5n6, 13, 46, 87, 146, 229; coverage of Nazi trials in Frankfurt by, 134–35, 189; divorce of, from Mary Slattery, 94; in Great Depression, 179; Jewish identity of, 230; and Marilyn Monroe, 94–97, 100n13, 101, 101n14, 104–6, 126, 241, 241n36; marriage of, to Inge Morath, 104, 106, 134; political activism of, 147–48, 184; as president of PEN, 148, 166, 176; and religion, xii, 158–59; themes and beliefs of generally, x–xiii, 179–80, 239, 247–49; and travels to Soviet Union and Eastern Europe, 148, 166; at University of Michigan, 1, 3, 13, 62, 88–89, 92n47, 110, 180; and work in auto parts warehouse, 88–89, 89n46, 92n47. *See also* specific plays

"Miracles" (Miller), 166
Mirren, Helen, 194n36
Misfits (Miller), 57, 57n64, 94–105, 131
Monroe, Marilyn, 94–97, 95n2, 100, 100n13, 101, 101n14, 104–6, 113, 123, 126, 241, 241n36, 245n38
Montezuma, 7–8
Moral responsibility. *See* Responsibility theme
Morath, Inge, 104, 106, 134, 135n2
More, Sir Thomas, 63–70, 72–76
Morley, Christopher, 229
Morrison, Toni, 219
Morse, David, 43n28
Mosher, Gregory, 207n49
Moss, Leonard, 96, 108, 108n27, 111n31, 161n36
Mother-son relationship, 115, 116–18, 117–18n40, 120–21, 124, 125, 127, 128, 129
Mottram, Eric, 30, 33n14, 135n5
Mr. Peters' Connections (Miller), x, 38, 221, 239–46
Murder. *See* Crime
Murder in the Cathedral (Eliot), 73–74
Murphy, Brenda, 11, 29n8, 39, 42, 54
Murray, Edward, 118
Music, 183, 184–90, 201, 205, 208, 226, 227, 240
Myth of the American West. *See* American West myth
Mythological themes. *See* Cain and Abel; Fall myth; Jacob and Rebecca

Nathan, George Jean, 55–56
"Nature of Tragedy" (Miller), 26, 55
Naughton, James, 146
Nazism, 69, 111, 115, 117, 118n40, 124, 129–30, 133, 134–45, 135n2, 142n10, 153, 184–90, 215, 229–34, 236–38
"Nazi Trials and the German Heart" (Miller), 189

Nelson, Benjamin, 4, 17, 44, 78n27, 101, 103, 128n47, 131n49, 140, 144, 158
Nietzsche, Friedrich, xii, 30n10, 32, 68
Nolan, Paul, 109
Nordenson, Lars, 60
Notes from Underground (Dostoyevsky), 110
No Villain (Miller), 1, 2–3, 64, 146

Oates, Joyce Carol, 29–30n8
Oedipus/*Oedipus the King*, 22, 24, 29, 29n8, 30, 34, 35–36, 40, 41, 43, 44, 48, 57n63, 76, 80, 84, 230
Oedipus complex, 41–42, 49–50, 57, 118
Old age and aging, 192, 200–203, 209, 213–14, 240, 240–41n35. *See also* Death and dying
Old Testament. *See* Cain and Abel; Fall myth; Jacob and Rebecca
Oliver, Edith, 88
O'Neal, Michael J., 74
O'Neill, Eugene, 13, 25, 27–28, 29, 41, 62, 149
"On Social Plays" (Miller), 26, 34–35
On the Waterfront, 78n26
Operas, 62, 80n29
Original sin. *See* Fall myth
Orr, John, 78
Othello (Shakespeare), 29, 85
Other, 20, 70, 209n50
Otten, Charlotte F., 29n8
"Our Guilt for the World's Evil" (Miller), 112
Överland, Orm, 136n5

Paralysis, 230–39
Parker, Brian, 43
Parody tragedy, 158
Pathos, 31, 51, 56, 90, 161
Peck, Bob, 194–95n36
PEN, 148, 166, 176
Personal responsibility. *See*

Responsibility theme

Pinter, Harold, 157, 169, 230

Pirandello, Luigi, 65

Playing for Time (Miller), 178, 184–90, 230

Poetics (Aristotle), 30, 45, 149

Poling, James, 47n43

Popkin, Henry, 82n34

Porter, Thomas, 49, 56n62

Postmodernism, 38, 68–69, 170–71, 177, 190, 229, 229n20, 243, 246

Press, David, 99, 102, 102n16, 104

Price (Miller), xn2, 2, 105, 106, 145–58, 166

Prideaux, Tom, 114

Prisons and prison imagery, 4–6, 4n5, 16–17, 16n15

Prudhan, N. S., 108

Psychiatrists and psychiatry, 196, 221–28

Psychoanalysts and psychoanalysis, 131n50, 135n2, 139–45, 205–6, 230

Puritanism, xiii, 9, 62, 71n15, 108, 120, 180, 184. *See also* Guilt theme

Pussycat and the Expert Plumber Who Was a Man (Miller), 1

Pyle, Ernie, 13

Rabe, Davi, 106

Rajakrishnan, V., 111–12n31, 230

Reagan, Ronald, 212

Reality and illusion. *See* Truth and illusion theme

Redgrave, Vanessa, 184

Reilly, Peter, 159, 195n37

Religion. *See* Cain and Abel; Catholic Church; Christian myth and Christ images; Fall myth

Reno, Raymond H., 24n28, 108n27

Responsibility theme: in *After the Fall*, 124, 126n46, 128, 131–32n52; in *All My Sons*, 15–19, 21–23; in *American Clock*, 179,

183–84; in *Archbishop's Ceiling*, 176–77; Bigsby on, 39, 39n21, 238, 248; in *Broken Glass*, 237–38; in *Clara*, 206, 208–9; in *Creation of the World and Other Business*, 162, 163; in *Crucible*, 74–76; in *Death of a Salesman*, 50–51, 53; in *Elegy for a Lady*, 191; in *Golden Years*, 8; in *Half-Bridge*, 6; in *Incident at Vichy*, 135, 135n5, 142–43n11, 143–45, 144–45n14; in *Last Yankee*, 227; in *Man Who Had All the Luck*, 10–11; Miller on, 75n23; in Miller's plays generally, xi, xiii, 2, 248–49; in *Misfits*, 98; in *No Villain*, 3; in *Playing for Time*, 189; in *Price*, 152, 154–58; in *Ride down Mount Morgan*, 213, 216–20, 220n12; in *Situation Normal*, 13; in *Some Kind of Love Story*, 195–96, 199, 199n41

Revery form, 191

Revivals of Miller's plays, x, xn2, xi, 16n14, 22n24, 25, 29n8, 36, 42–43, 46, 47, 62–63, 87, 88, 105, 111n30, 123n44, 145–46, 148, 149, 210, 239

Richards, David, 228, 233

Ride down Mount Morgan (Miller), x, 38, 210–20, 210–11n1, 220nn12–13, 221, 240, 241

Ritt, Martin, 76–77, 92

Ritter, Thelma, 97

Romantics, 112, 133, 161

Rosè, Alma, 185–87, 185n21

Rosten, Norman, 1

Rothenberg, Albert, 82

Roudané, Matthew, 27, 38, 51–52, 57n63, 143

Royal, Derek Parker, 110n29

Rube, David, x

Rubin, Gayle, 44

"Ryan Interview" (Miller), 240–41n35

Salem witch trials. *See Crucible* (Miller)

Sartre, Jean-Paul, 65n8, 110n29,

142n10

Savran, David, 44n33, 95, 101,
101n14, 103, 105, 117–18n40,
120n42, 205n48, 209n50

Scanlon, Tom, 18

Schissel, Wendy, 70, 70–71n15

Schizophrenia, 195–99

Schlueter, June, 23, 38, 51, 54,
111n31, 124, 126, 126n46, 135,
138, 157, 161, 167, 174, 195n36,
212n5, 213, 219

Schneider, Daniel E., 41, 49

Schroeder, Patricia, 113n35

Schvey, Henry I., 83n36, 142n10,
163–64

Screenplays. See Films

Sexism. See Feminist criticism;
Hegemonic masculinity

"Shadow of the God" (Miller), 248

Shakespeare, William, 29, 30, 33, 41,
85

Shapiro, Eugene, 82

Shaw, George Bernard, 31

Shaw, Sam, 95

Shelley, Percy Bysshe, 161

Siegel, Paul N., 29n8

Sievers, David, 53

Sign of the Archer (Miller), 13, 239.
See also All My Sons (Miller)

Simon, Josette, 123n44

Simonson, Robert, 223

Situation Normal (Miller), 1, 12–13,
23

Skin of Our Teeth (Wilder), 163

Slattery, Mary, 94

Social drama, 33–34

Social responsibility. See Responsibility theme

Socrates, 170

Solzhenitsyn, Aleksandr, 148

Some Kind of Love Story (Miller), 38,
190, 191, 195–99

Sophocles, 27, 35, 80

Sorcières de Salem, 65n8, 68n12

Soviet Union, 148. See also
Communism; McCarthyism

Spiller, Robert, xiii

Stambusky, Alan, 18, 78, 105–6n23,
135n5

Stanton, Kay, 45, 46

Starkey, Marion, 62

Steiner, George, 32, 87n43, 170,
170n8

Stinson, John J., 111n31, 124

Streetcar Named Desire (Williams),
39, 46

Strindberg, August, 239

Styan, John, 78

Styron, Rose, 29n6

Suicide: in After the Fall, 106n23,
112, 114n36, 121–22, 123, 125,
127; in All My Sons, 17, 18–19,
19n19, 21, 40; in Camus's The
Fall, 112, 114n36; in Death of
a Salesman, 19, 21, 38, 40–41,
47, 53–57, 54n56, 55n57, 58–59;
in Last Yankee, 224; of Marilyn
Monroe, 97, 104–5, 113; in Price,
154; in Ride down Mount Morgan,
213, 214, 216; in View from the
Bridge, 85–86

Survivor guilt. See Guilt theme

Tannen, Deborah, 45n36

Taubman, Howard, 135

Taylor, Frank, 100

Television productions, 165, 184–85,
184n19

Terkel, Studs, 165, 178, 182, 184

Testament of Mr. Mabuse, 51n51

That They May Win (Miller), 1

They Too Arise (Miller), 1, 2, 3, 64,
117n40

Thompson, David W., 36

Tillich, Paul, 112

Tolstoy, Aleksey, 110

Toubiana, Serge, 95n2

Tragedy: Aristotle on, 30, 31n12,
149; Bentley on, 26, 33–34;
Broken Glass as, 228–29, 238; and
catharsis, 54–55; Clara as, 204;
Creation of the World and Other
Business as, 161, 163; Death of a
Salesman as, 25, 26–38, 29–30nn8–

10, 31n12, 41, 49, 51, 53, 54n56, 55, 58–59; definitions of, 66; demise of, 32, 87n43, 170, 170n8; of displacement, 34; Dukore on, 53; and existential vision, 75n23; and female characters, 20; feminist criticism of, 45; and free will, 11–12; *Golden Years* as, 7n7; Heilman on, 31, 31n12, 66, 68; melodrama versus, 3, 31, 34, 55, 59, 66–67, 66n10, 69, 75, 76, 85, 88; and Miller, xi–xiii, 11–12, 26–29, 27n2, 28–29n6, 32–35, 55, 75, 87, 132, 158, 229–30; *Misfits* as, 102n16; Nietzschean tragedy, 30n10; O'Neill on, 27–28; parody tragedy, 158; pathos versus, 31, 51, 56, 161; *Price* as, 157–58; and religion, xii, 32–33; *Ride down Mount Morgan* as, 219; Shakespearean tragedy, 29, 30, 33, 41; *View from the Bridge* as, 78, 84–85. See also Greek tragedy; Ibsen, Henrik

"Tragedy and the Common Man" (Miller), 26, 33, 34

Trial (Kafka), 136

Trials. See *Crucible* (Miller); Law and lawyers

Trowbridge, Clinton W., 79, 106n24

Truth and illusion theme: in *Elegy for a Lady*, 190–95; in *Ride down Mount Morgan*, 211; in *Some Kind of Love Story*, 195–99

2 by A.M. (Miller). See *Elegy for a Lady* (Miller)

Two-Way Mirror (Miller), 190–99, 209

Tynan, Kenneth, 64, 64n7

University of Michigan, 1, 3, 13, 62, 88–89, 110, 147, 180

Unwin, Paul, 11

Up from Paradise, 164

Upham, Charles W., 65

Valente, John, 69, 71n15

Vaudeville form, 165, 178–79

Vercors, Jean Bruller, 104

Vietnam War, 147, 148, 149, 157, 184, 242, 247

View from the Bridge (Miller), xn2, 12, 26, 76–88, 77–78nn26–27, 85n40, 90, 105, 109, 146

Vogel, Dan, 41, 54

Wallach, Eli, 97, 101n14

Walters, Julie, 16n14

Wang, Qun, 146n18

Wanger, Walter, 110n29

Weales, Gerald, 40, 57, 103, 111n31, 156

Weinstein, Arnold, 80n29

Welland, Dennis, 58n67, 96, 130–31n49, 138n7, 146n18, 164n39, 179–80, 191, 199n41

Wertheim, Albert, 88, 118n40, 145

West. See American West myth

"What's Wrong with This Picture?" (Miller), 166n2

When We Dead Awaken (Ibsen), 177

Whitley, Alvin, 30

Who's Afraid of Virginia Woolf? (Albee), 169, 171

Wild Duck (Ibsen), 23

Wilder, Thornton, 163

William Ireland's Confession (Miller), 1

Williams, Raymond, 18, 41

Williams, Tennessee, 29, 39, 46

Witch trials. See *Crucible* (Miller)

Women characters. See Female characters

World War II, 1, 12–13

Zeifman, Hersh, 14, 107, 124

Zeineddine, Nada, 24n27, 57, 83n37, 87, 187n24

Zhu Lin, 47